Praise for *Sh*  *Myth*

"Saving money can ~~ ~~ of revenue than making money. Dappen shows why ~~ ~~ offers a blueprint for a saner life."
—Vicki Robin, coauthor with Joe Dominguez of *Your Money or Your Life*

"Finally a book that challenges the baseless group-think of the day—that two people have to work to make ends meet and make life worth living. Dappen tells it like it is: Two incomes aren't the answer, they're the problem."
—Bill Birchard, contributing editor, *CFO Magazine*

"Dappen has a message Americans need to hear."
—Paul Gonzales, talk show host, United Broadcasting Network

"A quality life is one that is created by making conscious choices: Save your money and give yourself the gift of time, or spend it and stay on the treadmill. This book gives you the tools you'll need to make that choice."
—Janet Luhrs, author of *The Simple Living Guide*

"This kind of self-help book is long overdue and one I've been waiting to recommend to clients...read it if you want a healthier and happier life and environment."
—Larry Gaffin, director of Center for Life Decisions, Seattle

"At last a guide to swapping the daily grind for a sensible lifestyle that fosters healthy families."
—Bob Quick, business writer, *The Santa Fe New Mexican*

"Everyday spending decisions are likely to have more impact on your financial well-being than investment decisions. This book will make you a smart spender."
—Paul Richard, director of National Center for Financial Education

"An anecdote-filled, insightful primer on how modern families can survive and even thrive on a single income."
—Doug Tolmie, special project producer, KOMO TV, Seattle

"A must for working couples. An entertaining, step-by-step approach for cashing in a non-stop lifestyle for one rich in quality."
—Carol Keeffe, author of *How to Get What You Want in Life with the Money You Already Have*

"A book that will benefit any family, single-income or not."
—Colleen Cramer, author of *Gifts on a Shoestring*

"Dappen shows why more money doesn't bring happiness. Then he presents a day-by-day plan for living a rich life with less. A great resource."
—Jacque Blix and David Heitmiller, authors of *Getting a Life*

"When I can't pay my bills, I close my eyes and open the book to a random page. I follow the directions and, within a couple of weeks, I have enough money to pay up."
—Steve Carlson, *Big Books from Small Presses*

"Both philosophic and pragmatic, this book explores the means and meaning of living on one income."
—Lynn Rosen, KVOS TV, Bellingham

"Had enough of the fast-paced, latch-keyed, two-earner treadmill? This book can help put quality back into your family's time."
—Marc Eisenson, author of *The Banker's Secret*

"Every bride and groom should be given a copy of this book as a wedding gift."
—Steven Lorton, Northwest Bureau Chief, *Sunset Magazine*

Shattering the Two-Income Myth

Daily Secrets for Living Well on One Income

by

Andy Dappen

Brier Books, Brier, Washington

Printed in the United States of America

Editor: Florence Hansen
Cover Design: Bob Lanphear

Library of Congress Cataloging-in-Publication Data

Dappen, Andrew R.
Shattering the two-income myth: daily secrets for living well on
    one income / by Andy Dappen.
        p. 416   cm. 22
    Includes index.
    ISBN 0-9632577-1-4: (pbk.) $14.95
    1. Home Economics.   2. Consumer Education.
    3. Thrift and saving.
640.42—dc20   CIP   97-93080

Contents

Acknowledgements

Many people contributed to this book through their willingness to share case studies, finances, experiences, advice, and lessons learned from the school of hard knocks. The real-life details and insights of those interviewed for this book, add strength, depth, and richness to the message. So to people like Joel Babione, Kim Bassey, Bryan Dickinson, George Elting, Leah Gary, Bonnie Glavas, Judy Harrison, Sue Ibarra, Mark Jenkins, James LeDuc, Melanie Naeger, Juliana Nievergelt, Gary Reid, Dana Sullivan, and Pam Withers, I owe my gratitude.

I also owe my gratitude to individuals whose finances are discussed in this book but whose names were changed for reasons of confidentiality. To you of fictitious names but of factual financials—thanks.

Special gratitude goes to my editor, Florence Hansen, for all those aggravating hours of copy editing. Readers may grumble that this book isn't cheap enough, but Florence's contributions have saved you a dollar or more. That gives you reason to thank her too.

Finally my deepest thanks to my wife for her moral support, advice, editing...and for the whip she brandished on sunny days when I wanted to go skiing.

Chapter 1:
The Myth

Get Richer: Quit Your Job

"Today, families need two incomes just to survive."
We've all heard versions of that remark, or have read stories in periodicals like *Time*, *Money*, and *The Wall Street Journal*, contending that families without two incomes are likely to find themselves in foreclosure.

It's out of necessity rather than choice, we are told, that about 60% of all American and Canadian families now rely on two incomes, even though a Decima poll reported that 70% of Canadian families with children would prefer to keep their children out of daycare and live a one-income lifestyle. But how would they survive?

We hear from young couples who can't pay their bills, older couples who can't afford to retire, Republicans blaming Democrats for higher taxes and lower wages, Democrats accusing Republicans of the same sins, and journalists creating ink about this modern dilemma. Everyone is voicing complaints, but is anyone making sense? Those who accept the premise that the modern family requires two incomes to stay afloat have entrusted their lifestyle as well as the financial, emotional, and spiritual health of their family to a half-truth.

Intuition propagates this half-truth. After all, if a family is having trouble living on one income, then two incomes must be necessary by merit of the logic that if one is good then two must be better. Furthermore, many couples (most notably those with no children or older children) insist that dual careers give them financial freedom and personal fulfillment.

But such testimonies depict only one side of a complex issue. The country has many citizens like Dan and Dana Sullivan of Omaha, Nebraska who were actually paying for the privilege to work. And it's brimming with people like Jim and Angela Benson, a couple from Snohomish, Washington, whose combined household income is $135,000 per year; whose liquid savings are non-existent; whose consumer debts total $46,000; and whose home and car loans total up to another $223,000 in unpaid debt.

How can a couple with combined earnings of $135,000 per year be having trouble making ends meet? How can it make sense to break their downward spiral by living on one income? And how can a single-income couple like Betty and David King of Gresham, Oregon live comfortably on $20,000 per year *and* save 25% of their income?

When you understand that you spend money—lots of money—to make money, and that a dollar saved is worth much more than a dollar earned, you begin to grasp the secret.

To Make Money Costs Money

In 1989, Dana and Dan Sullivan of Omaha, Nebraska were a two-income family making a combined income of about $41,000. Dana's salary (about $15,000/year) as the supervisor of a cleaning company was small, but because she worked nights and could swap child-care duties with Dan, her contribution made a difference.

When Dana grew tired of working nights and switched jobs to work days, the equation changed. Suddenly daycare for two children was costing the Sullivans $105 a week. That expense, coupled with taxes, ate up her earnings. And when she threw in the other work-related expenses (transportation, eating out, reliance on convenience foods) it was easy for Dana to see, "I was actually paying to work."

It's easy to blame a low salary as the problem here. But the cost of having both spouses work is far higher than most people think. A Labor Department study has shown that the *average* dual-career family loses up to two-thirds of its second paycheck to work-related expenses.

If children in need of daycare or after-school supervision are part of the equation, the picture can be even worse, but don't let the lack of children lull you into believing that the two-income lifestyle isn't expensive.

Take just one category of expenses: food. In the 1970s only 20% of the household food money was spent on meals eaten away from the home. In the 1990s that figure has risen to 40%.

Karen and Tim Blake, a childless couple from the midwest, began keeping a monthly tally of both the time and the money it took to earn their income. They noted the time spent preparing for work, commuting, working, and decompressing from their jobs. Then they calculated the money spent on commuting, work clothes, dining out, taxes, and hiring others to maintain their home.

The figures were dismal. To earn their combined yearly gross income of $46,000, they logged 108 hours during each of the 50 weeks they worked. If, like most Americans, they wanted to deceive themselves, they could claim they earned $8.52 per hour for their trouble.

But that would be a lie. To truthfully calculate their wage, they would first need to subtract all work-related expenses from their income. In the Blake's case, they spent nearly $30,000 each year on work-related expenses (including taxes), which meant they spent 108 hours a week to clear $16,000 a year. The real payment for their trouble? A meager $2.96 per hour.

These couples are not alone; they are representative stories of life in the 1990s. Their predicaments explain why a 1992 Merrill Lynch bulletin reported that the average 50-year-old has set aside only $2,300 for retirement. Their predicaments explain why, according to the American Bankruptcy Institute, bankruptcy rates are triple what they were in 1981.

Making money requires spending money and, if no one is home to look after children, maintain the house, buy food intelligently, prepare meals, purchase clothes on sale, obtain price quotes for major repairs...you'll be spending big bucks for the privilege of joining the nine-to-five parade.

A Dollar Saved

Ben Franklin is credited with saying, "A penny saved is a penny earned." His mind was in the right place but he flunked math. A penny saved equals two or three pennies earned.

Consider the Blake's case. They spent $30,000 to make $46,000. In other words, they spent $2 to earn $3. But suppose through smarter spending habits—by stocking up on food items found at loss-leader prices, by getting their teeth cleaned for half price at the local community college, by reducing heating bills 30%, by slashing Christmas expenses $500, by sharing a trash can (and the trash bill) with the neighbors, by putting $50 extra toward the principal of their mortgage loan each month—the Blakes slashed what they spent on personal expenses by $10,000. In their case, where their net income is only one-third of their gross income, a savings of $10,000 is comparable to earnings of $30,000.

Saving money does require time, but devoting one person to 'working the home' provides that time. For the Blakes, where their true hourly wage was about $3 an hour, the extra hour spent to save $20 on food sales, the 45 minutes spent and $15 saved on getting wardrobe items on sale, the half-day spent painting a room rather than paying a painter $100...these savings are big, tax-free earnings.

All of this reinforces the wisdom of Cicero who in 46 B.C. said, "Men do not realize how great an income thrift is."You, however, are getting the picture.

More to the Myth

Societal expectations are also interwoven into our acceptance of the two-income lifestyle. We live under the perception that nowadays wages are too low for the one-income family to acquire The American Dream. Maybe it was inflation that killed the purchasing power of the dollar or maybe it was suppressed wages fueled by corporate greed that killed our earnings. Either way, something or someone else is culpable for ruining the good life we believe we deserve.

In reality, the culprit stares at you through the mirror each morning. The 'they' you blame is you. And, like it or not, you're unlikely to keep the economics of the family off the rocks until you shoulder the responsibility for your difficulties.

The cost of living is not significantly greater now than it was 20 years ago, 40 years ago, or 90 years ago. In fact, in real dollars (dollars adjusted for inflation) what you pay today compared to yesteryear has dropped. Gas for the Ford is cheaper now than 20 years ago, the costs of consumer electronics have fallen to the basement, staple foods have dropped slightly, cars are so reliable that the lower main-tenance costs offset the higher sticker prices.

Mark Jenkins of Laramie, Wyoming, a self-employed writer lacking many of the benefits corporate employees take for granted (health-insurance, retirement plans, sick leave, vacation time), says that living on one income has not caused a financial crisis for his family—that the lifestyle is within the grasp of most middle-class citizens. "Most Americans have no concept of how wealthy they already are compared to the bulk of the world's populations, but they expect even more."

And therein lies the heart of the problem for it is our expectations more than the cost of living that have inflated. Look at houses alone. In 1953, the average residential space devoted to each American was 312 square feet; by 1993, the figure had swelled to 742 square feet. The median-sized house was 1,100 square feet in 1949 but had ballooned to 2,060 square feet by 1993. In 1970, only 34% of new homes had central air-conditioning and 58% had garages; by 1994, the figures were, respectively, 79% and 84%.

These days we need trophy houses to prove we are playing major-league corporate ball. These vacuous homes then must be filled with furnishings and gadgets that impress peers and simplify life.

Unfortunately, to finance the trophies and life simplifiers we 'need,' we are no longer their owners but their slaves, and every able-bodied family member has been sent to the fields. Hence the explosion of two-income families. In the mid-1970s only 17% of American families had both spouses working full time; by the mid-1990s that rate had climbed to the point that two-income families were the norm.

We've also had to raid the family savings. In 1973, Americans allotted 8.6% of their disposable income to savings; by 1993, that figure had dropped to 4.2%. In 1995 (after the coffers were drained paying for the four-bedroom houses, 28-inch-screen televisions, $3,000 computers, $25,000 Chevy Blazers, $1,500 stereos, and $100 Nike cross trainers) a million Americans filed for bankruptcy.

What Has All This Accomplished?

While this escalation in consumerism was presumably about buying The American Dream, about finding the good life, about demonstrating our worth, the chalice of our pursuit has proven to be an empty one. Our Holy Grail is leaving families financially, emotionally, and spiritually bankrupt. Consider the following:

◆ Compared to 1969, the modern American logs 163 more hours of work each year.
◆ The divorce rate in the mid-1990s is 34% higher than it was in 1970.
◆ Of 4,126 male executives polled in a survey, 48% saw their lives as "empty and meaningless."
◆ In recent studies, 69% of Americans report they would like to slow down and live a more relaxed life; 70% of Americans making over $30,000 per year say they would give up a day's pay each week for a day off; 75% of Americans between the ages of 25 and 49 report they'd like to see a return to a simpler society with less emphasis on material wealth; and 42% of Americans claim they are used up by the end of the work day.
◆ Studies of lottery winners consistently report that money is not synonymous with happiness. Five years after they got lucky, a majority of winners report being *more* depressed, alienated, and discontented.
◆ The 1996 *Index of Social Health* reported that while the country's Gross Domestic Product had risen steadily for 25 years, so had the percentage of teen suicides, child abuse, and drug abuse.
◆ While American parents spend an average of six hours per week shopping, they spend a mere 40 minutes per week *playing* with each of their children.

♦ Lawyers and doctors are among the highest paid professionals, but studies also report these professions have the highest percentage of unhappy people.
♦ In 1986, 32% of Americans between the ages of 18 and 29 believed the American Dream was an obtainable goal. By 1990, only 23% of that age group believed they could obtain The Dream.

These are not favorable signs that our love affair with consumerism is delivering the fruits we desire. One of the most damning indicators of all was reported in *The Wall Street Journal* when the results of a massive survey linking happiness to income level found that people making $0 to $1,000 per month had the same happiness quotient as those making $5,000 to $6,000 per month.

These figures are consistent with those from Harper's Index which reports 5% of Americans with a yearly income of $15,000 believed they had achieved the American Dream while only 6% of workers making over $50,000 a year believed they had arrived.

We've heard it everywhere from the Bible to Beattle verses—money won't buy happiness. Thornton Wilder said, "The difference between a little money and no money is enormous." The difference between a little money and a lot of money, however, seems to be negligible. Contentedness, fulfillment, realization...these are the spoils of completely different crusades.

Changing Attitudes

If you can embrace one simple idea, the rest of your life could become both easier and fuller. It's an idea that runs contrary to what we expect as Americans. It contradicts both what we were taught and what we have convinced ourselves we deserve. But it's time to stop dreaming of roses and start wrestling with the brambles. Making your life happier, more directed, and less stressful distills down to the acceptance of five simple words: You can't have it all.

No one wants to admit that you can't be rich and still have all the time you want for family and fun, that you can't have a trophy house and car without mortgaging yourself to banks and bosses, that you can't have a meaningful career without making concessions to children and spouse. But as Lisa Skalski, who walked away from a $36,000 job with IBM, stated in *Kiplinger's Personal Finance Magazine*, it's a matter of priorities. "You either spend time with your child or not—there's no such thing as quality time."

Nationally recognized business gurus and authors, Tom Peters and Nancy Austin, agree, "We have a number of friends whose marriages or partnerships crumbled under the weight of their devotion to a (career) dream. We are frequently asked if it is possible to 'have it all'—a fully satisfying personal life and a fully satisfying, hard-working one. Our answer is: 'No'."

Think about it. Does anyone you know have it all? Those who have it all are the ones you see Barbara Walters interviewing. You admire them until, a few months later, *People Magazine* writes about their drug dependence or pending divorce. Then it's back to Barbara Walters to find a new idol.

Good News For Modern (Wo)Man

The good news is that you *can have enough*—enough money to live comfortably; enough energy for family and self; enough time to do more than commute to work, make meaningless products, battle the traffic home, and decompress in front of sitcoms before repeating the ritual.

Having enough is vastly different from having it all, for it involves making choices and establishing new priorities. The fact that you've picked up this book indicates you're considering these choices, that old priorities aren't cutting it any more, that the treadmill you're on is leading nowhere. Apparently it's time for you to answer the tough questions:

♦ Do you want to make money and impress people with your corner office, $50,000 Mercedes, 4,500-square-foot house, tailored suits, swimming pool, Sun Valley-acquired tan...? If these are your goals, tuck your kids into daycare, drink your milk of magnesia, and stop simpering about 60-hour work weeks. You've made your choice.

♦ Do you want to enjoy a slower-paced life, take on the blessings and burdens of raising your own children, explore personal interests, volunteer time to worthy causes...? These are aspirations this book affords, but they come with a price. You may need to settle for a 2,000-square-foot house rather than one of the sprawling palaces your college classmates 'own'. You may need to traverse town in a six-year old Toyota rather than a new Infiniti. You may need to visit the neighborhood Thai restaurant on a quarterly basis rather than a weekly one.

These are tough choices, and if you believe there is an easy solution—that you simply need to keep looking—you'll simply delay the day that you come to terms with the rude truth: There are no easy solutions, only those that are better or worse for you. Ultimately, you must decide in principle (though not to such extremes) whether you side with the goals of Donald Trump or Mother Teresa.

More Good Reasons

The one-income lifestyle can do more than offer your family a road to fulfillment.

The lifestyle also reduces consumption. Many chores of the dedicated homeworker involve reusing, fixing, and recycling items two-income families are apt to throw away. Other methods of earning your keep at home will have you conserving energy and water. Others still will have you reducing your automobile dependence. In concert, these activities, whether motivated by environmentalism or capitalism, produce families with more sustainable habits and appetites. In a time when an escalating population uses resources like oil 100,000 times faster than that resource was created, this lifestyle is a notable contribution to the planet's future.

On another level, society may actually need parents who are less concerned about providing their brood with 500 square-foot bedrooms and private-school educations, and more concerned about actually parenting their children.

Studies, like Fordham Graduate Center's work with the *Index of Social Health,* seem to be validating this notion. For 25 years, Fordham University has monitored the national incidence of 16 social problems (including child abuse, teen suicide, drug abuse, high-school dropout rates, poverty rates, homicides, alcohol-related traffic fatalities) to compile its yearly index—a number that by itself means nothing, but when compared to previous years gives a basis by which to determine whether the nation's social health is increasing or decreasing.

From 1970 to 1977 the trend in the country's social health mirrored the rise and fall of the nation's Gross Domestic Product. Since 1977, however, the country's Gross Domestic Product has steadily risen while the Index of Social Health has steadily dropped to a point that is now 52% lower than the high point established in 1973. Roughly translated, the index shows that while the financial health of the country has continued to improve, the nation's social health has worsened.

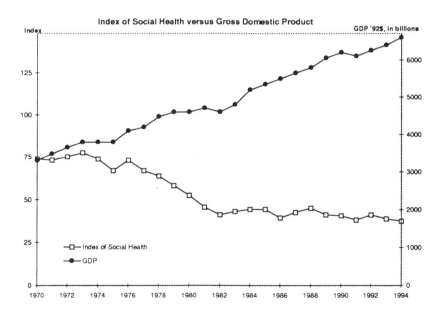

Reprinted with the permission of Fordham's Institute
for Innovation in Social Policy.

Since 1989, the country's social health has dropped 9%. This is true even though a quarter of the 16 variables measured (infant mortality, children living in poverty, unemployment, average weekly earnings, and poverty among seniors) are improving. The variables that are worsening (child abuse, teen suicide, drug abuse, and high-school dropout rates), however, are dropping at a faster rate and, tellingly, many of these variables are the ones involving children.

It is curious that since the mid-1970s, a period when the Gross Domestic Product has steadily risen (largely because of the 56% increase in families with two working parents), child abuse, teen suicide, drug abuse, high-school dropout rates have all worsened by more than 50%. Coincidence or connection?

Connection, say many single-income advocates. A frequently repeated theme of families who choose to keep one parent home until their children are at least of school age is the opinion that parents who opt for possessions over time spent with their children will pay for it later. Several parents interviewed for this book voiced this sentiment, "If you don't make the commitment to parent your kids, you're going to be dealing with a mess when adolescence rolls around."

Our social fabric is disintegrating in other ways as well. In *Saturday Night*, a major Canadian publication, a Toronto woman describes what is now endemic to modern life:

> She has four brothers and sisters, many of whom live nearby. "We don't help each other out," she shrugs. "My sisters and sisters-in-law all work. Everyone is too busy, too into their own lives...."
>
> With this comment she acknowledges, without resentment, one of the starkest changes that has taken place between this generation of women and the last...the move of women into the workforce vanquished the traditional community of at-home support. When she grew up, she continues, "there were always aunts and uncles around, and cousins....They paid for it by being thrifty."

Not only has our immediate family unravelled, so have the ties, the emotional support, and the values propagated throughout the extended family. Meanwhile, the demands of work have left Americans with less time and energy for other things that matter: schools, churches, charities, and non-profit organizations. *The Economist* reported that between the early and late 1980s the percentage of American adults volunteering for a cause dropped from 52% to 45%.

If it helps you make the leap to the one-income lifestyle, think of volunteerism as something that's greater than yourself. Think of it as something that's good for society as a whole. Maybe you should think of it as your patriotic duty.

Joining the Movement

If, for whatever reason, the one-income lifestyle speaks to you, you are not alone. Burgeoning movements from both the political left and political right are embracing concepts related to living on one income: concepts like frugality, simplifying needs, downsizing, downscaling. Increasing numbers of people are yearning to live rather than living to earn.

A poll funded by the Merck Family Fund in 1995 reported that among the 800 people interviewed in a nationwide survey, 28% had simplified, downshifted, or deliberately cut back on their income potential over the past five years as a result of changing priorities. Of those interviewed, 82% agreed, "We buy and consume more than we need."

Meanwhile, people from around the world—both famous and anonymous—have had plenty to say about the topic. Let some of their words inspire you to join the movement:

♦ We want a good future for our kids, so we work harder or become a two-income family and relegate raising the kids to day-care centers or nannies. We buy them the newest toys to prove our love. We earn for their college educations but relinquish the opportunity to spend time with them during their formative years. We bemoan the influences of 'bad company,' but we ourselves have never been in their company long enough to influence them. (Joe Dominguez and Vicki Robin)
♦ We work at jobs we don't like in order to buy things we don't need, so that we can impress people we don't care about. (Anonymous)

♦ A man may be very industrious, and yet not spend his time well. There is no more fatal blunderer than he who consumes the greater part of life getting his living. (Henry David Thoreau)

♦ High thinking is inconsistent with the complicated material life.... (Mohandas K. Gandhi)

♦ The love of money is the root of all evil. (the Bible)

♦ Where there is most labour there is not always most life. (Havelock Ellis)

♦ All work is empty save when there is love. (Kahlil Gibran)

♦ Men for the sake of getting a living forget to live. (Margaret Fuller)

♦ Most people spend most of their days doing what they do not want to do in order to earn the right, at times, to do what they may desire. (John Mason Brown)

♦ I don't know anyone who wished on his deathbed that he had spent more time at the office. (Peter Lynch)

♦ He who loves money will not be satisfied with money, nor he who loves abundance.... This too is vanity. (the Bible)

♦ Superfluous wealth can buy superfluities only. (Henry David Thoreau)

♦ In our rich consumers' civilization we spin cocoons around ourselves and get possessed by our possessions. (Max Lerner)

♦ The newer people of this modern age are more eager to amass than to realize. (Rabindranath Tagore)

♦ Reduce the complexity of life by eliminating the needless wants of life, and the labors of life reduce themselves. (Edwin Way Teale)

You are in good company in this effort to carve out a more meaningful life. When biblical writers, Gandhi, and Thoreau all support your principles, you are standing on high ground.

It is not, however, inaccessible ground. Thousands of everyday people like Melanie Naeger of Sugar Land, Texas, who gave up a career as a chemist, have realized that the sacrifices made to work the home are small next to the benefits received. "Staying home has allowed me to do a lot of volunteer work. I have been able to spend time with my kids and 'be there' for them. My faith has grown because I have more time for prayer and Bible study. And I have time to enjoy things I like to do...if I want, I can blow off everything to read a good book."

Working the Home

If you decide money (or a career) is *not* your principal priority, this book will demonstrate that you can quit working.

Several years ago, *Money Magazine* published the case of a couple from Redmond, Washington who, for the benefit of their children, decided to step off the two-income tread-mill. After taxes and all work-related expenses were sub-tracted from the wife's $30,000-per-year salary, the couple determined she was only contributing $4,000 to the coffers. They reasoned that if by 'working the home' (shopping intelligently, cutting energy use, performing more repairs, researching expenditures, visiting consignment stores, etc.) she could save $4,000, then the financial picture of the family would be a wash. Here is what shocked them: By working the home, she cut their expenses in half and saved $16,000. Her contribution on the home front didn't penalize the family but left it far richer.

Meanwhile, if your family is already living on one income (by choice or by the axe of corporate downsizing), don't blindly believe that sending your stay-at-home spouse back into the workplace will benefit the family's financial picture.

When Juliana Nievergelt, a stay-at-home mother from Foxboro, Massachusetts was considering whether to accept a sales job paying approximately $30,000 a year, she calcu-lated she would incur the following expenses: taxes of $9,300/year; clothing expenses of $800/year; dry cleaning costs of $350/year; lunching-out receipts of $1,200/year; dinner-out-with-the-family expenses amounting to $1,900/year; latte costs of $250/year; additional home-maintenance fees of $1,500/year; computer, monthly cell-phone bills, home-office expenses amounting to $4,000 the first year; and miscellaneous bills of $500/year.

Nievergelt already knew that by ignoring the perks she'd buy if money were no object (more clothes, a new computer, new living-room furniture, a home in a more expensive neighborhood), her family could live comfortably on her husband's salary. That made the proposition of working full time with these expenses ($19,800) marginal at best. However, when she added in one last expense (day-care: figured at $9,950/year), the thought of working was idiotic while the proposition of staying home and stretching one income was, indeed, a lucrative alternative.

Most people have no concept of just how lucrative. Using this book as a daily guide, the average family can realistic-ally expect to shave $13,000 to $14,000 from their annual expenses. And as you have now learned, those savings are the same as $40,000 in earnings.

Jettison the idea that staying at home means you're unemployed and embrace the concept that making one income go twice as far is, indeed, a job. Instead of working for someone else, you've become the Chief Financial Officer of a business: your home.

Those on the career track may demean this job as mundane, unchallenging, and unfulfilling, but you're quickly going to learn how naive they are. Unlike corporate jobs where you're confined to the cage of a specialty, home workers must be generalists. On consecutive days your work may have you determining the wattage of microwaves, comparing insurance policies, insulating heat leaks, reset-ting thermostats, formulating household cleaners, stockpiling food, and maintaining cars. Contrary to its unheralded status, working the home is an ever-changing job that delves into everything from appliances to zinfandels.

And when executed with diligence and motivation, it pays huge dividends. Says Betty King of Oregon, "Even though we gross only $20,000 per year, we feel like we're living on three times that amount because of what we do with our money."

One–A–Day Vitamins

Not only are the tasks of a home worker diverse but they offer flexibility. Some activities are likely to form the skeleton of your day—transporting kids to school, lessons, or practices; cooking; caring for sick parents; or exercising. But in between these activities, you will have time.

Some of that time should be devoted to your pleasures (reading, hobbies, keeping in touch with friends) and some of that time should be devoted to your job—the job of making half as much money go twice as far.

That's where this book helps. It gives you a task to pursue each day. Think of that task as your One-A-Day vitamin for financial health. Sometimes the daily task requires all of 15 minutes. Sometimes it will consume eight hours and stretch over several days. No matter. Success lies not so much in instigating hundreds of money-saving practices all at once as in maintaining the effort.

It's like sanding. Keep rubbing the shackles of your financial worries—sometimes with coarse sandpapers that save you hundreds of dollars, sometimes with fine papers that save several greenbacks—and you'll gradually turn the shackles to dust.

Chapter 2:
Getting Ready

Foundations and Preparations

Late in 1996 when Sarah Gunderson, a stay-at-home mother from New Hampshire, let friends talk her into helping a floundering business in need of her skills, her family felt the blow. Says her husband, formerly the family's only wage earner, "Used to be that we'd hit the sack at 10:30 or so. Now we go to bed almost every night after midnight. It's hard to even find time to grocery shop, make more than a meat-and-potatoes meal, or keep up with the laundry. Most nights we hit the rack exhausted, having spent no time even talking to each other."

Sarah notes, "We seem to cease doing any long-range thinking—we only have time to take care of immediate needs like preparing food or paying bills. The weekend is the only break, and increasingly we use that time for catching up...recreation used to be the focus of every weekend." She also notes, "The kids get less undivided attention. We put in time with them, but our minds are often not on the kids but on problem-solving related to jobs."

The Gunderson's already know they can survive on one income and, having seen both sides of the coin, long to return to the single-income lifestyle. This chapter may help you come to the same realization. Exercises define what attracts *you* to living on one income; they will help you define your desires. These desires are vital motivators. In Japan it is said, "wholehearted desire will pierce even a rock."

Additional exercises will put your finances under the microscope. The decision to drop a second income may be much clearer after you've analyzed just how much of that income pays the governor, is appropriated by the IRS, is consumed by work-related expenses...and how little actually gets deposited in the family vaults.

Working in concert, these exercises may indicate that your exit from Wall Street is more imminent than you imagined.

Beyond Gender Roles

Is *working the home* woman's work?

No! It's a job for whoever is attracted or best-suited to the role.

My family illustrates several aspects of the issue. My wife, Jan, has educational degrees, business skills, and a wage-earning potential that surpass mine. She's an excellent problem solver and knows how to get employees under her charge to focus their talents. All these skills make her our varsity corporate player.

I, on the other hand, am more interested in (and work harder at) saving money. I purchase fewer goods, investigate second-hand options, research purchases to find the best value, monitor sales, and fix broken possessions to ridiculous levels. All this makes me our family's ideal work-the-home candidate.

Which is what I did for a short while. When our first daughter was born, I scaled back my writing work. While Jan worked, I parented and performed the types of money-stretching tasks this book advocates. The chores we both hated (cooking, cleaning), we divvied up.

Because Jan's ultimate goal was to oust me from the home seat (she didn't like being an absentee mother), we wanted my work to progress. So when she returned from work, I'd escape to the home office to clock a half-day of writing.

Before long, Jan began working half-time and I logged more hours writing. Then, when our youngest daughter was two, Jan's company merged and her work evaporated. She was delighted.

For the past several years, she has maintained the home front and I have manned the word processor. As a freelance writer I have no benefits (disability insurance, medical insurance, retirement plan) and the fruits of my profession are half of what she earned.

Through smart use of the money I earn, however, our family of four maintains a comfortable lifestyle. Our yearly expenses of $20,000 pay for a nice (though unassuming) three-bedroom home; reliable (though plain) cars; adequate insurance (medical, life, and homeowner's); above-average amounts of travel; and all our day-to-day expenses (food, clothes, utilities...).

Our family illustrates a possibility that was rare 30 years ago but common today: The possibility for the roles of career and home to flow fluidly between genders. Many families have the ability to choose their wage earner and home worker from either side of the coin.

And many families are exercising that flexibility. Says James LeDuc of Biloxi, Mississippi a health-care professional who gave up his job to raise his two girls, "We felt it would be better for the girls if they had a more stable home life and if one of us was the primary care giver. As my wife is very career oriented, and I am not, we chose to have me stay home and assume the homemaking responsibilities and to have Julie focus on her career."

Enough families have reversed roles that there is a quarterly newsletter called *At-Home Dad* (61 Brightwood Avenue, North Andover, MA 01845-1702) to help the two million American men who stay home with their children deal with issues common to home-based fathers.

It's still more common, however, to divide responsibilities by sending husbands into the work place and delegating wives to working the home. While such families may resemble, in appearance, those of the 1950s, they are quite dissimilar.

As children age, one wage earner tires of a job, new careers emerge among the partners, or important causes capture the ideological imagination of a spouse, the modern family has the capacity to be extremely flexible. There are no hard-and-fast rules about who should and shouldn't be working—inside or outside the home.

Says Gary Reid of Canoga Park, California, "My wife has found it easier to find work and is now making nearly twice as much as I could. She is in mortgage banking, and people seem to trust women more with their money. I stay home and take care of a 17-year-old. I am not seeking employment now so that I can be there for him. That decision has improved his school work nearly 100%."

Joel Babione of Orlando, Florida says he's semi-reclusive and for 25 years held some 30 jobs which ended due to personal problems with managers and co-workers. For the past nine years, he's found more personal contentment taking care of the household and letting his wife, a partner at a CPA firm, concentrate on the earnings.

Bill Sanders of Bozeman, Montana spends several hours a day managing household chores and the remainder of most days skiing or bicycling. His wife, a lawyer, gets her adrenaline fix in the courts and does not take umbrage with her husband's lack of professional motivation. All of which has Sanders saying he has a match made in Heaven.

Many couples actually have the possibility of creating a heavenly match if each partner ignores the traditional expectations of what a man or woman should do and provides his ore her partner with the support needed to pursue driving interests, motivations, and purposes.

Why would you want it any other way? Wasn't it these interests, motivations, and purposes that attracted you to your partner? Why would you try to steer those qualities in a different direction from what you fell in love with?

Are You Suited To This?

Before you commit yourself to the idea of living on one income, make sure your goals and values are compatible with the lifestyle. The following list is a litmus test.

Be honest. If you thrive on the prestige and possessions money buys, seek social status, enjoy garnering power, admit it. You can always erase your answers later so that others won't know you're a money-grubbing, power-hungry, status seeker. Likewise, if you're a graduate of the Harvard Business School and are ashamed your goals are so unambitious, mundane, and common as to want to be a good parent, own up to it.

The point is to fashion a lifestyle that is fulfilling to *you* and that brings *you* happiness. That's impossible if the influences of family, friends, classmates, colleagues, and neighbors dictate how you answer these questions, as well as how you spend your time and money.

Read through the following list, marking each line accordingly: 1=very important, 2=somewhat important, 3=not important.

MY MAJOR MOTIVATORS INCLUDE:

____ Being looked up to and admired.
____ Excelling at the profession I trained for.
____ Being a good parent.
____ Cultivating a large circle of friends.
____ Living consistently within my religion or beliefs.
____ Spending quality time with friends and peers.
____ Being of service to others.
____ Helping my parents in their graying years.
____ Having an impact on others/society.
____ Being "a success" or "making something of myself."
____ Winning at whatever I decide to pursue.
____ Continuing my own growth and education.
____ Traveling widely.
____ Acquiring money.
____ Serving God.
____ Garnering power within my circles.
____ Maintaining the image/reputation of my family.
____ Pursuing recreational interests or hobbies.
____ Keeping pace with friends, peers, and/or colleagues.
____ Living in a way that does not overtax the world's resources.
____ Slowing down the pace of life and reducing levels of stress.
____ Living a life that is outwardly simple but inwardly rich.
____ Being considered a shaker and a mover.

The general trend of your answers reveals whether you're a good candidate to work the home rather than massage a career. If it's money, influence, status, power, prestige, and "success" that sparks you, you're probably not reading this book. You know that staying home will deprive you of the strokes you hold near and dear. Unfortunately, if you're on the money/status/power track, statistics do not support that this will buy you happiness. In his book *Modern Madness*, Psychotherapist Douglas LaBrier, documented that 60% of "successful" professionals who define their identity through money, prestige, and position are depressed, stressed, or victims of other job-related maladies.

If the general trend of your answers points to such values as being a good parent, pursuing recreational interests, slowing down the pace of life, cultivating friend-ships, living simply, helping others, or living consistently within your religion, then your aspirations are suited to jumping off the nine-to-five train.

Your Mission Statement

If you aspire to live on one income, take careful stock of what attracts *you* to the lifestyle. On days when you're dealing with screaming kids, fixing plugged toilets, or attending to other disagreeable duties, a mission statement will remind you of the underlying principles (children, religion, environmental ethic, personal growth) that make the unpleasantries tolerable. Like Nietzsche said, "If we have our own *why* of life, we shall get along with almost any *how*."

Use the following two lists to create a mission statement that defines your "why". Mark the lines of each list with: 1 = very important, 2 = somewhat important, 3 = not important.

I BELIEVE:

____ Superfluous wealth can buy superfluities only. (Thoreau)
____ Great wealth and contentment seldom live together. (English proverb)
____ The greatest wealth is contentment with little. (English proverb)
____ A great fortune is a great slavery. (Seneca)
____ Riches rather enlarge than satisfy appetites. (Thomas Fuller)
____ The larger a man's roof, the more snow it collects. (Persian proverb)
____ Enough is better than too much. (Dutch proverb)
____ Solvency is entirely a matter of temperament and not of income. (Logan Pearsall Smith)

____ He is rich that is satisfied. (Thomas Fuller)

____ Pearls around the neck—stones upon the heart. (Yiddish proverb)

____ Character is corrupted by prosperity. (Anonymous)

____ Health is better than wealth. (English proverb)

____ Our costliest expenditure is time. (Theophrastus)

____ He that has time has life. (English proverb)

____ He that gains time gains all things. (English proverb)

____ What the parents are, so will the children be. (Philippine proverb)

____ What the mother sings to the cradle goes all the way down to the coffin. (Henry Ward Beecher)

____ It is a wise father that knows his own child. (Shakespeare)

____ With your mother you will not want, but alone you will. (African proverb)

____ He who has neither father nor mother has no wisdom. (African proverb)

____ You shall have joy, or you shall have power, said God, you shall not have both. (Emerson)

____ What the superior man seeks is in himself. (Confucius)

____ It is better to be the head of a mouse than the tail of a lion. (Spanish proverb)

____ It is far better to borrow experience than to buy it. (Charles Caleb Colton)

____ You should be content with your lot; one cannot be first in everything. (Joseph Jacobs)

____ He is poor who does not feel content. (Japanese proverb)

____ My crown is called content—A crown it is that seldom kings enjoy. (Shakespeare)

____ Well-being is attained by little; nevertheless it is no little thing. (Zeno of Citium)

____ Let us endeavour so to live that when we come to die even the undertaker will be sorry. (Mark Twain)

____ God does not want men to overtax themselves. He wants men to be happy. (Henry Miller)

LIVING ON ONE INCOME WOULD...

____ Lessen the frantic, out-of-energy feeling of our family.

____ Eliminate the stress and anxiety of the daily commute.

____ Lower other stresses in our life. (Elaborate)_____

____ Allow us to spend more time with our children.
____ Let us (rather than the daycare) raise our children.
____ Leave time for hobbies and personal interests (list those of import)._____
____ Let us volunteer time to:_____.
____ Help us to better practice our religion. (How)_____
_____
____ Help us get involved with our schools.
____ Permit our children to be more involved with the following extracurricular activities:_____
_____
____ Give our family more flexibility. (Elaborate)_____
_____
____ Encourage us to travel more. (Where would you go)
_____
____ Reduce our environmental impact. (How)_____
_____
____ Facilitate a lifestyle that is simpler but richer.
____ Help us care for others who are in need (parents, disabled friends).
____ Other. (List)_____

After mulling over the philosophies of the first list and the benefits of the second, personalize this into a summary. Not inspired to wax poetic? Fine, just condense these lists down to line items defining your beliefs and expectations. On the top half of a sheet of paper use the first list to state your philosophies and priorities. For example:

"I believe:
♦ More money from two incomes does not equate to more happiness.
♦ Time is life and it should be devoted to more than the pursuit of money.
♦ Health is more important than wealth, and to maintain health requires concessions in how we live.
♦ Making enough money is preferable to making too much money.
♦ Too many people are the slaves of their possessions.
♦ Teaching, molding, and rearing my children is not a job I want hired out.
♦ Putting children above careers will produce children who put their children above their careers.

- Social status and power are not ambitions that will bring me contentment.
- Society will profit if I work less and volunteer more."

On the bottom half of your sheet, use the second list to target the benefits you expect to gain. For example:

"By working the home, I hope to:
- Slow down life at our house and reduce our stress levels.
- Find time for exercising, relaxation, and reflection.
- Enjoy time with our kids, teach them our values, and build a strong foundation for this most enduring of all human relationships.
- Appreciate simple pleasures and hobbies (music, writing, gardening, reading).
- Help the family financially by simplifying our needs, working the home, and economizing.
- Volunteer four hours a week to....
- Give us the increased flexibility to travel."

Post your statement where you will see it often and where it will inspire you to make the leap toward a more fulfilling lifestyle. Or, if you're already living on one income, keep that statement visible so that it continues to remind you of the big picture.

Affording the Jump

Can you really afford this one-income lifestyle? It's a question you're undoubtedly asking. If you've had trouble saving money on two incomes, the thought of downsizing to one is not only frightening, it runs contrary to common sense. But as emphasized earlier, it takes money (often lots of money) to make money.

The following exercises will produce hard numbers and mathematical confidence that living on one income is not financial suicide or fiduciary seppuku. Do these exercises.

In fact, you should do them twice. The first time through you'll get the general picture of what is spent to earn your second income. These figures won't be extremely accurate because many of your work-related expenses are not recognized as such. Consider the $2-a-day latte habit, toys bought out of guilt to appease kids who spend most of their waking hours with a sitter, expensive convenience foods many two-income families rely upon, unresearched car repair bills...they all have a work-related component that should be calculated. Until you know how to account for these expenses (I'll get to that), the best you can hope for is a sketch of what happens to your second income.

Collect your financial records, last year's tax return, and your daily calendar and start in on that sketch.

INCOME STATEMENT

Which family member would be quitting his/her job to work the home? What is the value of that person's:

_____ Yearly income.

_____ Benefits (e.g., stock options, insurances, retirement plan).

_____ **Total income.**

EXPENSE STATEMENT

Expenses that can legitimately be pegged to the second income include:

_____ Taxes paid on that income (include federal and state taxes). If your combined income bumps you into higher tax brackets, these higher rates should be assigned to the second income.

_____ Withholdings for redundant benefits (i.e., ben--efits you pay for but which would be received anyway through spouse's work).

_____ Transportation/commuting costs (gas and appropriate amounts for insurance, depreciation, repairs). It may be easiest to multiply job-related miles by a cost-per-mile figure that incorporates depreciation, licensing, taxes, repairs, insurance, and gas. Use *The Complete Car Cost Guide* (reference area of the library) for an exact figure of what it costs to drive your car. To guesstimate the cost of driving, figure that to drive one mile costs: 34¢ for subcompacts, 39¢ for compacts, 43¢ for midsize vehicles, 49¢ for large cars, and 70¢ for luxury cars.

_____ Image expenses. How much more per year does it cost to drive the right car, belong to the right clubs, be seen at the right functions?

_____ Tools of the trade. Is a car phone an important tool for work? What about a portable computer; specific software; a modem; business books; supplies for the home office; a fax machine; subscriptions to trade magazines, business papers, or on-line services...? Total 'em up.

_____ Clothing expenses (yearly expenses for work-related clothing).

_____ Cleaning expenses (yearly expenses to dryclean or launder the above).

_____ Grooming expenses (hair cuts, makeup, toiletries nail care, cosmetics). What is over and above your stay-at-home needs?

_____ Daycare and babysitting totals. Note: Day-care kids acquire more illnesses, so add in a percentage of doctors' bills, too.

_____ Lunch expenses. If you don't brown bag it every day, how much is spent eating out? If your spouse would switch to brown-bag lunches (if you had time to make those lunches), add the yearly totals of what (s)he spends lunching out, too. Note: A homemade lunch prepared by the average shopper costs about $1.25.

_____ Dinner expenses. How often are you eating out because you lack the post-work energy to cook? Are children in tow (if so, add their expenses; if not, add babysitting fees)? Note: A homemade dinner prepared by the average shopper runs about $2.75.

_____ Guilt expenses. Do you buy your children unplanned treats at the supermarket, impulse purchases at Toys R Us, or meals at McDonalds to appease the requests of children who spend much of the week with a sitter?

_____ Pick-me-up expenses. Lattes in the morning, a sweet roll during coffee break, microwave popcorn at 3 o'clock...add up all the bribes used to lubricate your eight-hour contribution to the corporate cogs.

_____ Decompression expenses. The flip side of the last expense: What do you spend to relax or forget about work? For some it may be a drink or three, for others a video, and others a drug. Also, add up what you spend on yourself by rationalizing, "I work hard and deserve this."

_____ Food. If you don't plan your food menu around the weekly sales (I'll get to that later) you're spending *at least* 30% (maybe even 40%) more than you should. If the lack of time keeps you from being a smart food shopper, take 30% of your yearly food bill and treat it as an expense.

_____ Home maintenance. Housecleaning, mowing, raking, window washing, gutter cleaning, fertilizing, gardening, landscaping, painting.... How much are you spending on maintenance jobs you would do yourself if time allowed?

_____ Unresearched expenditures. Do you lack time to comparison shop and/or to research large expenditures? Then you undoubtedly overspend on goods (cars, furniture, insurance, electronics, appliances, sports equipment, photography gear) and services (car repairs, remodeling, legal advice, consulting fees, home maintenance, equipment repairs). Figure that on all unresearched expenditures over $100 you overspend by 20%. Treat that as an expense.

_____ Miscellaneous expenses. Include additional expenses peculiar to your job: continuing education fees, job-related medical expenses, phone bills you absorb.

_____ **Total expenses** related to your second income (add together all of the expense categories).

YOUR DISPOSABLE INCOME

$_____ Subtract total expenses from total income.

This is it—the amount the second income contributes to the family's wealth. Look at the figure and weep.

YOUR TRUE HOURLY WAGE

Don't dry your eyes—there's more bad news coming. Open the daily calendar, study a typical six-month period, and carefully calculate how much of the average day and the average weekend is devoted to the job. Besides the time when you've punched the clock, how much time is spent: grooming in the morning, delivering children to daycare, commuting, parking the car, working overtime, fetching the children, attending business dinners, unwinding from the day, completing homework? And how much of the weekend is work related: getting suits dry cleaned, ironing shirts, catching up on paperwork, getting that slick corporate haircut, attending training workshops?

_____ Average hours per week devoted to work.

_____ Hours per year devoted to the job (multiply the figure above by the number of weeks you work; exclude paid holidays and paid sick leave).

Divide your true contribution to the family (disposable income) by the number of hours devoted to the job each year, and you've got your true hourly wage.

In your case, this works out to $_____per hour. Need another tissue?

Play It Again, Sam

The last several exercises are, at best, guesstimates. How can you pinpoint your expenses into the categories mentioned when you've never accounted for them this way? How do you account for your work-related time investment when you've never paid attention?

Nevertheless, the exercises show the general picture of what's happening to your money and time. The real picture is probably worse because in constructing this sketch from memory, you've forgotten many small expenditures of both time and money.

To crystalize the picture, get a 3" by 5" notebook for your pocket or purse and, over the next two months, record *every* expenditure made—even if it's just a measly quarter. Enter a code next to every work-related expenditure (e.g., C=clothing, Cle=Cleaning, De=Decompression, Di=Dinner, D/S=Daycare or Sitting, Gl=Guilt, Gr=Grooming, H=Home maintenance, L=Lunch, M=Miscellaneous, P=Pick-me-ups, T=Tools of the Trade...). List the miles you drive each day to work, the sitter, and the cleaners. Also, note food purchases (F) and unresearched expenditures (U) so that you can calculate the portion to be treated as an expense.

In the same notebook keep a time log. Over the two-month period, list all weekday and weekend hours devoted to the job.

After two months, use your notebook to create a more accurate picture of your disposable income, time outlay, and hourly wage.

When Bad News Is Good News

The truth of these exercises may jolt you. You are not unusual if you spend a total of 62 hours a week making a salary of $30,000 a year. And you are not unusual if, after taxes and expenses, your contribution to the family war chests is only $9,000. That makes your time worth $2.96 per hour.

Think about that. You're selling your life to create a marshmallow ad, defend a wife beater, engineer an electric pencil sharpener, sell wallpaper, or to perform one of a thousand jobs of dubious value. And you're selling your life for what? Under $3 an hour?

When your life is completed, will you look back proudly at how you doled out your most valuable gift—time? Will you say, "Those marshmallow ads really influenced society," or "My big regret is that I didn't get more wife beaters off the hook," or "Selling those cosmetics really fulfilled me!"?

All this bad news is good news if it forces you to reevaluate how you're spending the finite time you've been given—if it has you seeing that the simple road home could be more fulfilling than the cash-flow road to work.

Cash Flow

Of course you still need to know what would happen to your family's cash flow if you quit work today. The previous exercises may have proved that your *true* contribution to the family's total income stream was substantially less than you thought. But it's still a matter of thousands of dollars and you need to know whether you can cover your expenses without that contribution. A few hours of work will supply the answer.

INCOME

_____ Calculate your spouse's yearly take-home pay (an accurate figure is crucial). After social-security withholdings, insurance payments, and savings-plan contributions are deducted from earnings, how many dollars are coming home each month?

_____ Total up other sources of income augmenting your family's income each year (e.g., investment income, liquidated assets). Predicted earnings from the state lottery don't qualify.

_____ **Family's total income** without your wage.

FIXED EXPENSES

_____ Taxes. Unfortunately, the family income, small as it is, will have the mayor, governor, and president rubbing their greedy hands. Calculate what all those bureaucrats demand in income and property taxes. Remember, for the purposes of this exercise, you are not working. That probably puts the family income in a lower tax bracket.

_____ Loans. Add up the yearly outflow of money to all creditors (include what you pay on house, bank, credit-card, school, and car loans).

_____ Insurance. Some insurance payments (medical, dental, and life insurance) may be deducted from your spouse's paycheck before it comes home. Add up those premiums that are not deducted.

_____ Transportation. What's the minimum you'll pay to gas, maintain, and depreciate the family wheels (see entry for June 18 for help)?

_____ Food. Use figures from past years. Or, if you're committed to relying less on convenience foods and restaurants, figure that you can eat well for $5/person/day (cut the amount in half for young children).

_____ Utilities. Water, phone, electricity, gas, oil, sewer, garbage. Add 'em up.

_____ Maintenance. Use an average figure from years past to calculate what should be set aside for home and appliance repairs.

_____ Work related expenses. Wardrobe, continuing education....

_____ Other. Add up other fixed expenses unique to your family—medications, therapies, continuing education...

_____ **Family's total expenses.**

Bear in mind that this book *will* dig a deep divot in your fixed expenses. You'll learn how to drive down debt load, slash food expenses, nickel-and-dime your utilities, curtail your maintenance woes, eliminate unnecessary insurance... However, let's not get ahead of the game. How does the picture look at this moment? Without including discretionary expenditures you could eliminate—expenses like entertainment, dining out, donations, cable TV, club dues, gifts, superfluous clothing—is your total income enough to keep you afloat or are you going to drown?

If you're floating, you're nearly ready to make the move and the activities in Chapter 5 can make the lifestyle more lucrative than you may have imagined possible. This is no false promise; neither is it a promise to make life easy. These activities require that you devote energy to working the home. On many days you'll earn your keep by saving the family money. On some days you'll earn it by streamlining your wants and needs. On other days the smart consumer you will become will steer clear of costly blunders. And on other days still, you'll re-educate your family and make them accomplices in your mission.

If your cash-flow summary indicates the family is going to drown without your income, don't quit work yet but *do* proceed with the tips in this book. These tips will stretch your income and reduce your debts so that a year down the road your family may be ready to realize the one-income lifestyle.

Debt

Thoreau said, "I have found that, by working about six weeks in a year, I could meet all the expenses of living. The whole of my winters, as well as most of my summers, I had free and clear for study."

By living simply, Thoreau had 46 weeks a year to pursue his interests. You're working to accomplish a similar goal—to spring one person free 52 weeks of the year to pursue the interests of the family, whether that's children, charity, or chess.

If the cash-flow summary you just prepared proves that your expenses are too high to sacrifice that second income, accumulated debt is probably your problem. Debt by definition means you're living beyond your means and it has the ugly habit of siphoning the present paycheck to pay for past purchases. That is the start of a nasty spiral that strips you of financial freedom.

People who are out of debt (except for what is owed on a home) will find that the one-income lifestyle is not difficult to attain *if* they prioritize what's really important to them, accept the fact that they can't have it all, and employ the practices discussed in the following chapters of this book.

Unfortunately, if you've accumulated substantial debt (school, credit-card, and/or car loans) you will probably need to eliminate that debt (or consolidate it within a low-interest mortgage loan) before you can adopt the single-income lifestyle.

This book is not specifically about getting out of debt. Yes, the money-stretching advice it shares will add up to huge savings that disciplined families can use to eliminate debt. But strategies to keep compulsive spenders off the rocks of financial ruin are beyond this book's scope. Those who are burdened by debt and who want to break its strangle-hold should seek help.

One source of help is the Consumer Credit Counseling Service (CCCS) in your area. Look them up in the White Pages of the phone directory. Working with a counselor from the CCCS you'll destroy your credit cards, prepare and live within a budget, and receive something no book can provide—the moral support of others in similar predicaments. It's not an easy road to travel, but it will lead to a better life.

Other helpful tools? Library books (search under *Debt*). One interesting book to peruse: *How to Get What You Want in Life with the Money You Already Have* by Carol Keeffe (Little, Brown and Co., 800-759-0190). This book understands that people with spending problems (debtors) have completely different mindsets about spending and receive radically different emotional responses from their purchases. The book attacks the problem of personal debt from a platform that doesn't always make sense to money experts (most of whom are not debtors) but that seems to lead people with money problems out of their tailspins.

Once your debt is under control and you're committed to a few obvious principles (e.g., don't spend what you don't have, and tomorrow's earnings are *not* used for today's expenditures) you're ready to shatter the two-income myth.

Chapter 3:
Obstacles

Stumbling Blocks

Families that are tempted to abandon the two-income lifestyle for what they hope to be a healthier, more meaningful life still have important issues to address before they join the movement. While many of the financial implications of the switch have been addressed, what happens if a change of fortune (a job loss) changes the equation? Or what happens if divorce alters the picture?

Then there are issues of image and status to consider. For those of you accustomed to the image of being a professor, a financial analyst, or a doctor, will stripping your stripes down to those of a humble homemaker be too drastic a drop in status?

These issues are all hurdles that keep two-income families from pursuing a new course, a new direction, a new life that their hearts say would be better for everyone concerned but that their heads say are too risky to pursue.

This chapter looks at those hurdles and helps you follow your heart.

Emergency Funds

Tragically, what-if scenarios keep many couples married to a two-income lifestyle that has grown stale and exhausting. Many couples commit themselves to working two incomes so that financial ruin will not befall the family *if* one partner loses a job. A hypothetical future shackles the family to an unpleasant (and very real) present.

A better solution to this particular problem? An emergency fund.

Before leaving your job, build up at least three months of savings (preferably six) in case the job market rains on your parade. Should that rainy day arrive, remember that you can both seek employment, shortening the period of wagelessness.

To build your emergency fund, start living on one income now and devote all take-home pay from the second income to savings. The exercise not only builds your emergency fund, it's a trial run to see whether you can live this way. If you can live on one income while you both work, living on a single income later (when you will be working to stretch that single income) will be cake.

Divorce Insurance

In families with children, more often than not it's the mother who lobbies for the single-income lifestyle and who inherits the role of homemaker. It's not just the day-to-day finances, however, that worry women as they contemplate the leap. Some are unwilling to leave the work place because they perceive their careers, in part, as a form of divorce insurance.

This line of reasoning contends that, should a marriage go sour, working women (and the children of working women) will not become financial victims of the collapse— they'll have more options available. Although many women relate to the argument, another line of reasoning contends that rather than pouring major energy into divorce insurance, husbands and wives alike should be pouring their energy into *preventing* divorce in the first place.

Judith Wallerstein, a clinical psychologist and leading authority on the effects of divorce, says in her book, *Good Marriages*, "In today's marriages, in which people work long hours, travel extensively, and juggle careers with family, more forces tug at relationships than ever before. Modern marriages are battered by the demands of her workplace as well as his, by changing community values, by anxiety about making ends meet each month, by geographical moves, by unemployment and recession, by the vicissitudes of child care, and by a host of other issues."

In her book about two-career marriages titled *The Second Shift*, author Arlie Hochschild, a sociologist at the University of California, Berkeley, looks at our family-unfriendly society. Lack of day-care options, flex-time, job-sharing opportunities, personal time, and energy leaves the American family (and especially the American woman) overworked, overworried, and overwhelmed. Hochschild maintains that marriages often suffer because of these added strains.

Over the past 20 years, a period when the number of two-income families increased by nearly 60%, it's quite feasible that the strains of added fatigue, frustration, futility, guilt, and alienation explain why divorce rates have increased 34%. It's quite feasible that these strains explain why, at a time when some 2.3 million people tie the knot each year, another 1.2 million people cut the cord.

The irony here may be that while the two-income lifestyle does provide options to both partners in the event of divorce, it may be creating the very monster it is supposed to guard against. Furthermore, as writer Elizabeth Gleick notes in *Time Magazine*, "Despite their work outside the home, most women still suffer a severe income drop after divorce. The by-product of what remains the world's highest divorce rate is millions of children thrown into poverty, millions more scarred by bifurcated lives and loyalties....The breakup of families is increasingly seen not only as a personal tragedy but a social crisis."

Wallerstein, meanwhile, notes, "I am sometimes criticized for being overly pessimistic about the long-term effects of divorce, but my observations are drawn from the real world. Only if you see the children and parents of divorce day in and day out can you understand what the statistics mean in human terms."

It's enough to make you take serious stock of your marriage and to put whatever effort you can into nurturing and strengthening it. It's enough to make you treat this relationship (especially if children are involved) as though divorce were not an alternative. Maybe it's even enough to make some dual-career families realize that sacrificing one career is preferable to the options.

Certainly a repeating theme among the one-income families interviewed for this book was this: Life is far less stressful when one partner manages the home. And almost all families interviewed reported that stress reduction translated into happier, closer-knit marriages as well as better parent-child relationships.

The Image Gap

A problem awaiting newcomers to the single-income lifestyle is not financial at all. It's the identity our society attaches to what you do. You are a writer, a doctor, a professor and, mysteriously, that garners more respect than the job of keeping the household solvent, or of raising well-adjusted children.

In surveys of couples who scaled back to one income, nearly 30% of home workers say the hardest part of the transition is the loss of identity and the absence of professional status. Prestige, it seems, does not ride on the coattails of being a homemaker. Cultural stereotypes cast homemakers as unambitious, uninteresting, or shallow.

You may wrestle with feelings of failure and inadequacy when you no longer have impressive job titles or business accomplishments to report to your alumni magazine. Says Kim Bassey of Winnipeg, Manitoba, who took a two-year leave from her post selling surgical equipment for Johnson & Johnson, "Raising children is probably the most important duty a parent has, but I didn't feel like I had an identity when I left my job. It's one of the main reasons I went back to work."

Bassey admits that the identity crisis is self-imposed—that after getting an education and embracing the concept that modern women can have meaningful careers she was betraying her training and modernity by staying home.

And in her case she's trapped in a no-win situation: Away from work she wrestles with the identity issue, away from her kids she feels guilty. "Education and feminism were supposed to give women choices, but it has backfired and left us with a dilemma."

Education and history are not much kinder to men who consider working the home. Men have traditionally been the primary providers of their families, meaning that many will find their machismo sorely challenged if they tend the nest while their wife brings home the bacon.

As is the case with women, however, the identity issue may well be self-imposed. Even in the testosterone-charged atmosphere of the armed forces, James LeDuc, a house husband living on a military base in Biloxi, Mississippi notes, "I have found that men in the military are more accepting of my role than their wives."

LeDuc goes on to say, "Rather than feeling less manly, being at home has given me the opportunity to experience more. It has made me more secure in who I am and strengthened my relationship with my wife and children."

Bryan Dickinson, who spent 12 years in the United States Marine Corps, agrees that the identity issue is mainly mental. "When I tell women that I am a house husband, they make all kinds of encouraging comments."

Dickinson now lives in Waynesboro, Pennsylvania with his family and refuses to let tradition mold him. "I am just as much a man now as in the marine years. I can ensure that my children feel as strong about themselves as I do about myself....there is no shame in taking responsibility for the upkeep of the family."

At-home spouses who can't shake the identity issues through mental adjustments alone, should look to charities, schools, and non-profit groups for help. These organizations give many professionals who have abandoned the workplace an outlet for contending with the identity dilemma.

Volunteering allows you to apply your skills to a worthwhile cause. Because you are volunteering, you can decide when, where, and how long you will work. The work, however, gives you an opportunity to interact with adults on matters that transcend the family. The organizations you help are normally extremely appreciative of your effort. And by assuming a little responsibility, you'll often be given the chance (if you want it) to assume much more.

Although Janet Stewart of Lynnwood, Washington worked as a mortgage banker, financial analyst, and software consultant before adopting the single-income lifestyle, volunteering as the treasurer of the PTA organization at her daughters' school has brought her as much satisfaction as any of her paid positions. "It feels good for the soul to donate time to something I really believe in—like schools—rather than to a commercial cause that revolves around making a buck. And it feels good because as a volunteer you're really valued for your contribution."

Stewart also emphasizes that volunteering has helped satiate her need for adult interaction, one of the ingredients she missed most about leaving the workplace. "I've gotten to know parents who are in a similar stage of life and who have had careers as medical researchers, doctors, lawyers.... These are interesting people I would never have rubbed elbows with in my past work."

It's also been said by many homemakers that they feel like they receive short shrift at social gatherings—that the eyes of career types glaze over in boredom when speaking to someone who simply manages a family.

Bonnie Glavas, formerly a legal assistant who now lives in Tulsa, Oklahoma, has noticed none of this. "Most people respect our decision...many are envious of the fact that I don't have to work."

Sue Ibarra, a Spanish lecturer at the University of Wyoming who left her teaching post to raise her two children, concurs. "I've yet to hear a negative word or get a cold shoulder from colleagues, students, men, or women about my decision. Most tell me they think it's great. Many tell me they'd do it, too, if they could afford it."

Ibarra admits that she worried about the identity issue before leaving her job. "I'd been teaching for 10 years and I wondered whether raising a family would be enough. Was I blowing it? Would I be able to talk to adults again?

"I talked to a lot of people who had left their jobs— mostly women, but some men—and no one was sorry about their decision. Most were really happy.... All of them were supportive, telling me this was something more important than work."

All of which raises the question: Do corporate types actually snub those who assume the lowly position of a homemaker or is this loss of identity merely a monster of one's own making? Likely, the answer is: Some of both.

Regardless of root, this is a serious issue to be grappled with before leaving your job. How will you contend with new acquaintances who want to leave your company as soon as they discover you don't have a *real* job? How are you going to respond to questions like, "Don't you miss working?" or "What do you do all day?"

The latter question is actually one that should bolster your self-image. It should give you considerable pride. Why? Because working the home requires broader skills than those employed by most corporate drones. How many people can honestly say they are child psychologists, teachers, disciplinarians, chauffeurs, chefs, bookkeepers, purchasing agents, researchers, repairmen, handymen, schedulers, and comptrollers at their nine-to-five jobs? How many can say they do everything from the chores of the janitor to those of the CFO?

So whether you tell yourself that everyone defines meaning differently and ignore the snobs who treat your definition as a lowly one, or whether you opt to challenge their presumed superiority, the important point is not to let the beliefs of others mold you. Like John F. Kennedy said, "Conformity is the jailer of freedom and the enemy of growth."

Spousal Respect

The respect of a spouse is another topic of concern for those contemplating the mothballing of their pinstripes. Says Pam Withers, a publisher and editor from Vancouver, British Columbia, who has no intention of leaving her career, "In my experience, men treat their wives with more respect and assist more with the housework when their wives have careers away from the home. Stay-at-home women are more likely to be taken for granted."

It's an observation that also plagues stay-at-home men. Husbands who question whether running the household is fitting work for a man will wonder how their wives could respect such milquetoasts.

Sometimes these are real concerns. Just as often they are imagined. Leah Gary of Las Cruces, New Mexico, says she believes her marriage has benefited greatly because she *does not* work outside the home and can, therefore, spend far more time with her husband. About matters of respect she says, "He helps out around the house, realizing how difficult my job can be raising kids, cleaning, cooking...."

Julie LeDuc, a nurse for the Air Force, is inclined to believe that the loss of a spouse's respect is the creature of a couple's own making. She says of her stay-at-home husband, "I respect him a great deal for taking on this role.... Masculinity is not determined by a paycheck nor is it demeaned by taking on the child-rearing role."

There is no definitive answer to whether spouses who work the home are taken for granted or are more revered. Testimonies abound to support both sides of the claim. What's important is that you discuss the matter in detail with your spouse *before* you embark on this new path.

Heart-to-heart talks, regular planning sessions, church retreats, marital workshops—they are all avenues to facilitate the discussions that must take place if this change is to work. Living on a single income is a doomed prospect if both partners aren't behind the goals, aren't in agreement about how the family will benefit, aren't willing to pull together to make the lifestyle work, and aren't fully supportive of the role each partner plays in the arrangement.

For most young couples, part of that support is an understanding that adopting the single-income lifestyle is not a confession that the family wants the clocks rolled back to the age of June and Ward Cleaver. Research indicates that only a small percentage of young Americans would be happy in the strictly defined, stereotypical roles of the past.

Living on one income is unlikely to work if the change significantly worsens the stay-at-home spouse's status or access to family funds. Spouses who work the home but whose contributions (contributions that are very significant) are not appreciated or are even belittled, will have their efforts and egos undermined. And spouses who work the home but who must grovel for the expenditures they need to make are going to feel like prisoners caught in a trap rather than partners contributing to a shared dream.

There's little to prevent couples from working out these matters of respect. As mentioned in the previous section, the tasks tackled by the home worker are usually more varied and often just as complex as those the corporate worker faces. The competent home worker is a Benjamin Spock, Bob Vila, Helloise, Ralph Nader, and Sylvia Porter rolled up into one package. All of which means the issue of respect is largely one of perception—of opening the eyes of a spouse who underrates the job, of not underrating the job yourself.

Finally, these matters of respect boil down to what you demand. If you demand to be recognized and respected, you're likely to garner that respect whether you're a CEO or an OEC (Official Excrement Changer). And if you exhibit the backbone of a doormat, you'll get treated like one.

The Big Empty

Judy Harrison, the publisher of *Canoe & Kayak Magazine*, but a stay-at-home mom when her children were growing up, says that one-income families were more abundant 20 years ago. "I had more support among friends and neighbors, than the modern family. My sense is that people who come out of school, move immediately into a career, and then think about staying home panic over what they are going to do all day."

By Harrison's reckoning, people are afraid to be with themselves, afraid they don't have the interests or imagination to fill all that time, afraid of the lack of structure.

Melanie Naeger of Sugar Land, Texas, has been a stay-at-home spouse since 1979 and confirms Harrison's suspicions. "I'm sometimes jealous of my husband because he has somewhere to go every day. It can be lonely at home. Many of my neighbors are working. It is a bigger effort to find friends."

Parents who stay home for the benefit of their children will find their worries about the Big Empty are unfounded; children suck up time faster than a vacuum cleaner works on dirt. But what if you decide to work the home and don't have kids? If the Big Empty is a problem, the solution boils down to three words: Get a life.

Getting a life is as easily said as done. Take courses through the community college; start exercising; take music lessons; join local clubs (pick up a list of the possibilities at the library); get involved with a local church, mosque, or synagogue; volunteer time to a non-profit organization or charity; participate in activities through the local library, recreation center, or neighborhood association. The modern homemaker needs more imagination to meet people than in bygone days but, if you want to be busy and aren't, you aren't trying very hard.

George Elting of Burien, Washington, a house husband who once worked in the aerospace industry, states that besides caring for children and tending to chores, he runs a local computer bulletin board service (BBS); is the vice president of the Parks, Arts, and Recreation Council in his town; is on the 4th of July Parade Committee; and is active in a grassroots park bond issue. His advice to people who worry about what they'll do with their time? "Don't let the laundry pile up too high or you'll never catch up."

Future Employment

Another fear keeping people tied to the work place is that of losing skills and qualifications if and when they decide to don the pinstripes again. Popular dogma contends that once out of the job market you become progressively less employable.

"It's not necessarily because you lose your skills, but because there are a thousand people out there who want—and can do—your job," says Kim Bassey of Winnipeg, Manitoba who, after spending a year and a half at home with her young children, became increasingly nervous about becoming obsolete. "You feel that gap in your resumé is going to weed you out of the selection process."

The concern is legitimate. If you decide to live on one income and circumstances change (e.g., your spouse is fired), will you be able to pinch-hit and help pay the bills? But it's also a hypothetical concern and, if you're going to play that game, there are equally legitimate hypothetical questions to sway you the other direction. For example, should you let future possibilities (possibilities that may never occur) chain you to an unfulfilling present?

And while we're speaking hypothetically, if circumstances forced you to work again, would you even *want* to go back to the job you're hoping to leave? After being out of the job market for several years, will you be attracted to a different career—one where new training may be required, one where your past career (and departure from it) might be of little consequence?

Euripides said, "What we look for (in the future) does not come to pass—God finds a way for what none foresaw."

Meanwhile, Thomas Fuller said "He that fears not the future may enjoy the present."

The point?

Don't let fear of the future anchor you to a present you're ready to change. Roll the dice. It takes courage, but you won't reap the rewards unless you take a chance. Many who adopt the one-income lifestyle will find that it suits them. They'll find working the home and the connection this builds with their family and community more meaningful than amassing profits for a corporation's shareholders.

And some who adopt the one-income lifestyle will find that either for financial or personal reasons, they are eventually drawn back to the work place. Should that happen, take note of this advice from Marcus Aurelius, "You will meet the future, if you have to, with the same weapons of reason which today arm you."

If your path does lead you back to the work place, trust that options will be available to you. Maybe you will find an employer who admires the values and perspectives of those who took time to raise a family. Maybe you will have a friend who wants to hire you.

Maybe you will find that self-employment is a viable option. Currently 14 million Americans work full time out of the home and another 13 million run part-time home-based businesses. There are home-based opportunities for: resumé writers, credit consultants, interior designers, craft-business owners, gift-basket makers, collectibles brokers, part-time secretaries, herb farmers, child-care providers, apartment cleaners, house cleaners, window washers, landscapers, contractors, janitors, computer consultants, computer programmers, computer software instructors, career counselors, bridal consultants, dating-service owners, event planners, home health-care providers, image consultants, mobile DJs, personal shoppers, pet sitters, professional organizers, security patrollers, private investigators, writers, language translators, seminar promoters, public relations advisors, desktop publishers, graphic designers, newsletter publishers, advertising copywriters, bed-and-breakfast owners, hair stylists, pet groomers, physical fitness consultants, house inspectors, house painters, pest-control experts, plumbers, electricians, beauticians, food deliverers, chauffeurs, bookkeepers...

Bonnie Glavas of Tulsa, Oklahoma didn't let worries about the future torment her when she took a leave from her career, "It is a sacrifice to leave the workplace if you enjoy your career, but when you realize the importance of being there for your children during their early, formative years, time spent away from a career seems insignificant. There will be time for you to carry on after your children are set on the right path. Why have children if you are going to let someone else take care of them?"

Meanwhile, when Mark Jenkins and his wife Sue Ibarra decided to adopt the single-income lifestyle, they didn't let Mark's rather unpredictable future as a self-employed writer deter them from what they believed was important in the present. Says Mark, who in earlier times has washed windows, worked on oil rigs, and done construction work, "The truth of the matter is that most middle-class Americans, especially those with an education, can find work if they must. Making enough money to get by is not hard in this country."

The other truth is that most people who adopt the one-income lifestyle will make it work and will not want to return to those harried days of working two jobs. "Almost every day," says Sue, "I remind myself how happy I am that we made this decision."

Chapter 4
First Steps

First Things First

We had entered the black hole of entropy. It had started in April when our three-year-old fell off a slide and broke her arm. Over the next six months the timer on the microwave died, my work computer crashed randomly, the rim of the mountain bike absorbed a fatal bend, the new VCR proved itself a lemon, our sewage pump jammed, a speaker woofer developed a maddening bark, the lawn mower died, and both my wife and I cracked a tooth.

That was the top half of the list. Also, one car or the other was continually under the wrench, the movement sensor of our outdoor security light stopped sensing movement, roots from the cottonwood trees buckled the driveway, the bathroom sink suffered a fatal chip, a skylight developed a skyleak, the dishwasher racks kept jumping their tracks, a car tire took on a maddening leak, the no-stick frying pan started sticking....

Life vacillates through such cycles. You float between financial doldrums and tempests. And the people who weather the onslaught well are those who recognize that misfortune and fortune are the braided strands of the same rope and prepare accordingly.

Your chore today is to begin building the infrastructure that readies you for Mr. Murphy's visit. When the shirt hits the flan and you need a stain remover, when the Model T needs Mr. Goodwrench, when the broken arm needs Dr. Welby, or when the VCR needs TLC, readiness has you dealing with the problem promptly and profitably.

Supplies

Preparedness requires a few supplies. Over the course of the next year you will be keeping notes, addresses, and phone numbers about scores of repairmen, services, doctors, consultants, experts, and companies, all of whom deliver outstanding bang for the buck. You want this arsenal of advice at your fingertips when the doldrums shatter.

◆ Keep your notes and phone numbers in either an alphabetized notebook that travels with you (good for travelers), a computer database (good for trend setters), or in a Rolodex (good for traditionalists). Personally, I favor 3"x5" index cards, a medium-sized card file or recipe box (footprint of 5"x5½"), and alphabetized dividers to help me quickly file and find cards.

Index cards, unlike Rolodex cards or the lines of address books, are large enough to note multiple sources on cards dedicated to subjects like Appliances, Car Repairs, Dry Cleaners, Doctors, Grocery Stores, Libraries, Mail-Order Houses. They're also large enough to keep notes on individual companies or to list important tips about dealing with these companies.

Unlike an address book, index cards can be rewritten when extensive changes make them unreadable. And unlike a computer, you don't have to boot up an index card to find a phone number.

Decide for yourself how you want to organize the information you unearth. Flip ahead and browse through random pages of the book. Once you understand the type of information you'll be collecting, you can decide how to file it. Then it's off to the store.

◆ While you're purchasing supplies, pick up a weekly or monthly calendar: Like any other job, you will need to organize your time. Also, buy two boxes/packets of colored (e.g., orange) self-adhesive dots. The dots in one box should have a ¼" diameter, the other a ½" diameter.

These dots function like strings around your finger. When a particular chore requires follow-up, contemplation, or additional phone calls, a dot on your watch, fingernail, or refrigerator handle reminds you of your unfinished work. At other times you'll be putting these dots in places where children and spouse see them. When they drop the question, "What is this for?", you'll have their attention for discussing their role in a particular project.

Just Do It

Dots may seem an unsophisticated trick for implementing action, but until you adopt a better technique to jog the memory and spur you into action, use them. Transforming you into a fount of information on how, in theory, you can stretch your dollars is not the intent of this book. Getting you to *act* on the ideas is. It's the implementation of ideas, not the ideas themselves, that's money in the bank.

Keep that point front and center: It's action that really counts. Genius has been said to be one percent inspiration and 99% perspiration. The same applies to prosperity.

When you worked for a business, you gave people you may not have even known, liked, or respected the best energy of your life. You gave them action and that made them money. Now it's time to give that energy to what you care about most—your family, yourself.

In the years ahead you can get what you want *most* for both your family and yourself. It's as simple as this:

1) define and remain focused on your goals
2) make the necessary choices to reach those goals
3) act on those choices

Unfortunately, simplicity is not the same as easiness. As time rolls on, it's hard to remain focused on goals (hence the importance of reviewing goals often by hanging them in a visible place). It's hard to remember that in every situation you do have choices (many more choices than you first recognize); good choices *will* lead to what you want most, bad choices steer you off course. And it's hard to summon yourself to act.

But once you have identified your goals and made the choices necessary to pursue those goals, *action* is all that separates you from success. So that's what the rest of this book provides. On the pages that follow, you'll find an action for every day of the year. Some of these actions will be finished in five minutes. Others may require five hours of your day.

Don't let the inability to do the task all in one push keep you from starting. Begin when you have five minutes to spare. Then throughout the day, chip away at the task 10 or 15 minutes at a time. You *can* complete these jobs.

In the name of action, place this book where you will bump into it each morning (on top of the toilet?). At that time, turn to the appropriate day and receive your assignment. Work that assignment into the course of the day. Then give yourself the satisfaction of checking off the assignment when it's done.

Naturally you'll need to use discretion in deciding which tips are relevant to you. The suggestions that follow are ideas, not commandments. Read them and implement those that make sense for your situation. A tip that seems like too much effort for the return is, perhaps, one that's best ignored. One that seems to offend your sensibilities is worth thinking about—why does it rub you the wrong way? Is it you or me that's off base? Still, if you decide the tip doesn't fit your lifestyle or temperament, ignore it in good conscience. Even if you ignored half of the tips that follow, there would still be nearly a thousand suggestions that will keep you working the home profitably.

Throughout this book I give a number of product and service suggestions that my experience (or research) indicate are worth the money spent on them. I urge you *not* to take these recommendations as gospel but to use them as a starting point for research of your own. See if you can best my recommendations. And if you unearth better alternatives, tell me (send information to me care of the publisher) so that my advice evolves.

Keep in mind that there is a paradox to some of these recommendations as well—should you spend money to save money? So before making outlays on any such recommendations, ponder whether the product or service really applies to your needs, and whether it will give back more than you lay out.

But don't get too embroiled in thought. Remember, action is what you're after. Keep working steadily and diligently through the body of tips in this book and they will create a vehicle to carry you down the road you want to travel. An action a day *will* change your life. Now turn to the appropriate page and DO IT.

January

A major goal of this book is to tear your family away from the disastrous habit of impulse buying. Impulse buying comes in two forms: You see something at the store—a bag of chips, a latte, a pair of pants—and decide on the spot to purchase it, or you suddenly get the notion that you need a new blouse or deserve a new computer game, so you rush out and purchase.

Both behaviors are killers. The unplanned bags of candy and the computer games you deserve all bleed you of your finite income. Singly, these purchases seem harmless, and therein lies their danger. They are not single phenomena. Add up the yearly impulse expenditures at the grocery store alone—the candy bars, pop, coffee, cookies, chips—and you're the average consumer if you've frittered away $600 a year on foods you hadn't expected to buy. Apply this same concept to items bought on impulse at department stores, clothing boutiques, pharmacies, book stores, gas marts, auto shops, discount malls, music shops, computer emporiums... and we're often talking about thousands of dollars *a year* that leak away from you.

It's easy to rationalize these expenditures. Internal voices say, "Life wasn't meant to be completely disciplined," or "You worked hard today; you deserve a reward," or "The kids have been ignored lately and need a little boost," or "Your friends have this, why shouldn't you?"

But think back to the beginning chapters of this book and remember: You can't have it all. Every action has a reaction, and every purchase robs from other opportunities. The opportunities these impulses rob from are posted on the Mission Statement you prepared in Chapter 2. These opportunities are what you identified as being *most important* to you. They are obtainable but you'll need to exorcise impulse buying from your *modus operandi*.

Pam O'Reilley of Arlington, VA has been living on one income for nine years since leaving a career as a public relations writer. Her purchasing rule: "I never buy on impulse. I make myself wait at least 24 hours."

You'd be surprised how much money this saves. The $2 bag of potato chips you see, the $5 toy the kids just grabbed, the $10 hat... all these things are avoided because, once the moment passes, you realize you don't need them.

♦ Today, prepare your Master Purchasing List. This is a register for everyone in the family to list those items they want/need in the immediate or distant future. Partition a sheet of paper into columns, giving each family member one column. Also make a column labeled "Household" to record such items as a lawn mower, knife sharpener, bathroom tissue, dishwashing gloves—items the household *needs*, as opposed to those things you *want* to spiff it up (those items go in your personal column).

Post the Master Purchasing List in a central location (like the refrigerator if it isn't already swamped with papers) and discuss its purpose and use with your family this evening. From this point forward, the goal is to record all wants and needs on this list at least two weeks before they are actually purchased.

Obviously, emergency purchases will arise that can't wait that long, but play hardball with both yourself and your kids—if nonessentials haven't been on the list for a few weeks, they don't get purchased.

♦ Why the emphasis on waiting? Because:

After a few weeks of incubating, many items you wanted (or even needed) are seen for what they are—impulse buys. Often you'll realize you'd rather pass on frivolities than compromise important goals.

The interval gives time for research. What make and model of the product is best for the family, and who sells it for the best price?

Time helps you find the item on sale, through a mail-order outlet, in a secondhand shop...

The list allows you to combine shopping sorties, thereby reducing the time and money spent driving around town.

♦ Lists for food items and other consumables (cosmetics, cleaners, kitchen supplies, etc.) are discussed on July 12.

═══════ **January 2** ═══════

A Zen story tells of a man who, while dining at a friend's home, thinks he sees a baby snake swimming in his tea. Not wanting to embarrass his friend, the man closes his eyes and swallows the tea in one gulp. Shortly thereafter he becomes very sick.

The story deals on one hand with the placebo effect, for it was not a snake but a reflection the man saw. But the story is also intended to make us examine how narrowly we define our choices. Most of us confine our options to choice A (drink the tea and, perhaps, get sick) or choice B (embarrass our friend). We don't make a habit of examining our assumptions—maybe our host would want to know about the snake—or what about the illogic of a snake being able to swim in near-boiling tea. And we don't make a habit of considering less obvious choices: fondling the drink and pretending to sip from it, spilling the drink and embarrassing ourselves rather than our host, asking for a glass of water and disposing of the tea while the host is gone.

We make monetary choices every day like the man who closes his eyes and swallows a snake. When the television dies we replace it. We don't examine living without it, asking friends if they have a used one they could sell, shopping garage sales for second-hand replacements.

♦ Today, look at your calendar and your to-do list. Make a list of those things that will be costing you money today—transportation costs for the errands you will be running, food costs for the special ingredients a recipe is calling for, equipment costs for the soccer shoes your child needs, repair costs for the broken dishwasher...

Under each item list different options—even those that, on first analysis, seem crazy. Examine each option to see if it merits attention. Maybe not taking in the broken Nintendo would be a smart move after all. Maybe it would give your children time for more redeeming activities (reading, playing with neighbors, homework).

♦ Put an orange sticker on the face of your watch. Every time you see it over the coming week, ask yourself, "What are my options for what I'm about to do?" Looking for new solutions is the first step toward reducing the expenses you incur every day.

January 3

Some consumer advocates like Ralph Nader recommend eliminating plastic from your financial life. Except in the case of truly compulsive people, I disagree.

Credit cards have their evils, but they offer you tangible benefits as well—they help you order bargains through the mail; give you muscle in fighting vendors whose products, services, or warranties don't meet advertised claims; and they make national and international travel immeasurably easier.

The trick is to avoid the evils of the card and employ its benefits. Which brings up the Prime Rule of credit card ownership: Carry one in your wallet/purse only if you pay off the balance each month. Paying 18% each month on an outstanding balance is a financial shot in the foot.

If, like two-thirds of all Americans, you violate the Prime Rule and *do* carry over a balance from month to month, follow these instructions now:

♦ Take your cards from your wallet, put them in a Ziplock bag, fill the bag with water, and throw the works in the freezer. Or take your herd of cards to the bank and store them in your safety deposit box. The cards are now available should you really need them, but the defrosting process will give you plenty of time to cool off and contemplate discretionary purchases.

♦ Make a plan for ridding yourself of the outstanding balance. Study your investments and liquidate less profitable ones to pay off the outstanding balance.

Why? Because you're probably paying an interest rate of 18% on that outstanding balance, meaning a $5,000 debt (not at all atypical) is costing you $900 per year. Meanwhile a lower paying investment, like a $5,000 certificate, may be earning $400 or less per year. It doesn't take a degree in mathematics to see the obvious here.

 January 4

Yesterday's suggestion for eliminating credit card debt assumed you had investments to liquidate. Sadly, many Americans don't have that luxury. What are your options now?

♦ If you're an average card-holder, you're paying interest rates of 18% on your outstanding balance. The first order of business is to switch over to a card company charging lower interest rates. The annual cost of a typical balance ($2,500) at an average rate (18%) is about $450. Paying a card company to carry your debt at a rate of 10% costs you $250. And 10% isn't the basement rate these days.

Card companies based in Arkansas are a good place to start the search. State law here prohibits high credit-card rates. Some reputable card companies include: Simmons First National (800-636-5151 or 501-541-1000) or Arkansas Federal Savings (800-477-3348 or 501-224-7283). Bargain interest rates on Visa and MasterCard can also be found at People's Bank (800-426-1114) and Ohio Savings Bank (800-860-1445).

♦ Over 5,000 different financial institutions issue credit cards and there is no reason to pledge your allegiance to a local one. Card*Trak* (800-344-7714), publishes a monthly report of 500 bargain cards offering low interest rates, no annual fees, and rebates: cost is $5. "Your Money Monitor" in *Money* magazine (visit the library) gives a monthly listing of the best half dozen bargain cards. And the government publishes *Shop...The Card You Pick Can Save*

You Money, a 17-page booklet comparing the vital stats of 149 different cards. Order this booklet (#349C) by sending $1.50 (covers publication and postage) to the Consumer Information Center—6A, P.O. Box 100, Pueblo, CO 81002. Get the same publication free off the Internet by accessing the Consumer Information Center's on-line catalog (http://-www.pueblo.gsa.gov/textonly.html).

◆ Many card companies offer interest rates of 6% to 8% as teasers to get you on board. After several months they hike you up to much higher rates (like 18%). Read all the fine print of the initial agreement and later provisions before you bother to switch accounts.

◆ Assuming you have a good credit history, many card companies will want your business—they are, after all, going to make money off your debts—and they'll make it easy to make the switch. Sign their forms and let them know which credit-card balance they will be assuming. The new company will pay off the old one, assume the loan, and start billing you at the new, lower rate.

═══════════ **January 5** ═══════════

Studies show that consumers wielding credit cards at the mall spend 30% more on their sprees than those who pay cash. Paying with plastic, apparently, deadens the reality of what you're doing. So if you decided not to put your cards on ice and are still toting them with you, today's task will help give you a reality check every time you reach for the card.

◆ Order the credit-card condoms for safe spending issued by the National Center for Financial Education (NCFE). These are durable envelopes that fit over your credit cards. They're stamped with the bold reminder, "For safer spending and the prevention of debt." The few seconds it takes to remove the card from the envelope reminds you that this purchase may be a shot in the financial foot. It gives you the chance to evaluate whether impulses are getting the best of you. Order 10 of these credit-card envelopes by sending $3 and a SASE to NCFE (P.O. Box CT 34070, San Diego, CA 92163-4070).

♦ Better yet, make your own credit-card covers by folding and taping paper into sleeves that slip over the cards. On the outside of the sleeve, write a poignant note (e.g., "**Stop!** In a week will I regret this purchase?"), or attach a picture representing what you most desire—a home, a Hawaiian holiday, a piano. You want to *see* what's at stake every time you extract the card.

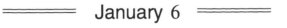

January 6

A statistic of interest: If you charge $2,000 on a credit card and then pay only the minimum amount due each month, it will take about 25 years to pay it off. Besides the original balance you'll spend another $7,000 in interest.

Few who see these numbers disagree that what they are paying in interest is drowning them. They understand that they need to annihilate that outstanding balance. And they see why the traditional dogma financial experts espouse (to pay off as much of the balance as possible each month, not just the monthly minimum) is the road to financial freedom.

The experts are right. People who pay more than the minimum each month (and who refrain from adding to the debt they've already created) bound ahead. Thousands of debt-ridden people who have paid their debt on the accelerated plan and pinched pennies in the interim, have proved the approach works. For some.

For large numbers of others riding the downward spiral of their finances, however, the advice doesn't wash. The paycheck arrives, a larger than minimum payment goes to the credit-card company, no money goes into savings, and in a few weeks the family is out of money paying for day-to-day expenses with, yup, their credit card.

If this is your family's predicament, Carol Keeffe, author of *How to Get What You Want in Life With the Money You Already Have*, takes a heretical stance: Pay only the minimum due, she says, **but stop using the card**. Take your extra money, the money experts maintain should go to the credit card company in the form of a larger payment, and earmark most of it for the month's survival (remember you're not going to use the credit card to bail you out), and put some of it (even if it's only $5) into a dream box (a box that is actually labelled for something you badly want, something that's truly important to you, something that **motivates** you).

It's a counter-intuitive approach that has worked successfully for the debt-ridden people who attend Keeffe's money seminars. It works because it pays the debtor first and creates positive energy and enthusiasm about the present. Paying larger installments than you can really afford to neutralize old bills enslaves you to the past—it establishes a tradition that has you permanently atoning for water under the bridge, it gives you nothing to get excited about now, and it creates a cycle of depression that has you using the credit card to buy yourself little pick-me-ups that siphon money away from what you want in your heart. As one of Keeffe's disciples says,

> "If you're paying minimum payments of $10 or $20, it bugs you more than using the credit card. You know if you keep using it, you'll have the bill for the rest of your life. When you were paying $100 and $200 toward the bill, you felt more free to keep using the card because you thought you were paying it off."

If you're living with credit-card debt, if you recognize it's strangling you (both financially and emotionally) yet you can't shake free of its pernicious bite, don't be too quick to cast off the counter-intuitive approach. Obviously, the popular dogma isn't working, so try something different. Take a look at Keeffe's book (published by Little, Brown and Company).

═══ January 7 ═══

Yet another approach to dealing with the hole dug by credit cards and other forms of consumer debt:

♦ First, stash the cards as emphasized several days ago. To cure the problem, you must stop adding to it.

♦ *Money Magazine* gave the following advice to a couple who were the parents of 12 and who lived off one $41,000 income:

"The Lather's biggest monthly hurdles are the $618 payment on their 9.5% mortgage, plus credit union and auto-loan payments of $952 (note: the credit-union/auto loans incur much higher interest payments than the mortgage loan). By taking out a new 30-year fixed-rate loan for 80% of their home's current $95,000 value, they could pay off the $49,900 balance on their original mortgage, cover closing costs of roughly $2,000 and wipe out their $22,600 in other debts (note: the credit-union and auto loans). They'd be left only with a monthly mortgage payment of $761, assuming an 8.75% loan—or roughly half what they pay now to service their debt."

♦ Assuming your home's current value is considerably higher than the balance due on your original mortgage, and assuming you have outstanding consumer loans whose hefty interest rates are really nicking the monthly finances, *Money's* strategy is a sound one. Working with your current mortgage-loan lender will probably be your easiest (and cheapest) option. Make informational calls now.

January 8

Credit-card users who heed the Prime Rule of credit cards (pay the outstanding balance each month) should use the day to establish their accounts with institutions issuing free cards. There's absolutely no reason to pay $20 a year for a Visa or MasterCard when you can get one free.

While researching the matter, be sure to ask about the grace period of each card—you want at least a 21-day grace period between the billing date and your payment-due date.

♦ Thousands of banks around the country issue credit cards and there is no reason to use a local bank, so shop for an institution issuing free cards and granting reasonable grace periods. A few of the possibilities: USAA Federal (800-922-9092), Amalgamated Bank (800-365-6464), Abbott Bank (800-288-3560), and Fidelity National Bank (800-753-2900).

For a far larger pool of institutions issuing free cards send a SASE and 55¢ to Consumer Action News (116 New

Montgomery Street, Suite 233, San Francisco, CA 94105, 415-777-9456) and request its annual credit-card survey. Or order reports from the sources listed in the entry for January 4.

Cheap Trick:
Want to forego annual fees, but avoid the hassles of switching companies? Next time you are billed for the annual fee, call the institution's customer service department and tell them you will be switching card companies if the annual fee is not waived. Squawk and you shall receive—most companies will waive the fee.

Note: You'll still be billed for the card each year—so, until you switch to a no-fee company, be prepared to squawk each year. Make this painless by listing the appropriate phone numbers and contacts in your Rolodex.

═══════ January 9 ═══════

Used cunningly, a credit card actually saves you money on some purchases. If you make large credit card purchases at the very beginning of a billing period and then pay off your debt at the end of your grace period, you've effectively borrowed money, interest free, for about 50 days.

Say you purchased a computer worth $3,000. By keeping your money in a money-market fund paying 6% during those 50 days you'd earn $25. That's $25 you'd be without had you written a check.

There's another big advantage to making credit card purchases at the beginning of a billing period: You have more time to activate a chargeback. In the case of the computer just purchased, you'd have six or seven weeks before you paid the bill to test that the machine worked and had been accurately advertised.

◆ Pull the credit card statements for each card you own and make a summary listing for your Rolodex (to be filed under *Credit Cards*) that notes each card's billing period, grace period, and payment-due date. Also note the customer service number of each card.

═══ January 10 ═══

Pull your latest phone bills (from both your local and long-distance carriers) and calculate what your interstate and intrastate long-distance calls cost (per minute) during peak hours (8 a.m. to 5 p.m.) and discounted hours (5 p.m. to 8 a.m.).

Write down these per-minute rates. You'll be using the figures tomorrow.

═══ January 11 ═══

AT&T, MCI, Sprint—which one really saves you money? Recently, my wife took a close look at who would save us the most money. After the smoke of discounts and promotions was blown away, her conclusion was that for small businesses and residential customers, there was little difference in the rates. On any given month, the promotions of one would better the other two. She decided that if we were going to stick with the big boys, price was basically a wash. Therefore, going with the company offering the best customer service was the issue—which left us linked to AT&T.

If you're willing to look beyond the Big Three, however, you can cut your phone bill in half. In 1995 after my discounts with AT&T, I was paying 27.5¢/minute to place calls during business hours and about 16.5¢/minute for calls logged during discounted hours. For intrastate calls (in-state long distance), I was paying an average of 19¢/minute to call during peak periods, 14¢/minute to call after 5 p.m.

When I switched my long-distance service to Arcada Communications (206-441-5022 or 800-925-2280), a small carrier servicing Western Washington, I started paying a flat fee (same fee regardless of the hour of day) of 12.5¢/minute for interstate calls and 10¢/minute for intrastate calls.

Almost all calls on my business phone occur during working hours, so Arcada Communications has taken a 56% divot out of that bill. My personal phone sees savings of 25% over AT&T's discounted hours and 56% over its peak hours. On average we pay about 35% less with Arcada.

On intrastate calls, my business line reaps a 48% savings while savings on the personal line average between 35% and 40%.

What did we give up for these savings? The clarity of the calls is no different. Out-of-state calling is no different (dial 1 plus the phone number). In-state long distance requires a five-digit access code, so we've programmed that code into memory, meaning we hit one more key than before. Customer service was a concern so we switched only after calling several references to see if current customers were happy with the billing and resolution of problems. They were. Now we are too.

♦ To the Yellow Pages you go. Under *Telephone Companies*, look for companies promoting long-distance service for less. Around Seattle, for example, you'd come up with firms like Arcada Communication (800-925-2280 or 206-441-5022) and Fox Communications (206-562-2900 or 800-488-2312).

♦ Call your local discount carriers and request literature on their different programs and rates. Also request a short list of current customers. Before you switch carriers, call some of these customers and ask them about the service, billing, customer service... Have problems been encountered? Have there been billing surprises? Is it easy to get through to customer service personnel?

♦ If the Yellow Pages don't deliver, call these national discounters and get their literature coming your way: Telephone Express (800-976-4685) and Excel Telecommunications (800-875-9235). These programs are not as competitive as my local discount service, but they still put the Big Three to shame.

January 12

You can't teach an old dog new tricks. You, however, are not an old dog and the reason you are consulting this book is because you want to learn new tricks. This ability to keep learning, to keep changing, to keep adapting is one of the blessings of our species. And on an individual level, the ability to keep adapting is what differentiates those who gain control from those who lose control of their lives.

Over the coming year you will be changing many details of day-to-day living that have not borne fruit: You will adopt new techniques and try new ideas. Often you will be fighting the momentum of old habits. This isn't easy. We have the ability to buck tradition, to change, to remake ourselves, but we are also creatures of habit.

Breaking our own habits is hard enough, but messing with the habits of others can make them extremely prickly. Therein lies the importance of getting matters out in the open—of discussing with the entire family your new goals, new directions, possible problems, and anticipated obstacles.

♦ Schedule a family forum this evening. Explain the issues at stake—the time problems of working two careers, the monetary realities of living off one income. Clarify changes that may occur, family traditions that may be questioned, old habits that may die, new conventions that may be adopted. Emphasize that not much about the day-to-day details of living is sacred.

Everyone in the family should understand that changes are in the wind. Some of these changes are painless, others may involve musclepower, brainpower, or, worst of all, willpower. But these changes will give much in return: a saner lifestyle, family time, flexibility, happier parents, and time to live rather than forever "earn" a living.

Get the entire family to buy into the concept. Get kids and spouse alike to acknowledge with their own voices that they're not afraid of change, that they can accept new solutions, that they won't cling to old dogma. This *does* lighten your load and your worries when for the hundredth time over the coming year you announce, "I've got an idea we should all consider," or, "From now on we should do this a different way."

After tonight's meeting, your family should expect to hear these words from you—often.

═══════ January 13 ═══════

Longer life, better looks, improved self-image, elevated energy, arrested aging, enhanced sex, and increased happiness have all been flaunted as the benefits of exercise. About the only claim proselytizers avoid making is that exercise will make you rich. In fact, with rapacious stars vying to sell you their newest video, health clubs hounding you to join, and Nike ads telling you to "Just Do It" (with their $120 shoes), exercise can leave you destitute.

Financial pain, however, is completely unnecessary to reap the gains of exercise. Recent studies, like an important one from the Institute of Aerobics Research in Dallas, show that sedentary people have higher mortality rates. But men and women alike who incorporate low-intensity exercise (such as 30- to 60-minute walks) into their daily regimen sharply reduce their death rates. Interestingly, the death rates of low-intensity exercisers is only slightly higher than hard-core runners logging 40 miles a week.

Many people (parents and corporate drones alike) insist they are too busy to exercise. Rubbish. Daily exercise in the form of mowing, gardening, raking, vacuuming, or chopping wood at a vigorous pace can actually save you time. Meanwhile, bicycling to the store, walking (rather than driving) the kids to school, and encouraging your spouse to walk or bicycle to work is not only good for health, it can slim the miles you drive each week. Remember, each mile not driven is a minimum of 35¢ saved.

To use daily life as your workout, dust off your duff and speed up the chores you need to accomplish anyway. Exercise each day and strive to burn *at least* 1,100 calories a week on some combination of the following tasks.

Brisk walking = 320 calories/hour
Stair climbing = 420 calories/hour
Rigorous gardening = 330 calories/hour
Mowing = 450 calories/hour
Raking leaves = 405 calories/hour
Turbo housecleaning = 320 calories/hour
Steady-paced bicycling = 405 calories/hour
Stair climbing (fast) = 510 calories/hour.

January 14

Low-intensity workouts are enough to bag significant health benefits—a recent, well-respected study shows those who walk a minimum of a mile a day are seven times less likely to suffer a stroke than those who are inactive. Nonetheless, low-intensity workouts won't transform the temple of your body into an awesome fitness machine. That requires a more rigorous aerobic regimen aimed at conditioning the cardiovascular system.

Toward such an end, the American College of Sports Medicine (ACSM) recommends three to five aerobic workouts each week. To score maximum benefit, the session should keep your heart pumping within its "target rate" for 20 to 60 minutes. To calculate your target rate, subtract your age from 220 to obtain your maximum heart rate (MHR). Multiply the MHR first by .6 and second by .8. Now exercise at an exertion level that keeps your per-minute heart rate between these two figures.

If you are 40 years old, for example, your MHR is 180. Exercise so that your per-minute heart rate is between 108 and 144. If you're aerobically fit, work out in the higher end of the range. Use the lower end of the range if you're just starting a fitness program or are fatigued from yesterday's activities.

Such workouts do not require the services of a swanky health club or stylish clothes. And they need not consume time you don't have. Any steady movement that maintains your target heart rate—be that jogging, bicycling, shadow boxing, or dancing—will keep you aerobically fit. The options here are limited by your imagination, but here are some ways to incorporate aerobic workouts into your week without wasting time or money:

♦ Jog to the store (with a pack) for groceries, walk home at a brisk pace.
♦ Jog back and forth to the video store.
♦ Jog while mowing the yard. Don't bag the clippings. Either let them lie or, following the mowing session, rake them up with a round of double-speed raking.
♦ Jump up and down and side to side while vacuuming.
♦ Jog while pushing a child in a stroller. Or, if you have older children, have them accompany you on their bikes while you jog.
♦ Ride a bicycle (and push yourself) on local errands.
♦ Play outdoor games with your children—tag, one-on-one soccer, race each other at a local field or track.

January 15

Although aerobic exercise is most important for maintaining fitness, the American College of Sports Medicine also recommends that adults incorporate strength-training into their weekly regimen. At least twice a week, do repetitions of 10 different exercises that tax the body's major muscle groups (each muscle group should be very fatigued after eight to 12 repetitions of a specific exercise).

You don't need the $2,000 Nautilus machines for this. Pull-ups, push-ups, sit-ups, squat thrusts, knee bends (not too deep), and other calisthenics employing the body's weight for resistance work just fine.

♦ Free weights, like barbells, are also excellent for strength-training but are quite expensive. Make your own eight-pound weights by filling gallon milk (or bleach) bottles with water. Make 15-pound weights by filling the same bottles with sand and water. Make four-pound weights by filling ½-gallon bleach bottles with water.

Now use a bottle in each hand for arm raises, twirls, and pumps. For bench presses, curls, shoulder presses, upright rows, and squats, make a barbell by sliding a 1-inch dowel (or broomstick) through the handles of several milk bottles. A 5- to 6-foot dowel will easily handle five or six bottles.

Would-be Arnold Schwarzeneggers may need heavier weights to build bulk, but for most of us, pumping 50 to 60 pounds of milk bottles is remarkably effective strength-training.

♦ Pumping rubber is another inexpensive alternative to pumping iron. Products like the *Lifeline Gym* and *Pumping Rubber Xercise Kit* are made from a length of heavy-gauge rubber tubing and have a handle attached to each end. These products, which weigh under two pounds and occupy less room than a dictionary, can compete with a Universal Gym in their ability to exercise all the major muscle groups in the body. The *Lifeline Gym* is so effective that a long list of professional athletes, astronauts, mountain climbers, and military personnel use it to build muscle and maintain stamina.

The *Lifeline Gym* is quicker and easier to use than free weights, does not clutter up the basement or garage, travels with you on business trips, *and*, at $60, costs a fraction of what weights cost. For information, contact Lifeline International, 1421 South Park Street, Madison, WI 53715, 800-553-6653 or 608-251-4778.

January 16

If you have time to watch television, you better not complain about lacking time to exercise. That's not to say you should give up time spent in front of the boob tube, but it is to say you should be multi-tasking. Rather than letting television contribute toward gel in the belly and cellulite in the thigh, use TV to sculpt a hard body. Use the time in front of that box to stretch, pump rubber, crank off sets of calisthenics, stair step, shadow box...

So while you watch:

♦ Use your milk-bottle weights or Lifeline Gym for strength training.
♦ Use your body for strength training—do calisthenics.
♦ Make your own StairMaster from a plastic milk crate. Turn the crate up-side-down in front of the television and start stepping. Unlike most stair steppers, which cost a fortune and clutter the family room, the milk crate can actually store sundries in the closet when it is not in use.
♦ Build gripping strength by squeezing old tennis balls until your forearms feel like rocks.
♦ Stretch your neck, back, hips, arms, and legs if you're not in a vigorous mood.

Warning: If you are a long-time tuber, get a medical checkup before you "just do it." These pointers aren't cheap if they induce a heart attack.

January 17

You take it for granted until it gives out. Then you understand how fundamental to life a strong back is. In

1988, a study performed by the National Institute of Occupational Safety and Health (NIOSH) found that back problems were responsible for the loss of 500 million worker days—only the common cold had Americans missing more work. Furthermore, the study said that 25% of all disabling work injuries were back-related and that bad backs accounted for one-third of the nation's worker-compensation bills.

Obviously, this is not a problem to turn your back on. Take appropriate measures to prevent back problems in the first place, or to help a back that's been finicky over the years. Here's a quick course on developing a stronger back that has nothing to do with the $39 gizmos sold on late-night TV. Do these *free* exercises while you watch television, or each morning in bed, or each evening before bed.

♦ While lying on your back, pull your right knee up to your chest and hold it there for 10 seconds. Do the same with your left knee. Do five or 10 repetitions with each leg.

Still lying on your back, with your knees bent and your feet flat on the floor, move into abdominal crunches. Lift your head, shoulders, and arms off the deck, letting the palms of your hands ride up your thighs toward your knees. Don't lift so high that your lower back comes off the floor. Hold the upward position for several seconds, then smoothly lower your shoulders and head down to the floor. Over time, work on strengthening your stomach so that you can do three sets of 30 crunches.

Now, sitting on your bottom with one leg bent (foot by your groin) and the other stretched out in front of you, stretch the hamstring and lower back by slowly reaching out with both hands toward your outstretched foot. Hold the toe of that foot for 10 seconds. Reverse leg positions and stretch the other side. Repeat several times.

Lie on your stomach with arms stretched out overhead. Simultaneously raise your left arm and right leg six inches off the floor and hold the swim-like position for 10 seconds. Lower those limbs and lift the opposite ones for 10 seconds. Repeat until you feel fatigue in your lower back. Gradually build up the number of repetitions performed.

Still lying on your stomach, put your elbows by your ribs and the palms of your hands flat on the floor, just above the shoulders. Arch your head and back up slowly into a cobra position, relying mainly on your back muscles to get your navel off the floor. Hold the position eight to 10 seconds. Work up to doing 10 repetitions.

♦ Many doctors recommend *Treat Your Own Back* by Robin McKenzie (Orthopedic Physical Therapy Products, 800-367-7393) to people wanting to treat or prevent back problems.

January 18

It's called the boob tube for good reason, but with a few smarts you can make time spent in front of that mind-numbing box productive rather than wasted. The secret is to multi-task as you watch. Grab a sheet of paper and list the chores you're going to accomplish in the days of viewing ahead. Some possibilities for your list:

♦ Cut cereal and cracker boxes into postcards.
♦ Exercise and/or stretch.
♦ Mend damaged clothing.
♦ Create pads of paper.
♦ Make wrapping paper.
♦ Snip pictures and headlines from magazines for special-occasion cards.
♦ Slice old inner tubes into squares of firestarter.
♦ Glue/repair broken household items.

Once your list is complete, lay it next to the television and pick a chore to work on each time you view.

January 19

Have you cleaned your VCR since we invaded Grenada? Probably not, so give it a little attention (just a little) before it develops an expensive complex. Some thoughts to ponder:

♦ To clean or not to clean—that is the controversy. Many repairmen condemn all cleaning cartridges for VCRs and camcorders, saying that the abrasiveness and improper tension of these cleaning devices often damage the heads and guide rollers. An added danger, according to some repairmen, is the public's perception that, if using a cleaning tape once is good, using it often must be gooder. Wrong—unless sanding the face off the heads is the intent. If you own a cleaning cartridge that uses any kind of liquid or rubs the heads with some kind of fabric swab, throw it away. Really.

One cleaning product that most repairmen will recommend for your VHS systems is the *Scotch Cleaning Tape* (about $11). All video tapes have cleaning agents bound to the oxides in the tape. The *Scotch Cleaning Tape* cleans the heads because it contains a higher ratio of cleaning agents and a lower ratio of oxides. But because it is a normal magnetic tape, it is not abrasive. Tests conducted by *Electronic Servicing and Technology*, a trade magazine for professional technicians, proved that the damage inflicted by this tape is negligible and that it will clean your heads. For 8mm camcorders, the *Sony Cleaning Cassette* employs the same principles. Put these items on your shopping list if they aren't already part of your home maintenance kit.

Use these cleaning tapes for 15 or 20 seconds when you notice a degradation (snowy image, lines in the screen) of your picture quality. Take the machine in for servicing if the tape fails to improve the image.

♦ To clean often or rarely—that is another controversy. Repairmen will tell you to bring your VCR and camcorders in for cleaning a minimum of once a year (semiannually for heavy users). Are these cleanings (averaging about $50) necessary?

Yes and no. More important than the months or years between cleanings is the hours of use. Most manufacturers recommend that the heads, guide rollers, pinch rollers, pressure rollers, impedance rollers, idlers, pulleys, and capstan be cleaned every 500 hours. For people using their VCR once or twice a week, it may take two or three years to amass 500 hours.

And if you wait more than 500 hours between professional cleanings, are you destroying your machine? Some parts, like the pinch roller, may need replacement sooner than normal but the money saved by not cleaning as often may offset replacement costs.

Not everyone agrees with me, but here are my thoughts on professional cleanings. If you own a low-end machine, schedule professional cleanings less often (about every 700 hours) because the benefits may not justify the cost. With a high-end machine, the relative cost of the cleanings is a smaller percentage of the machine's value, so a stricter maintenance schedule prolongs the life of your investment.

◆ To avoid dust and dirt—that, at least, is something on which everyone agrees. Dust your VCR (and your other electronic equipment) frequently. Also, use a canister-styled vacuum with a brush attachment to clean the machine. And keep pets away—their fur and dander are trouble.

January 20

Yesterday you took steps to put a dent in your reading budget. Time to hammer the dent into a hole. Call neighbors, nearby friends, and local relatives to discuss:

◆ Sharing the subscription costs of newspapers and magazines. A good match for the paper is a family with a modus operandi opposite to your own (e.g., if you read the paper the same day, look for a neighbor who lets theirs pile up). With monthly magazines, families that read the magazine immediately should receive the subscription. The family interested in saving the magazine should end up with it or get it back later.

◆ Swapping back issues of different magazines. You know, I'll swap you my *Reader's Digest* for your... *Rolling Stone*? Well, you need to share some interests.

January 21

Most magazines (with the exception of weekly news and business periodicals) are not particularly time sensitive. Read them now or in three months and you get the same benefit. So why pay for such information when libraries supply it free? Every month I check out six to 10 back issues of magazines—several for myself, several for my wife, and a few for the kids. If the stuff never gets read, we may feel intellectually bankrupt but at least we escape the dollar doldrums.

♦ Visit your local library today. Research which magazines are received each month. Ask about the check-out policies for back issues (can back issues be checked out, how many back issues can be checked out at a time, for how long?). Ask whether back issues of the magazines you desire are actually on hand or whether they are always checked out (women's magazines, for example, are often in high demand). Oh, and don't forget to bring home your first armload of back issues.

♦ Back at home decide which magazines you'll be cancelling and make the calls. If the magazine's satisfaction-guaranteed warranty provides a refund in the event of an early cancellation (as many magazines do), terminate your subscription. If there is no refund, resolve not to renew that subscription next time around.

January 22

You've whittled down the magazines you intend to purchase to skeleton crew. Now it's time to get those few magazines at rock-bottom prices.

♦ Most magazine readers subscribe directly with the publisher, but you can arrange a better deal buying most magazines through a middleman—which makes no sense at all. Look up what you're paying for your favorite magazines, then compare those prices to what you would pay ordering from Delta Publishing Group (800-728-3728) or American Family Publishers (800-237-2400). Call for quotes of the magazines you want, but also ask for a complete price list. If you're going to renew a subscription with one of these groups, note when your current subscription lapses. Then, to insure that you receive uninterrupted service, put a notation in your daily calendar to place an order through your new source two months before your subscription lapses.

I used to pay the publisher $61 for a year's subscription of *Time* magazine. Now I pay Delta Publishing Group $30 per year. Here are other examples of the 900 magazines available (publisher's subscription price first, then Delta's price): Atlantic Monthly $18 versus $10, Backpacker $27 versus $13, Esquire $16 versus $7.50, Fortune $53 versus $25, Ladies' Home Journal $20 versus $11, McCalls $16 versus $8.50, Newsweek $42 versus $24, Parenting $18 versus $10, Sports Afield $14 versus $7, Sports Illustrated $80 versus $38, Woman's Day $16 versus $11.

January 23

Where do you buy replacement checks for your bank account? If you buy from the bank, you're paying twice what you should. Purchase your replacement checks from *Current* in Colorado Springs (800-426-0822) or *Checks in the Mail* in Texas (800-733-4443). The new checks are guaranteed to work at your financial institution.

Your first order will need to be mailed and must include one of your current checks—this lists all vital bank and account numbers. Call the phone numbers above and request catalogs and introductory order forms. You should be paying about $6 for your first order of 200 checks, about $7 for subsequent orders.

Cheap Trick:
If you run out of checks, use the deposit slip in the back of your checkbook. These slips have all the vital information found on a normal check—the bank's identification number, the account number, your name and address—and are valid tender if the vendor accepts them.

When writing checks to the bank, use these deposit slips to save your normal checks.

January 24

For two decades banks have conditioned us to save money by turning us into helpers capable of withdrawing or depositing cash at automated teller machines (ATMs). But over the past several years, services that were once free—including the chores we executed on ATMs—are growing the scorpion tail of charges.

While most banks still allow free use of the ATMs at their branches, there may well be a transaction fee of 75¢ to use bank ATMs located away from a branch (say at a supermarket); $1.50 to use ATMs that are not owned by your bank; and $2 to use out-of-state, non-bank ATMs.

◆ With so many ifs and buts, it's easy to get nickeled and dimed out of $40 a year using the wrong machines. Make it your job today to call your bank and find out exactly how you are charged for different ATMs. Ascertain where the closest free machines are and which machines your spouse could visit while commuting. Record this information on the Rolodex card for your bank.

◆ Once you've got the hot poop, pass it on to your spouse.

Cheap Trick:
The checkouts at many grocery, convenience, and department stores are outfitted with pay points for your debit cards. You slide your card through the machine, enter your personal identification number (PIN) and, behold, the groceries are billed to your checking account.

This system has several beauties. You don't need to carry much cash, and most systems charge you nothing for the transaction; that's cheaper than writing a check. Also, if you need cash, tell the cashier you want "cash back." The money received will be debited against your checking account and, unlike using an ATM, you duck the transaction fee.

=========== January 25 ===========

Imagine the perfect checking account. This account has no minimum balance, no monthly fee, no transaction fees for ATMs, no stipulations on how many checks you can write, no fees for visiting a real teller. Naturally, there would be no limits on the number of free telephone transfers you could make and the money you had sitting in the bank would earn hefty interest rates. Maybe the bank president would call for a friendly chat and to thank you for your business.

While no account offers these qualities, you will find different banks and different accounts giving you combinations of several of these benefits. Today it's time to determine whether your account is nicking you for the way you use it. If it is, it may be time to establish a new account.

♦ Step one. Depending on how you use your checking account, prioritize what is most important for you. Is it the ability to use a teller free because you frequently have transactions an ATM can't handle, free use of ATMs because you're not frequently near a branch bank, free phone transfers so you don't have to write reams of checks, the convenience of a local bank to minimize driving (remember, it costs a minimum of 35¢/mile to drive)...

♦ Step two. Identify the possibilities. If convenience is your biggest priority, the job of choosing the nearest bank is a no-brainer. Almost. Most banks have several types of accounts and one of these accounts will serve you better than others.

If convenience isn't the be-all and end-all, then you've got an hour or two of telephoning ahead. Make a work sheet: The qualities mentioned in the perfect account above (minimum balance, monthly fees, ATM fees, teller fees, number of free transactions per month, interest paid, etc.) go across the top of the sheet to create column heads, while the different accounts (and banks offering these accounts) are listed down the page to create rows. Now fill in the matrix you've created as you talk to different banks.

♦ Step three. Call your spouse at work and ask whether being an employee of that company gives your family rights to bank at a credit union. You'll want to know by tomorrow.

January 26

Before you jump on board with a new bank, you'll also want to investigate credit unions. You'll find most of the services a bank offers at these nonprofit cooperatives but you'll need to learn the right lingo: checking accounts are called "share-draft accounts", savings accounts are called "share accounts", and certificates of deposits (CDs) are called "share-certificate accounts".

Unlike banks, credit unions don't have owners or investors to placate with profits, so they generally pay you more for deposited money and charge less for services and/or loans. Sound good?

Here's the catch: Credit unions aren't open to all. You qualify through your employer, church, or a charitable or nonprofit organization to which you belong. One such connection in some states is the region's local chapter of the Funeral and Memorial Societies of America (see October 21). For example, a lifetime membership ($10) in Washington State's People's Memorial Association (206-325-0489) qualifies you to join Group Health Credit Union.

♦ Call those credit union(s) you are eligible to join and add their vitals to your work sheet.

♦ This evening, go over the work sheet with your spouse and see whether you have consensus on whether your account should stay put or take a hike.

January 27

While interviewing retailers and manufacturers about the tricks of smart furniture purchases, I learned some interesting lessons I now pass onto you.

♦ Be suspicious of those furniture stores (or for that matter, any store) that always have sales: Memorial Day Sales, Fourth of July Sales, Ground Hog Day Sales.... Stores can't be offering off-price sales all the time and remain in business.

♦ Many furniture manufacturers offer retailers special prices during January and February and again in July and August (wholesale prices may drop 10%) so these are the two times of year furniture is most likely to be discounted.

♦ Several manufacturers told me department stores were not the preferred place to buy furniture. With VPs, buyers, catalog producers, store managers, floor managers, department managers, and salespeople, department stores have tiers of overhead that dedicated furniture stores lack.

♦ "When a department store says it has marked down its furniture 60% for a sale, it's B.S.," said a particularly blunt manufacturer. "Totally ignore the 'regular-price' stickers on the furniture; this is often inflated to create the illusion that the sale is a super deal."

♦ Retailers typically sell furniture for at least twice its wholesale price. After paying employees, leases, advertising, and the like, the retailer who simply doubles wholesale prices is often operating on only a 3% to 5% level of profit. Department stores and those outlets continually throwing extravagant sales are likely to be tripling (sometimes even quadrupling) their wholesale prices and then marking down from there. Their sale prices may be no lower than regular prices at stores who don't play games. Example: an upholstered chair my wife saw (and wanted) at a department store had a 'regular price' of $850 that had been 'slashed' to $599 for the store's Super Sale. When I called a local warehouse specializing in quality furniture, I discovered I could order the same chair with the same upholstery (which I was told was not a good grade of fabric) for $376.

♦ Furniture these days offers consumers a lot of value. When freight was deregulated, quality furniture coming from low-cost corners of the country like North Carolina could infiltrate the national market (shipping furniture from North Carolina to the West Coast often adds only 5% to the cost of goods).

===== **January** 28 =====

If new items of furniture are on your Master Purchasing List, make preparations today.

♦ January/February or July/August are likely to be the preferred times to buy. Decide if either of these windows will work for you, then mark your calendar accordingly.

♦ Write to the Chamber of Commerce, P.O. Box 5025, High Point, NC 27262 and to the Chamber of Commerce, P.O. Box 1828, Hickory, NC 28601. Tell both you will be making future furniture purchases and would like lists, brochures, and information on the mail-order retailers in the area who represent North Carolinian manufacturers. These retailers sell quality brands of furniture for 30% to 50% below the manufacturer's recommended retail price.

January 29

John Ruskin said, "It is as unwise to pay too much as it is to pay too little." The quote certainly applies to furniture where mid-range goods deliver the best bang for your buck. For a new upholstered sofa, for example, it's unwise to pay less than $800 or more than $1,200. Pay much less than $800 and you're getting a product in which light springs have been installed, cardboard fills out the arms, staples hold together the joints.... You'll end up with a product in need of replacement after four years. Spend $1,000 and you may need to reupholster your sofa after a decade, but you'll have a frame made to last for decades to come. Spend $2,000 on a sofa and you're buying name-brand recognition, more quality than you need in this lifetime, or designer fabrics.

♦ How do you identify the price range for any given product? Compare warranties. In the case of sofas and stuffed chairs, look at products offering lifetime warranties and buy into the low end of that price range. Some products offer only limited warranties (e.g., mattresses) so identify the products offering the best warranty and buy in on the low end.

♦ Most furniture stores fit into a price niche—that is, they specialize in low-end lines, mid-range lines, or high-end lines. You'll want to gravitate toward those outlets that give you plenty of mid-range selection. Find them with your old friend, the Yellow Pages under *Furniture—Retail*. Look for stores that have been in business a long time (they're probably doing something right), and for those mentioning quality brands.

♦ When calling stores, find out whether their product line caters to price-conscious or high-end buyers. Over the phone tell them what you want (be that a sofa or dining room table), emphasize that you're purchasing for the long haul, but also stress that price is an issue. Then ask what manufacturers you should be looking at and what kind of price are you likely to be paying. Take notes. As you call different stores, ask what they know about the makes other stores mentioned. After eight or nine calls, you'll have given yourself a good education on what constitutes a quality product, the approximate price of the goods you should be considering, manufacturers worth investigating, furniture whose reputation is built on hype rather than quality, and which stores are worth visiting.

♦ Warehouses most often deal with low-end products for price-conscious shoppers, but a few offer the warehouse advantage (lower overhead and lower prices) on quality merchandise. They aren't easy to find but, like MacLeod's Warehouse Showroom in my environs north of Seattle, they do exist. Seek them out while you're making your calls.

═══ January 30 ═══

Two days ago you wrote away for more extensive lists of mail-order retailers who sell furniture over the phone. The advantage of these retailers? They may be able to supply furniture (home or office) at prices 30% to 50% below what your local retailers charge. With the cost of freight being what it is (reasonable), having goods shipped may cost no more than the sales tax you'll save by buying out of state.

To order (or to get an exact quote) from these retailers, you'll need to know the manufacturer, model number/name, color, and desired finish of what you want. That means looking locally and zeroing in on items you like before calling for price quotes.

Working with these firms has some drawbacks—you may need to pay 50% of the order up front, and delivery (depending on what you want and who builds it) can take anywhere from weeks to months, and complications (if you, or any company involved, make a mistake) can get messy.

Still, if you're patient (you've lived without this item all your life so what's a few months?) and if you are meticulous about details while ordering (and about having those details read back to you when ordering), you can do your budget a lot of good.

Even if you're not inclined to order furniture this way, knowing what a mail-order retailer would charge can save big bills. Find a mail-order retailer handling the item you want and get a price quote. If it's significantly less than working through a retail store, call the store manager, politely explain what you're interested in, mention you'd like to support a local business, but announce you can order exactly the same item for $X less. Is he willing to discount your purchase (after all, making less off you is better than making nothing from you)?

Some mail-order retailers to consider:

♦ Cherry Hill Furniture, Carpet, and Interiors (High Point, NC, 800-328-0933 or 800-888-0933) has been in business since 1933 and can supply furniture, floor coverings, and business furnishings from over 500 manufacturers. Call for a listing of brands or for a price quote.

♦ Blackwelder's (Statesville, NC, 800-438-0201) has been in the furniture, and carpeting business since 1938 and is well-regarded for both their savings and efforts to insure customer satisfaction.

♦ Loftin-Black Furniture Company (Thomasville, NC, 800-334-7398) has been selling quality home, office, and patio furniture as well as bedding and accessories for 50 years. They represent hundreds of top names in furnishings. Call for a brochure or price quote.

♦ Quality Furniture Market (Lenoir, NC, 704-728-2946) has represented hundreds of manufacturers of accessories, bedding, and indoor and outdoor furniture for over 40 years. Call for a brochure or price quote.

♦ Shaw Furniture Galleries (Randleman, NC, 800-334-6616) has represented over 400 manufacturers of home furnishings for over 55 years. Call for a brochure/quote.

═══════ **January** 31 ═══════

To keep down the price of furniture, don't overlook companies specializing in "knock-down" wares. Generally, furniture-in-a-box (commonly referred to as ready-to-assemble furniture) from such companies as Ikea (410-931-8940 in the East, 818-912-1119 in the West), Dania/Plummers/Scandinavian Design (888-333-2642), and Crate & Barrell (800-323-5461), tend to favor more contemporary designs. If they fit your taste and you don't mind using instructions, screwdrivers, and elbow grease to assemble your purchase, you can acquire well-designed merchandise at prices traditional furniture stores can't touch. Order catalogs from these firms today and check your Yellow Pages for local retailers specializing in the jack-in-the box approach to furnishing your home.

February

In the 1500s, Montaigne wrote, "The soul that has no established aim loses itself."

Remember the Mission Statement and the goals you drafted as you read Chapter 2? You should be remembering them. Often. It is your aim. It is the guide that keeps you from losing yourself.

♦ Find that sheet and refamiliarize yourself with the ideals you hold most important—the ideology behind the lifestyle you have chosen (or would like to choose).

♦ In your daily calendar make a notation at the beginning of each month to spend 15 minutes reviewing your Mission Statement. Reviewing it at frequent intervals provides a constancy of purpose and, like Benjamin Disraeli said, "The secret of success is constancy of purpose."

You can spend a fortune raising children. But the much-embraced concept that kids are expensive is something of a myth. My brother is raising 10 children on a missionary's wage—a wage low enough that the IRS keeps none of his withholdings each year (a status he enjoys without even claiming all exemptions for his dependents). While his children are anything but typical among American kids who drown in material goods, these are healthy, happy kids. They spend few hours each day interacting with merchandise and most of their time interacting with people—family, relatives, friends, schoolmates, and church members. They are caring, hard-working, respectful children who make you wonder: If less money and more time were invested in children, would social problems evaporate?

My brother is but one of a thousand testimonies to the fact that children need not be expensive. What makes children expensive is the choices we make. They are expensive because we choose to send them to private colleges even though excellent state universities could educate them for a fraction of the cost. They are expensive because we endow them with Nintendo and Sega Genesis when books and soccer balls might be healthier for mind and body. They are expensive because we want to *give* them the world even though, as Ghandi asserted, "Wealth without work is a sin."

What we pass on to our children—the values they learn from us, the tenacity that drives them, their contentedness in who they are, their dexterity at balancing the pressures of life, the enthusiasm with which they embrace life, their optimism about the future, the ability to sidestep harmful diversions, the backbone of their personality—is the foundation they build upon. This foundation is a far more important prerequisite for mental, physical and spiritual health than a Harvard education. And if some sacrifices must be made because you devoted time to *raising* your children rather than *providing* for them, it's not a foolish sacrifice.

Rather than a "do" day, today is a "feel good" day. Simply take time to feel good about your decision to raise your own kids. Commend yourself for worrying more about their personality than their possessions.

February 3

No. It's a short word. And incredibly powerful.

Say it several times. Say it with authority. Say it until it rolls easily off your tongue. Now for the hard part: Say it to your children. Harder still, say it often.

That one word is the key to keeping your kids from costing you a fortune.

Don't let child psychologists (most of whom disagree with each other) give you angst over wielding this important ax. "No" is one of the most important words in the English language and if you're too spineless to refuse a child giving you the full-court press for new court shoes, toys, or games, how do you expect that child to develop the backbone to say 'No' to the peer pressures of smoking, drinking, taking drugs, or having sex?

Like it or not, your children will learn from and emulate your style. So give them a healthy model to emulate in refusing requests that are not in their best interest. Make a pledge not to shy away from the 'N' word.

Of course how you present negative news determines whether your child boils with bitterness or accepts the verdict. Following are some defensive maneuvers to parry the pocketbook offensive waged by your kids. Study them carefully and consider scenarios in which you could use each to best effect.

Twelve ways to say 'NO.'

♦ Sorry, but that's not on my shopping list (yet another good reason to shop with a list).

♦ Mom makes $5/hour and this toy costs $21, so here's the choice: Mom can work on Saturday to buy this, or she can spend the day at home with us (most children, especially young ones, value parental time over possessions).

♦ If you brought your own money, you can buy that.

♦ Yes, I can buy that now but you'll need to repay me once we're home. Do you have enough money saved up? Do you want to use it on this or on ____(remind them of things you know they really want)?

♦ If you'd like to earn the money for this, I'll expect ___ hours of work from you. Which of the following chores would you like to do for me?

♦ If you really like that, let's put it on your Christmas or birthday list.

♦ Sure, we can get this but it will cost you your allowance for the next ___ weeks. Do you want to do that?

♦ Let's put it on your master list at home. If it's still at the top of your list in a few weeks, we'll figure out how you're going to pay for it.

♦ I'm only saying this once. We didn't come here for that. Pester me again and I won't bring you with me next time (live up to your ultimatums).

♦ First you have a little research to do. I'll help you call a few stores to see who's selling this for the best price. Then we'll look at your savings and see how you're going to pay for it. (Your role in the research process is to help your child figure out whom to call. Let your child place the calls).

♦ Show me what you like about this (get excited with your child, talk about its features, share ideas on how the item could be used). We can't afford this now, so let's put it on your list and see if you're still interested when Christmas/your birthday rolls around. Note: The ability to share your child's excitement and the reality of whether you can purchase an item are independent issues. Encourage a child's excitement and joy, but make it clear that shared excitement is not an obligation to buy.

♦ No! (Use it when you're just too frazzled to rely on anything but the eloquence of brevity). Say it powerfully and severely with a tone implying, "Push any more buttons and you're toast."

February 4

Want a year's worth of entertainment for your kids that has nothing to do with television, video games, or spending big dollars, and everything to do with creative play? Then find either of these books: *365 Outdoor Activities You Can Do With Your Child* and *365 TV-Free Activities You Can Do With Your Child*, both by Steve and Ruth Bennett.

The books are packed with free (or almost free) activities for children between the ages of four and 11. A tiny sampling of these activities includes: balloon volleyball, bean-bag Olympics, ambidextrous activities, backward spelling bee, cereal box city, body traces, bubble basketball, bug motel, cloud watching, coin-toss games, crazy Olympics, dino bone hunt, food faces, indoor safari, magnet fishing, milk-jug catch, obstacle-course races, popsicle-stick architecture, shoe-box gardening, and pop-bottle bowling.

See whether your library carries the books. If not, purchase them ($6.95 each, plus shipping) from Bob Adams Inc., 260 Center Street, Holbrook, MA 02343, 800-872-5626 or 617-767-8100.

Cheap Trick:
Keep these books in mind as birthday or Christmas gifts for relatives and friends with young children. The cover price is cheap, the information between the cover is not.

February 5

Teaching kids to be money wise and advertising savvy will save *you* thousands of dollars. After all, some of the 15,000 TV advertisements that the average child sees each year will hit their mark. That means your children will be hitting you up for money.

Unfortunately, as your children grow, they may become less inclined to listen to you (a teen-age belief is that no one is stupider than parents), so it may be difficult to teach them the facts of smart spending.

A possible solution? Visit the library and check out back issues of *Zillions—Consumer Reports for Kids* . The magazine appeals most to children ages 10 to 14 and reports on things they care about: clothes, skateboards, videos, shoes, fast food. Products are tested by kids and advice comes across as kid-to-kid gospel. The magazine will not only help children spend wisely, it will teach them about earning and investing.

If the library doesn't handle *Zillions*, it's worth the $13 to subscribe for a year. Even if your kin give it sporadic scrutiny, the magazine is likely to save the family much more than it costs. Order it from Delta Publishing Group (1243 48th St., Brooklyn, NY 11219, 800-728-3728).

♦ *The Peanut Butter and Jelly Game* by Adam Eisenson is a full-color children's book with a valuable lesson for kids between the ages of 5 and 8. Each year, the average child is exposed to 30,000 to 40,000 commercials telling him to spend. This picture book of a gorilla who spends his money foolishly, appeals to a child's stomach and shows what happens when money is misused. The story also tells how to right a wrong. Check the library for it. Or call the publisher (Good Advice Press, 800-255-0899). If the book helps your child understand the woes of the spend-spend mentality, it is worth the $15 investment.

February 6

Teach children that turning lights and appliances off, using hot water sparingly, turning down the heat, and using less water are all money savers.

To emphasize all of this, make a chart with a column for each of the following: Lights Off, Short Showers/Shallow Baths, Heat Down, Water Saved. Hang the chart in a central location and attach a pencil or a supply of stickers (more fun for young kids).

Come evening tell the family what this is all about. Explain that anyone who turns off unused or unneeded lights, dials down the heat, shortens (or takes fewer) showers, or bathes with less water can put their initials (or a sticker) in the appropriate column.

Explain that you'll be comparing the new utility bills with the old ones and that money saved goes toward family fun—a night at the movies, an evening of bowling, a pizza dinner. It's important to share these savings with your children to motivate them in playing their part.

At bill time, if the kids have been partaking in the conservation program, reward them—even if the savings don't pay for the activity planned. You're molding new habits, habits that are likely to stick with your children and save you money month after month. Over the months, take them on several fun outings as a kickback.

Once the desired habits are second nature—lights are turned off, hot water and heat are not squandered, water is conserved—phase out the chart.

February 7

Children, especially grade-school kids, love receiving mail. Doesn't matter whether the envelope is personal or junk mail, whether a package is cheap or expensive. What grabs kids is the anticipation of it all, the feeling of importance when something arrives with their name on it.

Free Stuff For Kids is a book providing hours of cheap entertainment that feeds off this interest. The book lists hundreds of free (and nearly free) items that kids can order by mail. To order the $5 book, contact Meadowbrook Press, 18318 Minnetonka Blvd, Deephaven, MN 55391, 612-473-5400 or 800-338-2232.

Another source that fuels this interest is *Freebie Magazine*. Merchandise that's said to be free (most vendors charge a one- or two-dollar shipping charge) can be ordered from the magazine. For the current issue of *Freebies*, send $2 to Freebies Publishing Company, 1135 Eugenia Place, Carpenteria, CA 93014-5025, 805-566-1225. A yearly subscription for five issues of the magazine runs $8. The magazine also compiles a yearly book called *Freebies for Kids* ($5) which is published by Lowell House Juvenile, 2029 Century Park East, Suite 3290, Los Angeles, CA 90067.

◆ Put an educational twist on this game of receiving free stuff by making your kids write the envelopes and letters for all requests. They'll learn how to format letters and refine their writing skills. Pull out a typewriter and they can develop typing skills. Use a computer and they'll learn word-processing skills.

February 8

How often do new toys become dust collectors after several uses?

Pretty often.

How do you keep a child's unpredictable taste from becoming a waste?

By borrowing as many toys as possible.

◆ An interesting source of borrowed toys is the USA Toy Library Association, a non-profit organization promoting this very concept. While 50% of the country's 500 affiliate toy libraries are geared toward specialized groups of children (disabled children, sick children, preschoolers), the other half are happy to let any child check out toys. To find out about toy libraries in your area, send a SASE to the USA Toy Library Association, 2530 Crawford Avenue, Suite 111, Evanston, IL 60201-4954.

◆ Another option: Start a borrowing program with your friends and neighbors. Draft a letter listing the benefits of borrowing (a chance to expose kids to new toys without any expense, the chance to see whether certain toys are worth buying, the opportunity to visit each other more often). Also, list the rules everyone agrees to abide by (borrowers will clean items before returning them, lenders can call in borrowed items at any time, borrowers will replace or repair what they break, and participants will lend in roughly the same quantity that they borrow).

◆ A final option for making sure your toy purchases don't collect dust: Research your acquisitions and hone in on those products receiving rave reviews. *Zillions* (see February 5) is one resource for such research. Also, call the library and reserve a copy of *The Best Toys, Books, and Videos for Kids* by Joanne Oppenheim.

February 9

As consumers, it's not uncommon to pay top dollar for items you could easily and inexpensively make yourself—if you only knew how. So...I am going to reveal some deeply held secrets behind the making of several putties, clays, and solutions. Kids love the products, parents the price.

◆ Finger paints. Mix ¼ cup cornstarch with 2 cups cold water and boil the mixture until it thickens. Pour into suitable containers, then mix in food colors.

◆ Play dough. Mix 2½ cups flour, ½ cup salt, 1 tablespoon alum, and 1 package Kool-Aid (unsweetened packet). Add 2 cups boiling water and 3 tablespoons vegetable oil. Mix the works together, then dump out the resulting dough on the counter and knead in an additional cup of flour. Add additional flour if the dough is still sticky. Store the dough in an airtight container at room temperature and it will last many months.

◆ Bubble solution. Add ¼ cup clear dishwashing detergent (e.g., *Dawn*) and 1½ tablespoons glycerine (from a drugstore) to 4 cups warm water. Mix gently so as not to create a frothy solution, then use a variety of circular objects as wands.

◆ Giant Bubbles. Mix together ½ cup of Karo Syrup, 3 cups of Joy Liquid, and 3 cups of water. Stir very gently to avoid making bubbles in the solution. Add glycerine (from the drugstore), one tablespoon at a time, and experiment with the bubbles. Experiment also with different bubble wands (hangers, 6-pack rings, etc.).

◆ Modeling Clay. Mix together a 16-ounce box of baking soda and a cup of cornstarch. In another container, stir drops of food coloring (you decide how much) into 1 ¼ cups of cold water, then pour the liquid over the powder mixture. Stir. When smooth, microwave on high for five to seven minutes. Stop the microwave every minute and stir. Once the mixture is firm, cover it with a damp rag and after it cools, knead it into a smooth clay. Store your clay in airtight jars or Ziplock freezer bags.

◆ Silly Putty. To a ½ cup of Elmer's Glue, stir in small amounts of liquid starch. Once the mixture clumps up, begin kneading it by hand and continue to add small amounts of liquid starch. In total you'll use about ¼ cup of liquid starch to get the putty to the right texture and consistency.

◆ Sticker Glue. Boil ¼ cup of vinegar, then turn the heat to low and add 2 packets of unflavored gelatin (like Knox). Stir until the gelatin dissolves, then add ½ teaspoon of flavoring like peppermint extract. Paint your concoction onto magazine pictures, cards, photographs, comics... whatever you want to make into a sticker. Let the sticker glue dry and you're done.

========= February 10 =========

Never sentence broken mechanical or electronic devices to the trash—until you've dismantled them. That's right, for your education take apart all dead gadgets. Study how different devices work and, if the inner workings don't make sense to you, grill a friend who can explain the basics of the springs, gears, and circuitry.

It's a habit that will instill curiosity and erode the mystery surrounding the devices which serve us. Before long, you'll start seeing problems you can actually fix—wires you can reconnect, levers you can bend slightly, screws you can tighten, belts you can replace. And if you never find the problem, don't worry, it was dead anyway.

To start this new tradition, scour the house looking for a dead device to operate on. Then round up the screw driver and pliers, put on the surgical gloves and mask, and have yourself a session of Chicago Hope.

♦ If after operating, you pronounce the device permanently dead, salvage parts. Having a good selection of nuts, screws, bolts, washers, cords, connectors, and springs will help your future efforts (old jars, particularly plastic ones, make good storage containers). You never know when a salvaged part is going to save the next patient.

♦ Let your kids operate, too. Make a medical game out of these procedures and it can be so much fun your children won't realize they're being schooled.

========= February 11 =========

More fun than complaining about a crummy product or crummy service is complimenting companies that have pleased you. While some people pass on their gratitude to corporations because their heart overflows with love, we who are mercenaries (and are not ashamed of it) have found that flattery is profitable business.

When you find products/services you like, call the company's customer-service department (use the 800 number listed on the product's packaging) and tell your representative (who is probably accustomed to death threats rather than praise) how much you've enjoyed the product. Tell them you'd appreciate receiving coupons for that product to make it more affordable to you and to the friends you'd like to introduce to the product. Ask whether they have samples of other products they would like you to try. And tell them you would appreciate being notified when new products are developed.

In the event that there is no convenient (or free) number to call, send a letter to the company's marketing director with all these comments and requests. To speed up this process, file copies of your first few letters and plagiarize them for future requests. Or, if a computer is an esteemed member of the household, draft a form letter and fill in the blanks to personalize any flattery campaign you decide to wage.

Test the power of praise. Go through the house in search of products you truly like, that legitimately earn your praise. Get the manufacturer's name, address, and phone number from the packaging and start brown nosing by phone and by plume (I prefer the phone, because it's faster and usually free). Now sit back and wait. You'll be surprised by the stuff (coupons, samples, information) sent to those who ask.

Cheap Trick:
Know the company's name but not its phone number? Call the 800 Directory Assistance (800-555-1212) and request the company's toll-free number. Unlike normal directory assistance, this is a free call.

═══ February 12 ═══

A thorn of capitalism that pricks at the nerves of my sensibility is the multi-billion dollar industry revolving around special-occasion cards. We've been conditioned to feel like insensitive, impersonal brutes if we don't send cards on Valentine's Day, Mother's Day, birthdays, anniversaries... So how do we show just how sensitive and personal we are? We send a mass-produced card. Apparently, the fact that we spent $2 proves we care.

Time to eliminate the costly, mass-produced missives.

♦ Make your own cards. A homemade Valentine's Day card costs pennies, but the effort involved gives the end product more value than its store-bought cousin. One of a dozen pictures (or cartoons) from any magazine can form the theme of your card. Alternately, the words from Shakespeare's sonnets, Kahil Gibran's writings, or Paul McCartney's songs can become the nugget of your card.

Other card possibilities: clip your partner's horoscope from the paper and use it as the basis of the card, use a lottery ticket as your theme (gamble on me—be my Valentine).

♦ While you're at it, designate a stationery box to be your "Future Cards" box. As you encounter pictures, ads, and headlines that are good stock for future cards, cut 'em out and add 'em to the box.

═══ February 13 ═══

Romance has little to do with the money spent on a person and much to do with the attention given a person and the manner in which that attention is given. Keeping that in mind, consider these inexpensive but romantic ways to prepare for Valentine's Day.

♦ Give your Valentine a romance jar. In a small jar or vase, fold up five or six pieces of parchment describing niceties you are willing to deliver in the weeks that follow. Each week your Valentine draws one piece of paper and you pay up on the I.O.U. Examples of what you might offer: massages; flowers (you choose the type); a day off from the cooking; a homemade, candlelight dinner; an evening stroll under the stars.... Not only is the romance jar affordable, it prolongs the romance of the day.

♦ Send your partner one rose. The elegance of simplicity is as powerful as the boorishness of extravagance.

♦ Ignore roses altogether. On Valentine's Day they are both conventional and costly (expect them to double or triple in price). Be different. Find a flower that reminds you of your Valentine or that forms the basis of a love poem or letter (tulips and forget-me-nots offer obvious possibilities).

♦ Hide a dozen love notes around the house (in books, magazines, dressers, cabinets, closets...). Your partner will be finding these for weeks to come.

♦ Bestow your Valentine with a bowl of Hershey Kisses. Each Kiss must be redeemed with a real kiss.

February 14

Mandatory and *romantic* are not words that compliment each other well. That's why the notion of mandatory romance each February 14 seems insincere. Still, since you can't lick the movement, here's how to join it without making *mandatory* synonymous with *expensive.*

♦ Bake a heart-shaped pizza.
♦ Prepare a candlelight dinner at home.
♦ House-swap with friends for the big V-Day: It won't cost a thing, yet the change of environment casts a romantic spin on the evening.
♦ While you are out on a romantic stroll, have a friend deliver a gourmet dinner to your home, complete with candelabras, silver, and a Sinatra CD. Repay the friend by reciprocating in the future.
♦ Create a power outage at home. Trip the main circuit, dig out the candles, and cuddle up on the couch.
♦ Use a bed and breakfast clearing house to plan a getaway that suits your taste and budget. Contact Bed and Breakfast Reservations, P.O Box 282910 San Francisco, CA 94128-2910, 415-696-1690.
♦ Get a book of constellations from the library and arrange an evening stroll, allowing time to identify constellations. Bring a thermos of hot chocolate and steer clear of parks where you're likely to get mugged.

There are 364 days each year when these romantic activities would be more unexpected and, therefore, more memorable.

═══════ February 15 ═══════

Although many people hate it, complaining does pay—the squeaky wheel does get oiled. Years ago when my mother opened a can of corn and found a dead worm inside, she sent the president of that company the dried remains of the worm with a note, "I see we're getting meat along with our vegetables now." As an apology, she was sent a case of corn and was assured it would be meat-free.

Several years ago I received contemptuous treatment over the phone trying to make dinner reservations for eight at a popular restaurant. The hostess all but called me a dolt for believing that a restaurant of such import could make room for eight nobodies without at least a fortnight's notice. I wrote a polite letter to the manager explaining that, thanks to this treatment, there were now eight nobodies who would not be helping his restaurant maintain its important reputation. The manager sent me an apology and bribed me to reconsider. I swallowed my pride and used the $30 gift certificate.

To prepare yourself for those times when you need to complain, and to make sure those efforts will be effective, send away for the following resources:

♦ *How to Write a Wrong* (publication #D1126), from the AARP, Consumer Affairs Section, Program Department, 1909 K Street NW, Washington, D.C. 20049. It's a detailed guide for handling problems with door-to-door salesmen, mail-order firms, and normal businesses.

═══════ February 16 ═══════

Yesterday you sent for a resource to help you lodge effective complaints. Take a few minutes now to think about products/services that have recently disappointed or failed you. List companies that deserve the wind of your ire.

Yes, it is worth the time—especially with brand-name merchandise and organizations peddling high-quality services. More often than not, companies will try to make amends. Sometimes, they go way out of their way—the good words you spread to friends is bankable PR for them.

◆ If it's a newly-purchased item that's defective and you want a refund or an exchange, contact the store where you bought the item, describe the problem, and explain what you want. A salesman who doesn't give you good results is not worth your effort; move on to the store manager. Most problems will be resolved at this level.

◆ A problem with merchandise purchased some time ago (beyond the warranty period), a problem the manufacturer rather than the retailer should answer to (a worm in your canned food), or a problem the local retailer won't attend to, should be taken directly to the manufacturer. Address your complaints to someone high enough to make an action decision. In the case of defective merchandise, send the letter to the president of the company. He or she may never see it, but it will get properly directed. Matters relating to poor service are usually best taken up with the manager of an establishment.

◆ Make your letters short, listing: facts about where and when you purchased the item (or service), model and serial numbers (if relevant), nature of the problem, extenuating circumstances that have resulted. Include copies of documents, correspondence, or bills that pertain to the problem, and explain what you want: a refund, replacement, apology, new Rolls Royce.... Make copies of all letters sent.

◆ Keep complaints cordial. If you were on the other end, would you rather help an arrogant S.O.B., or let him rot?

◆ I recently sent this complaint to the president of a juice company. It earned me a $5 coupon to be used on any of the company's products. Refer to it as a model when voicing your own complaints.

Dear Sir/Madam,
    My family and I have enjoyed your apple juice for many years, have recommended it to our friends, and have almost always found its quality to be topnotch. Recently, however, we received a gallon bottle that was the exception to the rule.
    This bottle was sour when opened. I'm not sure if this was a freak bottle or whether you may have had

problems with your machinery over a particular period of time. On the chance that the label can help you identify when the juice was bottled, I've included it in the envelope.

I would appreciate receiving a coupon to replace this tainted bottle. Also, if you have coupons promoting new products, please send them.

February 17

Test your computer knowledge—then implement what you learn.

♦ True or False: It's safe to plug your computer directly into the wall socket.

It is standard practice, but it isn't safe. Voltage spikes and surges through the power lines can fry the electronics of your computer and printer, making a good surge protector far better insurance for your machines than an extended-warranty policy. Excellent products at a reasonable cost are available from American Power Conversions (800-800-4272) and Office Depot for $30 to $40.

♦ True or False: Computers don't like being turned on and off.

Off is no problem, but they don't like being turned on due to the surge of power that suddenly streams through the circuitry. The chance of failure at this time is high enough that many businesses never turn off their machines. Running a home computer full time makes little sense unless you use it long hours each day, but turning the machine off and on several times daily is equally nonsensical. If you step away from the computer and intend to return within three or four hours, keep it on.

When taking a break from a computer that is 'on', protect your monitor from "burn in" with a screen-saving or screen-blanking program. Alternately, dim the screen manually before walking away.

♦ True or false: There's not a lot you can do to extend the life of your hard drive.

When you save new information to an old file, the new information is *not* stored on the hard disk (or floppy) with the original data—it is tacked onto the disk elsewhere where space is available. The next time you retrieve that file, the disk's read-write heads must travel to several locations to gather up all parts of the file. These heads are mechanical parts and the extra travel increases their wear (i.e., reduces their life). By periodically running a disk-optimizing program like *Speed Disk* (part of Norton Utilities), you gather all parts of a file and store them together. The result: "Mileage" on the drive's read-write heads is greatly reduced.

♦ True or False: Files copied from bulletin boards, friends, networks, on-line services are best stored on your hard drive.

Viruses are the AIDS of the computer world. Some viruses are harmless—they'll flash an occasional message. Others are lethal—they'll obliterate your information. Before introducing files of unknown extraction (disks from friends, disks with data you downloaded from bulletin boards and on-line services) to the soul of your computer (your hard drive), scan them for viruses. Learn to use a virus checker like Microsoft Anti-Virus (MSAV) which is now a standard feature of DOS and can be run from DOS or Windows by typing MSAV.

February 18

Regularly backing up the data files containing your phone directories, investment spreadsheets, financial reports, word-processing files, databases, journal entries, recipes... is a crucial chore of computer use. It's not enough to have this information on the hard drive alone—a day will come when a power surge, virus, or mechanical failure of the drive will deny you access to your information. If you don't have that information backed up on floppy disks or a tape drive, you're driving the Sahara without a spare tire.

♦ Standard operating procedure to be practiced by everyone (you, kids, spouse) from now on: Always plug your own floppy disk into the A drive. While working, save your file every 20 minutes, saving alternately between the A and C drive (i.e., use the opposite drive every time you save). Whenever a file is closed for the day, its last incarnation is saved on both the hard and floppy drive.

Now in a worst-case scenario, (the death of your hard drive), you'll never have lost more than 40 minutes of work. In a more common crisis (a power outage that temporarily kills the machine) you've lost less than 20 minutes of work.

◆ A complete and regular backup of your computer's hard drive will save you days of frustration on that fateful day when (not if) it crashes. It will also save you *beaucoup* bucks. Restoring a crashed disk is likely to entail reformatting it, and reformatting erases all stored information. If you need to get that data off because you have no other backup, the process could easily cost you $500 to $1,000.

By comparison, the money spent on a quarter-inch cartridge (QIC) drive for backing up your data is cheap. With street prices of $125 to $150 the Travan-format drives like Conner's Tapestor 800 (800-426-6637), Iomega's Ditto Easy 800 (800-944-0936), or Colorado Memory System's T-1000 (970-635-1500) are the best values on the market. The TR1 tapes for these drives use the QIC-80 format, have a street price of about $30, and can store 800 megabytes of memory.

Many home users ignore tape drives and choose to back up their hard drive on floppy disks. Unfortunately, that process is so tedious that the job is rarely, if ever, done. Consequently most people, myself included, experience the bitter taste of loss before they invest in a tape drive. But if you use your computer regularly, the money spent on this technology will someday seem like an act of inspired brilliance.

February 19

Computers these days offer you hardware peripherals up the ying yang—scanners, modems, multi-media kits...you could spend the better part of a year's salary souping up the machine. You can live without all these bells and whistles, but if you have kids, and have a relatively modern machine (486 chip or better), the multi-media kits—most of which sell for $250 to $350 for a CD-ROM, sound card, speakers, and 10 to 20 software titles—are a good investment.

These kits eliminate expenditures in gaming hardware (video games are, after all, what will immediately appeal to your kids). Far more virtuous than the gaming side of multi-media kits are the low-cost educational materials that will run on CD-ROM. As part of your multi-media kit you're likely to receive such titles as The Grolier Multimedia Encyclopedia, which has 21 volumes of information packed into one disk (the paper version of this encyclopedia alone costs over $500). The kits also include educational titles with dictionaries, atlases, detective games, math games, geography games, problem-solving games, tools to create multimedia videos, music programs, language programs... High on the list of good values in multimedia kits are those assembled by Creative Labs Inc. (800-998-5227).

If you see multi-media as being part of your family's future, contact several local computer retailers and compare prices. Also ask about installation fees (if you're not knowledgeable about installing hardware, hire out this chore).

◆ Apart from the kits, a huge world of other educational materials awaits. The reference power of some of these titles boggles the mind. Type in a phrase or subject—like *Mason-Dixon line* and a diskette on U.S. History will search over 100 fat history books for all listings.

Some other great references: *Bookshelf* from Microsoft ($55) provides a good dictionary, thesaurus, atlas, almanac, book of quotes, and a ho-hum encyclopedia all on one diskette. *Street Atlas USA* from DeLorme ($70) offers state maps of the country or street maps of any city, be that Washington D.C., Walla Walla, or Winnemucca. And Correl Gallery ($40) gives anyone wanting to add graphics to their documents some 10,000 images of clip art from which to choose.

◆ In terms of sheer information, *Library of the Future* (World Library Inc., 800-443-0238), is one of my favorite titles. One disk packs away over 3,500 classic books, stories, plays, poems, religious works, historical documents, and children's stories. You can read the text of these books;

search the entire disk for a word, name, subject, phrase, quote, or date; print a quote, a page, or a book; or import any part of a book into another document. To buy paper copies of the literature contained on this $70 disk would cost over $7,000.

◆ Learning foreign languages on these multi-media systems is another superb application of the hardware. This includes the foreign language of music. With the Piano Discover System made by Jump Software (800-289-5867 or 415-917-7460) you get a four-octave keyboard that plugs into the computer and plays through the sound card. You can practice or jam on the system like a normal keyboard. But quite unlike a normal keyboard, the system's software has tutorials and instruction for players of different skill levels. The computer screen becomes your music instructor as it teaches you basic music theory, piano techniques, piano fingering, and how to work with both the bass and treble clefs. The system demonstrates how pieces should be played. And it lets you accompany computer-generated musicians and playback your own efforts. For the hardware alone, the street price of $200 seems reasonable, but considering that everyone in the family gets music lessons out of the deal, you're talking about a steal.

◆ Regarding software: find excellent prices on bundled titles and individual titles from Educorp Computer Services (7434 Trade St., San Diego, CA 92121-2410, 800-843-9497) and TigerSoftware (1 Datran Center, 9100 S. Dadeland Blvd., Suite 1500, Miami, FL 33156, 800-888-4437).

═══════ February 20 ═══════

Regardless of whether you're talking about traditional software or CD-ROM titles, there's enough choice on the market to bankrupt even the likes of Bill Gates. Some ways to keep the costs down:

◆ Shareware is not a type of software but a method of marketing software. The try-before-you-buy concept of shareware allows people to use (and thoroughly test) a program at home before purchasing it. If you decide to make the plunge and become a registered user, the cost of doing so is typically far less than buying comparable commercial products through a computer store.

The Software Labs (100 Corporate Pointe, Suite 195, Culver City, CA 90230, 800-569-7900) sifts through thousands of shareware programs available and produces a catalog featuring the cream of the crop. The company offers inexpensive educational programs, business programs, writing and graphics programs, games, utilities.... Shareware games sell for as little as $10 and a WordPerfect-type word processor sells for about a quarter of its name-brand brother.

◆ If you are adamant about sticking to big-name software, investigate mail-order prices before making the plunge. Mail-order prices are often lower and purchasing from out-of-state firms lets you avoid the noose of state sales tax. Typically, this more than offsets the cost of shipping.

Software is an ideal mail-order purchase—the package is already shrink wrapped for mailing and has nothing mechanical to break. Also, because computer users call the software company's technical support number when they encounter software problems, the need for local service is a moot point.

Mail-order houses to contact include: Computer Discount Warehouse (800-326-4239), Micro Warehouse (800-367-7080), Midwest Computer Works (800-669-5208), PC Connection (800-243-8088).

Call the 800 number of these companies today and get catalogs coming your way.

February 21

Buy state-of-the-art computers and they come with state-of-the-art prices. Settle for used equipment, however, and you'll get into the personal computing game for a third or a half of what techies demanding the fastest chips pay.

Most of us really don't demand a lot of muscle from our machines. We need them for word processing, accounting, tracking investments, storing addresses, playing games, using the CD-ROM, sending e-mail, and preparing our taxes. We aren't, however, trying to beat Gary Kasparov at chess, solving complex statistical studies, reconstructing the images Voyager sends back to Earth, or computing what happened a billionth of a second after the Big Bang. For the vast majority of us, our life does not revolve around the computer, so machines with slightly slower chips and clockspeeds (i.e., a generation or two old) are perfectly adequate. Furthermore they'll save us about $2,000.

As I write this in 1996, a relatively hot Pentium machine with a good monitor, a big drive, abundant RAM, CD-ROM, sound card, and considerable software sells for $2,300 to $3,300 (much depends on whether you're buying a clone or name-brand machine). Meanwhile, a good 486 machine with monitor, big hard drive, and lots of software sells for $800. And a 386 machine, which is more than adequate for word processing, accounting purposes, and databases of moderate size, sells for $300 to $400.

For an up-to-date look at what you might to expect to pay for a used machine, check the American Computer Exchange Index of computer prices. The index lists the average sales price of 20 to 40 different systems. Call your local library and ask about the listing or call 800-786-0717 and ask what papers in your area publish the index.

To find a used computer:

♦ Check the classified adds in the paper.

♦ Use the Internet—it's a burgeoning bulletin board of buy-and-sell information. Just one of many possibilities: Enter the search engine Yahoo (www.yahoo.com) and under its *Computers and Internet* section run a search on *used computers*. You'll get hundreds of listings, one of the more useful being *Business & Economy: Companies: Computers: Retailers: Used* which lists about a hundred retailers around the country dealing with used hardware.

♦ Check *The Yellow Pages* (Computers—Used) for local dealers of used equipment.

♦ Call the American Computer Exchange (800-786-0717). This company acts as a broker in the sales of some 80,000 used machines each year. Working through American Computer, sellers list their machine (and the asking price) in a database. Buyers calling the service are polled and their wants/needs are matched to suitable entries in the database. Price negotiation takes place anonymously through the service. Once a price is agreed upon, the seller sends the computer to American Computer and the machine is checked before it goes to the buyer. The buyer, meanwhile, sends a check to American Computer and that check is held in escrow several days while the buyer makes sure the purchased machine works. Once the buyer is satisfied, the seller is paid. For this, American Computer receives a commission of 10% (paid by the seller).

February 22

Time to give thought to paring the cost of keeping your computer printer up and running.

♦ Owners of laser printers have a hefty expense ahead of them when their "disposable" toner cartridge needs replacing. For popular laser printers—like those made by Hewlett Packard, Canon, and Apple—new toner cartridges cost $100 to $130. New cartridges for many other machines, like the NEC printer I own, can cost $230.

Slash these costs by recycling your "disposable" cartridge. Many companies refill old cartridges for less than half the cost of a new cartridge: Hewlett Packard cartridges can be refilled for $55 while the cartridge for my NEC printer can be refilled for $100. In the early days of refilling, the results were not always satisfactory; nowadays a refilled cartridge prepared by a reputable company will give you flawless performance.

Find local refillers in the Yellow Pages under *Computer Supplies*, *Desktop Publishing*, or *Office Supplies*. Some businesses also accept empty cartridges and ship the refills by mail. A company I've used for years is AMS Laser Supply (430 S. 96th #9, Seattle, WA 98108, 800-289-5277). AMS guarantees a two-day turnaround after receiving your empty cartridge.

♦ Willing to get your hands dirty in order to drastically lower your printing costs? Then consider refilling the toner cartridge of your laser printer yourself. Computer Friends (14250 NW Science Park Dr., Portland, OR 97229, 503-626-

2291 or 800-547-3303) assemble TonerBucket Kits (average cost $125) containing a video and all the supplies you'll need to refill 30 of the most popular toner cartridges on the market. The kit pays for itself on the first recharge and from that point on the cost of the toner purchased for recharges is about one-tenth the cost of purchasing a new toner cartridge.

◆ Because they are both affordable and deliver high-quality printing, inkjet machines are currently the tool most home users are employing for their printing needs. Like cartridges for laser printers (above), the cartridges of inkjet printers can be refilled for about half the price of purchasing new cartridges. Example: the 51626A cartridge used by the HP Deskjet, Deskwriter, and several other machines costs $32 if purchased new. Refills cost $14.

Check the Yellow Pages for a local refiller or mail your empty cartridge to AMS Laser Supply (430 S. 96th #9, Seattle, WA 98108, 800-289-5277). They will refill your cartridge and have it back in the mail within two days.

If you want to learn how to refill your own inkjet cartridge, request a Jet Master price list from Computer Friends (14250 NW Science Park Dr., Portland, OR 97229, 503-626-2291 or 800-547-3303). The company offers Jet Master Kits for nearly 200 different printers. These kits reduce the cost of recharging such cartridges as the 51626A (used by popular machines like the Deskjet and Deskwriter) to $3.12 per pop. Furthermore, some of these kits support color printers.

February 23

Yesterday's tricks to control computer printer costs assumed you owned a relatively modern printer. What if that ain't so? What can you do if you rely on ancient machines using impact technology, machines like dot-matrix or daisy-wheel printers?

◆ Rather than purchasing new cloth ribbons *ad nauseam*, consider re-inking your faded cloth ribbons. Re-inking entails the use of lubricated dot-matrix ink (non-lubricated inks will ruin your print head) and a machine, costing about $80, to apply ink to ribbon.

The casual computer user won't print enough to justify a re-inker, but because the replacement cost of most ribbons runs between $8 and $15, a re-inker can pay for itself after six to 10 ribbon changes. The same ribbon can be reused 50 to 100 times and the quality of the printing after re-inking is virtually as good as that of a new ribbon.

The MacInker (available by mail order from the distributor: Computer Friends, 14250 NW Science Park Dr., Portland, OR 97229, 503-626-2291 or 800-547-3303) is a popular re-inker. You buy a universal cartridge base ($70) and a specialized kit ($10) to adapt the re-inker to your type of ribbon.

♦ Impact printers are fast becoming the dinosaurs of the printing world. But if you like your dinosaur and it is still in fine shape, you should either stockpile new ribbons or get a re-inker so you won't be put of business when the manufacturer suddenly stops producing your ribbon.

♦ Restuffing is another option that can lower the cost of fabric dot-matrix and daisy-wheel ribbons. Mail your ribbon cartridge to a company like Northwest Ribbon Recycling and Supplies (8175 SW Nimbus Ave., Beaverton, OR 97005, 800-648-5156 or 503-641-5156). They will pull the old ribbon out of the cartridge and insert fresh ribbon.

Inexpensive ribbons, like those for the Epson MX80 printer, are cheaper to buy than restuff. But you can save 25% to 60% by restuffing medium-priced and expensive cartridges. The ribbon cartridge for the Okidata 393, for example, retails for $29 but can be restuffed for $10.

In the event that ribbons for your printer are no longer available (this is happening with alarming frequency now that laser and inkjet technology has overtaken the printing world), restuffing old cartridges may provide the oxygen needed to keep an old printer breathing.

February 24

This book is not about investing—dozens of books drum that topic to death. Though investing may be over-emphasized (saving money so that you have money to invest is equally important), investments are crucial to improving the financial health of your family. The thousands of dollars this book saves you will grow into tens of thousands of dollars if you develop and practice sound investment strategies. Consequently, you would be remiss not to be a practitioner of monetary dualism.

On the one front (the one this book emphasizes) is your attempt to spend less, save more, stretch the dollars you already own. On the other front is the concept of growing your money.

So, to the library you go. Check out materials with sound investment information. Magazines: *Money Magazine* (particularly each February's issue), *Bottom Line Personal*, *Consumer Reports*, *Kiplinger's Personal Finance*. Books: *Get a Financial Life* by Beth Kobliner (Simon & Schuster), *The Wealthy Barber* by David Chilton (Prima), *The Common Sense Investment Guide* or *The Stitch-In-Time Guide to Growing Your Nest Egg* by the Beardstown Ladies (Hyperion), *The Investor's Guide to the Net* by Paul Sarrell (Wiley & Sons), *The Hulbert Guide to Financial Newsletters* by Mark Hulbert (New York Institute of Finance).

Cheap Trick:
Once you're ready to invest (be that in stocks, bonds, Treasury bills, mutual funds, IRA plans, Keogh plans, CDs, or money markets) consider working through a discount broker like Charles Schwab (101 Montgomery St., San Francisco, CA 94104, 800-435-4000). Other brokerage firms provide more hand holding, give more advice (both good and bad), but most of these charge higher commissions (about 50% higher), more transaction fees, and apply more sales pressure. And unlike many of the Merrill Lynches and Dean Witters of the world, Charles Schwab has no annual fee, requires smaller initial deposits, and discounts its commissions. Call for information.

February 25

Many readers may lack the time, the money, or the expertise needed to play the investment game just now. That doesn't let you off the hook from using what resources you do own to help the financial picture of the family. Most of you have one huge blackhole of debt you can attend to with pocket change—your home loan. Until you've developed the knowledge and established the infrastructure to invest in your own securities and funds, devote surplus dollars to paying off your mortgage.

Those who rent homes complain that paying rent is like pouring money down a rat hole. But home owners have a rat hole of their own: interest. By the time home owners pays off a 30-year, $100,000 loan, they will have paid a total of $264,157 at 8% interest and $315,928 at 10% interest. That's a huge rat hole.

If your financial institution allows it (and most do), put whatever extra money you can each month toward a principal payment on your house. We're talking about big savings here. For example, if you have an 8%, 30-year, $100,000 loan, your monthly payment is $733.77. If, however, you paid $771.82 each month (only $38 more), you'd neutralize the loan in 25 years (instead of 30) and pay a total of $231,546 rather than $264,157. That's a saving of $32,611. That's no misprint: you'd save nearly 33 grand.

The same mathematic principles explain why you save so much with a 15-year loan versus a 30-year loan. Paying off a 15-year, $100,000 loan at 8%, you'd pay $991.32 per month (versus $733.77 per month for 30 years). Over 15 years you'd pay a total of $178,437 (versus a total of $264,157 for a 30-year loan). Your savings: $85,720.

Points of Interest:

◆ If you're in the process of purchasing a home, a 15-year note will save a roomful of money. Many financial experts, however, still recommend you negotiate a 30-year loan. Shop extensively for the lowest interest rate and make sure the loan allows you to apply extra payments toward principal whenever you want. Then, treat your loan exactly like a 15-year loan, making those larger payments that save you a ton of money. Why bother getting a 30-year loan if you intend to pay it off in 15 years? Because if times get tight, you are not trapped into higher payments—you can drop back to smaller payments until the family's cash flow improves.

♦ Why worry about paying off your 8% mortgage when you've got the 18% stinger of credit-card debt skewering you? If you haven't paid off all your other consumer loans (credit-card payments, auto loans, etc.), whittle away at them each month. After the consumer loans are eliminated, whittle away at the home loan.

===== **February** 26 =====

The importance of *not* accumulating debt cannot be overstated. The pressure of having debts hanging over your head (mortgages, credit-card payments, car loans) creates stresses that can, literally, have you worried sick. But even if you dismiss such emotional ills, it's easy to see the financial evils of debt by putting it under the analytical microscope of mathematics. Here's a small example illustrating the problem.

Say you purchase a $2,000 computer with a credit card and then pay only the minimum amount due each month ($30.35) at 18% interest. It will take 25 years to pay off the debt and besides the $2,000 owed, you'll pay an additional $7,105 in interest for—a total of $9,105.

How much better off would you be if you invested what money you had in a mutual fund and waited? Obviously it depends on the amount invested and the return (interest rate) of the investment, but just out of curiosity what would happen to that $30.35 payment going to a card company each month if it was sunk into your own investment (paying 10%) for 25 years? Besides the $2,000 needed for the computer purchase, your monthly installment to yourself with the compounding interest would give you another $38,269.

Accumulating $38,269 for yourself versus paying someone else $7,105 in interest. The difference on a $2,000 purchase between paying on credit and paying when you can afford the purchase could amount to $45,474. Yes, the case is extreme (you're unlikely to take 25 years to pay off your credit card debt) but it illustrates the point: Haste makes waste.

In this case, the haste to own something now, before you can afford it, costs you $45,474 more than purchasing it at a time when you're in a position to let your money work for you. Early in the game it seems like you're depriving yourself of what you deserve, but later in the game you're on Easy Street rather than out working the streets.

♦ Place a stick-on dot on the face of your watch. Whenever you see the dot the next few days, remind yourself to make purchases only when you can afford them outright. Promise yourself you will no longer borrow money for any nonessential. Remind yourself to be patient—that good things will come of that patience. An African proverb says, "Begin with patience, end with pleasure." In the East Indies it is said, "Patience is a dish of gold." And the Japanese say, "Patience is bitter but its fruit is sweet."

February 27

Another example to drive home yesterday's message that it is time to stop borrowing money. You purchase a $1,500 stereo and use the store's credit line (18% interest) to pay off the stereo with 24 monthly installments of $75. In total you pay $1,800 so you figure, big deal, you lost $300 over two years to afford a pleasure.

Not so fast, Bucko.

Someone else who puts that same $75 each month into investments earning 10% would have a fund worth $1,983 after 24 months. Now if Ms. Patience took the $1,500 cost of the stereo from her account, she would not be $300 in the red but $483 in the black. Do you see how patience on just one acquisition has made her $783 richer than you?

Furthermore, after two years you'll be lucky if you can fetch $750 for your $1,500 stereo and Ms. Patience could go out and buy a *used* stereo every bit as good as yours for $750. Consequently, at the end of the two year period she could actually own the same quality stereo as you and have $1,533 more in investments than you.

The true cost of making hasty purchases on credit, with loans, by borrowing should be slapping you awake and making you see the whole picture. To know the true cost of borrowing money you must not only calculate the interest you're paying others but the income opportunity of which you're depriving yourself.

All of this illustrates, on a micro scale, just how important it is to get out of debt. Stop worshipping materialism (at least for now). Slam the brakes on all discretionary spending that feeds your debt. Commit yourself to a lifestyle of temperance until the red tide turns black and your money earns profits for you rather than for billion-dollar financial institutions.

Your work for today:

♦ Pick up or copy a set of amortization tables (bookstores will have them, as will the reference areas of most libraries).

♦ Reread this information until the numbers and concepts make sense.

♦ Have your spouse read and reread this until it clicks.

♦ Discuss discretionary/unnecessary expenditures you're willing to forego until you can buy them outright, rather than borrow money. Up for discussion are: new cars, remodeling, wardrobe additions, new furniture, children's toys, meals out, electronic toys...

♦ Make a pact with your spouse that you will eliminate all debt (except your mortgage loan) by _____. You'll do this by paying $_____ per month to rid yourself of debt (use the amortization tables from the library to figure out what size payments will make this possible).

February 28

Is it worth ___ hours of my spouse's life?

That's the question you as a home economist should be asking before each purchase.

How much is your spouse's time worth? Employing the exercises from Chapter 2 calculate your spouse's true hourly wage. From his or her salary, deduct taxes, withholdings, and work-related expenses (wardrobe, grooming, commuting expenses) to determine the actual take-home pay.

Then calculate the total amount of time (including time devoted to commuting, grooming, homework, decompression) needed to earn these dollars that make it home.

Divide actual take-home pay by total hours devoted to earning that money and you'll be left with a fairly dismal picture of your spouse's true wage. Don't faint when your spouse's $40,000/year salary—an expansive sounding figure—translates into a true wage of $7.33/hour.

So is it worth 10 hours of your spouse's life to buy those cool, $70 court shoes your child wants (and that he'll outgrow in five months)? Ten hours of life for one item is a steep price. What about pants, shirts, books, food, insurance, entertainment, and education for that kid? What about shoes, pants, shirts, books, food, insurance and entertainment for yourself? If you don't keep asking the question, 'Is it worth ___ hours of my spouse's life?,' you'll consume that life with a closetful of clutter.

◆ On a bookmark-sized piece of paper write the question, "Is it worth ____ hours of my spouse's life?" Put that paper in your wallet where you will encounter it often as you reach for the dollars to pay for your purchases.

February 29

Vicki Robin, the coauthor of the best selling book *Your Money or Your Life*, lives off the $6,000 that her investments generate each year. Yes, she could easily make and spend more, but having the time to pursue her passions is far more important than earning money she doesn't need.

Living on this sum is unfathomable to many Americans, and journalists who interview her invariably ask, "Don't you ever go out to eat?" To that question she replies that she visits a restaurant for dinner about four times a year.

Robin says that, for her, going out less delivers more from the experience. It makes the evening an anticipated, savored one. "I enjoy my nights out in a way that people who dine out frequently can't."

It's a solid point. You may decide that dining out more than four times a year is a priority, but keep in mind that doing it less delivers more from the experience.

Also, if cost is the only reason you don't dine out more often, you'll help the cause tremendously by smarting up. Points to keep in mind:

♦ If young children will be in tow, feed them first— they'll enjoy the 89¢ can of Spaghettios at home more than the $7 plate of fettucini.

♦ For older kids, order one adult entree (rather than two kids' plates) and split it between them. Obviously, this doesn't apply to teenagers.

♦ Have hors d'oeuvres and cocktails at home. Nothing turns a meal into a financial disaster faster than appetizers and alcohol.

♦ Desserts are another belt- and budget-buster, so pass on them altogether or split one.

♦ What should you drink? Best values include ice water with a slice of lemon and coffee (with the meal). Should you order a soda, ask the waiter to hold the ice—soda is almost always refrigerated so you'll get twice the soda for the financial pop.

Do such antics ruin the experience of a night out? For some, yes. But try them before you condemn them. By sticking simply to a nice entree and a simple drink, you can eat out twice for the cost of one night of splurging. Many find that trade-off a good one.

March

===== March 1 =====

Aristotle said, "All that we do is done with an eye to something else."

The problem is that most of us don't actively define and focus on that something else. We haphazardly define our desires as life passes by and we reach mid-life in a financial state where all that we do is done to pay off the something else of credit card debt, mortgages, and car loans.

Change that.

♦ This evening get together as a family and decide upon something *fun* to save for. It can be simple—a dinner at the local pizza parlour, family night at the movies, a Saturday at the local amusement park. Or it can be a big dream—a ski vacation, a trip to that Mecca of Marketing (Disneyland), a computer... Visualize this dream, talk it up, ignite the flames of excitement.

♦ Now find a nice box/chest/container. On the container (or a card attached to it) write the family's dream, and start saving for your future goal. Funds that are saved through anyone's sacrifice go into the box. Spare change from the pocket goes in. The contribution of kids who take short showers, or turn off lights, or sacrifice on the purchase of new clothes, or refuse a snack all go into the dream box. With a fun goal to motivate your family, money will build up in the box. Like Emerson says, "A good intention clothes itself with sudden power."

Keep your dream box in constant use. When one dream is fulfilled, assemble the family and pick a new one.

══════ March 2 ══════

Expensive options for your car—ABS brakes, dual airbags—*do* make life out on the highway safer. However, your driving habits are what really determine whether your vehicle is a lethal weapon or a safe haven. *You* determine whether you will be involved in one of the 6.5 million car accidents each year. Consequently, the most important way to stay safe on the highway has little to do with gadgets and everything to do with judgment. The following defensive driving tips should be taught to everyone in the family.

♦ Drinking and driving. You're living in a vacuum if you don't know that drinking and driving are about as healthy a relationship as Romeo and Juliet's. According to the National Safety Council, drunk drivers cause one in four fatal accidents while Mothers Against Drunk Drivers (admittedly a biases source) says 26,000 people are killed in alcohol-related car accidents each year. It is the root of most fatal accidents. Don't do it. And avoid driving late at night when drunks produce the most carnage.

♦ The heart of darkness. Driving after dark doubles your chances of being in a fatal accident and the weekend hours between 11 p.m. and 3 a.m. are the most dangerous of all.

♦ The big sleep. Some 30% of single-car accidents and many fatal head-on collisions result from snoozing behind the wheel. Make a habit yourself and encourage your kids to pull over and nap when droopy eyes hit—arriving somewhere late is better than not getting there at all. Keep a blanket (for comfort) and a travel alarm clock (to prevent oversleeping) in the vehicle for just this purpose.

♦ Use the belts. If you're not using them, or are not forcing the kids to buckle up (even on short jaunts), begin today. Statistics consistently verify that seat belts reduce automobile fatalities by over 40%, serious injury by larger percentages still. Use both lap and shoulder belts when available. Without a shoulder belt the possibility of back, spinal cord, head, spleen, and liver injuries rise—that's why all cars since 1990 have been outfitted with lap and shoulder belts in the front *and* rear seats.

◆ Speed kills. Statistics prove that slower is better. Highway fatalities have increased by 20% a year on rural interstates that increased the speed limit from 55 to 65 mph. Also in 33% of fatal accidents, authorities list speeding as a contributing cause.

◆ Stop tailgating. Tailgating is an amazingly effective means of transforming a $15,000 machine into scrap metal. As a rule, give the car in front of you at least one car length of distance per 10 miles an hour of speed—more if the roads are wet or icy, and more if the cars ahead are tailgating each other (such cars will come up on you far faster if they don't come to a rolling stop).

◆ Kill the phone. A well-researched Canadian study, published in 1997 in *The New England Journal of Medicine,* indicates that drivers using cell phones are *four* times more likely to reach out and demolish someone. That's why some countries (Israel, Switzerland, Brazil) have outlawed the use of cell phones while you're driving. The only safe way for a driver to use these phones is to stop the car first. Moving calls should be made only if the traffic is extremely light. Anyone who believes his genius allows him to conduct business over the phone while navigating the rush hour is way too dense to be placing calls.

◆ Give them room. If you see drivers using cell phones, stay out of their blind spots and follow them from a safe distance—there's no predicting when a preoccupied driver will swerve or realize, too late, that the traffic ahead has stopped.

◆ Ahead or behind. Lingering at the side or in the blind spot of other cars on the freeway invites accidents. If crisis or carelessness causes such cars to swerve, you're mangled metal. Either pass cars to your side quickly or back off.

Likewise, if another driver boxes you in, speed up or slow down—you need swerving room, too.

♦ **Fast lane or slow lane.** From the standpoint of swerving room, the far left and the far right lanes of a freeway give you the largest margin of safety. If debris or other drivers force you to swerve, these lanes offer you a shoulder's worth of elbow room. Middle lanes lack these safety zones.

♦ **Attention on the road.** According to the National Highway Traffic Safety Administration, one out of 12 fatal accidents is precipitated through eating, talking, fiddling with tapes, or other inattentive behavior.

♦ **Slip-sliding away.** Accident probability rises 40% when you're driving in the rain. Promptly replacing worn tires (especially the front ones) is good insurance for accident avoidance (check the tread of your tires now). At 60 miles per hour, the line between a controllable car and an execution chamber may boil down to a ¼" of tread. Other wet weather tips: Keep wipers in good working order, and the windshield cleaner reservoir filled.

♦ **Back to school.** Defensive driving courses can cut 10% off your insurance premium. They can also save your body and property. Find out about local courses through either your insurance broker (ask how much your premium will drop while you're at it), the local community college, or the National Safety Council (800-621-7619).

Just as important as learning these habits is their enforcement. Family members who violate these practices should have driving privileges suspended (that goes for parents as well as kids). Inconvenience (be it a kid walking to school or a parent taking the bus) is a great motivator for getting back on the straight-and-narrow. This evening, discuss these defensive driving habits with your family and define how infractions will be punished.

March 3

Driving is especially scary when kids are behind the wheel. Scary because your children are the last people you want in an accident yet, statistics say, are among the first to cause them. For example:

◆ Turning left across traffic is dangerous—it accounts for nearly one million accidents each year. Interestingly, teenagers are five times more likely than adults to cause a left-turn accident.

◆ Teenage drivers don't drive the same with their peers as they do with their parents. With peers in the car they are distracted, take risks, and are more likely to speed.

◆ According to the Insurance Institute for Highway Safety, 82% of fatal accidents involving teenagers resulted from driver error. For fatal accidents involving adults between the ages of 20-49, 62% were caused by driver error.

So, if you have children who have recently reached (or are about to reach) the driving age, develop policies which will better protect them. Discuss these policies with your children. Points to consider:

◆ While the law of most states allows children to drive unattended at the age of 16, consider increasing that by a year. At the very least, don't let your children chaperon peers around until they have a year of experience under their safety belts.

◆ Place the financial burden of paying for all tickets and accidents squarely on the shoulder of your children—make them aware of the costs involved.

◆ Emphasize that speeding tickets will result in the loss of driving privileges for a predetermined amount of time.

◆ Driving after drinking (or riding with others who are driving under the influence) should suffer tougher penalties (perhaps twice the speeding penalty). Give the support needed to make this work—don't grumble or sermonize about midnight calls for a ride home, don't complain about a late-night taxi bill.

None of this will work if you don't walk the talk yourself. That means buckling up, driving defensively, traveling within the speed limit. It means being willing to call your driving-aged children for a ride home should the spirits leave you tipsy.

═══ March 4 ═══

Consider the pocketbook ramifications of driving fast. When you double your speed, you nearly quadruple your air resistance—which explains why a car getting 28 miles per gallon at 55 mph travels only 22 miles per gallon at 65 mph. As a rough rule, figure on losing two miles per gallon for every five mph over 50 you drive.

Recalibrate the time you think it takes to reach each driving destination and from now on give yourself a few extra minutes.

Driving slower is good for more than your wealth. Giving yourself extra minutes to reach your destinations will also keep you from tailgating, speeding, and passing unsafely— tactics that tardy drivers routinely use to make up minutes. That's good for your health.

═══ March 5 ═══

Less is often more. The concept applies to all aspects of life, but I'll illustrate the point with the soaps and cleaners with which we surround ourselves.

♦ While expensive cleaners are made for every room and every fixture in the house, you don't need them. In fact, the same all-purpose cleaner used in the kitchen will clean the bathroom fixtures just fine, yet cost about 50% less. If mold and mildew are problems in the bathroom, eradicate them for pennies (rather than dollars) with a home-made brew made by mixing one part bleach with three parts water.

◆ Drain cleaners are extremely corrosive and, if your house is old, these chemicals could eat through the pipes and cause more problems than they solve. Better to practice an ounce of prevention by pouring boiling water down the sinks every week or two.

◆ You don't need expensive detergents to hand-wash delicate fabrics. Most any brand of liquid dishwashing detergent or shampoo is gentle and will do an excellent job. To use: Add 1 teaspoon detergent/shampoo per quart of water.

◆ Commercials for laundry boosters promise you dazzling results. If, however, you compare the stain removal powers of most boosters to that of a good detergent alone, you won't notice a difference.

◆ Tinted, in-tank products may make your toilet bowl *look* cleaner, but if you think these products will keep your bowl clean without the occasional scrub, forget it. These in-tank products mainly camouflage, rather than prevent, dirty bowls. That's little benefit for the bucks spent.

◆ Cleanliness freaks won't go for it, but slothful chefs can often get away without cleaning their oven. Assuming you use the oven frequently and you mop up the major spills inside the oven, you can reach an equilibrium where grime burns off as fast as it goes on.

March 6

What detergent are you using in your dishwasher? Some detergents cost upward of 45¢ per dose and clean no better (or even worse) than ones selling for 11¢ per dose. In nonpartial product reviews, the following cleaners delivered the best bang for the buck. If you're not using one of these cleaners, put them on the Master Purchasing List and wait for a sale.

DISHWASHER DETERGENTS: BEST PICKS
Palmolive Ultra Concentrated Lemon (powder): .11/dose: A+
Par Lemon Scented (Safeway, powder): .11/dose: A-

Kroger Bright Lemon Scent (powder): .12/dose: A-
Electrasol Ultra Concentrate (powder): .10/dose: B+

DISHWASHER DETERGENTS: LACKLUSTER PICKS
Cascade (powder): .17/dose: B
Kmart's Dazzle Lemon Scented (powder):.18/dose:B
Amway Crystal Bright (powder): .45/dose: A
Sun Light Lemon Gel: .26/dose: C+

Products delivering less value than the previously mentioned best picks: All, Shaklee Basic-D, Dial Lemon, Sun Light With Fresh Lemon Scent, Albertson's Lemon Scented, Target, ShopRite Dishwash Lemon Freshened, Seventh Generation, and many gels. Gels as a group cost more and are less effective than powders.

═══════ **March 7** ═══════

Imagine cutting your use of consumables in half. Products would last twice as long and you'd spend half as much money.

Interestingly, many manufacturers routinely recommend using more of their product than necessary. Why? To ensure their products, despite the conditions they are used in, live up to the advertised claims. And, let's be honest here, to increase profits. After all, the more product you use, the more you buy.

Try these tricks and prove to yourself that half as much is sometimes twice as good.

♦ My parents, who have sensitive skin, have discovered that washing clothes with half the prescribed amount of laundry powder not only gets the clothes clean, but allows clothes to rinse better, thereby reducing laundry-induced rashes. Note: If your local water is extremely hard or mineralized, you may need to stick to the manufacturer's recommendations.

♦ Filling the dishwasher's detergent bin is overkill. Experiment with half that quantity and increase the amount as necessary. I don't pre-rinse my dishes (that's the dishwasher's job, right?) so I fill the detergent bin just over the half-way mark.

◆ When handwashing dishes, use a teaspoon to measure your detergent. People who eyeball it use more than necessary. One teaspoon of a *quality* detergent (e.g., Sunlight or Dawn) polishes off a load of dishes.

◆ Whether you're using an all-purpose, bathroom, porcelain, or window cleaner, go easy on quantity. Use just enough to create a thin film over the area in need of cleaning, or use elbow grease to spread a little cleaner a long way. Excess lather is unused cleaning power, and sending loads of it down the drain is no different than opening your wallet and rolling out coins.

Today, put red stickers on the bottles and boxes of all these cleaners. These stickers remind you to cut consumption and, when your family asks about their meaning, you can indoctrinate them as well.

March 8

Yesterday's half-as-much-is-twice-as-good philosophy applies to body cleaners as well as to household cleaners. The following tips may only pinch a penny at a time, but they require no extra effort and *will* nip your use of toothpaste, soap, and shampoo. Get everyone in the family educated and, over the year, the savings add up to serious denominations.

◆ **Toothpaste.** Television ads subtly influence us to smother our brushes with an inch-long bead of paste. But a quarter-inch dab is enough. Dentists say toothpaste is almost incidental to keeping teeth clean. It's the mechanical action of brushing (and flossing) that counts most.
◆ **Mouthwash.** You'll get the same benefit using a third of the recommended amount. Rather than filling the wash's dispensing cup or cap, use just enough to swish around your mouth.
◆ **Liquid hand soap.** When washing hands with liquid soap, a little dab—one with a pea-sized circumference—will

do ya. A full stroke of the pump delivers two to three times more soap than you need.

♦ **Bar soap.** Smothering your hands or limbs with a heavy lather is wasteful. As long as the film covering your hands remains slippery, you've got enough for the job.

♦ **Shampoo.** Use just enough shampoo to create a thin halo of lather around the entire head. Remember, lather is cleaning power that has not been used, so the thicker the layer of lather, the more you've wasted. As for washing your hair twice with each shower, it's unnecessary. Save the shampoo, water, and time.

Once again, go around the home affixing red reminder dots to those tubes and bottles. Sticking a dot to bar soap is tricky, but a sticker on the packaging of all stored soaps is a useful reminder. Over the year as you pull out new bars of soap, the dots remind you that half as much means twice the mileage.

═══════ March 9 ═══════

Shopping 25 years ago was noticeably simpler than it is today. That was before the age of specialization, before we had a cleaner for every household object, and a cosmetic for every body part.

Some of today's cleaners are, indeed, better mousetraps. Many products packing the shelves, however, are special only in their price, not in their composition. Over the next week, you will be making many of these not-so-special products. These cleaners are easier to brew than a cup of coffee, *and* you can make them for a 10th of store-bought products.

Truth be told, you can make just about any cleaner for the house, kitchen, bathroom, windows, clothes, stereo if you have the following items on hand: bleach, vinegar, ammonia (sudsing preferred), isopropyl alcohol, dishwashing detergent, shampoo, clothes detergent, and baking soda. Check your cupboards and see that you have all these items—if not, add them to your Master Purchasing List.

In preparation for the week ahead, read through the next nine entries, decide which cleaners you will be making, and what supplies you still need to round up: chemicals, spray bottles, storage bottles, label supplies...

Get all these supplies together and prepare your bottles. For convenience, type or write each recipe you'll be using on a narrow slip of paper and, using clear, wide packaging tape or transparent contact paper, attach the recipe to the appropriate bottle. In the future when you're out of that cleaner, you'll have the information needed on the label to whip up another batch.

Remove any old labels from the bottles you're using and clearly mark each bottle (use Mr. Yuk stickers) as poison. You want children, who know the shape of pop and milk bottles, to avoid your cleaners.

March 10

The single most valuable cleaner for the kitchen and bathroom is a good all-purpose cleaner. With it you can clean counters, tiles, sinks, toilets, floors, appliance exteriors, tubs, fixtures.... Unless you have a problem that's gotten out of control—mildew sprouting in the bathroom, mold growing in the grout of your tiles—expensive specialty cleaners for the bathrooms, tiles, and porcelain are unnecessary. If you've found an all-purpose cleaner you really like (Fantastik, 409), and if you can purchase the cleaner in bulk, stick with it.

Consumers who have not forged an allegiance to a specific cleaner will find financial advantages to making their own. The following concoctions cost about 50¢/gallon to make; expect name-brand cleaners to run you some $12/gallon.

◆ **All-purpose cleaner.** To 14 cups warm water, add 1 cup washing soda (look in the detergent area of grocery stores) and 1 cup ammonia (either sudsing or non-sudsing). Fill a spray bottle with the cleaner and apply it (full strength) to spot jobs on tile, counters, metal, porcelain... For large jobs (floors, walls), use 3/4 cup cleaner per bucket of warm water. Costs about 50¢ to make versus $12 for a gallon of name-brand cleaner.

Note: Washing soda can be difficult to locate. Arm & Hammer manufacturers the product—call 800-524-1328 (or 800-624-2889 in New Jersey) to find a local retailer.

For a milder (no ammonia) all-purpose cleaner, add 2 teaspoons borax and 1 tablespoon liquid detergent to 1 quart warm water. Store in a spray bottle and apply directly to surfaces.

◆ **Chrome and stainless steel cleaner.** To clean chrome or stainless bathroom fixtures, moisten a tissue with isopropyl (rubbing) alcohol and wipe the fixture.

═══ March 11 ═══

Did you know that many professional window cleaners simply use warm water to clean windows? If your windows, glass table top, or mirrors are simply soiled (not greasy), try it. It works and it's free.

◆ For heavily soiled or greasy glass, use this formula for a window cleaner that is virtually identical to the best commercial products. Mix ½ cup ammonia (sudsy preferred), 1 pint 70% isopropyl alcohol, and 1 heaping teaspoon liquid dishwashing detergent to 13 cups warm water. Stir. To make your mixture look like commercial products, add a drop of blue food coloring. Pour part of your solution into a spray bottle and use it just like commercial window sprays. Cost: about 15 times less than name-brand products.

◆ Regarding a solution for your car's windshield, mix 3/4 teaspoon liquid dishwashing detergent with 1½ quarts water and you're ready to roll. This extremely inexpensive cleaner is for three-season use only. Come winter, revert to a store-bought alcohol-based solution that will not freeze.

═══ March 12 ═══

While an all-purpose cleaner may eliminate the need for many of the following cleaners, you may have specialty needs—mildew in the bathroom, grout that's especially soiled, stained tiles. If you need more abrasive or more powerful cleaners for the bathroom, use some of the following.

◆ **Mildew spray.** In a spray bottle, add one part chlorine bleach to three parts water. Spray the solution on any mildew forming in the bathroom and, if possible, let the solution sit several minutes. Pretest the solution in a hidden nook before spraying it on walls or wall paper.

◆ **Scouring powder.** Sprinkle baking powder or borax on the surface to be scrubbed. Alternately, mix 1 part soap flakes and 2 parts baking soda. Sprinkle the powder on stains or dirty surfaces and scrub with a wet rag.

◆ **Sink cleaner.** Whiten porcelain sinks by covering them with paper towels saturated with bleach (let the towels sit for several hours). An alternative: Plug the sink and pour in enough bleach to cover the bottom. Fill the sink with water, letting the sink soak in the water/bleach solution overnight.

◆ **Tile, grout, and porcelain cleaner.** To 14 cups warm water, add 1 cup baking soda, 1 cup ammonia, ½ cup white vinegar. Spray the solution directly on tile or grout and scrub. Or, spray a solution made from 1 part bleach and 3 parts water onto tile and scrub. Some name-brand tile cleaners are little more than bleach disguised with perfume and a coloring agent; the disguise sells for 25 times more than mixing generic bleach with water in a spray bottle.

◆ **Toilet bowl cleaner.** Use an all-purpose cleaner. Or, pour 1/8 cup chlorine bleach into the toilet bowl and let the water sit for half an hour. Return and swirl the bowl with a brush before flushing.

═══════ March 13 ═══════

Parents with infants will spend a lot of pocket change on diaper wipes before one of those blessed milestones of parenthood—the day when all your children are toilet trained. Until that far-off day, beat down the price of wipes by making your own.

◆ With a serrated knife, saw a normal roll of paper towels into two half-sized rolls. Pull the cardboard core from the center of each and place one of the mini rolls in a large coffee can or plastic tub. Feed the center sheet of the roll through an X cut in the plastic lid of the can/tub.

Mix 1 to 1½ teaspoons liquid dishwashing detergent with about 1½ cups water and pour the solution over the towels. The quantity of water needed depends on the type of towels used. Let the towels sit for 30 minutes and add water if the towels are too dry. For future reference, note the exact amount of solution needed for your brand of paper towels.

Besides using these towels as diaper wipes, use them as towelettes for dirty hands and faces.

Note: If using a coffee can to store your wipes, paint the can first. It adds style to the can and prevents the inside from rusting.

March 14

The home houses a panoply of possessions needing occasional attention. Here are nine miscellaneous chores you can finance for pennies.

◆ **Bug off.** Remove dead bugs from the front of the car by sponging on a paste made from ½ cup baking soda and 1 pint water. Let the paste sit for at least five minutes before *gently* wiping off the bugs.

◆ **Decal remover.** Coat decals with vegetable oil. After five or 10 minutes, decals will rub/lift off.

◆ **Dust spray.** Out of dusting spray? Would you believe that a damp (not wet) rag holds dust just fine? Would you believe there is life after *Endust*?

◆ **Gem cleaner.** Tooth brushes and toothpaste will keep more than your teeth pearly, they'll keep your gems glittering, too.

◆ **Leaf polish.** To 1 quart warm water, add 2 teaspoons soap flakes (shred the remains of bar soap) and 1 teaspoon wheat germ. Very dusty plants should be showered first. Then dampen a cloth with leaf polish and gently wipe leaves. Costs about 10¢ versus $10 for an equal quantity of brand-name product.

◆ **Silk-flower cleaner.** Put flowers in a paper bag with salt and shake.

◆ **Stuffed animals.** Put animals in a paper bag with salt, and shake. Or, put animals in a paper bag with baking soda, and shake. Remove animals from bag, let sit for over 30 minutes, then brush off the baking soda.

◆ **Vinyl cleaner.** Sprinkle baking soda onto a damp rag, then wipe the vinyl.

◆ **Wall cleaner.** To 15 cups warm water, add ½ cup borax, 1 tablespoon dishwashing detergent, and 2 tablespoons ammonia. For large jobs, add 1 cup cleaner to ½ bucket of water and wipe walls with a soft cloth. For spot cleaning, spray on solution undiluted.

══════ March 15 ══════

While an all-purpose cleaner handles most needs around the kitchen, there are several chores in need of specialty potions. Tackle these jobs today with the following home-brews.

◆ **Oven cleaning.** Relatively clean ovens: Scrub with baking soda. Filthy ovens: Turn oven on for 15 minutes (low setting), then turn off and place a bowl of ammonia on the top shelf and a pot of boiling water on the lower shelf. Keep the oven door closed overnight so that the steam and ammonia can loosen the grime. Next day, open the oven and let the vapors vent. Pour the remainder of the ammonia into a gallon of hot water and use this mixture to scrub the oven. Make sure the ventilation is good.

To simplify the job of cleaning a regular oven, dissolve ½ ounce baking soda in a cup of warm water. Wipe the interior of the oven when clean with the solution; next time you clean, the muck will scale off faster. Reapply the baking soda/water mixture after every cleaning.

◆ **Brass, bronze, or copper cleaning.** Make a paste by adding 1 tablespoon vinegar or lemon juice to 1 tablespoon flour and 1 tablespoon salt. Rub paste gently onto brass with a cloth or very fine steel wool. Wash well in warm, soapy water and dry.

Other options for copper: Rub items with ketchup or a mixture made from 2 tablespoons vinegar and 1 teaspoon salt. Then wash with soapy, warm water.

◆ **Chrome cleaning.** Use straight vinegar.

◆ **Pewter cleaning.** Make a thin paste from wood ash and water and rub it on the pewter.

◆ **Silver and stainless steel cleaning.** Make a paste by mixing baking soda and lemon juice (baking soda and water works, too). Rub the paste onto silver with a damp cloth or sponge. Rinse in hot water and dry.

═══ March 16 ═══

Give them periodic attention and they'll treat you well, ignore them and they'll make you sorry. It's good advice whether you're talking about men, women, children, or... drains. It's a lot easier (and less expensive) to keep your drains flowing than it is to unplug them.

Today, wander the house—visiting all sinks, showers, and tubs—armed with your medicine. At each drain, sprinkle in ¼ cup baking soda. Wash it down with ½ cup vinegar. Close the drain until the fizzing stops, then flush the pipes with three to four quarts of boiling water.

◆ Should you ignore this twice-yearly preventive procedure and end up with a plugged drain, dissolve 1 pound washing soda in 2 gallons boiling water and pour the solution down the drain. The solution will sometimes dissolve the clot by itself, but using it in tandem with a plunger or plumber's snake increases the odds of success. Call Arm & Hammer (800-524-1328) and ask which local retailers sell washing soda.

Can't find washing soda? Then pour bleach down the drain and force it along its way with a plunger (or a snake) and boiling water.

═══ March 17 ═══

Cleaning isn't only about eliminating grime, it's also about eliminating odors. Following is a list of some of the foulest, stinkiest, most filthsome smells you're likely to encounter. Implement the remedies that apply.

◆ **Gamy garbage disposals.** Run orange, lemon, or grapefruit peels through the disposal. Or sprinkle in about ¼ cup baking soda, and run.

◆ **Putrid pets.** Rover really reeking? Give him a bath with several cups of tomato juice mixed into the water. The juice neutralizes a whole spectrum of gamy smells. Don't have time for a bath? Rub baking soda into your pet's fur and let the soda sit several minutes before brushing it off.

◆ **Stinking sinks.** Plug the sink and pour in about a gallon of water and ¼ cup bleach. Wash the sink and then let the water drain out slowly. The bleach water will attack odors emanating from the drain.

◆ **Malodorous bathrooms.** If you don't have children living with you, keep a packet of matches on the toilet. To mask unpleasant smells: Light a match, let it burn a few seconds, blow it out, and let it smoke. Drop the dead match in the toilet—it's not cheap if, in the aftermath, you burn down the house.

◆ **Repugnant refrigerators.** Place a box of baking soda (opened), a dish of charcoal briquettes, or a lemon half in the back of the refrigerator. Replace every few months.

◆ **Pungent plastic containers.** Fill them with crumpled newspaper and cover, or wash them with baking soda and water.

◆ **Reeking rooms.** Leave an uncovered dish of ammonia or vinegar in the room overnight. The same remedy applies if smoke or paint odors overpower a room.

◆ **Fetid carpets and cars.** Sprinkle baking soda on the carpet before vacuuming. Sprinkling a powder made from 1 cup borax and 2 cups cornmeal also helps. Both methods work best if the powders sit for at least an hour before vacuuming.

◆ **Smelly sponges.** Wash in the dishwasher or soak in bleach overnight.

◆ **Feculent shoes.** Place crumpled newspaper in shoes. Or sprinkle in a little baking soda (wipe out the powder before wearing).

◆ **Caustic cutting boards.** Rub salt over wooden cutting boards. This eliminates most smells and stains.

◆ **Loathsome laundry.** To eliminate perspiration odors, dab the area with white vinegar just before laundering. Or wipe the underarms, collars, etc., with shampoo about 30 minutes before laundering.

◆ **Rancid trash cans.** Pour ½ cup baking soda into the can's bottom.

◆ **Foul air.** Make a spray deodorant by adding 1 cup baking soda, 1 tablespoon scent (vanilla extract, pine oil, lemon extract), and ¼ cup ammonia to 15 cups warm water. Keep some of this deodorant in an atomizer (spray bottle). Don't spray the solution over wooden furniture. Cost: 50¢ versus about $20 for same amount of name-brand spray.

═══ March 18 ═══

Time to turn the attention of your money-saving sanitation to clothing. As is the case with household cleaners, Madison Avenue does its best to sell you cleaners you don't need. A good name-brand laundry detergent, bleach, dishwashing detergent, shampoo, ammonia, and vinegar—that's adequate armaments to kill dirt and stains.

◆ **Diaper and soiled clothing presoak.** Toss clothes in the washer and cover with water. Add ½ cup baking soda and ¼ cup ammonia per gallon of water used. Soak items several hours before filling the machine with cold water, agitating, and spinning. Now wash as usual.

◆ **Grease cutter.** For really dirty work clothes, add ½ cup ammonia to the wash water.

◆ **Ring around the collar.** Simply rub shampoo onto the collar several minutes before laundering.

◆ **Silk cleaner.** Hand wash silk with liquid dishwashing detergent or an inexpensive shampoo. Use 1 teaspoon detergent per quart of water.

◆ **Spray and wash laundry spray.** To 8 cups water, add ½ cup white vinegar, ½ cup ammonia, ¼ cup baking soda, and 3 tablespoons liquid dishwashing detergent. Spray the solution onto soiled sections of clothing several minutes before laundering.

◆ **Sweat busters.** Wet new underarm stains with ammonia, old stains with vinegar. Let the garment sit several minutes, then rinse and wash in the hottest water that's safe for the garment.

◆ **Wool and delicate-clothing soap.** No need to buy a special product, use the same liquid detergent you'd normally use for hand washing dishes, or use a plain-Jane shampoo. Use 1 teaspoon detergent per quart of water.

March 19

Put a lid on the overly sanitary section of your mind for a moment and honestly ask yourself: Are you over-cleaning your family's clothes?

Most clothes don't need cleaning after a days' use, and many clothes are socially acceptable after several day's use—especially when owners take the trouble to air their garments between outings. Clothes suspended from hangers or hooks not only freshen up with time, they lose some of their wrinkles.

Visit the bedrooms of the house and work out systems that will encourage your spouse and children to cooperate. In the effort to eliminate haystacks of semi-clean but wrinkled clothing piled in each room, remove or relocate dumping chairs, and add wall hooks. Organize and purge closets to create more hanging space. And make sure each closet has plenty of empty hangers on hand.

Over dinner this evening, discuss the new systems that the garment Gestapo will be enforcing. "If zie clothes are not shtinky, filthsom, or in any other vay gross, vie vill again vear dem. Und vie vill not on zie floor our clothes throw. Dey vill, by hook or by hanger, each night be hung."

You may choose to discuss the financial reasoning behind all this. That washing clothes half as often saves water, electricity, detergent, sewage, and maintenance bills by hundreds of dollars a year. That clothing washed and dried half as often will last half again as long. That less time washing means more time living. Or you may just let the Gestapo handle this one, "Fail to cooperate und I vill enjoy making you wary sorry."

March 20

You'll accuse me of having stock in the company, but I don't. It's simply a good product that is also cheap. Baking soda's main drawback is that it is not space-aged or high-tech. If you don't subscribe to the mentality that new is necessarily better, put baking soda on the Master Purchasing List (see January 1) and stock up when it comes on sale:

◆ Used on a damp sponge or rag it will clean sinks, counters, microwaves, pots, pans, refrigerators, cutting boards, coffee pots, tea pots, tubs, toilets, showers, tiles.
◆ Sprinkled in garbage cans, diaper pails, litter boxes, auto carpeting, car trunks, shoes, and drains, it deodorizes.
◆ Spread with a damp rag it cleans toys, high chairs, car seats, and changing tables.
◆ Spread over rugs and allowed to sit an hour before vacuuming, it acts as a dry cleaner.
◆ Added to your laundry (use ½ cup) with normal detergent, it freshens and brightens clothes.
◆ Thrown over fires (especially grease fires), it extinguishes flames.
◆ Brushed over teeth, it makes a dentist-approved (though terrible-tasting) toothpaste.
◆ Mixed in water (½ teaspoon per 4 ounces water) it's an effective antacid.

══ March 21 ══

We all know the adage, "If it ain't broke, don't fix it."

Here's an axiom to tack onto it, "If it's broke, you don't need it."

At the turn of the century our grandparents dreamed that technology would not only free us from need, but free us from lives of toil. They imagined that their children and grandchildren would possess more material goods *and* would have more time to enjoy those goods.

The truth of the matter? Not only does a higher percentage of the population work today than a century ago, but Americans work longer hours than ever before. Rather than languishing in free time, we are suffering from a famine of free time.

It's not the pursuit of what we "need" that inflicts our suffering, it's the pursuit of what we desire. All of our labor-saving devices, toys of leisure, and symbols of status chain us to the corporate clock. And the purchase of these items is only the first step to enslavement. Once owned, we pay to use our purchases (utility fees to operate appliances, greens fees to use golf clubs, gas fees and lift fees to enjoy our skis, battery fees to run the kids' toys), pay to maintain them, and pay to insure them. To pay these bills, of course, we must keep punching the time clock.

The first step in breaking these chains is to recognize the sand traps of our consumer society—to recognize the irony of how easily we become the slaves of our possessions. The next step is to simplify. Avoid collecting all the consumer clutter that mysteriously transforms assets into shackles. And if you are already a victim of consumer overdose, avoid fixing broken items.

Obviously, it's no hard-and-fast axiom. If the roof is leaking, if your tooth is aching, if your tire is flat, fix it. But think hard about each non-essential repair. Put broken items in cryogenic storage (the basement) and try life without them. This applies even to such worshipped gods as the television. With it packed away for several weeks you may be amazed that you have found time to read, that actual discussions are now taking place in the house, that you play games with the kids, and that the kids are pursuing so many more mind-stimulating projects. After experiencing the benefits for a month, you may decide that the broken television is exactly where it should be.

Given the chance, even items you deem to be vital may assume a level of unimportance. A second car that dies may force you to use public transport, commute to work on a bicycle, or car pool with a colleague. Before long the reading you accomplish on the bus or the exercise you obtain on the bike—to say nothing of the money saved by not operating, parking, and insuring a second car—may encourage you to sell the mothballed four-wheeler.

To encourage you to participate in the if-it's-broke-you-don't-need-it program, clear a space for cryogenic storage in the basement or attic now. Clear a sizable area—more than broken equipment alone will be making the pilgrimage to this property purgatory (more about that in a few days). Now deposit the dead, dying, and downcast equipment from around home. See what items your world turns without. See if living with less isn't, indeed, more.

====== **March** 22 ======

I'm willing to wager most readers didn't condemn much property to purgatory yesterday, that they're questioning the wisdom of sentencing potentially valuable merchandise to careers as dust collectors. Probably you're one of the skeptics.

That's why I want you to tour the house, seeking out additional victims for cryogenic storage. That's why I also want you to make 15 to 20 copies of the following evaluation sheet, fill out a sheet for each major malfunctioning item in storage, tape the completed forms to the items in storage, and hang the blank sheets on the wall beside the storage area.

Completing this form clarifies the pros of letting some broken dogs lie. It helps you accept the notion that some of your toys do the most for you when you let them do nothing at all.

EVALUATION SHEET: BROKEN GOODS

Broken/Malfunctioning items in storage:

Guesstimated repair cost:

How many hours of your spouse's life would be spent paying for these repairs (use the true hourly wage calculated in Chapter 2)?

How many hours of your time will be spent fixing this item (finding a repair shop, getting quotes, delivering item)?

How long is the repaired item likely to last?

List the advantages or repairing the item:

List the advantages of *not* repairing the item (cost, other uses of time, benefits of not having item around):

Ideas for living without this item:

How could this item be fixed/replaced cheaply?

═══ March 23 ═══

You've stacked up broken items over the past two days. Now it's time to box up all the unnecessary clutter that surrounds you and move it into the same storage area. Webster defines clutter as, "A disorderly heap or assemblage; litter; state or condition of confusion; disorderly mess."

I define clutter as those items in the house that haven't been used in a year and which consume your living space, creating the disorderly mess to which Webster alludes.

Houses and clutter go together like pizzas and pepperoni. Look through your rooms, closets, medicine cabinets, dressers, basements, attics, kids' rooms, kitchen cabinets... and they're probably packed with clutter—items you haven't used in years that just get in the way of the items you do use. Now it's time to purge the clutter because all that clutter is costing you.

Costing you big time.

It's overflowing your home and when you and your family no longer fit in, you'll seriously entertain the possibility of moving to a bigger home with bigger insurance bills, bigger utility bills, and much bigger mortgage payments. It's also costing you time to clean and organize. And because the closets, cabinets, and drawers are already bursting, it's taking you twice the time it should to keep it all tidy. That's time stolen from pursuits you enjoy; time stolen from the activities in this book that earn you money.

Time is life and time is money. So eliminate the clutter that robs you of both.

◆ Collect a load of large cardboard boxes (visit hardware, grocery, furniture, or photocopy stores).

◆ Systematically move through the closets, cupboards, dressers, book shelves, drawers, storage nooks, cabinets, filing cabinets, wardrobes, desks, chests, and medicine cabinets. Items that haven't been used in more than a year go into one of two boxes:

Death Row. This box contains one-time treasures that are sentenced to life without parole somewhere other than in your house. Goodbye, adios, auf Wiedersehen, sayonara... this stuff is either garage sale or Goodwill bound.

Solitary Confinement. This is your undecided box. Items that you never use but can't bear to excommunicate go in here. But the law of uncluttering demands this: If the item has been collecting dust for 18 months and there is no immediate occasion to use it, into this box it goes. Be stern. You're not banishing these items (yet). If after six months you suddenly need or want one of these items, you know where to find it.

♦ Once full, boxes for Solitary go to the storage area. With a felt-tipped pen, prominently note the date (month and year) and a brief list of the contents (listing the date and contents on both the top and side of the box helps you find items later).

 **March 24**

It's going to take more than two days to classify, segregate, and purge your clutter. Continue where you left off yesterday, uncluttering your own possessions and the public spaces of the home.

During a break, draft some guidelines for the ongoing management of clutter. Discuss these guidelines (over dinner) with the family.

♦ Any on-going system of clutter management must revolve around the basic premise that for each new item of clutter entering the house, some old item of clutter should be leaving to make room. Einstein might call it the Conservation of Clutter. Newton might say that for every cluttering action there must be an equal but opposite anti-cluttering reaction.

♦ Consequently, kids and spouses alike must know that from this day forth that while clutter-fests like Christmas and birthdays are times to receive, they are also days to give up. It means that room for the new is made through sacrifice of the unused.

◆ Explain the two-box method of categorizing unused possessions to spouse and children. Then for the next several evenings, brandish the whip and send the rest of the family to their rooms, dressers, closets, drawers. Stress that all unused items they are waffling over will be going into storage, that it can be resurrected if needed.

With young children you'll need to unclutter for them. Do it when they're not around and they're unlikely to notice the items they no longer use are even gone.

March 25

When it comes to clearing the closets, do you own too many clothes and too little space? The same laws of uncluttering apply—if it hasn't been worn in 18 months, into a box it goes.

◆ Still short of hanging space? The answer is not in remodeling the closet but in chaining your hangers. Save the plastic rings formed when you open a gallon milk bottle with a screw-on cap. Slip this plastic ring over the hook of a hanger and you've created a place where you can hang one hanger onto another. This trick lets you link several hangers in a chain and effectively doubles or triples the amount of clothing you can pack in a closet. To implement this trick without drinking 50 gallons of milk, make rings (about 1.5" in diameter) from sturdy cord.

◆ Clothing sentenced to solitary confinement must be stored properly. You don't want garments ruined by insects. That cedar chests repel or kill moths is a myth. They simply keep moth larvae (the guys who do the munching) away from your clothes—the tight seal of a chest keeps egg-laying moths out. But dirty clothes that enter the chest with moth eggs or larvae on them will emerge later with holes. And the problem will spread to other clothes in the chest. So...the first rule of garment storage is to be sure all items were recently laundered (machine washed, hand washed, or dry-cleaned).

◆ Large garbage cans with tight lids make inexpensive storage containers for unused clothing (and for out-of-season clothing). Place garments in large plastic garbage sacks, tie the bags shut, place the sacks in the cans, and put a lid on it. The cans are bug and moisture resistant.

═══════ March 26 ═══════

What's the long-term status of items sentenced to solitary confinement? Each year, as new boxes of clutter move into storage, check the dates of the resident boxes. Any box sitting longer than 18 months needs to go—that means the contents have not seen active duty for almost three years (remember, these items were dust collectors before they ever entered the box).

The strong-willed can sell the contents of the boxes at a garage sale (your own or a friend's). If, however, you know that upon seeing these artifacts you won't be able to part with them, take the unopened boxes to the Goodwill.

Or take the boxes to a friend's garage sale, and leave your friend with strict rules of engagement: you want the stuff sold without your involvement (seeing, touching, pricing, etc.), and you want unsold items donated to charity (again, without your involvement). Offer to return the favor when your friend needs a dispassionate person to see him through the single most difficult step in the uncluttering process—actually saying goodbye.

═══════ March 27 ═══════

Over the past several days you and your family should have accumulated many boxes filled with gems sentenced to Death Row. Consider holding a garage sale to squeeze some pennies from these deposed prizes.

Before you hold your own garage sale, learn some of the insiders' tips.

◆ Call the library and ask what titles in the system cover garage sales. Have them hold those books. Titles to consider: *Garage Sale Magic* by Michael Williams and *The Fabulous Money Making Garage Sale Kit* by Diana Rix. These books help with the finer points of organizing, advertising, and signing your sale; they'll also help you display and price your merchandise for maximum effect.

◆ If you come up dry at the library, send away for *50 Ways to Make the Most Money Having a Garage Sale* by Cindy Skrzynecki (CMS Publishing, PO Box 583303, Minneapolis, MN 55458-3303, $5 ppd). It's a small booklet but has enough good ideas to more than offset the cost.

◆ Check the classified ads of the Thursday paper (under Garage Sales) and make a point of visiting a few local sales before hosting your own. Serious bargain hunters hustle to shop the opening hours of a sale, but as an information seeker you should make the rounds during the waning hours. Ask the organizing family whether their sale was a success and what factors made it fly or flop.

═════ March 28 ═════

Following is a reader tip that Mary Ann Leer sent to *Simple Living*, a thoughtful and valuable newsletter that focuses on living in a manner that is outwardly simple but inwardly rich.

"A few years ago I realized I probably had more clothes in my closet than many people in the world have in their entire lifetime. Then I decided to stop buying any new clothes for one year. I first began to look with new eyes at clothes I hadn't worn in a long time. I also put together new combinations. I can't say I wasn't tempted a few times when I saw something interesting in a store or catalog, but asking the questions, 'Do I really need this? Do I already have enough to wear?' helped to put things in perspective...

I made it through the year just fine. In fact, I enjoyed discovering some new clothes I hadn't worn in years and concentrating on what I had, instead of the bewildering array that is out there. Since then I've become much more aware of what I really need. I buy the best quality I can afford so they last longer, and buy clothes I really like. Then it doesn't matter if they 'go out of style' before you wear them out. Instead, you create your own style, which is more interesting and fun... Take a long look in those closets and drawers instead of another trip to the mall."

◆ I challenge you and your spouse to take the year-long plunge. Shake the dust from the clothes you already own, discover new possibilities from your old garments, chuck the catalogs peddling apparel you really don't need, establish your own statement of style rather than following the faddish flocks of fashion. As Mary Ann Leer will attest, the trial, while taxing at times, will be personally and financially liberating.

◆ For information about the newsletter *Simple Living,* contact Simple Living Press, 2319 N 45th Street Box 149, Seattle, WA 98103, 206-464-4800.

═══ March 29 ═══

Babies and young children don't care if their clothes are Gucci or gauche. They shouldn't be the only ones in the family ignoring what Ralph Lauren, Calvin Klein, or Armani proclaim as fashionable (what's being sold this year for way too much money) and what isn't (what was sold last year for way too much money). You and your spouse should see through the transparent game the fashion industry plays to steal the shirt off your back. If you have seen the light, then you're ready to profit tremendously from those who haven't. Which brings us to today's task:

◆ Pull out the Yellow Pages, call each listing under *Clothes & Accessories—Consignment and Resale,* and ask each of these consignment shops what their specialty is. Tell the shops the age, gender, and tastes of the family members you shop for; ask about the style and condition of the clothing each store sells; ask how much, on average, the clothing is discounted; and find out whether these stores have occasional or frequent special sales. Do the same with listings under *Thrift Stores* that you think might carry clothing. In your Rolodex (under Clothing), make notes about those shops that appear to stock apparel for someone in the family.

◆ Shopping the stores you've listed won't be like shopping department stores. Good consignment shops handle fashionable clothes that are in first-rate condition but stocks are limited. You won't always find what you want. Therefore, the art of purchasing the bulk of your family's apparel through consignment (and thrift) shops revolves around frequent visits. When errands have you in the neighborhood, pop in, take a quick tour, and keep your eyes open for what you'll need soon *and* what you'll need later. When you encounter a bargain you can't use for six or 12 months, snap it up and put it in storage. It's yet another example of stocking up when the price is right.

◆ Now, get out of the house and visit the promising consignment and thrift shops along (or close to) your normal travel routes. Find out for yourself which shops are a good match for your needs. Update your Rolodex cards with notes from your visit.

March 30

Foster fond feelings in your children about visiting rummage sales and thrift shops. If you make shopping at these meccas of bargain merchandise rewarding, your kids will enjoy returning. Give your youngsters some money (50¢, $1, maybe $2) to spend on whatever they please. Don't criticize their choice—better they blow a buck on junk here than a ten-spot on trash at Toys R Us.

March 31

Stockpiling the clothing you bring home from consignment shops, thrift stores, rummage sales, and garage sales is vital if you want to assemble a superior wardrobe from a paltry salary. But stockpiling great finds is useless if you can't find your finds, or if, by the time you need them, you've forgotten about your finds. In other words, stockpiling wastes money if you aren't organized.

So, get organized today. Decide where you will store future clothing for kids, spouse, and self, and devise an inventory system. Here's the system we use—adopt it if it makes sense to you, adapt it if doesn't.

♦ Clothes—whether they're from shops or are hand-me-downs—are stored in boxes in the attic. Different boxes are used to organize clothing by age and gender (e.g., one box might contain girls' clothing that's about a size 10). Each box is numbered on all four sides so that no matter how it is stacked it can be identified without moving it.

Now the part where most falter: Keep a file in a handy place (be that with the boxes or with other household records) listing the contents of each box. As items go in and out, update the sheet for that box.

These inventory sheets are the crux. If you need a particular item—a pair of pants, a coat, a sweater—the sheets lead you to the right box in seconds. If a department store runs a half-price sale on children's jeans or shoes, without opening a box you can decide whether to visit or ignore the sale. If a child will soon be into a new size, the list describing the next box indicates what items you better be searching for.

♦ Some exceptions to the rules stated above: Regardless of size, footwear (boots, shoes, sandals, sneakers) is all stored together in the same box. Of course, an inventory sheet of the footwear box describes the type and size of the boxed shoes. We've also found outerwear (raincoats, winter coats, gloves, and hats) easier to store by category than by size.

♦ All items in long-term storage should be clean before they are stored in a box that is double lined with heavy-duty, garbage bags. There's no economy in letting moths gnaw holes in your bargains.

April

Years ago I shared money-saving tips each week on several radio programs. One week a program focused on letting listeners share their thriftiest tips. Besides hearing from a man who saved his popcorn old maids for bean bags, and a computer hacker who viewed his antics to cheat the phone company as thrift rather than theft, we heard from a woman who won a frugality contest this way:

Each night she had her four kids brush their teeth with the same toothbrush and the same toothpaste (yes, used).

"To save toothpaste?" I asked in amazement.

"Partly that, but mainly because when one kid comes down with a bug, they all get sick together. That saves on doctors' visits."

That's taking frugality to a new level.

And that's exactly what you're going to peddle to your family today. Place stick-on dots on everyone's toothbrushes and toothpaste. When they inquire. "What now?" Tell them that the soft-core measures of saving are over. Now the family's playing hardball and because the American Medical Association has recommended this as a way to reduce family visitations to the doctor the entire family will share one toothbrush and one dollop of toothpaste. Parents, of course, brush first. Press the notion. See if you get anyone to raise used brush to mouth before fessing up that it's April Fools' Day.

══ April 2 ══

Do you use the last drop of the consumables you buy? Without a little salvaging effort, you may be needlessly tossing away usable product.

◆ **Sunscreen.** Bottles of creamy sunscreens may seem empty, but if you cut them open you'll find some 10% of the cream clinging to the bottle walls. Scrape it off (finger or small spatula) and store it in an empty 35mm film canister.

◆ **Shampoo.** If you've grown impatient waiting for a nearly empty shampoo bottle to deliver, you may, in frustration, toss the bottle before the last little dab does ya. Solution: Put a plastic cup in the shower and store the bottle upside down so that the shampoo is always near the cap. The same trick works for nearly empty bottles of ketchup and salad dressing stored in the refrigerator.

◆ **Toothpaste.** If you're dealing with plastic tubes, splay the empties open and mine the remaining deposits with your toothbrush.

◆ **Clothes detergent.** With liquid detergent, rinse the bottle out with several cups of water. Swirl the water around the jug and use the soapy water for a small load of clothes.

Walk around the house marking those bottles and products deserving of effort before they are tossed. Put a sticker on sunscreen bottles and toothpaste tubes with a reminder like "cut" on them. Mark shampoos and condiments with a sticker reminder to use the "cup."

══ April 3 ══

Time to move ahead with the planning of your garage sale. Pull out the calendar and decide on a date for your own affair (most run as a Friday-Saturday or Saturday-Sunday event). Don't run your sale on a day that competes with a big community festival—unless that event takes place near your home and you can capitalize on the increased traffic flow. And keep in mind that early spring, before serious garage salers have been numbed by the billionth sale, is typically a better time for a sale than late spring (although the possibility of cold, wet weather can change all the odds).

Call the newspaper(s) in which you might post a classified ad. Ask how much lead time is needed to post an ad, what ads cost, how many characters the basic ad gives, and the cost of additional space. Note advertising deadlines on your calendar (daily papers typically need one or two days' notice, weeklies need your ad several days before the paper goes to press).

Other considerations:

♦ Try selling big ticket items (anything priced over $25) through other avenues first—signs on the road, community papers, bulletin boards at spouse's work. Garage salers are notoriously low spenders.

♦ Plan your classified ad carefully. Key words that define your stuff (toys, vintage, housewares, tools, sporting goods, or books) will go a long way in pulling the right kind of shoppers. So will catchy titles that define your stuff (Toys R Us, Handyman's Heaven, Skier's Delight). And an indication that there's a ton of stuff pulls well (Four-Family Sale or Eighty Years of Grandma's Clutter).

♦ If you want merchandise to sell at a garage sale, items in good condition should be priced at 75% to 80% off their original retail price (i.e., an item costing $10 new should be priced between $2 and $2.50). Clothing is an exception—it earns even less. Really nice clothing is doing well if you can make 10% of its original price. Keep the money you generate on your person (e.g. in a fanny pack).

♦ Encourage your kids to sell lemonade, pop, brownies or cookies to generate some cash of their own.

♦ Lock the house and unless an adult friend is available to oversee the sale, don't let anyone in your house to use the phone or bathroom.

April 4

In 1995 the average residential carpet sold for $16 to $18 per square yard. Added to that were installation fees ($3.50/sq.yd.) and padding ($3.00/sq.yd.). Knowing that the replacement cost of the carpet in your home totals to some $24/sq.yd. gives you a powerful financial incentive to immortalize the carpet you already own.

One easy way to add years of life? Go Japanese. Leave the dirty shoes just inside the door and wander the house in socks or slippers. Pull out the slippers or heavy socks, and when children and spouse arrive home today, tell them the new rules of the home. School friends of your children are subject to the same rules.

Good mats located at the entrance of every outside door are also carpet life savers. According to the American Carpet Association, 80% of all carpet dirt and stains enter the house on your shoes. If you're currently living without such mats, pick some up today.

Besides saving your carpet, these tips save you from vacuuming so often. No complaints there, eh?

April 5

Even if your efforts to stonewall dirt at the doors is successful, other agents—wine-spilling friends, diaper-leaking children, spaghetti-splattering spouses—will take their best shots at damaging your carpet. Your defense: knowledge of how to oust the resulting stain.

A handy, inexpensive booklet with solutions to remove blotches caused by 300 different staining agents is published by the Carpet and Rug Institute (Publication Dept, Box 2048, Dalton, GA 30722-2048, 800-882-8846, 706-278-3176). Send $1 and your return address, for a copy of *Carpet and Rug Spot Removal*.

When the guide arrives, study its contents and arm yourself with some of the frequently used cleaners it recommends to fight stains. Store the booklet where you'll find it when crises strike.

===== **April 6** =====

Couch potatoes beware: If you don't clean your upholstered furniture from time to time, it may become soiled
enough to sprout tubers. Your defense? Get in the habit of
vacuuming your upholstered furniture when you're dusting
your wooden furniture.

If you've neglected this task for years and the couch is
as soiled as a potato patch, you can rent an upholstery
steamer. Though cheaper than hiring a pro, this is expensive unless you have lots of upholstery to clean or can split
the cost with friends. Expect rental fees of $25 to $30 per
day.

The cheaper, easier solution for small jobs is to buy a
spray-on upholstery cleaner. While many brands are
ineffective, the exception to the rule is *Blue Coral Dri-
Clean Upholstery and Carpet Cleaner* (available at automotive stores). This cleaner produces results that will compete
with a steamer. Before you attack the couch, however, test
the cleaner in an inconspicuous spot for adverse side effects.
And don't use it on velvets and silks.

Note: The effectiveness of *Blue Coral Velour and
Upholstery Cleaner* pales next to the aforementioned dry-
cleaning formula.

===== **April 7** =====

Frequent vacuuming isn't the only care your carpets
require. Every 12 to 18 months a more thorough cleaning
will remove ground-in dirt, pet dander, minor stains. Taking
area rugs to professional, out-of-house cleaners gives
excellent results. Unfortunately, professional, in-house
cleaning of wall-to-wall carpets is an altogether different
matter—consumer magazines that anonymously test carpet-
cleaning services often report mixed results.

Fortunately, a do-it-yourself cleaning system developed
by Host consistently receives good marks for cleaning soiled
carpets. And cleaning with Host is wallet-friendly compared
to hiring a pro.

Host Dry Carpet Cleaner is actually the consistency of
a moist sawdust. It is sprinkled over the carpet and

scrubbed into the pile with a power brush rented for the purpose or a scrub brush powered by your own biceps. This moist sawdust sits in the carpet for several hours (the longer the better) where it dissolves and absorbs dirt. Then the particles are lifted from the carpet with a normal upright vacuum cleaner.

If it's been more than 18 months since your carpet was cleaned (12 months if you have kids or pets), plan a thorough cleaning now. Rent the power scrubber and purchase a 14.5-pound box of Host (about $25) for each 1,000 square feet of carpet to be cleaned. To locate a local retailer handling the cleaner and power scrubber, check your Yellow Pages (under *Carpet—Rug Cleaning Equipment & Supplies*) or call Racine Industries (800-558-9439) and ask for a local dealer.

Cheap Tricks:
♦ You'll add years of life to your carpet by scrubbing Host into the traffic lanes every three months (two months if you have kids or pets). Although the power scrubber gives the best cleaning, working the powder into the carpet with a soft-bristled scrub brush provides good results (it's also an excellent upper body workout). Pull out your daily calendar and, using three-month intervals, note when you'll be Hosting again.

♦ To keep spills from metamorphosing into stains, immediately blot up as much of a spill as possible with dry rags or paper towels. Sprinkle the area generously with Host and scrub the powder deep into the carpet with a soft scrub brush (work the brush in all directions so every surface of the pile gets cleaned). Allow the Host to dry overnight, then vacuum up the powder.

♦ If you have trouble finding Host, check into Capture Dry Powder Cleaner sold through Sears. It, too, is well-rated for cleaning soiled carpets.

April 8

Ever take time to contemplate how people walk around the home? Frugality fanatics like myself worry about these things. And here's what we notice: Everyone walks in exactly the same place—down the middle of stairs, through the middle of hallways, in the middle of rooms.

That's bad news.

Why? Because the wear of many footfalls is confined to a few square feet of carpet rather than spread out over the square footage of the home. That means you're going to have to replace your entire carpet when the 5% where everyone walks wears out.

Starting now, buck the trend. Let your feet fall where others don't. Walk the stairs bowlegged—or, if you don't want to look ridiculous, walk up the stairs on either side of the middle. Pass through hallways close to the walls. Stay to the side of traffic corridors in the main rooms...

Spend time studying the floor plan of your home and learning to walk the house without contributing to its problems. As a stay-at-home spouse, your feet may contribute 25%, 33%, maybe even 50% to the floor's abuse. Spread your wear and you'll delay the day your floors demand expensive attention.

◆ While re-learning how to walk the house, consider ways to mitigate areas of extreme abuse. Mats or area rugs inside the main door will help preserve the carpet throughout the house. Area rugs in traffic corridors may concentrate abuse to items that are cheaper and more readily replaced than wall-to-wall carpet. Repositioning the furniture periodically changes the traffic lanes through a room.

 **April 9**

Driven by the hammer of feet, dirt is capable of sanding, slicing, and soiling your carpet. Let dirt lie, and damage to the wall-to-wall footing of your home mushrooms quickly. Consequently, an easy way to double the life of your carpet is to vacuum twice as often (several times a week).

This needn't take more time than what you currently devote to vacuuming; during the next week, simply try to redistribute your efforts. Rather than vacuuming the entire house, spend a few minutes every other day vacuuming the traffic lanes. It is here that double doses of dirt and twice the number of footfalls really shorten the life of your carpet. Every fourth or fifth cleaning, let your vacuuming forays venture from the beaten path into the dusty corners of the house.

Buying Tip:
In 1997, *Consumer Reports* gave the Sharp Twin Energy Vacuum ($150) better marks for its ability to clean than the Kirby G4 ($1,350). Kirby will tell you their product lasts for life. Perhaps. But if you bought nine Sharps instead of one Kirby, you'd spend the same amount of money and have vacuums enough for several lives.

===== April 10 =====

Keeping your electronic equipment clean adds to their life and performance. Make this cleaning day for the audio and video equipment around the home.

◆ Use a Q-tip dipped in isopropyl alcohol to clean the heads of cassette recorders, Walkmans, and computer disk drives. The heads of your audio equipment will be metallic or ceramic cubes that rub against the tape near the center of the cassette.

◆ Use a cotton swab dipped in photographic-lens cleaner (or *Windex*) to clean the lens of a CD player.

◆ Dust, whether it is inside or outside the appliance, contributes to overheating, and heat is one of the main enemies of electrical appliances. Vacuum the vents and dust the casings of all your appliances so they can shed heat. Cover valuable equipment (computers, stereos) when they are not in use.

===== April 11 =====

Whether you embraced its arrival or succumbed after much arm twisting, if a computer is now part of the family you've learned it's no petty-cash entity. After spending an arm-and-leg on it, you don't want this machine visiting the repair shop any time in this life, so adhere to that famous axiom: Cleanliness is next to cheapness.

♦ Establish quarters for your machine in a relatively dust-free room. Humidity, heat, and direct sunlight are additional carcinogens that will rob years of life from your computer, so choose a cool, dry room.

♦ Clean the heads of your computer's floppy drives using lint-free cleaning swabs purchased at electronic supply stores (these swabs are longer and thinner than Q-Tips). Dip the swab in isopropyl alcohol, reach through the front slot of the drive, and lightly scrub the heads of the drive. You'll need a flashlight to see the heads—look for two tooth-sized white cubes (one on the roof of the drive, one on the floor) along the centerline of the drive but behind its midpoint.

♦ Computer repairmen recommend cleaning your computer's central processing unit (CPU) at least once a year to exorcise dust, dander, and hair that can damage the electronics. It's easy to save money by doing the job at home. To clean the CPU, remove the case covering the electronics. This is no big deal, even if you know zilch about what happens inside this magic box. Unplug the computer, then remove the five or six screws (in the back) that hold the case on. If you want to unplug the cords and cables, fine, just take careful notes about which cable goes where. Slide the case forward and away from the electronics. Now blow air over the electronics, (using a vacuum cleaner set on "blow," or canned air) to blast away the dust. Keep the vacuum's nozzle a good eight to 12 inches away from the components. If for any reason you decide to touch an electrical component, ground yourself first (on the computer's power supply) to prevent static electricity from frying something it shouldn't.

♦ Dust sucked in through the front of your floppy drive adds to the drive's wear and tear. Once or twice a year, use a vacuum cleaner set on 'Blow' (rather than 'Vacuum') to blast air through the drive and carry out the accumulated dust.

♦ Spraying glass cleaner directly on the monitor's screen can cause damage. Spray the cleaner onto a soft, lint-free rag, then wipe the screen.

═══════ **April** 12 ═══════

Keyboards are the computer component most prone to problems. Dirt, hair, and food particles fall into the cracks between the keys and gum up the contacts. Or a coffee spill toasts the contacts altogether. Today you can immortalize your keyboard by performing one chore and completing one purchase.

♦ Vacuum the keyboard using a canister-style vacuum cleaner and a soft brush attachment. After vacuuming, set the airflow of the vacuum on "blow," tip the keyboard upside down, and blast the keyboard with air.

♦ They may cost you between $15 and $30, but over the long haul either a Keyguard or a SafeSkin keyboard protector is cheap insurance for your keyboard. These protectors are made from a clear, flexible, durable polymers (plastic). Different protectors are molded to fit over different keyboards (over 1,000 to choose from), so you're assured of finding a protector that fits the topography of your keyboard like a glove.

These protectors remain on the keyboard at all times, meaning the keyboard is permanently protected from dirt and spills. I didn't really believe the product would allow for decent typing. When I ordered mine, I expected to cash in on the manufacturer's satisfaction-guaranteed-or-your-money-back offer. I was wrong. Some products simply defy logic.

The SafeSkin Keyboard Protectors (Merritt Computer Products, 5565 Red Bird Center Dr., Suite 150, Dallas, Texas, 75237, 800-627-7752 or 214-339-0753) come in over a thousand different keyboard configurations and sell for about $19.

Meanwhile, mailers for the customized Keyguard Protectors (from Fellowes Manufacturing, 1789 Norwood Ave, Itasca, IL 60143, 800-945-4545) can be purchased at office supply stores like Office Depot for $15. These mailers come with a catalog listing some 1,500 different keyboards and a form on which to list your make and model number (check the bottom of your keyboard). Mail in the form and Fellowes mails back a custom-fit Keyguard.

April 13

In my book *Cheap Tricks,* I advise readers not to perform elaborate prerinses on dishes headed for the dishwasher. It's amazing how much hot water, energy, and time people spend washing dishes before the machine gets a crack at them. It's also amazing that dozens of people responded to this tip, saying that they just couldn't bear to put dirty dishes in the dishwasher—that's what saniphiles we've become.

Today I challenge you to a test.

Because this is a test, I implore you to ignore old habits and listen to me. For the purposes of science, you *will not* rinse your dishes before they enter the dishwasher—simply scrape the food scraps and major globs of sauce into the sink *without running the faucet.* Even if the dishes will be sitting a few days before you run the machine, thou shalt not use water to rinse thy plates. Same goes for the silverware, just get the excess food particles and globs off.

When the machine fills up, run it on the normal cycle. If your dishwasher is worth its keep, it will clean your dishes without any of the prerinses. First you'll be amazed by the sparkling results, then depressed about the countless dollars and hours wasted to prewashing.

Assuming your machine passes this test, try another one using the "Short Wash" cycle, an option consuming 25% less hot water. Many machines will still pass with absolutely no prerinsing.

Cheap Trick:

If your dishwasher failed my test, it is probably old. This is still no reason to waste copious quantities of hot water prewashing dishes. Here's what you do for geriatric machines: Pour a little cold water onto the food surfaces of the dishes and allow them to sit. When you've got a load of dishes, pour off the water (no additional rinsing or scrubbing), load the machine, and run it.

Cutlery is more likely to come away dirty than dishes and if your machine lacks muscle here, soak the accumulating dirty silverware in a plastic container filled with cold water. When it's time to do dishes, move the wet silverware directly into the machine and wash.

===== April 14 =====

Here are two more important tips for efficient use of your automatic dishwasher. Employ them from this day forth.

◆ Really fill up the machine. A family that runs the dishwasher daily will spend about $200/year on utilities (about half that if the water is heated with gas). If you consistently run the machine when it's only two-thirds full, you're washing your wallet of $65/year.

◆ Use air drying or overnight drying. This cuts dish-washing costs about 10%. Trick dishwashers lacking this feature by turning the machine off after the last rinse and opening the door.

===== April 15 =====

To run a dishwasher every day with 140°F water costs a family with average electric rates about $90 a year ($59 for families owning gas water heaters). Obviously, if you run the machine less, you'll spend less. In my family, we cut dirty dishes by using some more than once. We each have a spot on the counter for dishes we can reuse. After breakfast I rinse my cereal bowl, spoon, and glass with a cup of cold water and put the lot in my spot. I can use them all again at lunch. After lunch, the bowl may be greasy from soup, so into the dishwasher it goes. But my glass can be rinsed for another use. Meanwhile, if we only boiled or steamed vegetables in a pot, we rinse it and leave it on the stove for another job. All told, the process cuts our dishwashing in half. Equally nice, it saves time.

◆ Time for you to survey the kitchen and develop similar systems of your own. Designate a place for everyone in the family and start the routine today. Have them rinse appropriate dishes (glasses, bowls that contained only cereal, plates that simply held a sandwich...). You may want to use a coaster or a paper plate (with names) to mark each family member's spot.

If you're wondering about sanitary issues, keep in mind that most people use the same drinking glass in the bathroom for weeks at a time. They also use the same toothbrush for months on end without ill effect. Reusing relatively clean glasses, bowls, and plates several times between sterilizations is *not* going to poison anyone.

═══ April 16 ═══

You use it most every day, but are you using it well? These tips about efficient use of your range require only knowledge, not time, to employ. While they won't save you a lot, consider the Danish proverb, "He that does not save pennies will never have pounds."

Ovens:

♦ Stop peeking. Every time you open the oven door, you lose a quarter of the entrapped heat.
♦ Turn off the oven about 30 minutes before your food is done. The trapped heat will finish the job.
♦ Get organized and bake several dishes at once while the oven is hot.
♦ Run the cleaning cycle of a self-cleaning oven after baking or broiling. The oven is already fired up.
♦ A nail through a baking potato reduces its cooking time by 15 minutes. Slicing potatoes into halves and laying them, cut surfaces down, on a greased cookie sheet, cuts baking time by a third.
♦ After baking, open the oven door so the heat will warm the house.

Stoves:

♦ Match your pans to the burner size. A small pot on a big burner lets heat disappear into thin air.
♦ A watched pot never boils—probably because the lid is off, which increases boiling times (and power consumption) by 20%.
♦ Make lids even better at trapping heat by covering them with a hot pad. Obviously, such makeshift cozies are for stove-top cooking, not oven use.

- Once water boils, turn the heat to low: A slow boil is as hot as a rolling one.
- Pressure cookers reduce stove-top cooking times by two-thirds, saving you time and money.

===== **April 17** =====

Take the true/false quiz. Then forevermore, adopt these money-saving principles into your cooking habits.

Quiz:

1) For 85% of your cooking needs, a microwave will cut energy use in half.
2) Cooking potatoes in a microwave, rather than in a conventional oven, uses 45% less energy.
3) It takes 10% less energy to boil a quart of water on a stove burner than in the microwave.
4) Materials that get very hot in the microwave should not be used as receptacles to nuke your food.
5) Covering the food speeds microwave cooking and reduces energy use.
6) A problem with microwave cookbooks is that the wattage (strength) of the author's microwave may be quite different from your own.
7) A standard oven, not a microwave, is needed to restore old or stale food.

Answers:

1) True, according to a Wisconsin Power and Light Study.
2) False. Actually the microwave uses 65% less energy.
3) True. Large quantities of liquid are heated more efficiently on a burner, but heating just a cup or two of liquid is more efficient in the microwave because energy is not wasted while the burner heats and cools.
4) True. Unsure if a receptacle is microwave safe? Test the empty receptacle by microwaving it on high for one minute. If it is hot, don't use it in the microwave; if it is lukewarm, it's fine for reheating foods; if it's cool, use it for microwave cooking.

5) True. Paper plates make good covers—keep reusing them until they're dirty.
6) True. Cookbook authors are going to have good machines with high outputs. Knowing your unit's power and how this compares to those used in your cookbooks will reduce mistakes that ruin food. See no mention of your unit's power on the machine or with its instructions? Use this simple test. Pour exactly eight ounces of water into a glass measuring cup and place the cup (uncovered) in your unit. Microwave on *high*, timing how long it takes for the water to boil. If it boils in under three minutes, your microwave is a 600- to 700-watt unit; in three to four minutes, its power is 500 to 600 watts; in more than four minutes, its power is less than 500 watts.
7) True and false. A microwave can restore hardened brown sugar—zap it for 15 to 30 seconds, being careful not to liquify the sugar. To rejuvenate stale peanuts, spread them on a suitable baking dish; nuke them on *high* (three minutes per cup), stirring them once during the cooking; then let them cool before sentencing them to a jar. Extend the life of milk that is past its expiration date by heating it to 160°F in the microwave—you'll get 10 to 14 more days out of the milk.

April 18

This is the day to act on a long-term measure—it's the day to invest energy into a 401K plan for your future utilities. Regardless of whether you live in sun country or snow country, trees buffer your home from both heat and cold. In the summer, a shaded house needs far less air conditioning than an unshaded one. In winter, well placed trees buffet chilly winds and significantly reduce the heat sucked from your home. Start growing trees around your house, especially along the southern and western exposures, and by the time you retire to a fixed income, the trees will be reducing both your cooling and heating bills by 30%.

◆ In planning which trees to grow, ask your neighbors what does and doesn't thrive in your soil. Bounce the same questions off the employees of local nurseries. Ask a variety of people what distance these trees should be placed from the home (you want shelter, but the trees need adequate room to grow). Finally, get plenty of advice on what exposures need tree protection. Shade along your home's southern and western exposure is important for summer cooling. Find out from which direction the winds of winter strike and how to position trees to dissipate such winds.

♦ Determine what trees you are going to plant and where they will go today. Picking up those trees and actually getting them in the ground is a project for an upcoming weekend when you have the muscle power of more family members to help (put a date in the calendar).

♦ Call local nurseries: Ask advice from each and get price quotes for the recommended trees. Once you've settled on the type of tree needed, call wholesale nurseries for price quotes as well. After receiving their price information, tell them you are an end user and ask if you may simply pay cash for the desired trees. Many are happy to oblige—after all, a sale is a sale. If this is against their policy, perhaps friends who are contractors or landscapers will make the purchase for you.

April 19

Lawn mowers are expensive tools. Neglected, they may spend a lot of time with mechanics who charge $40/hour. Cared for, they can deliver season after season of faithful service. Following is a maintenance schedule you should apply toward your mower this year. Copy this page and hang it on the garage wall above the mower.

♦ Start the mowing season with new oil, a clean air filter, and fresh gas. Get out the owner's manual and attend to these chores today.

More About Maintenance:

♦ Much of the dirt entering a mower ultimately ends up in the oil where it can sand away at the piston and cylinder. Check your owner's manual for exact recommendations but, as a rule, change the oil after 25 hours of operation (SAE 30 oil). For most homeowners, that means changing the oil halfway through the mowing season.

◆ Check the oil often; run out of this cheap fluid and you'll be selling an expensive mower for scrap metal.

◆ Clean the air filter every 25 hours. Otherwise dirty air sucked into the carburetor will scour the moving parts. It's an easy job, but check your owner's manual for instructions if you've not done it before.

◆ In moist parts of the country, mower shops say the corrosion ruins the bodies of many mowers. Wet grass matted to the bottom of the housing, combined with fertilizer (which is very corrosive), can destroy a mower's body long before the engine dies. Solution: Spend a minute after mowing tipping the mower on its side and scraping away the wet grass matted underneath (disconnect the spark plug first).

April 20

An easy way to establish a healthy but inexpensive lawn is to keep the grass long. Grass survives by drawing water and nutrients from the soil (a function of the roots) and by photosynthesizing these raw materials into sugars for the plant (a function of the blades). Long roots have access to more water and nutrients in the soil (meaning less watering and fertilizing) while long blades produce more energy for the plant (meaning healthier grass).

To establish long roots, you cannot cut the grass short. The roots will grow deeper only if the blades are allowed to grow higher. Without finding this balance between root and blade growth, all your watering, spraying, and fertilizing won't create a healthy lawn.

Other benefits of long grass? First, its shading makes it difficult for sun-loving weeds and crabgrass to get a toehold in your yard. Next, because deep roots can store larger food supplies, grass bounces back more readily from dormancy. These same food supplies make the plant more vigorous and resistant to weeds and disease. Finally, you won't need to cut long grass as often; short grass grows faster because the plant must use its stored foods to grow back the leaf it needs to photosynthesize.

The exact cutting height depends on such variables as climate, soil type, and grass variety. As a general rule, grasses that thrive well in the northern climates should be kept around 3 to 3½ inches high during most of the mowing season. Cut your lawn short (about 2 inches) for a month in spring so sunlight reaches and warms the soil, then readjust your wheels for about a 3-inch cut. In October, as the cold temperatures return and the trees lose their leaves, *gradually* cut the lawn back down to the 2-inch range for the winter.

Southern grasses are different. Bermuda grasses, the most common grasses of the area, are long when kept in the 1½- to 2-inch range. They can be kept at this height all year long. Thicker grasses like St. Augustine's and many coastal grasses can be cut at a 2- to 3-inch height throughout the year.

To learn more about your lawn, take a clump to a nursery and have them identify your grass. Then, consult a book at the library, like *Building a Healthy Lawn* by Stuart Franklin, to determine the proper mowing height. Once you've decided on the height, readjust the wheels on your mower.

Regarding appearance, don't worry about the lawn looking shaggy. It's the evenness of the cut, more than the length, that defines whether your green patch is a pasture or a lawn.

April 21

Got problems with pests? Solve them today with low-cost remedies.

◆ Scare away roosting birds with rubber snakes purchased from novelty stores. Or hang strands of monofilament fishing line around the eaves, light fixtures, and down spouts where birds roost—the touch of the nearly invisible line startles the birds.

◆ Destroy ant colonies by pouring boiling water on them.

◆ Eliminate aphids and spiders by washing plants with a mixture of water and mild detergent. For large jobs, use a hose-end sprayer filled with detergent.

◆ Spray flies with hair spray; it immobilizes them long enough to kill them.

◆ Catch flies by dabbing honey on a strip of yellow paper. The yellow paper attracts them, the honey holds them.

◆ Stop moth larvae from eating holes in your garments by washing all clothes bound for storage. Then store those clothes in air-tight plastic bags.

◆ Keep small mammals away from your prize vegetables and flowers by sprinkling chili powder around the garden.

◆ Kill ants and cockroaches with a poison made from 2 cups borax (available at grocery stores) and 1 cup flour. Store the powder in a jar with holes punched in the lid. Sprinkle the powder around baseboards, sills, foundations...wherever you have a problem.

◆ Prevent dogs from chewing furniture or rug edges by sponging problem areas with a solution made from ¼ cup clove oil, 1 tablespoon paprika, and 1 teaspoon black pepper. Reapply as needed.

◆ Repel dogs, cats, raccoons, opossums from the attractive nuisance of your trashcan by spraying its outside with a mist of full-strength ammonia. If your can is particularly ripe, spray the inside as well.

April 22

Giving the beds in your garden a thick layer of mulch accomplishes many good things—it controls weeds, prevents erosion, slows evaporation, and, possibly, helps fertilize.

Around your prized beds of flowers and ornamental plants, the mulch is also intended to beautify, so loads of attractive bark, wood chips, or cocoa hulls are imported for the purpose. Unfortunately, these fancy mulches come with an equally fancy price.

Solution:
In the open areas of beds where you need weed control lay a thick layer of free mulch first. Grass clippings; old, matted leaves; chipped-up tree prunings (often given free by the local park department); pine needles (raked up from under pine trees) are several free options. Old newspaper is also free: Nowadays even the inks on the color pages of the paper won't harm the soil, so you can lay a substantial layer of newspaper (one-inch thick) throughout your beds. Few weeds can flourish smothered by all that bad news.

Over your inexpensive mulch, lay a thin layer of decorative mulch.

===== April 23 =====

Annual flowers are expensive when you factor in their yearly expense. Perennials are often cheaper over time but are pills for that first pop. So reserve some bed space for these bloomers: columbine, cosmos, candy tuft, gloriosa daisy, California poppy, foxglove, sweet alyssum, and larkspur.

These flowers are not expensive yet, if after they bloom, you leave several flowers behind (rather than trimming them), you'll have the stock to reseed the beds. Let several stalks of each flower type brown and shrivel. Once the plant is papery, cut the stalks and shake its seeds over the ground where you'd like to see next year's display.

Future flower shows without any cash flow—you've gotta like that.

===== April 24 =====

Create a card for the Rolodex today marked *Plant Sales* or *Garden Sales* and begin monitoring the plant sales this year. Even if you've done all your garden shopping for the coming year, you'll want to record when the sales occur for the different plants you buy each year (annuals) and the plants you'd like to purchase (e.g., shrubs) in the future.

♦ To give you general guidelines about when to move on certain purchases, record the following:
June: Annuals
July: Spring-blooming bulbs
September: Perennials, roses
October: Shrubs, shade and fruit trees

♦ Put plants from the aforementioned list that you want (and the date when they're likely to be discounted) on the Master Purchasing List. Also leave prompts in your daily calendar about when to monitor the nurseries—if you need annuals, for example, leave yourself a June 1 reminder to pay attention to annuals.

♦ As you notice significant sales, mark the date and place on your card.

═══ April 25 ═══

Today's tip consumes no time. In fact, if you implement this tip as you mow, you'll save time. You'll also save money. I'm talking about a habit which may upset your desire to convert your patch of green into a piece of Pebble Beach, but a habit that you should adopt. I'm talking about letting the lawn clippings lie.

Why?

For starters, clippings nourish your grass. They provide a 4-1-3 fertilizer (4% nitrogen, 1% phosphorous, and 3% potash), an ideal formula for your lawn and a cheaper one than a store-bought fertilizer. The clippings you leave behind will also create a mulch that keeps the ground wetter, minimizing water bills. Finally, letting the clippings lie will reduce trash bills and the time it takes to mow.

Mow when the grass is dry and before it gets too long and you'll hardly notice the clippings left behind.

Cheap Trick:
Aerating works wonders on a yard by getting water and fertilizer to the grass roots. Wear golf spikes whenever you

mow and you aerate with no extra time investment. If you don't own golf spikes, pick up a pair at a garage sale.

===== **April 26** =====

Many people believe that by not collecting grass clippings (yesterday's tip) you're guaranteed a thatch problem. Not so. Thatch depends on many variables—type of grass, climate, and how you maintain your lawn. Overfertilizing is the root of the problem because it promotes too much growth. Fast-release fertilizers also kill many of the soil bacteria that help break down thatch. Frequent, light watering is another cause of thatch—the grass roots are not forced deep in their search for water but are given reason to spread along the surface where they create the thatch mat. Pesticides and fungicides also aggravate thatch because they kill and weaken soil bacteria. To prevent thatch, go light on the fertilizer; use heavy, once-a-week waterings; and aerate the lawn to get water and nutrients down deep.

♦ Evaluate whether you've already got a thatch problem. With a healthy lawn, you should be able to stick your finger down through the grass and touch soil. Unhealthy lawns will snag your finger in a layer of thatch, a mat lying over the soil which is composed of grass stems, roots, clippings, and runners. If the thatch layer gets ½ inch thick, it will prevent fertilizer and air from reaching the soil. Also, it will encourage grass roots to grow in the thatch rather than the soil, making the plant very intolerant to heat, frost, and insects.

If you have a thatch problem, collect your clippings while mowing until after you've used a thatch rake to physically remove (rake away) the thatch. If you don't own a thatch rake, a cheaper—and in many ways superior—solution is to spray your yard with soap and beer.

That's not a misprint. The yeast in beer helps break down thatch into fertilizer your grass can use. In a hose-end sprayer, combine ½ cup of liquid dishwashing detergent per 16 ounces of beer and spray the lawn on a hot day. Don't worry about the brand—your yard has not cultivated a palate so don't spoil it with Lowenbrau when Buckhorn will do. A six-pack will cover a third of an acre, and leave a can or two for you. And you thought yard work was no fun.

◆ Even if your lawn does not have a thatch problem at present, keep your soil microorganisms happy by giving them a beer treatment at the beginning and middle of each growing season. Get the supplies together today and do the job on the next warm day. Also mark a date in late June for the next kegger.

══════ April 27 ══════

Leaving—rather than bagging—your grass clippings can greatly reduce your fertilizing bills. That practice, however, won't eliminate the need to fertilize your lawn because water leaches nutrients down into the soil, away from the lawn's reach. Occasionally you need to replenish these nutrients. Spring and fall are the best times, so prepare yourself for some fertilizing.

If you're using synthetic chemical fertilizers, *don't* apply them according to the manufacturer's recommendations. These amounts are more than a yard can use in one shot. The excess nutrients cause the plant to grow too quickly and without corresponding root growth, meaning your grass isn't healthier—it just needs more mowing. Also when you overfertilize, many of the nutrients wash away before the grass uses them.

Save money. Adjust your spreader so that the lawn gets half or a third of the recommended dosage. Several weeks later (mark your calendar), apply another diluted dose.

══════ April 28 ══════

The hay-fever season lurks on the horizon and, if members of your family are annually victimized, it's time to tool up for the season. Check the medicine cabinet to see if you're armed for the itchy times to come. If not, add an antihistamine to your shopping list.

One good choice: Chlor-Trimeton. Of course, that's the brand name and a generic form of this over-the-counter drug delivers the same relief for about half the price. At my local pharmacy, Chlor-Trimeton runs $12.79 per 100 tablets, while Clortabs (the pharmacy's generic equivalent) cost $6.

For good information about surviving seasonal allergies, order *Hay Fever* from the Asthma and Allergy Foundation of America, 1717 Massachusetts Avenue, NW, Suite 305, Washington D.C. 20036, 800-727-8462.

Cheap Trick:
Check that you have a good supply of petroleum jelly on hand for the allergy season ahead. Add it to the shopping list if your reserves are low. Reason: Coating the inside of the nose with petroleum jelly is an effective home remedy against mild hay fever and allergies. Use a finger or a *Q-tip* to coat the inside of each nostril with a thin layer of petroleum jelly (get the jelly at least an inch up each nostril). Reapply throughout the day as needed. The trick gets me through yearly bouts of hay fever with nary a need for drugs. It also significantly reduces the number of pills taken by my wife (who is more seriously affected by hay fever).

April 29

Spring and early summer are the seasons associated with allergies—perhaps that's because many of us open our homes to let in the fresh air when, in fact, that air is polluted with pollens and dust.

If you've been thinking that a good air purifier will reduce your allergies to homes, think again. Controlled studies show that air purifiers have little effect on reducing allergies. The *University of California at Berkeley Wellness Letter*, rated by many periodicals as the country's best health newsletter, says, "Unfortunately, even the best air purifiers are no better than air conditioners at ridding indoor air of allergens and pollutants." And air conditioners have never rated as a miracle cure for allergies.

Why? Because pollutants and allergens are not airborne for long. They settle onto the walls, furniture, and carpet where even $600 purifiers can't touch them. Before you throw money at expensive allergy remedies like air purifiers, attack the problem with inexpensive elbow grease first. Mop, dust with a damp cloth, and vacuum often.

When fumes or gases irritate you, open windows and turn on exhaust fans. Ban pets from the bedroom. Replace the furnace filter monthly. Wash all bedding often. On warm days, cool the house with an air conditioner—it recycles the inside air and keeps new allergens out.

===== **April 30** =====

Is the purchase of a major appliance on the horizon? Electric or gas water heater, electric or gas furnace, cooling system, air conditioner, dishwasher, washing machine, dryer, stove, microwave, freezer, refrigerator? If so, start researching—like the British say, "With time as an ally, a farthing will buy fat thrushes." Procrastinate and the hour of need erodes your advantage, leaving you thankful if a farthing fetches even a scrawny sparrow.

Purchasing Tips:
   ◆ As a rule, you get the best bang for your buck buying mid-priced appliances. Low-end products are usually made to attract price-point shoppers and often sacrifice quality and necessary features for a low-ball price. High-end products flaunt expensive features few people really need—features that are also prone to breaking.
   Mid-priced dishwashers, for example, cost around $350. Some machines with a plethora of special cycles sell for twice that price, but product reviews rate the pricey units no better for everyday dishwashing than their $350 brethren. Mid-priced dishwashers have a light, normal, and heavy cycle—just what most people need.

   ◆ The true cost of an appliance is the sum of its sticker price, lifetime maintenance costs, and lifetime operating costs. A refrigerator costing $150 less than another is actually far more expensive if it has a poor maintenance history and uses 40% more energy.
   Guesstimate maintenance costs of competing appliances by comparing their frequency-of-repair records in magazines like *Consumer Reports*. Calculate the lifetime operating costs by checking the EnergyGuide tags attached to refrigerators, freezers, dishwashers, air conditioners, water heaters, furnaces, washing machines, dryers. Multiply this figure by

the life expectancy of the machine. The results can be significant. The operating cost of an efficient refrigerator may be 1.5 times its retail cost, an inefficient refrigerator three times its retail cost.

♦ When buying a dishwasher, refrigerator, freezer, washing machine, or gas range, used appliances may not be your cheapest option. Over the last decade, the efficiency of these appliances has increased by more than 30%, making the long-term costs of running old appliances quite high. If you can't afford to buy new, look at used appliances that are only a few years old.

♦ Gas dryers are so much cheaper to operate than electric ones that you'll recoup their higher cost (about $50) in about a year. Electric dryers perform slightly better than gas, but the lower cost of gas more than compensates for these minor differences. As a group, gas dryers break down more often than their electric brethren, but by studying the frequency-of-repair records published in *Consumer Reports*, you'll find some machines that outshine most electric models. Gas dryers using pilot lights use 30% more gas than those with electronic ignitions, and increase fuel bills by over $25 a year.

♦ Based on the average cost of energy (8¢ per kilowatt-hour), running the cleaning cycle of a self-cleaning oven costs between 50¢ and 75¢. Chemical oven cleaners for standard ovens cost about $1 per cleaning. Over time, a self-cleaning oven will help pay for itself, especially if your electric rates are below average.

♦ Eliminating the pilot of a gas range (get an electronic starter) saves $25 to $30 a year.

♦ Top-freezer refrigerators are cheaper to buy *and* run than side-by-side refrigerator/freezers. The average side-by-side unit uses 35% more energy and will cost an extra $30 a year to run. Historically, top-freezer units also have fewer repair problems. Either type of refrigerator will give you fewer repair problems if you avoid frills like ice makers. Dispensers for both water and ice are particularly prone to meltdown and can increase refrigerator repairs by 50%.

◆ Horizontal-axis washing machines (popular in Europe) will undoubtedly start capturing more of the American market. They get clothes cleaner; take up less space; and, because they use so much less energy, water, and detergent, are 45% cheaper to operate than our top-loading, vertical axis machines. Although the horizontal-axis machines cost $150 to $200 more, the Washington State Energy Office reports that difference will be made up in energy and detergent savings after four years. From that point on, the savings earned are all gravy. The life expectancy of a washing machine is about 15 years.

These same arguments apply when comparing domestic dishwashers to non-domestic models made by Asco and Bausch. The non domestics use a fraction of the resources-over 10 years they'll save about $830 in energy, water, sewage, and detergent, thereby paying for themselves. They'll also last 50% longer (15-year life span for non-domestics, 10-year life span for domestics). Unfortunately the up-front cost of the non-domestics is about twice that of the mid-range domestics, so the break-even point is five to six years down the road.

Library Resources:

Consumer Guide to Home Energy Savings (Wilson and Morrill, the American Council for an Energy-Efficient Economy, 1001 Connecticut Ave. NW, Suite 535, Washington, DC 20036, $6.95). Consider this book to be required reading if you're mobilizing to purchase a major appliance. Also, check the index in the back of any *Consumer Reports* to find out when the appliance in question was last reviewed. Get that back issue from the library.

May

This is not an action day but a personal education one. Settle into the sofa and absorb the following information about extended warranties.

Whether you're buying a car, a major appliance, a television, or stereo equipment, warranties (which are very profitable for the stores and dealers selling them) are rarely a wise investment.

Consumers buy these policies as a form of insurance—spend a little now, save a lot later is the general gist of the argument. But insurance is usually a losing gamble. Taking a loss to protect yourself against catastrophes makes sense, but taking a loss to protect yourself against an oven meltdown or a fried computer does not. Simply pay for smaller mishaps, out of pocket, and you'll come out ahead.

Interestingly, extended warranties are often the most profitable "product" sold by appliance retailers. The cost of these warranties is substantial and consumer studies have reported that for every dollar paid in to extended warranties as little as 20¢ is paid out. If doesn't take a math degree to understand that's a crummy return.

Research your purchases and buy gear with a record for reliability. Ignore the arm twisting from salespersons professing the value of these warranties. Altruism does not motivate their persistence, it's the commission (up to 20%) they want.

When it comes to new cars, the service contracts (extended warranties) offered by dealers seem like a good idea. Consumer magazines and books, however, consistently advise against them—partly, because many contracts are riddled with more holes than a sponge (and dealers are adept at finding shelter in these holes), partly because dealers simply overcharge. In a suit against Nissan, for example, it was revealed that dealers paid back only 16.5% of the monies taken in on extended warranties costing $795. That's not a pretty picture. Save money by buying a car with a good manufacturer's warranty and/or one with a high reliability rating.

Now read tomorrow's chore and give thought to how you will execute it.

May 2

Count on it, your appliances and cars will occasionally break down. Rather than purchasing someone else's extended warranty package, invest in your own. Open a money-market fund, mutual fund, bond fund, or some other investment and make it your repair fund.

Whenever you buy appliances or equipment, ask the price of the store's extended warranty. Then, buy a warranty from yourself by setting aside that amount of money in your own fund. Most of your appliances won't break and the repair dollars set aside can be used to fix the few that do. In the interim between crises, your investments will earn money for *you*.

The type of fund you establish depends on the peculiarities of your finances and your personality. If you are financing a new purchase (not recommended), pay monthly warranty installments to yourself. If you are paying cash for your purchase (recommended), pay a lump sum to the repair fund as well.

Likewise, how you draw money out of your repair fund may vary. People with enough liquid funds for the day-to-day tribulations of fixing a broken computer, dead car, or flickering television can establish a high-interest, less-liquid repair fund. When repairs are needed, funds can be transferred between accounts at your leisure—or, after a repair, you may simply decide to leave the fund intact and ignore a future payment to be paid in. Those who live hand-to-mouth will probably need to keep their repair fund in a liquid, less-lucrative account like a money-market fund or a certificate of deposit (CD).

Your task today is to decide how you will establish and manage your repair fund and to actually set it up.

May 3

It's Efficiency Day for your refrigerator and freezer.

Did you know that each degree drop in the temperature of your refrigerator or freezer increases your power consumption by 2.5%? That means you don't want temperatures set any lower than necessary. On the other hand, keeping temperatures too high reduces the shelf life of your food. Frozen beef, for example, keeps for 13 months at 0°F, but only five months at 10°F. Milk and vegetables keep nearly twice as long at 36°F than at 40°F.

Get a thermometer—the cheap jobber hanging outside the house is fine—and check that the freezer is operating between -3° and 0°F, the refrigerator between 36° and 37°F. Check this several times a year.

Cheap Trick:
Defrost the freezer when it has accumulated ¼ to ½ inch of ice. The ice significantly reduces the efficiency of the freezer and its ability to fast freeze your food. To make quick work of defrosting, use a fan (the bigger the better) to blow air into the open (and empty) freezer.

May 4

More refrigerator and freezer chores:

♦ Dusty condenser coils (on the bottom or back of refrigerators and freezers) lower the efficiency of these appliances and shorten their lives. Clean these coils at least twice a year with a coil brush (from a hardware store) or a soft-bristle attachment to a canister-style vacuum cleaner.

Unplug the appliance first. And if the coils are under the unit, pull the appliance away from the wall so that you can reach (and clean) the coils from both the front and rear.

◆ Once the gaskets of your refrigerator or freezer start deteriorating, you're in for a big waste of energy and money. Prolong the life of these gaskets which seal in cold air, by wiping them regularly with warm water. And check their seal occasionally by closing the appliance doors on a sheet of paper (like a dollar bill). The sheet should be firmly anchored. Repeat the test along the length of the gasket. Adjust the door hinges or replace the gasket if the paper slides.

═══ May 5 ═══

Throw a bag of bread in the freezer and, without proper prepping, you cut its shelf life in half. To get the maximum shelf life (and taste) from foods you freeze, practice these two essentials: get all excess air away from the food, and surround items with heavy, moisture-proof wrapping.

◆ Get rid of excess air by wrapping items with a thin skin of plastic wrap or by vacuum-packing the food. To vacuum-pack you don't need expensive machinery, simply use the gifts you were born with. Put your food in a holeless plastic bag. Gather the plastic at the neck (as though you were going to blow air into the bag), but, instead, suck air out: Your lungs make an excellent vacuum pump. You will see the plastic shrink in tight around the food. Tie off the bag in a loose knot.

When storing food in a zip-lock bag, seal the bag from the two ends and leave a half-inch gap in the center unsealed. Push in on the unsealed segment to pucker the gap into a circle, then draw out the excess air and seal the bag. Practice this a few times and adopt the trick for both freezer food and refrigerator-bound leftovers.

◆ Thin plastic bags (produce bags, bread bags, sandwich bags) make a fine first layer around the food you intend to freeze, but they are not completely impermeable to air and moisture—ever notice how the smell of an orange can pass through bread bags and give your loaf a citrus flavor, or how cookies grow stale in produce bags?

This is no reason to buy "freezer" bags. Instead, let your waste stream supply you with a lifetime's supply of great freezer bags: Reuse the heavier, crinkly plastic bags surrounding your cereal, chips, and cookies as freezer bags.

═══ May 6 ═══

If you don't own a stand-alone freezer, it's time to decide whether you should—'tis the season that many freezers will be found on sale.

Properly used to store meat, dairy goods, bread, vegetables, fruit, and convenience foods, a new freezer will pay for itself in two years. Think about that a minute—how many stocks bonds offer a 50% return on your investment?

Why is a freezer so profitable? Because it lets you stock up on perishables sold at loss-leader prices. With the freezer full of top sirloin purchased at $2/pound, lean hamburger snagged for $1/pound, ice cream stockpiled at $1/half gallon, canisters of orange juice concentrate purchased for 50¢, cheddar cheese running $1/pound, bread costing 25¢/loaf, and convenience foods snared when marked down 40%, a freezer lets you stockpile the staples of your diet from sale to sale.

The other big advantage of a freezer? It eliminates many little trips to the store. Factor in what you pay on your car's depreciation, insurance, maintenance, and gas, and it costs about 35¢/mile to drive even a small car. It doesn't take many trips to the store for butter, cheese, bread, or hamburger to offset the freezer's yearly utility bill.

But a freezer is not for everyone. Owners full of good intentions fill them with foods that sit, and sit, and ... eventually go bad. In such hands these appliances drain on your finances.

Take the following test to see whether you're a good candidate for a freezer. Answer the following yes-or-no questions.

___Do you shop sales and stock up the pantry with canned or dry goods?

___Do you rotate items in your pantry or refrigerator so old products get used first?

___Do few stockpiled dry goods (cereal, crackers, noodles, flour, rice, etc.) spoil before they're used up?

___Do few leftovers in the refrigerator spoil before you use them?

___Does cheese in the refrigerator get eaten before it molds?

___Do you dislike running to the store for sundries like milk, bread, and fruit?

___Do you repackage bulk chips for sack lunches?

___Do you wash and reuse your Ziploc sandwich bags?

___Do you have the money to purchase a new freezer?

___Do you make and stick to lists?

___Are you inherently an organized person?

___Do you know where you'd put a freezer?

Most of your answers a 'Yes'? Then you're a good candidate for a freezer. Most of your answers a 'No'? Save your money. Are your answers split down the middle? Then leap only if you commit yourself to some form of freezer management (see May 8). Using a freezer to advantage means being meticulous (maybe even anal retentive) about staying organized, maintaining lists, and using old food.

══════ May 7 ══════

Assuming you've decided to spring for a freezer, you have several decisions to make:

◆ **Location.** Where will it go? Does this location dictate the maximum size of the freezer (take measurements)? Does it dictate whether you'll require a chest or upright unit? Do you have access to an electrical outlet?

◆ **Type.** Chest freezers use 10% to 15% less energy than uprights: partly because they are better insulated, partly because the heavy, cold air does not flow out when the door is opened. Uprights are, however, vastly easier to keep organized—everything is accessible without much digging and items are far less likely to become permanently buried. If you're at all worried about keeping control of this appliance, join the majority (75% of buyers purchase uprights) and get an upright.

♦ **Size.** The biggest mistake families report in purchasing freezers is buying too small. Figure on four to five cubic feet per family member, meaning a family of four should be considering at least 17 cubic-foot units. The two most common sizes of freezers are 12 cubic feet and 21 cubic feet, and because these units are produced in larger numbers, they're cheaper. For example, expect to pay about $460 for a 17-cubic-foot unit, $500 for a 21-cubic-foot unit. The energy consumption between the two units is negligible, so the 21-cubic-foot unit offers families of four or more better bang for the buck.

♦ **Age.** The major cost of owning a freezer is paying for the energy to power it—over the life of the appliance you'll spend far more on energy than you did on the appliance itself. Modern freezers are energy misers compared to old freezers, so, over the long haul, it's considerably cheaper to buy a new model than a 10-year-old one. New freezer codes implemented in 1993 demanded a 30% improvement in efficiency over the 1990 codes, so if you are going to buy a used freezer, look for a relatively new unit that a family outgrew.

♦ **Defrosting.** Auto-defrost freezers use about 40% more energy than manual-defrost models. Compared to manual-defrost models, auto-defrost freezers also cause much more freezer burn and reduce your food's shelf life. The convenience of auto-defrost may make sense for the refrigerator/freezer unit in your kitchen, but for a freezer dedicated to long-term food storage, a manual defrost (which is unlikely to need defrosting more than once a year) is a wiser purchase.

Buying freezers:

♦ About 60% of the freezers in the country are built by Westinghouse and then given names like General Electric or Kelvinator. The freezers vary little, but the warranties and service offered by the labeling company can vary a lot. At the time of this writing, General Electric offers the best combination of price, warranty, and service.

♦ Visit a major appliance store with a good selection of freezers and finalize what you want: chest or upright, big or small, inside light or not, white or cream, bread bin or shelves only. Check the warranties of different units. Compare the energy consumption figures listed on each freezer and calculate what it will cost to *own* (not just buy).

But don't buy yet, even if the unit is on sale. Go home and call the other appliance stores listed in the Yellow Pages. Hone in on the store that offers a great price *and* that treats you right.

♦ Don't purchase an extended warranty. Even salesmen (if you catch them in an honest mood) will tell you it's a waste of money.

May 8

Whether you already own a stand alone freezer or have just purchased one, you need to seize control of it. There's no one way to do this but today's assignment is to design a system that works for you. Here is a simple system that works for my family.

Logging food in:

♦ Keep loads of plastic bags (bread bags, produce bags, cereal bags...) stuffed in a box in the pantry. In a handy drawer stock rubber bands, masking tape, a felt-tip pen (permanent ink), and scissors. When food arrives from the grocery store, the freezer food is processed together. Bulk purchases are divided into meal-sized portions, then everything gets properly wrapped or bagged. Bags are sealed with a loose knot, rubber band, or tape. The date (month/day/year) is written on the outside of the bag with the felt-tip pen.

♦ Now, pull the master list of what's in the freezer (we hang a one-page sheet inside a kitchen cabinet) and add the new entries. Our master list is divided into four vertical columns (two on each side of the page) and each column corresponds to a shelf in the freezer. We keep columns for bread, meat, prepared meals, dairy products, fruits and vegetables.

In the appropriate column, we note the date and item entering the freezer (list the date first). Bulk items—like five pounds of hamburger that were divided into one-pound packages—are listed once with an appropriate number of hash marks after the entry.

◆ The food is freezer-ready now. On the appropriate shelf (we own an upright freezer), space is made available on one side by high-stacking older foods on the opposite side. As much as possible, we lay the new entries directly on the metal bars of the shelf and avoid stacking one new entry on top of another. This allows a fast freeze which helps preserve the food's taste and texture. This is especially important for meat.

◆ A few foods (bread, frozen juice) we don't log on the master list. These staples circulate so quickly we never worry about using them up.

Using the master list:

◆ Grab the master list whenever you're pulling items from the freezer. First, because you want to pull the oldest items and need to know which package you're looking for. Second, because you need to keep the master list current by crossing off what you pull.

◆ Check the master list whenever you're compiling a shopping list. Plan menus around what's in that big box, and note the ingredients (grated cheese, frozen peas, Italian sausage, etc.) that can be pulled to prepare other meals.

◆ Finally, consult the master list as you peruse ads for the weekly food sales. This keeps you from over-buying some items, under-buying others.

Long-time freezer owner:

If your freezer is currently an example of chaos theory at work, consider pulling everything out, labeling it with a best-guess date, compiling a master list, and segregating foods by shelves. Or, spend a few concentrated weeks foraging from the fruits of the freezer, empty out that black hole, and start over.

May 9

Another vital element in effective freezer management: Know the shelf life of what goes into cryogenic storage. Food left in longer than recommended will slowly begin to lose taste, texture, and nutritive value.

Keep a shelf-life list of freezer foods stapled to your master list. Until you find a better list, photocopy this page and familiarize yourself with these times. The following list assumes the freezer is kept at 0°F.

SHELF LIFE OF FREEZER FOOD

MEATS
-Roasts (beef and lamb), steaks (beef), chops (lamb): 9-10 months
-Chops (pork), ground and stew meats, variety meats (beef), liver, kidneys: 4 months
-Meat pies, stews, casseroles: 3 months
-Variety meats (pork), sausage (pork), cooked meats, gravy, ham (whole): 2 months
-Bacon, hot dogs, ham (slices): 1 month

POULTRY
-Chicken and turkey (whole), game birds, chicken (pieces): 9-12 months
-Turkey (pieces), duck & goose (whole), chunks covered with broth, casseroles, gravies, cooked poultry: 6 months
-Fried chicken: 4 months
-Stuffing, chunks not covered by broth: 1 month

FISH
-Fish (lean): 5 months
-Fish (fatty), shellfish: 3 months
-Cooked and smoked fish: 1 month

FRUITS AND VEGETABLES
-Frozen juice concentrates: 12 months
-Most fresh fruits and vegetables: 9 to 12 months
-Cauliflower, cabbage, leek, herbs, onions, purees: 6 months
-Citrus fruits, potatoes (French fries): 3 months
-Dried fruit, mushrooms: 2 months

BAKED GOODS
-Baked breads (brown and white), scones (cooked), biscuits (baked and unbaked): 6 months
-Cakes (undecorated, yeast types), cookies, pies (baked), pastries: 4 months
-Cakes (decorated), pastries (unbaked), souffles, pies (unbaked), puddings: 3 months
-Breads (quick), breads (unbaked): 2 months

DAIRY PRODUCTS
-Butter (unsalted): 9 months
-Hard cheese: 9 months
-Eggs (without shell): 7 months
-Butter (salted), margarine, semi-hard cheeses: 5 months
-Soft cheese: 4 months
-Quiche: 3 months
-Milk, cottage cheese, ice cream, sherbet: 1 month

MISC
-Candy, nuts (shelled): 12 months
-Most prepared dishes (casseroles, soups, stews): 3 months
-Leftovers (cooked), pizza, sandwiches: 1 month

═══════ May 10 ═══════

Summer in many southern cities can be unbearable without some air conditioning. If this is the year you're going to spring for a room air conditioner, now is the season to buy. Procrastinate until the hot spells come and the prices will rise with the mercury.

Your first chore today: Visit the library and read the most recent issue of *Consumer Reports* (usually the last June issue) tackling air conditioners. This will teach you how to calculate how big an air conditioner you need and highlight models worth your attention.

Chore two: Use the Yellow Pages to comparison shop. Call at least four major appliance shops for price quotes. See who has sales pending or in process, and don't be shy about floating lines like, "Sears has their units on sale, when do yours go on special and how much will they be discounted?" If you're given that information, run with it,

"If the units will be 25% off in two weeks, will you offer me that discount now?"

Other considerations:

◆ Reports found in *Consumer Guide*, found in the reference area of most libraries and published by Publications International (7373 North Cicero Ave, Lincolnwood, IL 60646), is another source of information for determining the best values on the market and the street prices you should expect to pay.

◆ The EnergyGuide tags put on all new air conditioners display the machine's Energy Efficiency Rating (EER), or the amount of cooling obtained from the electricity used. A rating of 8 is good and a machine with such a rating might run 700 hours for $55, but a machine with an even better rating of 10 will provide the same cooling for $44. A cheap air conditioner to buy may not be cheap to own.

◆ Used air conditioners may not be wallet friendly. Tougher efficiency standards implemented in January 1990, require that all new air conditioners have an EER of at least 8. The average unit sold now has an EER of 9, which is 10% more efficient than the average five years ago and 23% more efficient than the average 10 years ago. These are averages. Some old units are as efficient as today's models while others measure in with EERs of 5.5. Ouch.
Before buying used merchandise, verify its EER. Check for tags (sometimes located inside the front panel near the top of the coil), or call the manufacturer with the model number.

◆ In hot parts of the country, more and more homes have central air conditioning; it's cheaper. But if you rely on air conditioning through much of the year, a room air conditioner in the bedroom will pay for itself quickly. At night, turn off the home's central cooling and use the room air conditioner to sleep comfortably and economically.

◆ Install room air conditioners on north- or east-facing windows. South- and west-facing windows receive more sun and the extra labor that inflicts on the machine will cost you.

◆ Finally, how do you stay comfortable if an air conditioner just ain't in the finances this year? Fill a hot-water bottle with ice water and lay it on your belly. Ahhh...feels like an arctic blast.

═══ May 11 ═══

When my General Electric dishwasher broke down, I called the GE Answer Center and tapped into their over-the-phone repair instructions. A technician analyzed my problem and gave me a test to conduct. I called back with the test results, and was told which part to replace and where, locally, I could purchase the part. When the local outlet didn't have the part, I ordered it through the Answer Center using my credit card.

The part arrived two days later and, with the instructions the technician had given me over the phone, this electronic dimwit had no trouble getting the machine working. The process sentenced me to a few days of handwashing dishes, but saved me $75 in service fees. Plus, I got to run around the house, voltage-ohm meter in hand, singing, "I am Ohmman hear me roar...I can do anything." Drove my wife crazy—which made the dishpan hands worthwhile.

The point of all this is to prepare you for the day when (not if) *your* appliances belly up. Pull a blank card from your Rolodex file, label it *Appliances*, and make the rounds noting each major appliance and who manufactures it. Now, refer to the list below and copy the relevant phone numbers for over-the-phone repair instructions. When catastrophe strikes, these numbers may be the cornerstone of a cheap fix.

Over-the-phone repairs:

◆ **GE** gives repair instructions on all major appliances, though they are restricted in what they can tell you about gas ranges and microwaves (apparently hapless words here can transform luckless customers into crispy critters). GE also offers repair instruction on consumer electronics, though a high percentage of these products will need professional servicing. Call 800-626-2000.

◆ **Hotpoint**, Monogram, and RCA major appliances are actually manufactured by General Electric. Call 800-626-2000.

◆ **Whirlpool**, Roper, KitchenAid, Estate, and Holiday major appliances: Call the Whirlpool Consumer Assistance Center 800-253-1301. The center gives repair instruction on all its major appliances except microwaves.

◆ **RCAs** number for technical support and troubleshooting of its consumer electronics is 800-336-1900.

◆ **Maytag**: Call Customer Relations for over-the-phone repair instructions at 800-688-9900. Of course, if your Maytag breaks, that bored repairman from the ads is likely to talk your ear off. Other companies under the Maytag umbrella providing phone-assisted repairs include: Jenn-Air 800-680-1100; Admiral 800-688-9920; Magic Chef, Norge, Hardwick, and Crosley 615-472-3500.

◆ **Amana** will sell service manuals and parts over the phone but no longer offers repair instruction. Call 800-843-0304.

A final thought. You may have forgotten this exercise in preparedness by the time an appliance actually needs surgery. Consider putting a photocopy of this page in your Rolodex or with your warranty information.

May 12

Dining out is important entertainment for many couples. A tip listed in the *Simple Living* newsletter makes that entertainment more affordable. Says a Pennsylvanian subscriber,

"One of our biggest wastes of money was eating out. We would spend over $200 monthly on this and came up with a simple solution. It was really the entertainment we were seeking, not just the good food. Now we make simple meals and invite two or three couples over. Sometimes we all bring potluck."

◆ Think about that quote over the course of the day. Does it apply to you? Would gathering with friends provide what you need from a night out? Can you force yourself to simplify the food? And can you force yourself to simplify the preparations in having friends over—after all, get-togethers feel like more work than fun if you stress out making the house look perfect.

♦ Schedule an evening with friends for later in the week and force yourself to try out a new *modus operandi*—no elaborate meal, no elaborate preparations, just a pleasant evening with people you enjoy. If it relieves your anxiety, forewarn your friends not to expect the Ritz. Tell them you're turning over a new leaf, that you want to get together more often with friends, and that to make that goal more fun than stress, the meal won't be out of Gourmet Magazine and the state of the house won't win the Good Housekeeping Seal of Approval.

═══ May 13 ═══

Mother's Day looms. In preparation, husbands unwilling to face the bitter winds of cold shoulders will want to consider this advice.

♦ Supermarket flowers and bouquets are considerably cheaper than purchases from a dedicated florist.

♦ If there's reason to spring for a big floral show (have you been particularly neglectful lately?), look up *Flowers— Wholesale* in the Yellow Pages. Some wholesalers are happy to make cash sales that will set you back but a half or a third of what retailers charge. A local wholesaler will sell me 24 long-stemmed roses for $23, compared to the $36 to $45 (per dozen) that the retailers charge.

♦ More is not necessarily better. Single roses (or gardenias) make an elegant offering.

♦ Cut out pictures from magazines, paste them onto a folded card made of construction paper; scribble your own sassy or sappy observations, and *voila'* you've got a card— *sans* a trip to the store.

♦ Are you celebrating with your own mother or mother-in-law? A brunch makes the occasion easier and cheaper.

═══════ May 14 ═══════

Most metropolitan areas have a gaggle of writers who take cheap shots at their native cities. I'm not talking about disparaging, abusive, offensive remarks, but about inexpensive ones. This is the day to research your local prophets of the penny who can tell you where, in your own backyard, to eat, sleep, play, shop, relax, even die, for less.

In my neck of the woods (Seattle), books to stretch the dollar include *The Seattle Super Shopper* (where to snag the best buys on everything from aardvarks to zymometers), *Romance on a Shoestring* (inexpensive outings for two around the Puget Sound environs), *Seattle Cheap Eats* (inexpensive dining), and *Northwest Cheap Sleeps*.

Most other parts of the country have comparable resources—books like the *L.A. Bargain Book*, *San Diego's Best Freebies and Bargains*, *Northern California Cheap Sleep*, *Mr. Cheap: New York*, and *Let's Go: New York City*. Research, locate, look, and maybe even buy a few such books. Look for books dealing with your city and books focusing on destinations where travels take you.

◆ Start with the freebies. Call the local library and ask the reference desk what regional titles are in the system that would help you eat, sleep, shop, and play for less. Ask them to check *Books in Print* for money-saving titles pertaining to cities where you travel.

◆ Call the best bookstores in the city and ask the same questions. If they have interesting titles that were not available through the library, visit those stores the next time errands have you in the neighborhood.

◆ Entertainment Publications (2125 Butterfield Road, Troy, MI 48084, 800-445-4137) compiles discount coupon books for travelers. These books offer hotel rooms at half price (50% off the rack rates) and two-for-one coupons that can be used at restaurants, tourist attractions, theaters, museums, amusement parks, and other leisure activities. Discount coupon books are assembled for 140 major cities around North America, Europe, and Australia (priced from $28 to $48) and often pay for themselves the first time you use a coupon. For information about the discount coupon book for your city, call Entertainment Publications (local number listed in your phone directory).

Entertainment Publications also assembles general books for vacationers and business people traveling in wider circles, including *Entertainment National Hotel and Dining Directory* (lists half-price offers to 2,500 restaurants and 3,500 hotels around the United States, Canada, Mexico, and the Caribbean ($43 ppd), and *Entertainment Europe* ($40 ppd).

===== **May** 15 =====

Live theater is a caviar experience that those of us who make croutons from bread crusts believe we cannot afford. There's some truth to that belief: Professional theater around my home in Seattle runs $18 to $38 per seat at small professional theaters and $40 plus at the big-name venues. Fortunately, exceptions to the rule let penny-pinchers tap into quality performing arts at movie-theater prices.

Look up *Theaters—Stage* in the Yellow Pages and start working down the list of theaters near home. Call the box offices and ask about their prices on different show days (Thursday performances and weekend matinees are typically cheaper). Most small theaters offer affordable tickets (some as low as $10) with perfectly-adequate viewing.

Next, ask what last-minute tactics are used by the theater to unload unsold seats. Those tactics translate into discounts for you. Some theaters, like A.C.T. in Seattle, sell half-price tickets at the box office on show days—you can call the box office and make the purchase with a credit card. Others, like the Seattle Repertory Theater, sell "rush tickets" 30 minutes before show time for half price. Rush tickets may be unavailable for the Friday or Saturday showings of a popular play, but if you call the box office, they'll tell you which evenings have seats available.

Other theaters offer discount days or showings: You can see a show for half price during a matinee, or during a specified weekday evening. Then there are student and senior citizen discounts, which are typically 25% to 50% off normal prices. Some theaters offer a pay-what-you-can performance of each new show.

Because each theater has its own policies and programs, call and grill them all. List the promising theaters (their prices and discount programs) in the old Rolodex under Theaters. Get on the mailing lists of the theaters you can afford to attend—you want to know what's playing when.

While you're researching new and affordable entertainment, call the community theaters. In large cities the quality of the productions is high, the ticket price isn't (expect to pay $8 to $12 per person).

A city's semi-professional theaters also offer the opportunity to see excellent quality productions at mid-range prices. Find out about their last-minute sales of unsold seats and you'll see top notch performances at prices that won't leave you homeless.

Your city and county arts commissions (listed in the government pages of the phone book) are the best sources for listings of community, semi-professional and professional theaters. Or, if you know one community or semi-professional theater, its administrator can tell you the names of others. Most of these will also be listed in the Yellow Pages (under *Theaters—Stage*), but until you ask you won't know whether you are dealing with a professional, semi-professional, or community theater.

═══ **May 16** ═══

Enough talk of performance arts. Following are other forms of budget entertainment for the family.

◆ In most cities you'll find discount movie theaters featuring films that are neither fish nor fowl (i.e., neither first run nor in video). Because films reach this no-man's-land quickly and because discount theaters give you the big-screen effect at video prices ($1.50 to $2 per person), it's worth being a few months behind the times. Call all your local movie houses (*Theaters—Movies* in the Yellow Pages or those listed in the entertainment section of the newspaper), and make a card for the Rolodex listing discount operations and the matinee times of the local full-fare theaters.

♦ Local clubs catering to special interests can pack your calendar with activities and social functions for a low price.

Scope out the clubs in your area by looking under "Clubs" in the Yellow Pages or calling the Chamber of Commerce. In my town, a bedroom community of Seattle, the Chamber's list includes a coin club, stamp club, several garden clubs, opera club, music and art club, rock and gem club, 4-H Club, Boy Scouts, Girl Scouts, and Campfire Boys and Girls.

Also, contact the retail shops stocking supplies for your hobbies. By calling local outdoor-equipment stores, I unearthed contacts and phone numbers for a climbing club, orienteering club, bicycling club, hiking club, and canoeing and kayaking club. Computer shops will plug you into computer clubs, photography stores will expose you to photo clubs, craft stores can point out the needlecraft clubs...

Use the library to locate clubs. Call the reference desk and ask them where you can locate the nearest chapter of the club for orphaned twins, or one-armed sky divers, or left-handed sumo wrestlers. It's amazing what they'll find.

♦ The library itself is another entertainment possibility. It sponsors a roster of events: lectures, slideshows, readings, speakers, kids' programs. Get in the habit of picking up the calendar of events when you visit.

♦ Sports enthusiasts can watch cheap, live action by tracking their region's minor-league or farm teams. These teams are fun to watch; play in smaller, more intimate venues; and, unlike their big-league brethren, more truly embody the love of sport than the love of money. Call the sports department of your newspaper and ask which minor-league teams play in the area and how to track their scheduled games.

Cheap Trick:
Movie theaters and sports arenas glean hefty profits selling food and drinks. Popcorn costing 30¢ to make runs $3.50 at the theater. A quarter's worth of pop rings up at $2. Bring your own refreshments and escape the scalping. Theaters don't encourage these practices (lost revenue) so be inconspicuous: Carry the contraband in a small day pack or a woman's tote bag.

===== **May** 17 =====

Some final thoughts on filling your family's free time with affordable fun.

♦ Flip through the government pages of the telephone book, studying each listing. You'll discover a rich supply of resources and facilities for your entertainment. Under *City* listings you may find zoos, golf courses, swimming pools, community centers, parks, aquariums, dance studios, boating centers, theaters, libraries, and art commissions. Under *County* numbers you'll see libraries, parks, educational services. Under *State* listings, look up the parks. Under *Federal* listings you'll find many numbers to facilitate outdoor adventures—Forest Service and Park Service numbers, river information, whitewater and fishing hotlines....

Call those numbers that arouse curiosity, ask for schedules of events, get on their mailing list, and, of course, file those phone numbers that are helpful. Soon your family will be tuned into the local pools, libraries, zoos, aquariums, parks. Deciding which inexpensive outing to attend (rather than finding cheap entertainment) will be your curse.

♦ How about some high-brow entertainment on a low-life's budget? Use the Yellow Pages to contact the local art galleries (see *Art Galleries*). Ask the proprietors to mail you notices announcing the opening of new exhibits. At these openings you can view good art, hobnob with interesting people, and gawk at eccentrics who may prove more interesting than the art.

Poetry and book readings provide other forms of high-brow entertainment. Call the large, distinguished bookstores in your area and ask to be put on their special-events mailing lists. Listening to visiting authors read their work is mind-stimulating and observing the audience is of great rubbernecking value.

===== **May** 18 =====

Are you prepared (or at least partially prepared) for earthquakes and storms? Being ready is not just a money saver, it could be a life saver. Vital preparations include:

◆ Store four days' worth of water, allotting one gallon of water per person per day. Five-gallon plastic buckets with waterproof lids are excellent for the job (fast-food chains receive condiments in these buckets and will often give you their empties). Empty milk, and bleach jugs also work.

◆ Keep iodine on hand to purify water. Iodine purification tablets (available from camping and outdoor-sports stores) like Potable Aqua use tetraglycine hydroperiodide (TGHP) to destroy the microscopic worries you might have about storm-tainted water.

A cheaper alternative: Get a small bottle of 2% tincture of iodine and a pharmaceutical eyedropper (both available from pharmacies). Add five or six drops per quart of clear water and wait 30 minutes before drinking the water. Double the iodine dosage for cloudy or extremely cold water.

◆ If you own a camping stove, wood stove, and/or a propane barbecue, keep at least a week's supply of fuel on hand in case disaster disables the home's primary stove.

◆ Keep first aid supplies, flashlights, fresh batteries, nonperishable food, candles, and matches on hand. Also, plastic sheeting and duct tape will facilitate temporary repairs of broken windows and damaged roofs.

◆ Also, strap your hot water heater to the wall; position fire extinguishers in convenient locations; and learn how (and where) to turn off the home's electricity, water, and gas.

══════ May 19 ══════

Insurance—whether it's for your house, car, or life—is a losing game. It's a game worth playing to protect yourself against catastrophe, but you don't want to over insure yourself. So get ready for the tedious job of examining many of your insurance policies. Before getting down to specifics, commit these general rules to memory. They apply to any type of insurance.

1) **The Prime Rule.** Insure yourself against large or disastrous losses, but not against small risks you can afford to pay out of pocket. Insurance is a losing proposition—over the years most everyone pays much more than they collect.

2) **The Rule of Suspicion.** While it's commendable to ask questions and seek different opinions, take it upon yourself to really understand your insurance policies and the coverage you are purchasing. Insurance agents, even independent agents, make their daily bread selling salvation after scaring the hell out of you. It's not that they're lying—terrible things can happen. But how much of your present life are you going to waste worrying about and paying for future cataclysms that have a very small likelihood of happening? At some point you must accept the fact that life is a risky business and that too much payment toward the future ruins the now—which is the only sure thing you've got. At some point you've got to roll the dice and play the odds—even if it isn't a sure winner.

3) **The Rule of Differences**. Financial advisors and insurance agents make many recommendations about insurance on the assumption that you are playing the game by mainstream rules. But the fact that you're willing to snub the two-career lifestyle, that you haven't swallowed many American myths, that you don't accept that more is synonymous with better, that adjectives like new and bigger don't make them best for you, means many of these assumptions don't apply to you.

Today's chore:

♦ If your home were ruined by storm or fire, what essentials would you need to get back to everyday life? Wander the house, room by room, with pencil and paper, noting the items you'd definitely replace: clothing, bedding, essential furnishings, toiletries, pharmaceuticals, cookware, major appliances, dishes, cutlery, tools for home and hobbies, basic toys, office equipment and supplies, essential books and references, crucial consumables, vital jewelry, important appliances and electronics.... Estimate the replacement value of these items. Guess high—if you don't know an item's exact value, pick a figure you're sure would cover the replacement. Leave all those items your family never uses and which simply clutter up the house (a good 60% of your possessions) off the list.

♦ Review the finished list with your spouse to add or subtract items and to verify values.

══════ May 20 ══════

Today, pull your current homeowner's (or renter's) insurance policy and evaluate your coverage.

♦ Applying The Prime Rule to your homeowner's insurance, increase the deductible on your policy to $500 or even $1,000. Compared to a policy with a $250 deductible, your premiums will be 10% and 25% (respectively) lower. Statistics strongly indicate that over time these discounted rates will save you money. Also, refuse many of the specialized coverages available through your homeowner's policy—they often insure you against small risks you should cover yourself. Options to refuse include: stolen credit cards (card companies insure you against this already), fire department surcharges, debris removal, removal of damaged property, damage to vegetation (trees, shrubs, plants).

♦ With yesterday's list of essential possessions in hand and the Rule of Differences in mind, seriously examine the value of the possessions (personal property) you are insuring. Imagine the worst case scenario of being ruined by storm or fire. Would you really want to replace everything? A good 60% of what you currently own is simply in long-term storage and is unlikely to be used again. In truth, a disaster could eliminate a lot of deadfall that enslaves you. Then there are the sentimental objects that really have no financial value—they cannot be replaced, so why insure them? Instead, take measures to make copies and backups (see October 15) before disaster strikes. Now, use the list you prepared yesterday to determine what personal property is worth insuring and the value of that personal property. Reduce your coverage if you're overinsured.

♦ Get the best value from your policy by purchasing replacement-value coverage of your possessions (rather than market-value coverage). It may cost $1,500 to replace a stolen computer, but if you received market-value for a four-year-old machine you'd collect about $350. Replacement-value coverage of your possessions costs 10% to 15% more, but budget-minded experts believe it's the better buy.

◆ Insure only structures and possessions on your property. Land, which makes a huge contribution to your home's appraised value, doesn't require insuring.

◆ Know the true replacement value of your structure(s). Insure up to this amount. Additional insurance only wastes money—in the event of a loss, you will be paid only the replacement costs. Carry at least 80% of the replacement costs of your house, otherwise the insurance company penalizes you by the percentage that you are underinsured. Example: on a $100,000 home if you carry $60,000 of insurance you have 75% of the required $80,000 minimum, meaning you are 25% underinsured. In the event of a fire that caused $40,000 of damage, you would not be reimbursed $40,000 but 75% of that amount ($30,000).

◆ Renters should know (but often don't) that landlords are not responsible for possessions stolen from (or damaged in) your apartment. Protect yourself with renter's insurance. As explained earlier, opt for replacement-value coverage of your possessions.

◆ Tell your insurer if you have smoke alarms, are retired, live next to a hydrant, have a sprinkler system, are a non-smoker...these can all contribute to lower rates.

May 21

If you have had the good fortune of amassing a fortune, protect yourself with more liability insurance—otherwise a jury perceiving you as a deep pocket could make you a victim of your own pocketbook. The smart way to fortify the liability shield isn't to add huge coverages independently to your auto and homeowner's policy but to purchase an umbrella policy that protects you on both fronts.

These policies are inexpensive (around $170 for $1 million of coverage) but are not always well advertised (insurance agents don't make much on them). Ask for them.

To qualify for a personal umbrella policy, you may need to carry both your homeowner's and auto insurance with the same underwriter (not mandatory with all companies). You will also probably need certain liability limits on both your auto and homeowner's insurance (e.g., $300,000 and $200,000 respectively).

Investigate these policies today by calling the companies currently handling your homeowner's and auto insurance.

May 22

Car insurance is like every other commodity—different companies charge different rates for the same basic coverage. Many policies are quite competitive, but in any given metropolitan area, the best shopper may pay half of what the worst shopper pays for the same coverage. That difference amounts to hundreds of dollars a year. Today's task is to look at your current policy and decide whether to change your coverage. Tomorrow's chore is to comparison shop and to decide whether to change companies.

Examine your policy now to check your coverage.

♦ Liability coverage for the bodily injury you (or a family member) inflicted in an accident you caused is the most critical form of coverage. Without it you could go broke settling a victim's (or passenger's) medical, rehabilitation, or funeral bills. How much liability coverage should you carry? Experts commonly recommend (especially if you've accumulated a nest of assets) to insure yourself to the tune of your net worth. Liability insurance beyond the minimum required by the state is not expensive, it's a good value—it's the minimum amount the state requires that's ugly.

Incidentally, if you drink and drive, load up with as much liability insurance as you can afford. When alcohol contributes to fatal or injury accidents, settlements average over $250,000 and can balloon into million-dollar settlements which, appropriately, means a serious accident can ruin more than your victim's life.

♦ Liability coverage for property damage you cause in an accident pays for the vehicles (and other property) you ruin. Most states have low minimums but because cars are so expensive today, and because you can easily damage several cars in an accident, the extra cost of carrying $50,000 of property damage also delivers good bang for the buck.

◆ Many experts recommend getting underinsured motorist coverage that matches the dollar figure of your liability coverage. Underinsured motorist coverage pays for the bodily injury to you and your family if the driver causing the accident is not adequately insured (it also covers your family for hit-and-run accidents). Because underwriters pay out more dollars to this category of claims than any other, and because so many people in urban areas drive uninsured, matching your liability coverage is good advice.

◆ Your policy will also offer either Medical-Payments Coverage or Personal-Injury Protection. These coverages are variations of the same theme. Regardless of who is at fault, both coverages pay for medical expenses your family members incur from an accident (money is also available by collecting on liability coverage for bodily injury). These coverages also compensate the family for lost wages, or services hired as a result of disability.

To decide whether you need this coverage, study your health-insurance policy and read how well it protects you against car accidents. Unfortunately, while the costs of medical coverage have rocketed, the benefits enjoyed have not. Increasing numbers of health-insurance policies don't offer suitable coverage for the injuries sustained during a car accident. After reading your health-insurance policy, call your health-insurance provider and double check how thoroughly you're protected. If members of your family need extensive emergency care after an automobile accident would your health coverage keep you afloat or drown you in the red waters of debt?

Next, check what disability insurance the wage earner of the family carries—it's likely to duplicate benefits touted under medical-payments coverage or personal injury protection. Duplicate coverage boosts your premiums without significantly boosting your protection.

If you're well protected on the medical and disability fronts, keep this part of your auto-insurance coverage at the state's minimum.

◆ You may also want comprehensive coverage to safe-guard against non-collision loss (fire, theft) and collision coverage to fix your car if it's damaged in an accident. Applying The Prime Rule to these coverages, settle on large deductibles for both your comprehensive and collision coverages. The premium paid for a deductible of $200 averages 20% to 25% more than a deductible of $500 and up to 40% more than a deductible of $1,000. Low deduct-ibles cost enough more that over the years it would take multiple accidents to make them a better buy than higher deductibles.

Furthermore, once the blue-book value of your vehicle sinks under $2,000, cancel both your collision and com-prehensive coverages. At this point, the return from a stolen or totalled car is not enough to justify the cost of the coverage. Play the odds. A few people will get burned (though not on a disastrous level), the vast majority will come out ahead.

◆ Underinsured property damage protects your property (namely your vehicle) if an underinsured driver plows into you. It's cheap and has no deductibles but is best avoided if you carry collision insurance. If you don't carry collision insurance you might add it.

◆ A variety of other coverages, representing relatively minor risks, can be added to your policy but should be avoided. These include emergency road service (emergency towing), specialty coverage of your audio equipment, and rental coverage (in case you must rent a vehicle should yours be stolen or sidelined in an accident).

◆ Cars titled to young adults (ages 16 to 25) are an ugly sight when it comes time to ante up for insurance. If children insist on being independent and in placing a vehicle in their name, then insist that *they* pay the inflated insurance premium. If you're footing the bill, put your child's car on your policy and insure him or her as a driving-age child.

◆ Make a list of discounts for which you might qualify.
— Are any of your vehicles low-mileage cars (i.e., driven under 8,000 miles per year)?

— Does your vehicle have automatic seat belts, air bags, anti-theft security systems, or anti-lock brakes?
— Are you over 50?
— Do your drivers have spotless records for the past three years (no tickets or accidents)?
— Are your teenage drivers excelling at school and have they taken driver training?

May 23

The companies offering the best deals in auto insurance change from year to year, so occasionally it pays to give several companies a crack at your business. Spend a few hours today doing just that.

◆ First, call your current agent/underwriter and ask what you will be paying for coverage after you institute changes prompted by yesterday's readings and research. Mention any discounts (see yesterday) you qualify for.

◆ To get quotes from additional companies, they'll need to know the age, make, and model of your cars; approximate mileage on each vehicle; approximate miles each car is driven in a year; age, birth dates, and records (tickets or accidents) of each driver. They'll also need to know what coverages you'll want—how much bodily injury, property damage, uninsured motorist, and personal injury protection; what deductibles (if any) to assign to collision and comprehensive coverage; and which discounts you qualify for.

◆ A few companies that consistently offer competitive rates include: Aetna Life & Casualty Group (check Yellow Pages), Allstate Insurance Group (check Yellow Pages), American International Group (800-807-9458), Geico Corporation Group (800-841-3000), ITT Hartford Insurance Group (check Yellow Pages), Nationwide Insurance Group (800-356-6153), The Travelers Companies (check Yellow Pages), USAA Insurance Group (check Yellow Pages), USF&G (check Yellow Pages). Some of these groups will give you a quote over the phone, others work through agents listed in the Yellow Pages under *Insurance*. When calling local agents, don't get roped into having them visit.

If they're unwilling to give you a quote over the phone, bid them goodbye.

♦ If you live in New York, New Jersey, Pennsylvania, Florida, California, or Washington state, consider calling Consumer Reports' Auto Insurance Price Service (800-808-4912). After giving the service your basic personal information, the age and type of vehicle(s) you have, and the amount of coverage you want, you will receive a list comparing 25 of the least expensive policies. Cost is $12 for the first vehicle, $8 for each additional vehicle (getting just one vehicle quoted will still help you locate a good choice).

♦ Regardless of how you hone in on different companies, before signing on with any new underwriter visit the library and see if that underwriter is reviewed in *Consumer Reports'* most recent review of auto insurance. Then look up the underwriter in *Best's Insurance Reports* (reference area of the library) to see how they are rated. Deal with those companies with at least an A rating (A+ and A++ ratings are even better).

May 24

It should really be called "death insurance" because the intent of life insurance is to protect family members who are financially dependent on a wage earner who dies. The long-range goal of a family's wage earner is not only to pay the monthly bills but to build an estate with assets and investments capable of supporting the family once the wage earner is unable (or unwilling) to work. Each year the amount of death insurance required decreases because, theoretically, the growing estate is drawing closer to self-sufficiency. Until that time, however, death insurance is a stop-gap measure that leaves the family financially secure in the event the wage earner fills a coffin before the coffers.

♦ Whether you need life insurance at all is your first question. If you're supporting no children, have an employable stay-at-home spouse, and have an emergency fund capable of supporting that spouse for several months, life insurance may be unnecessary. If, on the other hand, you have children; want a good education for them; have a spouse with limited career experience who is unlikely to find a good job; or have considerable outstanding debt, then carrying term insurance may be a wise precaution. The face value of that insurance should be five to seven times the gross annual income of the family's wage earner.

♦ Interestingly, 10% to 15% of all life insurance covers children. If your progeny is Macaulay Culkin, you insure him, but parents who insure children who are not the wage earners of the clan don't get it. Life insurance should be taken out only on the wage earner upon whom the rest of the family depends. Insurance is not a wise way to save or invest money for your children.

♦ Most whole-life insurance, universal life insurance, and single-premium whole life insurance policies are a poor use of your insurance dollars. They provide "death insurance" but at inflated prices. The other benefits these policies tout (savings and investment plans, college funds, tax shelters, a full set of Ginzu knives) are usually a poor use of savings and investment dollars. True, a minority of whole-life and universal policies provide a reasonable return on your money. But if you buy inexpensive term insurance and invest the money saved in a *good* investment (e.g., a mutual fund), you'll outearn the best of these policies and avoid some truly horrid ones.

♦ Term insurance is the cheapest form of insurance. This is death insurance pure and simple: You pay $170 a year, for example, and your beneficiary receives $100,000 if you prematurely check into the Pearly Gates Motel. This can cost 75% less than the mumbo-jumbo policies noted above and buys you the same death insurance. And if you take the money saved and sink it into a real investment, you might actually pay for your kids' college tuition when that financially tragic day arrives.

♦ Several types of term insurance are available to you. *Decreasing term insurance,* in which payments are the same each year but the face value of the insurance drops, tends to be overpriced. That leaves *annually renewable term* (ART) policies and *level premium term* (LPT) policies as the choice buys for bargain hunters. Annually renewable term insurance is often the cheapest option. Once you qualify for the insurance, renewal is guaranteed the following year if you pay the premium—a premium that increases every year. Level premium term insurance lasts a given period (e.g., five, seven, 10, or 20 years)—and your payment and payoff remain the same during each year of the policy.

◆ Purchasing an adequate amount of term insurance and disability insurance gives you the coverage supplied by credit life insurance and credit disability insurance at lower prices. Therefore, credit life insurance (where upon death, the borrower's loans are paid off), and credit disability insurance (where upon permanent disability, the borrower's loans are paid off) should both be considered unnecessary duplicate coverage.

═══ May 25 ═══

Dig out your life-insurance policy and all literature describing your benefits.

◆ If you're currently investing in a form of life insurance different from term insurance (e.g., whole-life or universal life), call your insurance agent and discuss the consequences of surrendering your policy. Listen to what your agent says but don't take the advice as gospel. Remember The Rule of Suspicion? Get all the information about your policy's cash surrender value and its face value at maturity. Calculate how much this policy will have cost (in total) by the time it matures. Perhaps you'll discover that at this point in the game, you're entrenched in the policy and you should ride it out. But you may well decide your policy, when compared to the death coverage of term insurance, is costing way too much for way too little coverage and way too little invest-ment return. You won't know until you collect and study the numbers.

◆ Contact LifeRates of America (800-457-2837) a no-pressure, telephone brokerage that will take down the specifics of the insurance you want (be it term insurance or whole-life) and will then find you the lowest rates among the 200 best-rated underwriters in the country. SelectQuote Insurance Services (800-343-1985) is another firm that conducts its business over the phone and handles only term insurance. It sifts through the policies of about 15 different underwriters, all with at least an A-rating in *Best's Insurance Reports*. Both these companies will need to know your birth date, smoking habits, and the face value of the policy you desire. Call them and get some quotes coming your way.

◆ Initially, annually renewable term (ART) insurance is likely to be cheaper than level premium term (LPT) insurance (see yesterday's discussion). But because the premium of your ART policy increases every year, it will typically overtake the fixed premium of your LPT plan. You'll have to study the numbers of ART and LPT plans to decide which deserves your dollars.

May 26

What about savvy life-insurance buyers who have already seen the light of term insurance—what can they do to keep life-insurance costs down?

◆ As previously mentioned, ART rates start cheap and escalate slightly with each coming year. If you remain healthy and are physically able to qualify for a new ART policy, switch underwriters every three to five years. By sticking with the same underwriter year after year, you get stuck with higher and higher premiums. It's the old loss-leader scenario. The insurance company entices you on board with a low come-on, then it ups the rates each year, hoping the increase between any two years isn't large enough to make you jump. If you remain healthy, however, that's exactly what you should look into every few years. Jump ship and you'll capitalize on another underwriter's loss leader. Sometimes the grass *is* greener elsewhere.

======== **May** 27 ========

You pay hundreds of dollars a year for big companies to insure you. Today, for under a dollar, you will self-insure yourself against the loss or theft of a wallet.

♦ Take your wallet, all important cards, and all vital forms of identification to a photocopy machine. Laying multiple cards down on the machine at the same time, make two copies showing the fronts of all your precious pieces of plastic (license, social security card, voter's registration card, credit cards, debit cards, health insurance cards, living will, membership cards, calling cards...). Now flip the cards over and make two copies of the backs of all these cards (important phone numbers are often listed here). File one set of copies in a safe place at home, the other set in your safety deposit box.

♦ Make your spouse jump through the same hoops, using a photocopier at work.

♦ Rifle through your wallet (spouse's, too), making sure the PIN numbers affiliated with credit cards, debit cards, and calling cards are not within. If they are, write them in an unbreakable code.

How does all of this qualify as insurance? If your wallet is lost or stolen, it's going to take you hours or days to figure out what is missing, how to cancel financial cards, and how to replace this valuable deck of cards. These copies contain all the vital account numbers and phone numbers and will exponentially speed up this painful process.

And time is often money. Twenty minutes after one of my acquaintances had her wallet stolen, the thief had already extracted $250 of cash from her checking account and racked up another $200 on a charge card.

======== **May** 28 ========

Get this simple chore done fast, then go enjoy your kids, life, or a latte (homemade, of course). You'll want to perform this job two or three times a year, so get out the daily calendar and give yourself a reminder every four to six months.

Now, gather a length of hose, a bucket, some rags, and the manual for your water heater (if you can find it), and visit the water heater. You're going to drain a gallon or two of water and sediment from the faucet-like valve located at the bottom of the tank. Removing this sediment prolongs the heater's life and increases its efficiency.

With most water heaters, you'll screw the hose onto the faucet, twist the faucet counterclockwise (to start draining water and sediment), collect the soiled water in the bucket (keep draining water until the stream entering the bucket is clear), then twist the faucet clockwise to stop the flow. Naturally, if you found the manual to your water heater, you'll want to check its instructions. Men, of course, will ignore this last suggestion.

Incidentally, if you did find those instructions, keep them handy so you can ignore them again tomorrow.

═════ May 29 ═════

Another visit to the water heater to check the thermostat. First, however, turn off the power to the unit at the fuse box.

People commonly heat their water to 140°F, which is much hotter than necessary—to use this water, lots of cold water must be added. That's part of the reason the U.S. Department of Energy recommends setting your water heater at 120°F. The department also makes this recommendation to save energy. Every 10°F you turn down the thermostat, reduces the energy needed to heat water by 5%. Consequently, resetting the thermostat from 140°F to 120°F translates into savings of $60/year if you use electricity to heat water, $30/year if you use gas.

Unfortunately, not all dishwasher detergents dissolve at this temperature, so try yours. If you have dishwasher trouble at 120°F, try a new detergent or reset the thermostat to 130°F and try again.

Many water heaters have two thermostats. In this case, turn the top control to the desired temperature and set the bottom control 10°F cooler. Check your instructions to verify this is what your manufacturer recommends.

═══════ **May 30** ═══════

When you want to conserve the heat your body has produced, you wrap yourself in a blanket, right? That's exactly what your water heater needs if you want to cut your yearly energy bill by $35 to $51, depending on whether you heat with gas or electricity.

♦ First, call your utility company; many supply free (or very inexpensive) kits to insulate your water heater. If you strike out there, purchase a fiberglass-insulated blanket (sold for this very purpose) from a local department store. Average cost: $20.

♦ Second, install the blanket. Notice where the heater's thermostat controls lie, and, tape the blanket closed over these controls. On the outside of the blanket, use a pen to mark the position of the controls. Now, if you need to reset the thermostat, a short incision along part of the seam provides access.

♦ If you can't find a kit, wrap several length of 3½"-thick foil-backed fiberglass insulation (foil side out) around the water heater. Tape each wrap closed with contractor's sheathing tape along the axis containing the thermostat controls. Then, use horizontal strips of tape to seal the seams between the strips of insulation used.

♦ Not all blankets come with a hat—the piece covering the top of the heater. If absent, make a cap from a length of 3½-inch-thick fiberglass insulation or from a section of cushion-type foam. If the top of your water heater has vents, cut windows in your cap to allow the vents to breathe. Then, use contractor's sheathing tape to close the seams between the cap and the blanket.

May 31

The final measure to coax your tank into maximum performance is to install a timer, like the Little Gray Box (model WH40) or the WH80, both made by Intermatic Incorporated (Spring Grove, IL, 815-675-2321). Such timers shut off power to the water heater when hot water isn't needed (after bed, after the family leaves for work) and fires up the unit again when you need hot water (early morning and late afternoon). These units list for $85 and $112 respectively but will sell for about $60 and $76 at major home-improvement stores like Home Base. Considering a timer will pay for itself in two years, you're dimwitted not to spring for one.

Call Intermatic to find out where, locally, you can find their timers. Request a catalog describing the features these timers. Also, call local home-improvement/hardware stores to see which timers they stock and the benefits of their units.

Cheap Trick:

Whenever you leave home for more than a day, pinch pennies by heading to the fuse box and killing power to the water heater.

June

Sure, you have a lot to do, meals to cook, tasks from this book to complete, kids to get to appointments. But take time to slow down each day, too. Grab a bit of sanity each day. It's a lot cheaper than a therapist's couch when you blow a fuse. It's a lot cheaper than relying on drugs to unwind. It's a lot healthier than getting sick.

A few ways to slow down and/or gain more time:

- Keep the television off—keep it off for a week and you may be amazed how much more time you have.
- Don't jump whenever the telephone rings. You're not its slave, so when you're in the middle of something else, leave the phone to the answering machine.
- Do nothing. That's right, just sit for 15 or 20 minutes a day. Daydream. Let your mind roam while you sit.
- Listen to music. That's not the same as simply having it on. Sit down and listen to it. Listen to the instruments and what they are doing. Make sense of the lyrics.
- Keep a journal.
- Do something from childhood days—what did you really love then? Painting, riding your bike, collecting stamps, fishing.... Do it again.
- Spend quality time with your pet.
- Converse with your family—that's not the same as yelling instructions as you pass in the hall. Talk about

issues, feelings, books, movies. This is the verbal equivalent to keeping a journal.

◆ Just be. When eating a chocolate, concentrate on its smell and taste. When talking to people, give them your full attention. When walking, notice what's around you. Use your senses to their fullest.

June 2

With summer about to start, it's time to check that all family members own effective sunglasses. Good ultraviolet (UV) absorption is critical for sunglasses. The same UV rays that burn bare skin burn unprotected eyes, causing short- and long-term damage. Buy sunglasses that screen all UV radiation (100% UV filtration means all rays between 290 and 380 nanometers are absorbed). Most sunglasses (cheap and expensive) from outdoor specialty stores (skiing, backpacking, fishing shops) filter all the UV, but check.

After the UV rays come the violet/blue light (400 to 510 nanometers). Because recent evidence suggests these rays could be harmful to the eye as well, look for sunglasses that filter two-thirds or more of the blue light. Many manufacturers don't mention how much blue light their products filter, but nearly all lenses meeting the other criteria of good sunglasses filter out enough, meaning much of the blue-light hoopla is a marketing maelstrom. Beyond the filtration of UV and blue light, manufacturers boasting that their glasses screen more infra-red or mumbo-jumbo rays are simply creating hype to hike prices.

Good sunglasses should also limit the visible light reaching the eye. Experts believe that on bright days only 10% to 30% of this light should pass through the lenses, making sunglasses with a 20% transmission rate a good general-purpose compromise. Test this by donning sunglasses and looking in a mirror; your eyes should be very difficult to see. Skiers and beach bums need even darker glasses and should not be able to see their eyes when performing the mirror test.

Sunglasses worth owning should not distort your vision so the lenses should be ground, polished, and capable of passing prescription eyewear specifications. Hold the sunglasses at arm's length and look at rectangular objects:

The lines should be straight. If vertical or horizontal lines appear wavy or ragged, pass on the purchase.

Decent sunglasses should also be scratch resistant—i.e., made of glass, or covered with a scratch-resistant coating if made of plastic. Finally, they should be shatter-resistant and—for the truest color transmission—tinted gray, green, or brown.

To get all this you don't need to spend a fortune. Use these tests and read the literature accompanying the glasses and you'll find products that pass muster for under $20 (sometimes under $10 when purchased on sale). Pay much more and you're paying for name recognition or for fashion rather than function.

June 3

Summer and vacations—the two go together like, well, vacations and expenses. Because accommodations account for an elephantine percentage of holiday expenses, you have some homework ahead of you. Seeds planted now will bear cheap fruit later when those travels commence.

♦ A house exchange is a first-rate way for families to control lodging costs if their travels involve visiting one city for a week or more. Not only is lodging free but you may opt to swap cars, water each other's plants, feed each other's pets...options that all make travel easier and less expensive. Your homeowner's insurance should protect your home during a swap while your car insurance should cover your car (if the swapper uses it) and yourself (if you use the swapper's car). Call your insurance agent and ask about the limits of your coverage.

People living in or near popular travel destinations (Disneyland, ski resorts, Hawaii, New York City, etc.) are particularly likely to arrange a swap—such homes are in high demand. As a denizen of Okmulgee, Oklahoma, however, don't give up hope—miracles can happen.

Of the thousands of exchanges taking place each year, most are facilitated through home-exchange clubs publishing directories of people hoping to swap. Joining a club costs $50 to $80 and is a worthwhile expense because it gets your house listed in catalogs read by like-minded people.

Exchange clubs to contact today for their literature include: Vacation Exchange Club: Box 650, Key West, FL 33041, 800-638-3841 or 305-294-1448; Intervac US, Box 590504, San Francisco, CA 94159, 800-756-4663 or 415-435-3497; Trading Homes International, Box 787, Hermosa Beach, CA 90254, 800-877-8723 or 310-798-3864.

♦ Hospitality exchanges offer travelers another inexpensive lodging alternative. As a member of such a group, you are listed in a directory so that other members may arrange a short stay with you when they visit your area. In return, you may arrange to stay with any of the listed members when you travel. The goal of these groups is not simply to provide inexpensive lodging but to help travelers learn more about the area or culture they are visiting.

Organizations to investigate: U.S. Servas (11 John Street, Room 407, New York, NY 10038, 212-267-0252, about 14,000 members worldwide); INNter Lodging (P.O. Box 7044, Tacoma, WA 98407, 206-756-0343, mainly US members); The Hospitality Exchange (116 Coleridge, San Francisco, CA 94110, 415-826-8248). Call these groups and ask for their literature.

June 4

"The heaviest baggage for a traveller is an empty purse," says an English proverb. One sure way to empty your purse during summer travels is to pay full hotel fares. How do you beat paying $100/night for a pillow?

♦ Prepare to haggle. While people think of hotel rates as being fixed in stone, they aren't. They are commodities priced by the laws of supply and demand. Just as those rates can soar when a convention is in town, they can plummet when rooms lay idle.

Every city has its slack seasons—business centers like New York, Boston, and Chicago, for example, have slack seasons every weekend—and that's when visitors with the courage to ask, receive big savings. To talk your way into a discount, call several hotels late in the afternoon or early evening on the day of your arrival. By then, empty rooms are looking like lost opportunities. Working from a telephone, ask if the hotel has vacancies and at what rates. Casually query whether they offer discounts for AAA members, students, senior citizens, AARP members, government employees, frequent fliers, clergy members, nearsighted penny-pinchers, exconvicts....

If the hotel doesn't nibble, let your fingers walk to the next hotel listed in the *Yellow Pages*. If you do get a lower offer, don't take the first quote as final. Politely make a counteroffer—"That's a good rate but I can only afford a room costing about $X. Do you have a smaller room or can I qualify for a larger discount if I pay cash?"

If you don't get the rate you want, courteously say you need to consider the offer and that you'll call back if you want the room. Let a few more kids on the block bid for your business, then book with the wallet-friendly choice.

══════ June 5 ══════

The film canisters of 35mm film are extremely useful containers. Pull out a pad of paper now and think of 10 ways to put these receptacles to good use. Drawing a blank? Then circle some of the ideas below you could use.

1. Advent calendar. Cut a sheet of cardboard into the shape of a Christmas tree. Glue the bottoms of 25 canisters onto the cardboard. Glue a picture to the outside of each lid and place a surprise in each canister.

2. Condiments. Fill film cans with ketchup, mustard, or salad dressing for sack lunches and picnics.

3. Clamp protector. Glue the cap to the swivel end of a C-clamp to protect wood projects from clamp damage.

4. Drug and cosmetic receptacles. Kodak film canisters (with their tight-sealing lids) carry shampoo, hand cream, toothpaste, aspirin, sun screen, and other personals on short trips.

5. Electric cord holder. Remove the top and bottom of the canister. Use the hollow cylinder to corral the excess loops of electrical cords.

6. Fishing bobber. Lay the fishing line across the top of the canister and snap the lid on. To weight the bobber for improved casting, add water to the canister.

7. Hair rollers. Use as is.

8. Salt and pepper shakers. Poke holes in the lid with a fat needle (hot needles make the job easier and cleaner).

9. Spaghetti measurer. Stack uncooked spaghetti into an opened canister. A full canister makes spaghetti for two.

10. Swimmer's kit. Tape a lanyard to a Kodak canister. Use this floatable, waterproof container for keys and money.

11. Travel sewing kit. Load a canister with needles, buttons, safety pins, straight pins, and lengths of thread.

12. Weights. Fill canisters with sand to create weights to anchor your fabric while cutting.

===== **June 6** =====

Yesterday should have started the process. It should have had you wondering what other items could be resurrected from the trash and given a useful second life. Grab a sheet of paper and brainstorm about how you could reuse plastic bottles. Again, I've listed several suggestions that might spark ideas of your own.

MILK and BLEACH BOTTLES (PLASTIC)

♦ **Bailers.** Cut off the bottom of milk or bleach bottles, tape on the lid, and you've got a good bailer for a canoe or row boat.

♦ **Buoys.** Fill the bottles with styrofoam packaging peanuts and tape on the lid to make buoys marking crab pots, boat anchors, deadheads in the lake.

♦ **Bulk cleaners.** If you make your own cleaners, you will need a supply of gallon containers.

♦ **Clothespin holder.** Cut a fist-sized hole high in the jug, through which you can grab clothespins stored inside. Hang the jug on the clothesline by the handle and slide the bottle down the line with you as you hang clothes.

♦ **Emergency drinking water.** Clean bottles, fill with water, tape on the lid and store them in the basement for emergency drinking water.

♦ **Ice blocks.** Fill a milk bottle 7/8 full with water and freeze it. Then put it in your cooler for picnics or camping trips. After the ice melts, you have cold drinking water.

♦ **Old oil.** After changing your car's oil, store the old oil in plastic bottles. When the garage gets cluttered, dispose of the oil at a local recycling center.

♦ **Universal gym.** When filled with water, two bottles (one in each hand) serve as weights for myriad upper-body exercises.

PLASTIC POP BOTTLES (2-liter size)

♦ **Canteens.** Fill plastic pop bottles with water and take them on camping trips.

♦ **Bailers and scoops.** Cut off the bottom, screw the lid on firmly, and you're left with a bailer for small boats or a sand scoop for kids.

♦ **Funnels.** Cut off the bottom and throw away the lid and you've got a funnel. Cut the body down to make the funnel any size. Great for changing car oil.

♦ **Bowling pins.** Save 10 bottles, put a little sand in the bottom of each (for ballast), screw on the lids. Kids can bowl them down with a medium-size rubber ball.

═══ June 7 ═══

According to *The Green Lifestyle Handbook*, the yearly waste generated in the U.S. alone would form a convoy of 10-ton garbage trucks extending half way to the moon— 145,000 miles. The tips over last few days aren't going to solve the problem, but with the incentive that you are helping the planet while helping your pocketbook, think of more ways to reuse the items you normally toss.

On your pad of paper, make headings for old linens, newspaper, old clothes, coffee cans, egg cartons, margarine tubs, tin cans, jars, mesh bags, old socks and nylons, plastic bags, pie tins.

For newspapers you might decide to store the comics as gift wrap, shred some of it as kitty litter, and bury additional sections under bark dust in the gardens to inhibit weed growth. Coffee cans can be used as cooking on a camping trip. Egg cartons come in handy as a desk organizer in a child's desk, sock organizer in her chest, costume-jewelry organizer, or as a seedling nursery. Margarine tubs can become containers for leftovers, sandbox molds, camping bowls. Plastic pickle and peanut butter jars can store screws, nails, and sundries in the basement; or leftover paint....

June 8

In a review of plastic garbage bags, *Consumer Reports* found that many store-brands of bags were as strong as the national-brand bags and significantly cheaper (about 50% less in large sizes, 30% less in medium). Try several different brands and it won't take long to hone in on a store giving you high quality for a low cost.

♦ Of course the question that really begs an answer is this: Why do you use garbage bags at all? Not for your garbage—the plastic or paper bags that brought your groceries home from the store are perfectly adequate for handling your garbage—and they're free. Or why not throw your trash in the garbage can without a bag at all? Most waste management companies don't care. Sure, your can will cultivate an odor, but what's the big deal? A few times a year, throw in ½ cup of ammonia and a gallon of water, soak the can, scrub it quickly with a brush, and rinse.

June 9

Another lidded, plastic container should find its way into your kitchen. Place it next to the kitchen sink and deposit in it all your inedible, non-meat, food scraps (potato peelings, melon rinds, orange peels, coffee grounds, plate scraps). This is all material you can compost.

Composting in most people's minds means work—bins that must be built, rotting food that must be stirred, new dirt that must be redistributed. It means yet another junky-looking structure somewhere in the yard that will fall into disrepair when you tire of feeding it food scraps.

At its most basic level, however, composting is nearly effortless, it downsizes your trash (which saves you money by reducing the garbage you pay to have hauled each week), and it fertilizes your plants for free. Here's how lazy-man's composting works. Implement the system today.

◆ Start with the aforementioned plastic tub (about the size of a large coffee can). It lives beside the kitchen sink and, once full, is emptied into an outdoor compost can. Our outdoor can is actually a recycled plastic diaper pail with a 12- to 15-gallon capacity and a fast-on, fast-off plastic lid.

◆ Once the outdoor compost can is full (this takes a few months), bury the load in a hole dug in a flower bed, beside a bush, or along the perimeter of your property. The compost is not particularly smelly while it sits undisturbed by the side of the house, but some truly odoriferous slop will pour from the bucket when you dump it. That's normal.

◆ Mix several shovels of dirt in with this decaying matter, then cap the hole you've dug with the remaining dirt excavated from the hole.

◆ Give your compost can a quick rinse, drop a few inches of leaves or grass in the bottom (an optional maneuver to keep the bottom of the can cleaner), and you're done. Nature will gradually transform the buried food scraps into rich soil. It takes four to six months for that metamorphosis to occur, so in the intervening months, bury new food scraps in new holes.

June 10

Newspaper, magazines, writing paper, tin cans, aluminum, glass, and many grades of plastic—they're all recyclable. It would be a more agreeable world if everyone recycled for ideologic reasons—if they recycled because they recognized that while world population continues to balloon, forests, parks, wildlife, arable land, air quality, and water quality continue to shrink. It would be a more agreeable world if everyone contributed toward a solution rather than just to the problem.

But the truth of the matter is that many people who will not recycle for ideologic reasons will recycle for economic ones. If you happen to fall in with that crowd, I have money news for you: Recycling will help you cut your yearly payments to the garbage company in half.

♦ Do a thorough job of removing recyclables from your trash and the landfill-bound garbage you pay to have picked up will wither. If you pay your local waste-management company to haul away two garbage cans per week, change your service. You're likely to find a weekly "mini-can" will accommodate you. In my community, reducing the family's waste stream from two normal cans to a mini-can would save $131 per year.

My family handles our non-recyclable waste another way: We share a garbage can with neighbors who also recycle. Each week we carry our half-full can over to the neighbors who add their contribution and set the can out for the garbage truck. We receive one bill and split the damage. The joint effort saves a total of $214/year ($107 per family).

♦ Call your waste management company and ask what service options (mini-can, one can per week, one can per month) are available by slimming down.

♦ Rather than keeping up with the Joneses, join forces with them. Discuss sharing a trash can with some of the neighbors. Having two cans picked up at one residence (and cancelling service to the other residence) is another way to cooperate with a neighbor. Such an arrangement in my community would save you $73 per year.

The moral of all this: If your community has a curbside recycling program, get as much of your waste stream as possible—paper, cans, glass, and suitable plastics—into those curbside bins. If your community lacks such a program, contact the local *Recycling Services* listed in the Yellow Pages today and ask how to go about recycling your paper, cans, glass, and plastics. Ask how these items must be sorted and prepared, and when you can deliver them. Now make room in the garage and label a few boxes for the storage of recyclable paper, cans, glass, and plastics.

Next, clear room under the kitchen sink for a bag or box. Put empty bottles, rinsed tin cans (remove labels), recyclable plastics (squashed milk and pop bottles), aluminum, newspaper, magazines, and junk mail in this bag or box. When it fills, take it out to the garage and sort it into the appropriate boxes.

===== **June 11** =====

Envelopes are one of those products we use without thinking, but which we can happily survive without. Go to your desk and tie a shoestring around the box housing your envelopes. It's a reminder to do the right thing and an inconvenience when you do the wrong thing. Some ways to survive happily on a tiny supply of new envelopes:

♦ If you haven't purchased them already, put 1" X 3.5" envelope labels on your Master Purchasing List (see January 1). Boxes of 5,000 continuous computer labels can be purchased for $10 from the Office Depots and Costcos of the world and will give you a cheap, lifetime supply of stick-on labels. Use these to cover mailing addresses, return addresses, and postmarks on old envelopes worthy of reuse.

♦ Much of your mail does not need an envelope. Fold your letters in half (or thirds) tape them shut. Write the address on the back of the page, stamp it, then mail it.

♦ Send postcards. Not only do they fly for 38% less, but you can make free postcards from scores of materials around the house—photographic prints you no longer want, cut-up cereal and cracker boxes. Size requirements to receive postcard rates: no smaller than 3½" X 5", no larger than 4¼" X 6".

===== **June 12** =====

What do you do with the shipping boxes in which goods are mailed to you? You should save them. When you want to ship hand-me-downs to friends, presents to distant family, or defective merchandise back to the manufacturer, you'll pay a premium for new boxes. At the post office small boxes (6" X 6" X 6") sell for $1 and medium-sized boxes (20" X 14" X 10") for $2.50. Meanwhile, scavenging boxes from stores costs you time and mileage (35¢/mile). Today:

♦ Clear an area in the garage, attic, or basement for medium- and large-box storage. When you receive boxes, tear off (or black-out) the labels, slice the tape holding the box together, and collapse the box. A good collection of collapsed boxes can slip into narrow slots behind storage shelves, under workbenches, behind shelves along the garage walls....

◆ Also, find a crate or a box with about a 16" X 14" base. Use it to stack the padded shipping envelopes, video mailers, and small boxes you receive in the mail. Once again, tear off (or black-out) labels and collapse boxes before stacking them in your crate.

◆ Now all you need to mail your own parcels is packaging tape (use it to reassemble and seal your box) and a supply of stick-on labels for the shipping and return addresses. Note: 3" X 5" index cards can be used instead of labels—attach them by covering them with a few strips of clear packaging tape.

═══════ June 13 ═══════

Everyone wants your money. Sheriffs want to send underprivileged kids to the ball game (or jail), the Sierra Club wants money to fight the G.O.P., the G.O.P. needs money to defeat the Sierra Club, the high school wants to send the local band to Europe, and the mail arriving today has yet a new request.

So how do you keep from handing out so much that you're not the next one in need of a handout? And how do you accomplish this without feeling like you possess a raisin for a heart?

In an issue of *Simple Living*, a quarterly newsletter, readers shared their ideas on this topic. Following are some interesting ideas:

◆ Once a week and once a year. A reader from California reported that during the course of the year her family collects all requests for money in a file. Once a year (in December) the family does their budgeting, decides which organizations they will support, and doles out the funds accordingly. When they receive calls for donations over the rest of the year, they politely explain their policy, and wish the organization well. Regarding the innumerable requests the family receives from special interest groups trying to lobby government officials, the reader reported she sits down once a week and writes one letter on the issue that strikes her as most important.

♦ Pick a passion. Another reader from Washington says she picks a cause and volunteers time only. "Giving money may be quick and easy but who knows where your money is actually going?" How do you pick a cause? "Volunteer for one cause for three or six months, then try another until you find one that fits."

♦ Concentrate on a few. You can't fix all the world's problems and that shouldn't make you feel guilty. You can, however, help a few causes. Yet another Californian reader focuses her attention on several organizations she truly believes in and refrains from diluting her contributions. "Whenever anyone calls me asking for donations, I simply say that I'm already supporting other groups."

♦ The 3/3/1 System. A family from Wisconsin reported that at the end of each year they decide, as a family, who to support during the coming year. They dole out the amount budgeted to donations by giving first to three organizations they are committed to supporting each year. Then they give to three causes they are supporting that particular year—these three organizations may change from year to year. Finally, they save one contribution for a special occasion that is bound to arise during the year—like a donation to honor the memory of a special person. When they are approached during the year for contributions, they explain they make all their donations at one time but mention they will be happy to consider the group at that time.

I've adopted what several of these systems advocate (dealing with all requests but once a year) and I can report that it is both emotionally and financially liberating to have a system in place that dictates how you will respond to the sea of pleas. Time for you to choose a system.

If you decide to adopt a once-a-year system, label a file for all requests. As the pleas pour in, stack them together.

For information about the newsletter *Simple Living* contact Simple Living Press, 2319 N. 45th St, Box 149, Seattle, WA 98103, 206-464-4800.

═══ June 14 ═══

Rick Hack, a Seattle lawyer working downtown in a classy high-rise office, nets an income that makes free-lance writers like myself green, but I forgive him that trespass because he refuses to squander his earnings. Most admirable of his money-saving measures is his commitment to living with a single automobile. Not many Americans of Hack's means and marital status (married and the father of three) make this choice.

Hack's reasoning is partially economic—even an old car that is completely depreciated has insurance, licensing, operating, and maintenance costs that will siphon a bare minimum of $2,000 from the family. Add a newer car to the mix, whose high sticker prices should be depreciated as a yearly expense, and the cost of owning even a relatively plain-Jane compact averages some $4,500 per year. Furthermore, in Hack's case, were he to drive to work each day he'd pay $1,440/yr to park the beast.

Hack's commitment to the one-vehicle lifestyle is also a quality-of-life issue. He receives far more exercise than the average American. And while most families believe a single car would immeasurably complicate life, Hack insists the opposite is true. "You have to say 'No' to a lot of opportunities if you don't own vehicles to shuttle every family member everywhere they want to go. Being able to say 'No' really simplifies life. You become much more involved with your family, neighbors, the local community—and that enhances the quality of your life."

Finally, Hack believes in the power of example. "When I talk about making choices to save money or help the environment, it means something to my children because they see me making this choice."

How does the man make do?

Usually he rides his bicycle (an hour each way) to work. Compared to colleagues who battle rush-hour traffic in the car for 40 minutes and then take time from their schedule to exercise several times a week, Hack believes the bicycle commuting saves time and reduces stress. Hack used to take the bus to work, but now prefers the exercise and the time out in the elements.

Occasionally, Hack takes the family car to work and his wife is *sans* wheels for the day.

For some business occasions or special weekends, he rents a car (weekend rates for rentals are particularly cheap). He also calls on the occasional taxi for a ride. His $600 per year expenditures on rentals and taxis is pittance compared to car ownership.

Evaluate this issue today. Could your family eliminate a vehicle? Pull out city maps and research whether safe bicycle routes lead to the work place. What mass transit options exist to support your daily routine and your spouse's? Do your buses have bicycle racks (more and more cities are providing this option) so that a combination of busing and bicycling could get your spouse to work quickly? What car-pooling options exist?

Talk about this with your spouse and discuss mothballing a vehicle for a two-month trial. Like Rick Hack you might be surprised how many financial and emotional benefits stem from this one change.

═══════ June 15 ═══════

Yesterday's discussion may have inspired you to depend less on a vehicle and more on a bicycle. But exposing fragile flesh to tons of hard steel may strike you as foolhardy. Statistics beg to differ: The odds of death while biking are one in 88,000 per year while the odds of death while driving are one in 8,000 per year.

Statistics aside, don't let anyone in the family two-wheel the roads until they are properly equipped. Saving money on mileage isn't of much use if it lands you in the cemetery. Following are suggestions from Rick Hack, a lawyer who has bicycle-commuted the streets of Seattle for the past three years.

◆ While any bicycle can maneuver the streets, Hack, who has sampled many types of two-wheelers, finds mountain bikes the safest. The upright position is comfortable and puts you in a good position to monitor traffic. The wide tires increase safety when negotiating potholes, rough shoulders, wet roads, and unexpected obstacles.

◆ Of the 1,000 people who perish in bicycling accidents each year, 85% of the deaths are attributed to head injuries. Doctors say many of these deaths and thousands of additional cases of brain damage would be prevented if riders wore good helmets (ones that are ANSI or SNELL approved). Commuters, kids riding to school, and children riding tricycles in the driveway should all be wearing helmets.

◆ For efficiency, equip your mountain bike with a tire designed for pavement (like the Continental Top Touring).

◆ Front and rear fenders (like the full fenders made by Zefal) make wet-weather commuting far more pleasant. They also reduce the water and grime reaching the bike's components, cutting the maintenance a bike will require.

◆ Bicyclists are hard for motorists to see. Wear optic (neon yellow, hunter orange) jerseys or windshells. A hunter-orange, nylon-mesh vest with reflective strips that slips over what you're wearing is an excellent investment.

◆ Riders out around dawn and dusk should be especially concerned about being seen. Use reflectors on the front, back, and wheels of the bike. Wear a reflective vest. Also don reflective anklets or shoe straps. Nathan Reflective Wear (800-835-0800) makes a good line of inexpensive, nationally distributed products.

◆ For twilight and night riding, lights to be seen are far more important than lights to help you see—the ambient lights around most urban and suburban communities provide enough light to ride, but not enough light to make you plainly visible. Flashing lights (like Vista Lites) on the front and rear of the bike are crucial for night riding. One set of batteries will power these lights for months.

◆ Mirrors mounted to the helmet or handlebar ends help you monitor traffic from behind. They'll help you avoid overtaking vehicles that seem oblivious of your presence.

◆ Other important accessories: minimal tool kit, patch kit, pump, day pack or bike bag, U-lock, toe clips or clipless pedals, water bottle and bottle cage, chain/derailleur lubricant.

◆ Mail-order sources of these items: Bike Nashbar (800-627-4227), Performance Bicycle (800-727-2453), and REI (800-426-4840).

June 16

When you treat yourself to popsicles or fudgesicles, save those wooden sticks, run them through the dishwasher, and store them in a drawer.

Later, you can make your own ice cream bars during summer picnics and barbecues. Here's how.

Buy inexpensive half gallon cartons of vanilla, strawberry, or chocolate ice cream (yup, stock up during sales). When it's dessert time, open the carton to expose the entire box of ice cream. With the ice cream resting on one of its broadest side, use a carving knife to cut it along its long axis (longitudinally) into halves. Now cut across each of these halves (transversely) and partition each half into seven or eight slices of ice cream (each slice will be 1 to 1½ inches wide).

Poke a popsicle stick into each slice and you've created 14 to 16 "creamsicles" for under $2. For picnics, where you want to dress up the finished product, roll the bars in crushed nuts.

A point of interest: If you have kids interested in making money at local fairs, picnics, or parades, encourage them to set up a concession selling these bars for 75¢ to $1 each. Buy unused popsicle sticks at the store if you're going into business.

══ June 17 ══

Like most ex-VW Beetle owners, I've broken down on remote roads all over the country. I own real cars now, but I still carry a vestige from the old days—a box in each car with emergency tools and supplies. Even with real cars, those supplies have saved me from engine meltdowns, unplanned nights at roadside motels, and expensive tows.

What's in the box? Besides the standard stuff (tire jack and chains) I carry a selection of second-hand tools purchased at pawn shops: standard-slot and phillips-head screwdrivers, crescent wrench, box wrenches, needle-nose pliers, standard pliers, vice grips, hacksaw blades, socket wrenches, spark plug remover, pocket knife. Next there's the duct tape, extra motor oil, water for the radiator (at least a quart), spare fan belt, tubeless-tire repair kit and bike pump, plastic tarp to lie on, rags, flashlight (count on problems occurring at night), baling wire, nylon cord, and first-aid supplies. Then there's a miscellaneous selection of bolts, washers, sheet metal screws, and hose clamps. Finally come the items for personal safety: a blanket, first-aid kit, coat, matches, and umbrella.

My other vehicle—the one I have less confidence in—also packs a set of jumper cables and about 40 feet of thick rope for that day when I can't fix a problem and need a tow to the nearest service station.

Go around the house, collecting what you can for this cause. Flush out your car kit with visits to thrift shops, pawn shops, and discount department stores. Those items that cannot be found cheap, or are currently too burdensome on the budget, should go on the long-term shopping list today. Add them to your toolbox over time.

══ June 18 ══

Take a wild guess: What does it cost, on a per-mile basis, to drive your car? Ten cents a mile? Twenty-five cents a mile? Write down your guess.

The true cost of driving may surprise you, for it incorporates such components as: fuel, maintenance, insurance, depreciation, and licensing.

Call the library today and ask the reference librarian to look up the per-mile cost of driving your make of car in *The Complete Car Cost Guide.* Here are averages for vehicles purchased in 1995:

◆ Subcompact cars: 34¢/mile
◆ Compact cars: 39¢/mile
◆ Mid-sized cars: 43¢/mile
◆ Large cars: 49¢/mile
◆ Luxury cars: 65-75¢/mile

Write down the per-mile figures applying to your vehicles and tape these figures in prominent spots (the dashboards, the ashtrays) inside each car. Leave the figures in place for several weeks—they will remind the entire family of what these machines cost to operate and prompt all of you to forego frivolous chores.

═════ June 19 ═════

In a survey of master technicians certified by the National Institute of Automotive Service Excellence (these are the top mechanics in the country), 99% of those polled said that changing the oil and oil filter frequently were the most important chores in maintaining automobiles.

Oil has a monumental job to perform: It cleanses, cools, lubricates, and seals the space between the cylinder and piston rings. Its ability to do all these jobs diminishes with time and use. And as it soils with each mile driven, the suspended dirt grates away at the guts of your engine.

Your owner's manual probably advises an oil change every 6,000 to 8,000 miles or every six months (whichever comes first), but most mechanics believe an oil and filter change every 3,000 miles (or three months) adds years of life to an engine. This belief is supported by a *Consumer Reports* poll in which car owners, who had logged over 100,000 miles without major repairs, shared their maintenance secrets. The majority changed their oil and oil filter more frequently than normal (every 3,500 or fewer miles).

◆ Learn (or force another family member to learn) how to change the oil and filter in each car. As you'll see by consulting your owner's manual, it's an easy job. Although it will take you an hour to change the oil the first time, the job will take 20 minutes thereafter—that's far faster than taking the car to a garage. It's also cheap. The tools needed include a crescent wrench, an oil filter wrench, a plastic drain pan.

Dispose of your oil responsibly (i.e., not in the trash or down the sewer). Store it in old milk bottles and occasionally deposit it at a recycling center. Call a mechanic, parts store, or city hall for the whereabouts of such a center.

◆ On your daily calendar, estimate when each car will need an oil change during the year ahead and mark a day when the job is to be done. The average American drives 13,000 miles a year, so Mr. Average should have a reminder on the calendar to change the oil every three months.

◆ What oil should you use? Check your owner's manual or call the dealer for recommendations. At the very least, check the label to see that the oil meets new-car warranty requirements. Also, if your climate allows it, use 10-30 oil over 10-40—the extra viscosity gives added protection. Unopened bottles of oil do not have a shelf-life problem so stock up when you find a good sale.

◆ Regarding oil filters, don't assume that any filter that screws to your car will work. Different filters remove different-sized particles. You want your filter to eliminate the particle sizes that the manufacturer deems most damaging to your cylinders. Make sure your filter is recommended for your model of car and buy good filters (i.e., those that are mid-range or higher in price). Put oil filters on your long-term buying list and stock up when they come on sale—auto-part and department stores frequently discount them.

◆ Do you save money pumping your own gas? If so, don't neglect the other chores that go along with a full-service fill up. Chores like checking the oil. Let your car run out of oil (self-servers do this frequently) and the sage who pumps his own gas becomes a stooge. So...check the oil regularly yourself or get a full service fill-up from time to time.

June 20

Your car is going to need tuning, it will need preventive maintenance, it is going to break down. Where should you take it when it needs servicing: the dealer, an independent mechanic, a national chain? I avoid dealers as much as possible. Call around for what dealers charge—be it for a clutch replacement, new brakes, or a head gasket—and you'll discover they consistently charge one-and-a-half to two times more than independent mechanics.

How do they get away with such highway robbery? Car owners let them. Many owners take their car to the dealer by habit: After all, that is where they took the vehicle for all its warranty checks. Later when something goes wrong, (ding) the Pavlovian response is to visit the dealer. Many car owners also believe that only the dealer can fix their car. Not true, but it keeps the dealers busy enough to fleece their faithful sheep.

For a fairer deal, spend a few hours today searching out several independent mechanics in your neighborhood. How do you find good ones? Call several local auto-parts stores stocking parts for your make of car and ask for the managers or assistant managers. Tell them the type of car you own and ask if they know a good independent mechanic who can repair it. Emphasize that price is an issue: You want quality work at a reasonable price. These managers will most likely know several independent mechanics with good reputations who can work on your car. Note them on an *Auto Repair* card for your Rolodex—you'll be ready for that unpleasant day when the beast goes lame.

Following are additional tips for finding a good mechanic and protecting yourself from over-priced (or dishonest) ones.

♦ The nearest office of the American Automobile Association (AAA) can tell you which repair shops in your neighborhood are AAA rated. To get an AAA rating, the shop must meet equipment specifications, employ certified mechanics, and consistently prove it is providing high levels of customer satisfaction. These garages may not be the cheapest on the block but they do offer a guarantee of sorts, and guarantees are hard to come by in the auto-repair business. Any dispute with an AAA-approved shop is arbitrated by AAA and the shop must abide by AAA's decision.

◆ Ask friends, neighbors, and relatives about mechanics they'd recommend.

◆ Look for repair centers certified by the National Institute for Automotive Service Excellence (ASE) and check that some of the mechanics are certified with the ASE as Master Technicians. If the certificates aren't displayed, ask to see them. Check that the certificates are current.

◆ When your car does fall ill, getting a second opinion is as valid a practice in the mechanical world as it is in the medical one. If one mechanic paints a gloomy (and expensive) picture, fashion a feeble excuse (you've got to check your finances) and leave. Take the vehicle to one or two other mechanics before settling on a treatment plan. It is acceptable to ask that the price quote be written down and that the mechanic contact you if the work is to exceed the quote (put this in writing, too).

◆ Before work actually begins, ask that replaced parts be kept for you. Later, look at the parts, ask why they needed replacing, ask what warranties cover the new parts.

===== June 21 =====

Each year about 42,000 Americans die in car accidents. Think about that a minute. Over a three year period the highways will claim *twice* as many American lives as our decade-long involvement in the Vietnam War. In a country with a population of 250 million, each member of your family has—very roughly—about one chance in 6,000 of not surviving the war zone of the highway this year.

Fortunately, statistics don't account for driving habits, and you can dramatically boost your personal odds of survival by adopting smart driving habits. These habits not only significantly increase the chances that you and your family will die of old age, they'll decrease the likelihood of expensive fender benders. So...from this day on:

◆ Drive with the headlights on—regardless of the time of day. Studies from Finland, Sweden, and Canada show a 28% reduction in frontal and side accidents among vehicles using daytime headlights. Why? The headlights are far more visible to other drivers who may be changing lanes, pulling into traffic, crossing intersections, or passing.

In many newer vehicles, the headlights automatically shut off with the engine (even if the headlights are still on). In this case, keep the lights on permanently.

Older cars don't offer such intelligent electronics. It's up to your intelligence to prevail—kill the daytime lights or the battery dies. I rely on a reminder to accomplish this goal. I keep a clothes pin on the dashboard; when the daytime headlights go on, I clamp the clothes pin onto the door lock. When I exit the car, I encounter the clothes pin and am reminded to check the lights. Figure out a similar reminder system for your car.

Organized as I am, I'm still prepared for the day when my system fails: I keep jumper cables in the car. Sure, occasionally attending to a dead battery is inconvenient, but a fatal crash will really ruin your day.

June 22

Advertising has convinced many drivers to buy gas with more octane than they need. Premium gas does not deliver additional power or improved mileage, so get the cheapest gas that keeps your car from pinging (knocking) when it is working hard. Most cars in this country were designed for regular unleaded gas (87 octane). However, while only 10% of today's cars need a mid-level or premium gas (89 and 91 octane), over 30% of all car owners buy premium.

Look up your vehicle's octane requirements in the owner's manual. From this day on, save your money if you've been using Bordeaux to water a beast designed for Gallo.

June 23

The average American car travels about 13,000 miles a year. Because the average car gets about 25 miles to the gallon, figure your yearly gas bill is roughly $675 per car. Adopt the following driving habits and you can make each gallon of gas take you some 15% farther. That's a saving of $90 per car.

◆ Not using the roof rack? Remove it; cars with racks are 10% less efficient. Amazing how two bars affect aerodynamics.

◆ If you don't own radial tires, switch over next time you buy. Compared to bias-ply tires, radials deliver an extra mile per gallon. They last much longer, too.

◆ The Environmental Protection Agency (EPA) reports that you will save gas by turning off the engine if your car will be idling more than a minute.

◆ When you double your speed, you nearly quadruple your air resistance. That's why a car logging 28 miles per gallon at 55 mph receives only 22 miles per gallon at 65 mph. Slow down.

◆ Putting the pedal to the metal between city intersections may impress members of the opposite sex but it robs you of the money needed to take them out. It wastes gas, places unneeded strain on the transmission, and wears the brakes. Experts recommend you drive as though eggs were taped to your gas and brake pedals. Work the pedals lightly, as if trying to keep from crushing the shells.

◆ On the highway, cruise control is more efficient than speeding above, then coasting below, the speed limit. Cruise control is also handy for ticket prevention—most new cars cruise so smoothly it's easy to awaken from a daydream with the State Patrol on your tail.

◆ Idling your car for several minutes before driving is not a good use of gas. Furthermore, if the automatic choke is set so the car revs at high RPMs as it sits, that idling damages the vehicle. Avoid all the prewarming. Turn on the car and go. But do the car a favor and drive slow and easy for several miles while the engine warms up.

◆ A cold engine burns twice as much gas as a warm one, so run all of your driving errands at the same time to take advantage of your warmed-up engine.

◆ On the downhill, let gravity help you: Ease up on the gas. At red lights, slip vehicles with automatic transmissions into neutral: The habit reduces gas consumption and engine wear.

June 24

Washing the exterior of your vehicle is important to prolong its good looks and resale value, but washing the engine occasionally may be more important in prolonging the vehicle's life. Dirt and grease coating the engine trap in heat and can trigger a meltdown.

Pick up a can of engine degreaser from an auto-parts store (e.g. Engine Brite or Gunk's Steam). Now visit a car wash with a high-pressure hose. Spray on the degreaser (following instructions on the can) and let the degreaser sit for about 15 minutes. Then, with the car running, rinse the engine with a high-pressure water spray, being careful to keep the spray off the distributor and out of the air intake.

June 25

It's surprising how few people fail to hide a spare key on the exterior of their car. The money and time this saves on that day when (not if) you lose your keys or lock them in the car, makes it ludicrous not to have a backup handy.

No need to spend money on fancy magnetic key boxes— they are more easily located by thieves, are not waterproof, and can fall off the vehicle. Just locate a well-hidden spot on the chassis, clean it with a rag, center the spare key on a strip of duct tape, and rub the tape onto the chassis.

Get spare keys made for all your vehicles and find a hiding spot. Hint: Position the hidden key in roughly the same area of each car—a year from now when you've locked yourself out, it's frustrating not to remember if this was the car with the key hidden in the front or rear. Toward this end, place a cryptic reminder in your wallet (that will mean nothing to a burglar) directing you to the hidden key.

═══ June 26 ═══

The old television ads focused on diapered children playing as some authoritative voice proclaimed, "Michelin. Because so much is riding on your tires."

A lot *does* ride on your tires, so don't be crash foolish in your attempt to be tread wise. Check the tread thickness of each tire in several places with a ruler. Measurements below 1/16" (or if you can see tread-wear bars across the width of the tire) are illegal and unsafe.

Start thinking now about the replacement of tires that are nearing the 1/16" mark. Put them on your long-term shopping list and monitor the sales and wholesale warehouses. Toward the goal of making a wise purchase, keep the following in mind:

◆ Throughout much of the country, the use of all-season radials eliminates the need to purchase snow tires. All-season tires are the most frequently purchased tires, thus the best engineering goes into them. These tires remain soft at cold temperatures and incorporate an aggressive tread design—two features giving them reasonable traction in snow. They don't deliver the traction of a snow-and-mud tire, but they perform well enough to winter the roads around much of the country. This saves you the initial cost of purchasing snow tires and the annual cost of mounting them.

◆ The cost of a new tire is a poor indicator of quality. So is the brand name. Each major manufacturer produces some very good tires and some very mediocre ones. Spend an hour in the library thumbing through consumer and automobile magazines and you'll unearth valuable tips. For example, knowledge that the Dunlop Axiom not only outperformed the Michelin XA4 but cost $60 versus $95 per tire, would save you a hefty sum, especially when you multiply the savings by four.

♦ To help you interpret their size and quality, all-season tires come with a lot of information printed on the sidewall. Most of that information is in an obscure code you must learn to read.

The words "Tread wear" will be followed by a number like 100 or 300. This tells you, on a relative basis, how much life you can expect from the tread. Under the same driving conditions, a tire with a rating of 300 will wear three times longer than one with a rating of 100. A tire with a tread wear of 300 that costs $40 is a much better buy than a tire with a tread wear of 100 that costs $29.

The "Traction" rating ranks a tire's stopping ability on wet streets. Grade A is best, C worst.

The code following "DOT," tells you the tire's age. By looking at the last three numbers in the code "DOT XF E5 X JJX 405," any idiot would know the tire was *obviously* made during the 40th week of 1995. You want fresh tires, not ones that have hardened with age, so purchase those that are less than a year old.

===== June 27 =====

You checked them yesterday, now plan their rotation schedule today. Ideally you want to rotate your tires every 6,000 to 9,000 miles. The goal of rotation is to help the tires wear—and wear out—uniformly. Check your car manual for the recommended rotation scheme.

A common misconception about radial tires is that you must not change the direction the tire turns (i.e., wheels cannot be rotated between different sides of the car). This was the accepted practice in the early 1980s but no longer holds true. New radial tires can be rotated front to back *and* side to side without worry.

Assuming the tires on your vehicles haven't been rotated in quite some time (this is, after all, one of those tasks most of us manage to sweep under the car mats) assign a family member to that task. Also, pull out the daily calendar, guesstimate when each of your vehicles will be due for the next rotation, and enter the appropriate reminders.

If your car is older and the manual recommends moving radials only from front to back, you may not be maximizing the wear on your tires. Get a free copy of the *Consumer Tire Guide* (Tire Industry Safety Council, Box 1801, Washington, DC 20013) and check out the rotation scheme for your type of vehicle.

===== **June** 28 =====

About a week ago you learned the true cost of operating your cars and posted the per-mile price of driving inside each car. You've had a week to ponder the fact that frivolous driving is not frivolous at all; you've had time to think about how you can reduce the mileage you're adding to each car's odometer. Now it's time to really attack the problem.

◆ Toward the goal of reducing your spouse's work-related driving, thoroughly research the mass transit options today. Check out buses, subways, and car pools. Get scheduling information on these options over the phone, and ask that schedules for the appropriate buses and subways be mailed to you.

If the workplace, is nearby get your spouse to consider bicycling or walking to work whenever the weather co-operates—this hones both the body and the budget. Also, ask your spouse to talk to others at work—perhaps car-pooling with colleague makes sense.

◆ Toward the goal of reducing the miles you drive, investigate these same options for yourself. Does community transit make sense? How many of your errands (to drop off videos, pick up milk, mail packages) could be done by foot or bike, giving you a financial excuse to exercise? Are there neighbors you could pool with for running kids to school, with whom could you alternate running petty errands?

Consider, too, ways of ganging up your weekly errands so that they are all done in one grand circuit rather than in many petty junkets. How can your working spouse help here? Can you plan the pick-up and drop-off of kids, laundry, mail, groceries, and videos around the car that is already out on the road?

♦ Make a list of options that makes sense for your family and discuss these tonight. Set a target of reducing your driving by, say, 30 miles a week. For a mid-sized car, that translates into a savings of $12 a week or $600 a year. That's worth some walking.

══════ June 29 ══════

In recent surveys of the work force, only small percentages (2%) report that keeping up with the Joneses had any redeeming value. That public confession, however, is not consistent with the way people act in private. In truth, most of us spend vast sums of money and energy keeping up with those to whom we compare ourselves. Maybe you don't buy an Audi because your neighbor does, but if you're the only one in the neighborhood with an old car, doesn't it make you want a new one? When you visit the ski slopes, don't you want up-to-date gear? When you go out with friends, don't you worry about wearing something stylish? When you visit a college classmate in her 5,000 square-foot house, don't you feel like a trophy home would declare you a success as well?

Few things will keep you so enslaved to the monthly paycheck as competing materially with friends and neighbors. Many of you will deny you're a victim of Keep-Up-With-The-Joneses Syndrome but the first step toward curing the problem is admitting it. Answer the following true-false statements.

___After a car is three or four years old, I either get (or want) a new one.

___Even though I already own a home, moving into a new home is one of our family's top priorities.

___I feel like an underachiever when I compare my accomplishments to my classmates'.

___Year after year I turn over more than a third of my wardrobe.

___The impetus to buy many of our toys (adult toys or children's toys) originally came from friends and neighbors who told us what they own.

___If I won a $1-million lottery, our family wouldn't have trouble using all the money.

___I enjoy reading about the newest restaurants, movies, vacation spots, people, foods, music.

___I read these or similar magazines: Glamour, Vogue, GQ, Esquire, Cosmopolitan, Gourmet, Conde Naste Traveller, Mens' Journal, Home, House Beautiful.

Are four or more of these statements true for you? Then your tendency to keep pace with others is stronger than you think. You're unlikely to get your money to really work for you unless you stop playing Keep Up. It's to your own self that you must be true—get out the Mission Statement you prepared (Chapter 2) and put that sheet where you'll read it multiple times a day over the coming week. Hanging it on your headboard or beside the toilet are good bets.

You might also want to print a reminder on that goal sheet. Here's what works for me—I've written "Joneses" across the bottom of my goal sheet and crossed the word out with a big red X. It's primitive but it keeps reminding me to avoid a game I can't win.

═════ June 30 ═════

Rather than keeping up with the Joneses, have you ever thought about joining forces with them? Consider how many of your possessions—rototillers, garden tools, power tools, camping equipment, sports equipment, canoes, books, slide projectors—collect dust 95% of the year. You're not unusual. Each of your neighbors also has a large fleet of dust collectors. Which means there's a ton of money wrapped up in little-used possessions in your neighborhood alone. If you could lend and borrow amongst one another, everyone would benefit. That's where the concept of a borrowing exchange comes in. Follow these steps to establish such an exchange:

◆ Decide what you're willing to lend—go through the garage, attic, basement, and closets looking for tools, toys, gardening hardware, sports equipment, appliances, books, tapes, camping gear, and party supplies you're willing to lend. Make a master list.

◆ Draft a set of rules applying to your items. The rules should address: how long the borrowed items may be kept (e.g., two days unless otherwise agreed upon), your return requirements (borrowed items must be as clean or cleaner than when received), damage settlements (items damaged during use will be repaired at borrower's expense), damage settlements for failure resulting from normal wear and tear (mechanical items do break, even when properly used—a borrower shouldn't be fully responsible). It's your stuff; draft rules you can live with.

♦ Call friends/neighbors you would like to lend to and borrow from. Explain the concept of a borrowing exchange. If they're interested in the idea, send them your list and rules. They can send you their list and rules later.

Emphasize that your list is only for those you have given it to (you don't want it passed on) and that lists received are for you only (you won't pass them on to others). You may set up borrowing/lending agreements with quite a few families, but you want control over who is privy to your stuff (friends and neighbors who mistreat their stuff shouldn't get a crack at mistreating yours).

July

July 1

You probably know that using a vehicle's air conditioner reduces gas mileage—the belts engaged to turn the air conditioner increase the engine load and gas consumption some 7% to 10%. If 4/40 cooling (four windows down at 40 mph) can keep you comfortable, forget about the air conditioner.

But did you know that at freeway speeds open windows disrupt aerodynamics and can reduce a vehicle's mileage by as much as five miles per gallon? So during the hot months ahead, use your vehicle's air conditioner when traveling faster than 45 mph.

July 2

Air conditioning defiles the utility bill more than heating. On average, each degree of temperature drop precipitates a 5% increase in energy consumption. Keep the house at 77°F versus 70°F and you'll cut the cooling bills by over 35%. Resolve to keep the house a little warmer come summer, and use the day to prepare for the uncomfortably warm weather to come.

Walk the home, closing all vents to your forced-air heating system. Don't let the cool air from the air conditioner vacate the house through the ducts. Remember, cold air sinks.

July 3

Loose-fitting windows can leak cooled air five times faster than properly installed windows. Test yours on the next windy afternoon by moving a burning candle around the perimeter of each window (from inside the house). If gusts of wind disturb the flame, you need caulking or rope caulking to seal gaps around the windows.

Caulk from inside the house for best results. Caulking the outside creates a moisture barrier, but is not as energy efficient. If you're unsure about what caulk to use, ask a hardware-store employee. Before heading into the store, note the materials the caulk will be bonding to (e.g., wood siding on one side, metal window frame on the other), the color it must match, and the width of the gap to be filled (some caulks that bond and wear well do a crummy job of filling anything over a ½-inch gap).

Never caulked anything? It's easier than diapering a squirming two-year-old. Get the store employee to give you a quick lesson, or head to the library and ask the reference librarian for a book covering caulk talk.

Resources worth referencing or owning include: *Consumer Guide to Home Energy Savings* (by Wilson and Morrill, American Council for an Energy-Efficient Economy, 2140 Shattuck Avenue #202, Berkeley, CA 94704, $6.95) and *How to Weatherize Your Home or Apartment* (Massachusetts Audubon Society, Educational Resources, 208 South Great Road, Lincoln, MA 01773, $4.25).

July 4

A true attic fan is typically mounted horizontally in the ceiling of a room below the attic—that is to say, in the floor of the attic. In the evening of a hot day, (once the outside temperatures start dropping) the fan is switched on and air sucked from the cooler rooms of the house is blown into the attic to force hot air out the gable vents. Meanwhile, cool air from outside flows into the house to replace the air blowing into the attic. Come morning, when outside temperatures begin to rise, the fan is shut off for the day and the house is shut up to preserve the cool evening air trapped inside.

In northern latitudes of the country, an attic fan can eliminate the need for any air conditioning. Even when temperatures hit the mid to high 80s, such fans keep a house completely comfortable. Studies show that in southern climes attic fans decrease the need for air conditioning some 30% to 50%, hacking $150 to $200 off the yearly utility bill.

Attic fans keep temperatures pleasant at a pleasing price because they draw relatively little power. For example, a 400-watt attic fan costs 3.6¢/hour to run, a three-ton capacity air conditioner, by comparison, costs 38¢/hour.

In an ideal world, you'd hire a contractor to install an attic fan with louvers that automatically slide closed (to hide the fan) when the fan is not spinning, an insulated panel to seal the ceiling hole (to avoid losing atmospheres of hot air) in winter, and a timer to run the fan. The cost of such a system would run between $300 and $600.

In the real world of tight money, however, you can scrape by with a quality extension cord feeding electricity to a department-store 20-inch fan positioned over the entrance to the attic or even positioned to blow air out one of the gable-end vents. Operate the fan by plugging and unplugging the extension cord at the appropriate times. Or, use an inexpensive 24-hour timer (available from hardware and department stores) to activate and deactivate the fan.

═════ July 5 ═════

The summer heat wave is either upon you or will arrive soon. If you don't own an air conditioner—or simply don't want to use it (your utility bills will show you that cool comfort doesn't come cheap), use the following tips:

♦ Ventilate the attic in the evenings with an attic fan (see July 4).

♦ Fetch the sleeping bags from the attic. During blistering weather, bed your kids in a cool basement or outside on a cool porch. Inexpensive Coleman or White Stag sleeping bags are a tenth of the cost of a room air conditioner. Also, camping out on the porch or in the backyard makes an adventure out of a night's sleep.

◆ Barbecuing your dinners outside will keep both your abode and body cooler.

◆ At night, draw cool air into your home by opening doors, drapes, and windows. Come morning, close up the house to seal in that cool air. Close the drapes in the morning, too, to keep the sun's rays from undermining your work.

◆ Another evening task for blistering days: Hose down your roof with water (wait until the evening sun is no longer striking the house) and you'll shorten the time your home feels like an oven.

◆ Early in the century, midwesterners and southwest-erners relied on swamp coolers to take the sting out of hot weather. Water was dripped down through wood excelsior which absorbed the water. A fan would blow air over the wood excelsior and the evaporating water would cool the air.

Use the Edison in you to adapt this concept to your advantage. Direct the fan past a hanging, wet sheet; make a frame that holds strips of wet linen that will dangle in front of the fan; position a fan so it blows air over a pail of water...

Note: the swamp cooler is only effective in hot, *dry* climates. If your relative humidity is always high, you won't get much evaporation—and, therefore, not much cooling.

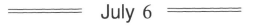 July 6

Whether the moisture comes from the sky or a sprinkler, established lawns require an inch of water per week to stay green. When the soil gets dry to a depth of four to six inches (use a trowel or a short length of pipe to get a core sample), it's time to irrigate. Here's how you should conduct those waterings to minimize cost.

♦ Most Americans over-water their yards by nearly 30%. How long should sprinklers stay on to deliver an inch of water? A simple test (performed once) answers that question. Set up four cans at different distances from the sprinkler and let the water run. Check the cans every few minutes and note the time it takes *each* can to accumulate an inch of water. Add these four times together, divide by four, and you're left with the average time to run the sprinkler.

♦ Water slowly so the moisture sinks in rather than runs off. Do the job properly and the soil will be moist down to a depth of six inches.

♦ You'll use less water (and time) giving the yard one good weekly soaking instead of several sprinkles. A thorough soaking is also better for the grass because, as the soil dries, the plant must maintain deep roots to find water. Sandy soils may require two waterings a week.

♦ Water your yard in the early morning or evening. Sprinkling at midday (or on windy days) can use three or four *times* more water. Experts greatly favor morning waterings so the grass can dry during the day (better for avoiding fungus).

♦ For more thorough—and free—information about watering, order the booklet *Efficient Use of Water in the Garden and Landscape* from the Texas Water Development Board (P.O. Box 13231, Capital Station, Austin, TX 78711, 512-445-1467).

July 7

To really shave the water bill, stop watering a well-established lawn once the drought days of summer arrive. The grass will go into a brown dormancy. Worry not, grasses survived for millenniums before we came along with our hoses. The grass will green up again when the rains of autumn arrive. In the event that those autumn rains never arrive, start watering again in mid-September to revive the grass and give it time to manufacture food for winter.

♦ While it's OK to cut juice to the lawn, don't abuse ornamental shrubs—if they brown, they're unlikely to green-up again. Here's a way to water those shrubs cheaply and with little time involvement. Put an end cap on an old hose (or one purchased at a garage sale) and run it past (or around) the shrubs in a bed. Drill a 1/64" hole at each shrub (don't over-do the size). Now you can deliver water (at medium pressure) to your shrubs without watering the space between shrubs where you want to discourage weed growth. The first time you use this soaker hose, time how long it takes to properly water the shrubs—that will make subsequent sessions a no brainer. Create a soaker hose for each bed you water, then use one feeder hose (connected to the faucet) to deliver the water.

══════ July 8 ══════

Coffee lovers should try this hot-weather variation of their favorite addiction:

Brew your morning coffee per normal but as soon as the coffee finishes dripping, get it off the burner and into the refrigerator.

Later in the day when you need a refreshing break, put a few ice cubes in a tall glass, fill the glass with a mixture of coffee and milk (I add a touch more coffee than milk), and sugar the concoction to taste. Sit down in the shade and, until the kids manage to seek you out and destroy the atmosphere, let your iced coffee and imagination carry you to places far from home. Consider this inexpensive break a valuable mood enhancer.

Encourage your spouse to try the brew at work as well. If s(he) has access to ice s(he) can tote the mixture of cold coffee and cold milk to work in a thermos and pour the mixture over ice during an afternoon break. Toting this coffee fix to work will set the family back about a fifth of the $2.50 that would be spent if your spouse orders an ice coffee from a coffee stand.

July 9

Statistics gathered by the United States Department of Agriculture indicate that in 1994 the average couple (without children) spent $3,845 per year ($10.54 per day) on groceries. My wife and I were feeling smug: Our yearly grocery bills for our *family* (we have two young children) came in at $3,768. Felt smug, that is, until we compared figures with my parents, who paid less per person still *and* who ate steak when we ate hamburger. It dawned on me then that the storekeepers loved me; I was financing the college education of their children rather than saving money to educate my own kids.

Which got me thinking—just how much can people pare down their food bills? By sticking religiously to the commandments of smart shopping that will be shared with you over the next 10 days, most middle- and upper-class Americans can slash those bills in half.

However, not all of the following commandments will make sense for your lifestyle. Employ those commandments that are easy to follow, skip those that aren't, and you're still likely to put a 30% dent in your bills. Not bad for embracing a few commandments.

#1: SHOP THE SALES, EAT THE SALES

This commandment gives you the most savings for the smallest time investment. Try it this week by changing the way you plan your meals. Rather than sitting down with your recipes and deciding what you will prepare, go right to the weekly ads of the grocery stores you regularly shop. With the sale items before you, plan your menus.

If chicken thighs, sirloin tip steak, and cod are at bargain prices, find recipes to capitalize on these specials. Check the pantry and freezer for foods to complement these meats, then scan the sales for additional vegetables and starches to round out your meals.

The same approach works for lunch. After noting which refrigerator and freezer foods should be used, plan the additional lunches needed around the cold cuts, cheeses, sandwich spreads, and soups found on sale. Buy vegetables, fruits, and snacks on special to complement the main fare. Ditto for breakfast.

Planning the weekly menus in this fashion takes little, if any, extra time. I find the process faster than browsing the recipe box because I deliberate less over what to make; the specials lead me to quick decisions.

My dad, who is the chef of his roost, shops the specials and visits two or three stores each week for their sale items. This gives him more diversity in deciding what to serve; it also allows him to stock his pantry with a wider array of sale items. I lack the time to shop many stores, so my selection is reduced. Nevertheless, I can buy 80% of the food needed for the coming week from the specials. Adhering to this one tip will slash your yearly food bill by at least 25%. Try it a while and get it working for you.

═══ July 10 ═══

#2: KNOW A GOOD PRICE

This is not a skill you'll develop overnight but one you should build upon every time you shop. Why bother? Because 15% to 20% of the items highlighted in the specials are listed at normal prices. You don't want to buy these "specials" under the illusion that you've scored a deal. Furthermore, in some stores the aisle-end exhibits (products you assume to be on sale) are not discounted at all; you need to recognize the impostors from the real McCoys. At other stores, you'll see yellow price-reduction stickers on hundreds of items. Unless you know prices, you can't identify the good pitches from the sucker balls.

The pitches to swing at are the ones giving you a discount of at least 25%. And when discounts drop to 40% to 50% below normal price, you want to stock-up big (see the Third Commandment).

I keep a master list featuring the several hundred foods, cosmetics, toiletries, and pharmaceuticals I buy. On this list I note the normal price, and sale prices I've seen for each item. Later, if I've forgotten these figures (it is, after all, difficult to remember prices of items bought but a few times a year), I can check my list to see how good a sale price is.

You needn't be this compulsive: Just don't shop like a zombie. Keep your brain turned on, pay attention to prices, and after five or six months you'll develop a sense for good deals.

================= July 11 =================

#3: STOCK UP

When a product is truly on sale (i.e., 25% off its normal price), and especially when it's offered at loss leader prices (40% to 50% below normal price), buy enough of the product to tide you over until it comes on sale again. How often items are discounted varies from product to product, but if at all possible (i.e., if freezer space or pantry space allows it) stock a three- to six-month supply of the sale item.

The goal is to *never* pay full price again. No one achieves that goal completely, but the more you stock when the price plummets, the less you'll need when it rises.

Pantry space is important toward this end. You may lack a huge kitchen pantry, so roam the house today searching and organizing usable nooks in closets, cupboards, the basement, the garage, beneath the stairs, under beds... Think about inserting more shelves in the existing cupboards, under sinks, or above the washer and dryer. Can more shelves be built in the basement? If you have an uninsulated garage with exposed studs, nail in dozens of narrow shelves between the studs and store nonperishables out there.

It's far easier to play the stock-up game successfully with a stand-alone freezer. Meat consumes about a third of the food budget, and a freezer lets you stock protein at digestible prices.

Consider this commandment more than a matter of food, consider it a form of investment as well. Stocking up on products sold at loss-leader prices gives you a 50% return on products used within a year. Furthermore, Uncle Sam is not taxing you on capital gains. Can you name a money market, mutual fund, stock, or bond that competes with that rate of return?

===== July 12 =====

#4: STICK TO THE GAME PLAN

Supermarkets are selling machines: The aroma from the bakery is meant to instigate a feeding frenzy, exhibits of food at aisle heads are traps for impulse buyers, staples like eggs and milk are purposely placed farthest from the entrance and cannot be reached without passing hundreds of other appealing products, candy is placed by the register where kids will pester parents for a purchase.

The Wall Street Journal reports that 53% of grocery purchases are made on impulse. Before you even step into the supermarket, food companies and manufacturers have spent some $6 billion a year on advertising to weaken your resistance. With all this working against you, studies have shown that shoppers often spend twice what they anticipated on their groceries.

Your defense? Arrive at the store with a grocery list and stick to it. Don't succumb to impulse buying. Remain flexible only to the extent that you will consider the unadvertised specials you find. Add these to your purchases or substitute them for other items on your list. Otherwise, stick rigidly to the list. This list affords a good excuse when your kids impulsively grab packets of cookies or candy. Tell them with a voice of finality, "Nope, it's not on the list."

Be just as hard on yourself when chips or pastries tempt your senses and override your sensibilities.

♦ How was this all-powerful list created?

It is the product of two grocery-store lists hanging on the refrigerator door. One list, the Batter's-Up List, features items needed to survive the coming week, regardless of whether those items are on sale. The second list, the On-Deck List, features items you don't need yet but whose stocks have run low and are in need of replenishing when the price is right.

Each week as the main grocery buy is being prepared, the current Batter's-Up List comes down (hang a clean sheet in its place). As you study the supermarket ads featuring the weekly specials, decide what meals will be prepared (see First Commandment) and add to the list accordingly. Now, check the On-Deck List and prepare to stock up on those items that are currently on sale.

July 13

#5: SHOP ONCE (AND ONLY ONCE) A WEEK

Yesterday I discussed tactics supermarkets use to tempt you into impulse buying. Sticking to your list (yesterday's commandment) is one defense. Another defense is to reduce your exposure to temptation by shopping but once a week.

The commandment has other benefits. It forces you to budget food efficiently during the week. If one night you scarf down the extra pieces of chicken you intended to use for the next day's meal, you may find yourself fasting. And it saves you from the hassles and expense of running back and forth to the store for a cube of butter, a few apples, snacks for the kids...

Everyone may have a harsh week or two adjusting to once-a-week shopping. But if you don't give in to kids who suddenly ran out of snack food, or if you learn to substitute another spice for the basil you forgot to purchase, everyone will adapt to this time- and money-saving way of life.

July 14

#6: SUBSTITUTE, EXPERIMENT

This commandment works nicely in conjunction with the last (shop for food but once a week). Many people worry about following the letter of their recipes as though the slightest deviation could transform ambrosia into Alpo. Lighten up. Recipes were not brought down the mountain by Moses, they were created by people who were dallying. Don't be concerned about dallying yourself—about finding a detour around an expensive ingredient you'd rather not purchase. If a recipe calls for half a teaspoon of a spice you never use, substitute a similar spice or omit it altogether. If a stew calls for a can of peas but canned beans are on sale, switch. If a recipe calls for a cup of bacon when you have leftover ham in the refrigerator, use the ham.

Following are ways to use cheaper products you may have on hand for costlier ones a recipe demands. Copy the list, hang it in the pantry, and add new discoveries of your own.

- Arrowroot (1 tablespoon): Substitute 2/3 tablespoon flour or ½ tablespoon cornstarch.
- Baking powder (1 teaspoon): Substitute ¼ teaspoon baking soda plus ½ cup plain yogurt; or ¼ teaspoon baking soda plus ¼ cup molasses.
- Brown sugar (1 cup): Substitute 1 cup white sugar and 1 tablespoon molasses.
- Butter (1 cup): Substitute 7/8 cup vegetable oil.
- Buttermilk (1 cup): Substitute 1 cup yogurt, or 1 cup milk with 1 tablespoon vinegar or lemon juice.
- Chocolate, unsweetened (per square): Substitute 3 tablespoons cocoa powder and 1 tablespoon butter.
- Cornstarch (1 tablespoon for thickening): Substitute 2 tablespoons flour.
- Corn syrup (1 cup): Substitute 1¼ cup sugar plus ¼ cup water; or 1 cup honey.
- Cracker crumbs (1 cup): Substitute 1 1/3 cup bread crumbs.
- Cream, heavy (1 cup): Substitute 1/3 cup butter plus 3/4 cup milk.
- Creamer, for coffee: Substitute powdered skim milk.
- Egg yolks (2): Substitute one whole egg.
- Flour, cake (per cup): Substitute 1 cup all-purpose flour. Replace 2 tablespoons all-purpose flour with 2 tablespoons cornstarch and sift several times.
- Flour, self-rising (per cup): Substitute 1 cup all-purpose flour plus 1½ teaspoons baking powder and 1/8 teaspoon salt.
- Lettuce for sandwiches: Substitute celery leaves or thinly sliced cucumber.
- Honey (1 cup): Substitute 1 cup sugar plus ¼ cup water.
- Milk, skim (1 cup for cooking): Substitute 1/3 cup instant dry milk (nonfat) and water to make 1 cup.
- Milk, whole (1 cup): Substitute 1 cup nonfat milk and 2½ teaspoons butter.
- Mozzarella cheese: Substitute equal amounts of jack cheese.
- Nuts, any kind: Substitute equal quantities of cheaper nuts.

♦ Nuts, for cookie recipes: Substitute equal quantity of oatmeal, puffed rice, or puffed wheat.
♦ Prunes, pitted and minced: Substitute equal quantity of raisins.
♦ Sour cream (1 cup): Substitute 1 cup plain yogurt.
♦ Tomatoes, chopped (1 cup): Substitute ½ cup tomato sauce and ¼ cup water.
♦ Wine, cooking: Substitute equal quantity dry table wine.

July 15

#7: TRY STORE BRANDS

In most supermarkets you'll find goods under three different labels: national labels (brand names), house labels (store brands), and economy labels.

National brands are the most expensive because they are heavily advertised. Consider a box of cereal: About 30% of the cost covers the food while 15% of the cost represents gross profits. The remaining 55% covers advertising, promotional games, coupons, and glitzy packaging. Much of this advertising and packaging brainwashes us into thinking we pay more because we are getting a higher-quality product. In truth, we pay an extra 15% to 20% solely to offset the advertising costs spent baiting us.

Store or house brands are typically of equal quality to the national brands. In fact, the same plants packaging brand-name foods often package the store brands for major grocers like Safeway, Albertson's, A&P, and Kroger. Stories abound of store employees opening cases of their house-brand and finding packages of name-brand product mixed inside. In many food-processing plants and canneries, the identical fruits and vegetables go into bags with different labels and different price tags. With canned soups, stews, chili, etc., national brands have their own patented recipes and may taste different, but the actual foodstuffs are of no better quality.

The benefit of store brands? The store, with a built-in market for its label, spends less on advertising and can offer products of equal quality for 15% to 20% less. Studies conclude it is cheaper to buy store brands than national brands with cents-off coupons. Unless you use your cents-off coupons in combination with sale prices (a valid practice but one requiring considerable time and organization), store brands save you time and money.

Some people steer clear of store brands altogether because a few have disappointed them. Undoubtedly they have also been disappointed by national brands—stews that offended the palate, cereals smacking more of cardboard than food—but they learned which products they liked and which they didn't. Store brands are no different—you'll find products you fancy and others you don't.

In your journey to experiment with new labels, be aware that major grocery stores usually stock both a house brand *and* an economy brand. Economy brands are often identified through a thrifty name like Scotch Brand or Cost Cutter and may cost 20% to 40% less than national brands. However, they can be lower-quality or irregularly sized goods. The food is safe and healthy—it must meet FDA standards and regulations—but the aesthetics or texture may not equal house or national brands. If you are unsure whether a label qualifies as an economy or a store brand, ask a store employee.

═════ July 16 ═════

#8 SHOP DIFFERENT STORES

Instead of pricing merchandise with a flat markup of, say, 20%, grocers use a variable system to price each item individually. Their goal: Lure you inside with their discounted specials and then quietly make a profit off the non-sale items that have been priced to earn back the discounts that lured you in.

Stores use variable pricing to their advantage in other ways. They keep a selection of visible staples at very low prices, often well below what competitors charge. They'll sell other staples at a mid-range price. Then they mark up less frequently purchased merchandise, merchandise buyers are unlikely to know the value of. Stores can make you believe their prices are lower than average when, across the board, they are mid-range or high-end.

By paying attention to prices (Second Commandment) you can beat the supermarkets at their own game. Shop several different stores to learn which staples each discounts. The local Safeway may discount mayonnaise, frozen orange juice, cheddar cheese, and flour, while the local Super Saver may offer excellent prices on milk, hamburger, sugar, bread, and canned soups. Consequently, the next time you are in Safeway purchasing the specials for the week, stock up on their discounted staples. Same goes for the Super Saver when the specials take you in that direction. Milk each store for its bargains and ignore the offerings designed to milk you.

An axiom to this commandment: Don't play supermarket games. Games encourage you to shop one store. Collecting trading stamps or receipts to claim prizes is sinful for the same reason. Shop at one store only and you become the victim rather than the master of variable pricing.

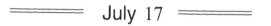

July 17

#9: BUY DATED GOODS

As a culture, Americans are incredibly spoiled. Bread turns a day old, we call it stale; meat sits in a cooler for a few days, we think it rancid; dairy goods pass their "sell-by", we call them toxic. We are so paranoid about old food that stores are hard pressed to be rid of it unless they slash prices.

Stores may still have difficulty selling it, which explains why tons of perishables (fruits, vegetables, dairy products, baked goods) get trashed every day. Before it gets trashed, however, you can often net a deal.

Beef sitting under fluorescent lights for a few days is often steeply discounted because it develops a greenish patina; it is still perfectly safe and perfectly delicious. Day-old bread may have lost its downy softness but is still fresher than the bread in your pantry that you've been eating without complaint. Dairy goods, if kept refrigerated, will keep long past the "sell by" date printed on the label. Vegetables that look shoddy will still be excellent for cooking if used promptly. Aging fruit will still be sumptuous for fruit salads, baking, or fruit milk shakes.

Today, call all of the grocery stores you frequently shop and talk to the store managers about how they handle their dated goods. Is there a particular area where dated goods are moved, are these foods grouped together on a particular shelf in their department, or are they simply given discount stickers and left alone? Are there particular days of the week offering budget shoppers the best selection of dated goods? Do certain times of the day (morning? late evening?) offer a better selection of dated goods?

Note the salient details of your research (in your Rolodex under Grocery Stores) and use the knowledge to advantage on future shopping forays.

═══════ July 18 ═══════

#10: COUPON LAST

Believe what the shopping experts demonstrate on television and you'd believe that with coupons and rebates you can buy the entire grocery store and get money back. Only in your dreams. Coupons and rebates *can* save you money, but they have major pitfalls.

For starters, these practices are time-consuming: The average devotee spends about eight hours a week for a 25% to 30% savings (people who are short on time can achieve the same savings much faster by shopping the sales). Coupons and rebates also encourage impulse buying: Studies show couponers are more likely to buy things they don't need just to use the coupon. Finally, cents-off coupons for brand-name goods won't save you money unless you combine their punch with a sale. Otherwise, it's cheaper to buy store brands.

All this said, if you enjoy couponing as a hobby and employ the coupons wisely (use them on sale items and resist impulse buying), you'll definitely spend less bread buying your bacon.

♦ Should any of your local supermarkets sponsor double-coupon days, the practice of couponing is instantly more worthwhile. On such days, the face value of the coupons you present is doubled (i.e., you'd be credited 50¢ for each 25¢ coupon). Most stores don't sponsor such days and the practice is absent in many communities. Nonetheless, take a few minutes now to call all your local supermarkets to ask whether they sponsor such days. If the practice is alive and well in your community, you may decide couponing holds far more value than I give it credit for.

═══════ **July 19** ═══════

#11: CHECK THE RECEIPT

Check what you're charged for groceries. Do it in the store immediately after you've received the receipt. Mistakes are common and, more often than not, they contribute to your impoverishment rather than your retirement.

It's not that the stores make dishonesty a policy, they simply may have mistaken your golden delicious apples (a sale item) for granny smith apples (a nonsale item), or their scanners may not have been reprogrammed with a sale price, or the code for the produce you selected (because it was the most affordable of the options) may have been incorrectly entered (meaning a higher-priced item is likely to register).

♦ For small mistakes, you may decide hassling the clerk is not worthwhile. But mistakes are often sizable. My wife, for example, just recently had an incorrect code entered and was overcharged $20.

♦ Many stores maintain a policy that if a scanner overcharges, you receive the item free. Therefore, the advantage of finding a mistake may amount to more than the quarter you're overcharged.

♦ The commandment works both ways. When you're undercharged (not that this happens frequently), pay up. There's a difference between frugality and dishonesty.

═══════ **July 20** ═══════

When you shop for food, be discriminating over the bag of carrots, potatoes, or apples you buy. Also be picky about the head of lettuce, the cucumber, the celery stalks, or the bunch of radishes you grab.

What do all these things have in common? They are usually sold at a set price. A two-pound bag of carrots sells for 89¢, a five-pound bag of potatoes for $1.19, a head of lettuce for 79¢. While the bag price of all the carrots or potatoes is the same, the weight of different bags can differ. Weigh a few bags of carrots and you'll find them to be a minimum of two pounds, but you'll discover that a few are a half-pound portlier than others.

Go through the same antics for celery sold by the bunch and lettuce sold by the head and you'll usually cart away an extra half pound of salad. Might as well take free food when it's offered.

===== ## July 21 =====

Remember the food commandment about not being concerned about substituting and experimenting? Following is a list of substitutes for seasonings, herbs, and spices. Study the list, copy it, and tape it inside the cupboard containing your spices.

SEASONINGS AND SPICE SUBSTITUTES

♦ Allspice (1 teaspoon): Substitute 3/4 teaspoon cinnamon, 1/8 teaspoon ground clove, and 1/8 teaspoon nutmeg.
♦ Basil: Substitute marjoram or thyme.
♦ Bay leaf: Substitute mint.
♦ Caraway: Substitute anise.
♦ Catsup (1 cup): Substitute 8 oz can tomato sauce, ½ cup brown sugar, 2 tablespoons vinegar.
♦ Cayenne pepper (1/8 teaspoon): Substitute 3-4 drops liquid hot pepper.
♦ Celery seed: Substitute chopped celery leaves.
♦ Chives: Substitute scallions.
♦ Cilantro: Substitute Italian parsley.
♦ Cumin: Substitute turmeric.
♦ Dill: Substitute caraway.
♦ Fennel: Substitute anise.
♦ Lemon juice (1 teaspoon): Substitute ½ teaspoon vinegar.
♦ Mustard, prepared (1 tablespoon): Substitute 1 teaspoon dry mustard.

- Onion (1 cup chopped): Substitute 1 tablespoon dried minced onions.
- Oregano: Substitute basil, marjoram, or thyme.
- Paprika: Substitute cayenne.
- Parsley: Substitute basil.
- Rosemary: Substitute mint or sage.
- Saffron: Substitute turmeric.
- Sage: Substitute rosemary.
- Tarragon: Substitute chervil.

July 22

Americans spend a third of their food budget on meat, partly because meat is expensive, partly because Americans eat 50% more meat than the government's recommended daily allowance (RDA) stipulates. Time to trim what you spend on meat.

◆ Casseroles, stews, and soups slash meat expenses without slighting the RDA for protein. Thumb through your cookbooks for recipes that go heavy on vegetables, pastas, rice, and beans, and light on meat. Mark or copy these recipes and experiment with them over the coming weeks.

◆ Stir-fry meals use half the meat of standard American dinners. Experiment with these recipes, too.

July 23

Your mission, should you choose to accept it, is to continue streamlining meat expenditures today. Pay a visit to the library and thumb through any interesting cookbooks you find, looking for casseroles, stews, stir-fry meals, pasta dishes, bean and rice recipes.... Check the vegetarian cookbooks for no-meat ideas. And look through promising specialty cookbooks that can arm you with both low-meat ideas—books like *The Incredible Potato Cookbook* by Consumer Reports, *The Brilliant Bean* by Sally and Martin Stone, and *Beans and Rice* by Williams-Sonoma.

Your job in evaluating these recipes is to avoid creations that, while they may be low on meat, rely on expensive or exotic ingredients. Your job is also to remember that you can substitute or eliminate the occasional expensive ingredient (see the seventh food commandment).

Copy a crop of promising recipes and then start in on the real Mission Impossible—preparing them for your family during the weeks ahead. Take credit for the hits and, for the bombs, let the Secretary disavow any knowledge of your action.

July 24

You've been gathering recipes for casseroles, stews, and soups. In the coming weeks as you prepare these meals, try this: Double the dishes you make and freeze one of the portions. Doubling your output increases your preparation time now by about a third. So while it costs you a little extra time now, it saves you loads of time *later*.

Equally important, it's going to save you loads of money. You'll save on foodstuffs because you can buy them in larger quantities. You'll save on utilities because the oven is already fired up. Mainly, on those days when you're too frazzled to face yet another tour of duty in the kitchen, you'll save yourself the expensive alternative—taking everybody out for pizza.

July 25

Some final thoughts about slimming what you spend on meat. Incorporate these tips into how you buy, prepare, and serve your meals.

◆ Once mayonnaise, onions, celery, and spices are added to tuna in salads and casseroles, the taste difference between expensive white tuna and cheaper chunk tuna is undetectable.

◆ A *Consumer Reports'* test of over 35 brands of pork bacon did not find consistent taste differences among the brands. The magazine recommended buying by price. Because different brands have different percentages of fats, the uncooked cost of bacon varies from the cooked cost.

Nonetheless, the cheapest uncooked bacon is almost always the best buy.

◆ Frying thin strips of ham is more economical than frying bacon. It's also healthier.

◆ Paying more for brand-name chicken is folly. Pick your label by the per-pound price. Then pick a package with plump thighs and breasts.

◆ Boneless chicken or turkey breast can be substituted for veal scaloppine or cutlets. The taste and the savings are both pleasing.

◆ Make good use of the freezer to stockpile meats purchased on sale.

◆ When meat is prepared as a stand-alone dish, serve small portions. Satiate your family's big eaters (teenagers) with large (or extra) helpings of fillers—potatoes, rice, salads.

◆ The serving of food is extremely psychological. Put a huge platter of meat on the table and your family (especially the men and teenagers) are likely to devour what you intended to serve as leftovers tomorrow. Put out only the meat budgeted for the meal, however, and civilized humans will pick out their share (re-educate children who behave uncivilly). So... make a habit of exhibiting only what is fair game for the evening. Or serve the food yourself in the kitchen, giving everyone their meat quota at that time.

Changing what you serve and how you served is likely to elicit grumbles from your family—people are narrow-minded about their stomachs. But while you may receive flack about uprooting family traditions, remain steadfast. It is important to buck counterproductive traditions. Like T.S. Eliot says, "A tradition without intelligence is not worth having."

Give it time. Your family will adapt. A year from now when you serve up a huge sirloin steak purchased at a give-away price, they may even tell you, "There's no way I'm eating that disgusting slab of cow."

═══ July 26 ═══

Next to meat, nothing bruises the food budget like snacks. Besides costing a pound of flesh, candies, chips, and cookies have the unpleasant habit of leaving unwanted pounds of flesh behind—or on your behind. The wisest advice is to avoid these foods. Keep them off your shopping list and, once inside the supermarket, stick rigidly to the list (the fifth food commandment).

When snackmania strikes, rely on one of these cheaper options: popcorn, peanut butter or jam on toast, graham crackers, raisins, peanuts, brown sugar and cinnamon on toast, carrot sticks, celery stalks (salted or topped with peanut butter), granola, English muffins and honey, pretzels, sandwiches, ginger snaps, instant pudding, saltines and peanut butter, fresh fruit, applesauce, fruit cocktail (canned), house-brand ice cream, or yogurt.

◆ A $15 hot-air popcorn popper has proved an amazing budget saver around our home. Several times a year we purchase 12-pound bags of unpopped corn at Costco (a membership warehouse) for $2.75. A huge bowl of popcorn for family snacks costs under a dime, and that includes margarine and utility costs.

═══ July 27 ═══

Simplify using carrots, celery stalks, broccoli, radishes, and raw cauliflower as snacks by washing and cutting these vegetables in quantity. Store them, immersed in water, in a plastic container. Now when someone requests a snack, these veggies are as convenient as cookies to serve.

◆ A no-cook, no-trouble method of extending the life (and improving the flavor) of cut vegetables is as follows. Wash 'em, slice 'em, and drop 'em in a clean jar. Then add a dill brine made from one part white vinegar, two parts water, and sprigs of dill according to your taste. Tomatoes, cabbages, cauliflowers, peppers, cucumbers all keep well this way. Refrigerate.

◆ Also, if you're fond of gourmet pickles, reuse the leftover brine when the pickles are gone. Cut up cucumber rounds, carrot sticks, celery stalks, and soak them in the leftover brine.

===== **July 28** =====

One trick that keeps snack foods from devouring the food budget is to employ the Dollar Rule: Any snack food costing more than $1 per pound doesn't come home with you.

Many of the options mentioned yesterday will always pass the test—unpopped popcorn, carrots, celery, toast with a topping, English muffins with a topping, seasonal fruit, applesauce, store-brand ice cream (half-gallon boxes weigh 2½ pounds), yogurt...

Many other snacks will make the grade only when purchased on sale. This includes such offerings as brownie mixes, fruit cocktail (canned), licorice, tortilla chips, pretzels, house-brand graham crackers, saltines, cake mixes, and ginger snaps. But, remember, if these items aren't on sale, they don't come home.

◆ Remind yourself to use the Dollar Rule by grabbing two red circular stickers and writing "$1/lb" on them. Place one sticker on your Batter's-Up List, the other on your On-Deck List.

===== **July 29** =====

Milk shakes without ice cream? Call this a cool (and cheap) way to while away the blistering afternoons of summer.

Place 2 cups skim or 2% milk in the freezer for 70-90 minutes (time varies depending on the temperature of your freezer). Pull out the milk when ice crystals have turned it into a slurry, add the desired fruit and flavoring, then blend (or shake). Try this today and decide whether to make the trick a summer staple.

══════ July 30 ══════

Here's the miracle of turning one gallon of milk into two—for 30¢. Add one gallon of milk to one gallon of water, then stir in 1½ to 2 cups of powdered whey.

Unlike extending real milk with powdered milk (which requires an acquired taste) this recipe is *almost* as good as the real McCow. Whey milk does taste chalkier, but if you didn't know the milk had been altered, you *might* not notice.

♦ Find a local source of whey. It can be expensive if purchased from a health-food store but should cost 60¢ to 70¢ per pound if purchased from a bulk-food warehouse, local mill, or the bulk bins of a supermarket. Purchase a few pounds of the powder (go easy until the stuff passes the taste test) and mix ½ gallon milk with ½ gallon water and 3/4 to 1 cup whey. Chill the milk.

Serve the concoction to kids and spouse without announcing that you've meddled with the milk. See if you get busted immediately or whether the concoction flies without detection. Obviously, the longer the milk goes unnoticed, the stronger the case for wheying your milk.

In the unfortunate event that your ruse is detected immediately, tell the family you want to test the altered milk for a week before the final vote is cast.

══════ July 31 ══════

Who says you can't compare apples and oranges? You can and you should. You should also be comparing asparagus and squash, corn and cabbage, bananas and grapes.

I'm talking about comparing prices, but the issue is not as simple as throwing these fruits or vegetables on the scale and weighing them. For the real per-pound price, you must know how much of the fruit is edible. In the case of oranges, a quarter of its weight is in its peel, meaning you must buy 1.33 pounds to get 1 pound of usable fruit. That makes the true cost of oranges 33% higher than the advertised per-pound price. One third of the weight of a banana is in its peel which means you must buy 1½ pounds to get 1 pound of useable fruit (50% more expensive than the advertised per-pound price). Melons are worse still. Up to 40% of the fruit is inedible, meaning you must buy 1 2/3 pounds to get 1 pound of usable fruit (66% more expensive than the advertised per-pound price)

Now for your quiz: If grapes are 80¢/pound and bananas 55¢/pound, which is the best buy?

◆ Next time you visit the grocery store, buy one sample of the different fruits and vegetables you normally eat. Weigh each of these items whole, then dissect them and weigh the edible portion. From these two weights you can calculate how much of each fruit or vegetable must be purchased to extract a pound of edible food. Then you can calculate the true cost of these foods.

August

At a camp I recently attended, an unusual but admirable lunchtime custom was practiced once a week. The camp called it their Solidarity Lunch and only bread, milk, and rice or pasta were served. The food was perfectly adequate to sustain energy, but its plainness made campers think about the billions of people around the world who eat this way meal after meal. The lunch reminded us how privileged we are and that the world is full of people who have been dealt a far harsher hand in the game of life.

It was also a meal meant to raise money. Each week the difference between what this meal cost (little) and what a normal lunch cost (a couple of dollars more per camper) was sent to two local charities—one for the homeless, one for battered women.

♦ Although middle-class Americans are prone to complain that they have little or no money for charity, for school fund raisers, or even for their children's college education, this is a hollow complaint. The truth of the matter is that they have no pleasures they're willing to sacrifice.

Today's call to action requests that you sacrifice at least one (and perhaps two) meals a week. Perhaps you will eat bread and rice for that meal, perhaps you will fast. Regardless of the details, determine how much your sacrifice (and the sacrifice of other family members) is saving. Donate that money to a cause that rises above the rumbling of your stomach.

Ideally, that cause will extend beyond the family to the community at large. But if you're unwilling to look that far, look at least at your family's grander needs—like the need to stockpile money in a retirement fund or for the kids' education.

═══ August 2 ═══

Potatoes are one of the world's wonder foods. What we consider an ordinary tuber is, in truth, extraordinary. A seven-ounce, unskinned potato delivers iron, potassium, B vitamins, a little protein, a lot of fiber, and about half the RDA for vitamin C. If you don't slather it with butter, its 200 calories are nearly fat free.

Considering their nutritional value and their price (normally about 20¢ per pound and 10¢ per pound on sale) your family should indulge in them often.

♦ Call the library and ask them to hold potato cookbooks with potato menus that will favor your economic and metabolic needs.

♦ Try these inexpensive, fat-free French fries today. Cut potatoes into half-inch-thick strips and soak the strips in water for a couple of hours. Bake the strips at 400° F on a greased cookie sheet for 35 to 40 minutes.

♦ Boiled bite-sized red potatoes are an inexpensive energy food used by endurance bicyclists. Boil the potatoes until they are firm to the stab of a fork (neither crunchy nor mushy), then pour out the boiling water and store them in the refrigerator. Use them for energy food (bicycling or hiking), to complement lunches, or as a snack. Surprisingly, these little potatoes are very moist and appetizing just by themselves. They're also filling.

Cheap Trick:
Reduce the baking time of potatoes about 15 minutes by impaling them, lengthwise, with a clean nail. Leave the nail

in while you bake. Alternately, cut the potatoes in half and bake them, cut-side down, on a lightly greased cookie sheet.

August 3

Next to dirty dishes, the only thing piling up faster in the kitchen are bread bags housing stale crusts. What do you do with all these crusts, besides harbor guilt about world hunger, as you trash them? A few possibilities:

- ♦ Freeze them for future duck food (particularly useful if you have young children).
- ♦ Freeze them for future breakfasts of French toast (this applies to stale bread as well). Many chefs insist French toast *must* be made from stale bread or crusts.
- ♦ Air-dry them for several days, then roll or blend them into bread crumbs. Store in a jar for future use.
- ♦ Use them as a frisbee (outside). When you tire of the game, shred and spread them for the birds.

August 4

Place a large, plastic tub (like a shortening container) with an airtight lid inside the kitchen freezer. Use the tub diligently to store all uneaten vegetables, spare scraps of cheese or meat, discarded leaves from celery, extra salad makings, unwanted lettuce and cabbage remains, unused pasta or potatoes, and/or excess spaghetti sauce. Keep freezing miscellaneous scraps of usable food and include the ingredients in your next batch of soup.

Use the tub religiously and you'll quickly fill it, meaning nutritious but inexpensive homemade soups will become frequent additions to your monthly menu.

♦ Meat drippings are a valued complement to these soup makings. To avoid mixing flavors, however, freeze drippings from different kinds of meat in separate, smaller containers.

♦ Good vegetable-based soups should have at least seven vegetables in them. Follow the rule of seven and your soups will improve dramatically.

August 5

Each year many dollars' worth of breads, pastries, cereals, and cookies are needlessly ruined by letting them go stale. On those occasions when you fail to prevent staleness (i.e., forget to properly bag and seal your food), don't discount it as ruined. Take this quiz and learn what to do.

Quiz:

1) Name a trick for salvaging dried-out cake—this includes those fruit cakes left over from Christmas.
2) Besides using them for duck food, what can you do about dried-out rolls?
3) How do you revitalize stale cereal, cookies, or crackers?
4) What can be done to transform stale donuts into a savory breakfast?
5) How do you use leftover hot dog or hamburger buns before they go stale?
6) How can you incorporate stale bread into an appetizing lunch or dinner?
7) Your child didn't eat all his cereal. What do you do with those soggy flakes in the bottom of the bowl?

Answers:

1) Poke holes in the top of the cake and spread a thin layer of frozen orange juice concentrate over the top. As the concentrate melts, the cake will absorb it.
2) Sprinkle them lightly with water, wrap them in foil, and pop them in the oven for several minutes.
3) Spread them on a cookie sheet and bake them for three or four minutes at 250°F. Dry out stale potato chips the same way under the broiler—watch them closely, there's a fine line between crispy chips and Crispy Critters.
4) Slice them in half (bagel style), dip them in egg, and fry them like French toast.
5) Use them as dinner rolls: Spread butter, garlic powder, and parmesan cheese over the top, then bake for several minutes.
6) Cover it with thinly sliced beef and gravy.

7) Spread them out on a cookie sheet and bake them? What, are you crazy? Throw them away. If this happens often, serve smaller portions.

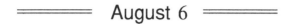

August 6

Storing food properly makes a huge difference in whether a human or a fungus will dine on it. Rummage through the refrigerator and pantry today, employing these measures to keep your food fresh.

♦ Throw away the plastic tabs sealing bread bags—they don't work well. Instead, suck or squeeze excess air from the bag, twist the end, and tie it into a loose knot. Don't cinch the knot.

♦ Use jars to store snack mixes, pretzels, nuts, etc. These goods stay fresher than those stored in plastic bags.

♦ Mushrooms last longer if stored in paper rather than plastic bags.

♦ Celery and lettuce both last longer when wrapped in a paper towel before being stored in a plastic bag. Alternately, store these items in paper bags.

♦ Fresh parsley stored in a sealed jar keeps well; frozen parsley keeps better still.

♦ Place a celery stalk or a slice of apple in with a loaf of bread that is not being used quickly. Either will keep the bread fresher.

♦ Refrigerating bread alters its carbohydrates, making it drier and tougher. Keep bread at room temperature or freeze it.

♦ Once bananas reach their desired ripeness, place them in the refrigerator. The skin will blacken, but this won't damage the fruit's taste.

♦ To prevent berries from molding, refrigerate them and don't wash them until you're ready to serve them.

♦ Keep dried fruit in the refrigerator or, if space allows, in the freezer.

═══ ═══ ## August 7 ═══ ═══

True or false: Bottled water is healthier than tap water. Bottled water doesn't need to meet any higher standard of safety than your municipality's standards for tap water. Some bottled waters are drawn from the local water system, and although they may receive additional filtration and treatment, they may not.

In fact, tests performed by reputable consumer organizations show that bottled water is no safer than the tap water from most municipal water systems and that some bottled waters actually contain disturbing levels of arsenic and fluoride. Consequently, if you're on the bottled-water bandwagon (this applies to seltzers, Perrier, and spring water), jump off. Simply drink your tap water.

◆ Local water that has an unpleasant aftertaste can be spruced up by adding several slices of lemon to a pitcher of water. Let the pitcher sit overnight (uncovered) in the refrigerator.

═══ ═══ ## August 8 ═══ ═══

Given that the cost of store-bought croutons is about $2 per box (or a whopping $4 to $5 per pound), it's worth making your own. Especially since old or dried bread from the kitchen works fine for the job.

◆ Make a batch of croutons today. Dice slices of dry bread and unwanted crusts into cubes. Sprinkle the cubes generously with garlic powder, then toast them under the broiler to the desired crispiness. Or, rather than toasting the cubes, bring two tablespoons of butter or olive oil up to temperature over a medium high burner. Saute' the cubes, sprinkling them with garlic powder as you cook. Store your croutons in a glass jar with an airtight lid.

═══ August 9 ═══

You've lowered the highest-priced portion of a salad, the croutons. Now mix several easy-to-make concoctions that will cut the cost of store-bought dressings 60% to 70%.

◆ **Blue Cheese Dressing.** Mix 2 ounces crumbled blue cheese, ½ teaspoon salt, and ¼ teaspoon pepper in 1½ cups mayonnaise. Stir well and store in a wide-mouth jar. Refrigerated shelf life: three to six months.

◆ **Italian Dressing.** Mix 2 cups vegetable oil; 1 cup wine vinegar; 1/3 cup grated onion; ¼ cup Parmesan cheese (optional); 1 teaspoon each oregano, basil and celery seed; sugar to taste (about 1/8 cup); and pepper to taste. Refrigerated shelf life: six months.

◆ **Russian Dressing.** Mix ½ cup plain yogurt and 1 cup mayonnaise together, using a whisk. Then stir in ½ cup ketchup and 1 teaspoon horseradish and mix well.

◆ **Herb Dressing.** In a jar with a good lid, mix ½ cup vegetable oil; 3 tablespoons wine vinegar; 1 tablespoon fresh parsley (chopped); 1 teaspoon fresh tarragon (chopped); and ¼ teaspoon dried thyme, dried marjoram, and dried basil. Shake hard after combining all ingredients. Allow dressing to sit for 20 minutes before serving. Refrigerated shelf life: eight months.

═══ August 10 ═══

Store-bought frozen pancakes and waffles are mostly air—expensive air. Freezing homemade pancakes (waffles) will not only save you pounds for the pennies invested, they provide tastier, healthier meals.

Plan a pancake or waffle breakfast for one of the coming mornings, and double the amount of batter. Prepare uneaten cakes (waffles) for freezing by putting a layer of cellophane or wax paper between each cake (prevents them from welding into a solid mass). Now place your stack in a heavy-duty plastic bag, draw or squeeze out excess air, and lay the parcel in the freezer.

When a family member craves pancakes (waffles), pull several from the freezer and reheat them in either the microwave or toaster.

===== **August 11** =====

A friend tells the story of a colleague who was a diligent brown-bagger. Over the years the man's devotion to his sack lunch was the source of good-natured jokes, but on that day when he arrived at work and declared his new Mercedes to be the payoff of his brown-bag parsimony, co-workers realized the joke was on them.

True, Mr. Brown Bag may have been a fool to buy such a transparent symbol of status, but you get the point—over the years lunching out at $4 to $5 a pop squanders more than petty cash. In fact, for the diligent brown bagger, whose lunch is unlikely to exceed $1.25 per day, the yearly savings can easily amount to $900.

◆ Assuming your working spouse lunches out often, your mission today is to temper the habit. Discuss brown-bagging this evening over dinner. The option need not be a north-to-south switch. Lunch is a social time and that brings more than monetary issues into the mix. Nonetheless, make a case for having your spouse brown-bag more often (maybe half time), then offer your help in preparing those lunches. It's a simple way to keep an extra $450 in the bank each year.

===== **August 12** =====

Preparing lunches while children blitz to catch the bus and spouses bolt to beat the clock may be a tough assignment. Solutions?

◆ Try an assembly line. You put the food out and put it away after the dust settles. But make your children and spouse responsible for gathering and wrapping what goes into their lunch bags.

◆ Regarding sandwiches, let everyone make their own (after you lay out the supplies) or make a week's worth of sandwiches yourself and freeze the lot. Lunch meats, cheeses, peanut butter, jelly, honey, mayonnaise, and mustard all freeze well. Toppings like lettuce, cucumber, and tomatoes should be added after sandwiches are pulled from the freezer.

══════ August 13 ══════

Smart food buying does not end at how intelligently you handle the supermarkets. There are other outlets for buying food. Once again pull out your friend—the Yellow Pages—and go to work researching new sources of inexpensive food. Salient finds go straight into the Rolodex.

◆ If anyone in the extended family runs a business, a copy of her business license is likely qualify you to shop at wholesale grocers. It won't matter if the family business is not food-related; virtually any business might need the paper products, cleaning supplies, or coffee makings that wholesale grocers typically carry. Look up *Grocers—Wholesale* in the Yellow Pages and call those within easy driving distance. Ask what product lines they stock (frozen foods, canned goods, produce, paper supplies, cleaning supplies); what licenses or papers qualify you to shop there; how you establish an account or, at least, on-going shopping rights; what is the minimum-order size; how you pay; and what the store hours are.

◆ Other Yellow Page listings to call include *Meat—Wholesale* and *Bakers—Wholesale*. Ask them the same questions you asked the wholesale grocers.

Any wholesale outlets that sound promising (sell products of interest, allow you to list several company representatives who can shop the store, welcome low minimum orders, accept company checks or cash) are worth a visit. Make a photocopy of licenses that may be required (e.g., business licenses) and then walk each store, making notes about the sizes and prices of products you might purchase there in the future.

═══ # August 14 ═══

"Ask and ye shall receive. Seek and ye shall find."
It's more than just good spiritual advice, it's also purchasing advice that you will apply today. Once again you'll need the Yellow Pages and Rolodex at your fingertips.

♦ Look up the following listings: Dairies, Dairy Products-—Retail, Meats—Retail, Fruits and Vegetables—Retail, Meat—Retail, Bakers—Retail, Bakers— Wholesale (scan this listing for bakery outlets). Call local businesses from each section of the Yellow Pages and own up to who you are—a penny-pincher sniffing out opportunities for those pennies. Ask each business about its products or services. Do these stores undersell the supermarket for any, many, or most of their products? Do they have sections of their store devoted to dated goods? How much are their goods discounted?

It's a shotgun approach and many calls will miss the target. But you'll find several stores that will permanently change where you stock up on particular foods. In my own search, I unearthed a bakery outlet where we save big on breads, rolls, bagels, and buns. I also found a butcher who sells all kinds of dated cheeses—from American Cheddars to Swiss Gruyeres—for 99¢/pound.

═══ # August 15 ═══

Starbucks has changed the morning ritual of the country. Unlike olden times when workers got their caffeine jolt in-house with free or cheap coffee, modern workers arrive at the office with latte in hand and $2 to $3 out of pocket.

If this sounds like a worker in your family, it's time to extinguish a habit that can be costing $600 a year—perhaps twice that if your addict is a multi-cup-a-day offender.

The habit to extinguish is not the actual consumption—giving the wage earner of the family a boost before he or she connects to the cogs of corporate America is a well-deserved simple pleasure. It's the habit of how that simple pleasure is acquired that needs extinguishing. Making that gourmet cup of coffee or latte at home costs about 15¢ in beans and a maximum of 15¢ in milk, flavorings, and sugar. So we're talking about a cup of coffee that is eight to 10 times cheaper if made at home.

◆ To appease the coffee snob in the family, resign yourself to several investments today. At the very least you'll need a coffee maker and good beans. You can grind quality beans at the store when they are purchased (cheapest option), or you can buy a grinder (about $20) and grind the beans as you need them (the option recommended by coffee connoisseurs). You'll need freezer space to house your grounds/beans because everyone knows only lowbrows, barbarians, and philistines store coffee at room temperature. You'll need a lidded cup (one that is microwave safe for preheating any milk that is added to coffee). And if your spouse harbors a multi-cup addiction, you'll need a thermos to store the afternoon's fix.

◆ Coffee making can get complicated if espressos or cappuccinos become part of the addiction. Start out simply with the basics mentioned above and expand into brews requiring additional hardware only after you've saved enough through your efforts to justify capital improvements.

====== **August 16** ======

No amount of money spent on the newest diet or scientifically formulated foods will change the facts—to lose weight you must consume fewer calories than you burn. Like it or not, that leaves you with only three courses of action: eat less, exercise more, or eat less *and* exercise more. None of these options is easy, for they all involve changing habits.

Two tips, however, will help you eat less while making you feel like you've eaten plenty. That means these tips will benefit the beltline. Even if you're not dieting, however, adopt these habits because less food eaten also benefits the bottom line.

◆ Much of the satisfaction of eating comes from the time it takes to complete a meal *and* the amount of chewing involved. By serving yourself half as much food, but chewing it twice as long, you can fool yourself into having a satisfying meal. Try it. Chew every bite of food today until it's liquid in your mouth—this takes considerable effort and by the time others have finished their meal, you'll have consumed only a fraction of what you normally eat. Still, you won't feel deprived.

The same applies to snacks. Chew that chip until it's water in your mouth and maybe you *can* eat just one (or two).

♦ Cut your food into smaller or thinner bites. Rather than quartering an apple, quarter the quarters. Visually, 16 slices of apples looks huge compared to four. And handling and chewing all those pieces will have you believing you ate far more than you did. One banana cut into 1/8" slices and eaten with a fork suddenly seems bounteous. Get creative with your cutting. Slice pizzas into thinner slivers, sandwiches into thin pie-shaped slivers, meat and cheeses into paper-thin slices, toast into checker squares, muffins into ¼-inch slices....

August 17

In blind taste-tests of orange juices performed by consumer groups, frozen concentrates typically score higher marks for taste than refrigerated pre-made juices. Furthermore, even the best frozen concentrates like Minute Maid or Florida Gold are about 35% cheaper than the best chilled juices like Tropicana Pure Premium. Meanwhile, some store brands of frozen concentrates (e.g., Albertson's Janet Lee and Lucky's Lady Lee) are half the price of chilled juices.

If you're currently a chilled-juice drinker, it's time to put frozen concentrates on both your On-Deck and Batter's-Up shopping lists (see July 12).

August 18

Failing to apportion portions: it's one of the deadly sins of snacking. It's also a deadly habit for the beltline and bottom line.

When the kids, your spouse, or you, for that matter, get into a bag of cookies or chips, what tells you to stop? Your guilt when there's one cookie left?

Change this. Start doling out the snack food to be consumed each day.

♦ Make a pile of the day's snacks on a kitchen counter. Pull out the number of apples, chips, and/or cookies allocated for the day. The rest of the food (and you must stress this to your family) is off-limits, verboten, taboo. Shut the pantry and, to keep passersby from feasting on forbidden fruits, keep it shut. At times I have gone so far as to tie the pantry shut to keep myself out. Untying the cord takes enough time to make me contemplate the unconscionable, despicable sin I am committing.

♦ Portion the food into equal parcels if you have kids. Place enough food out, but don't be wasteful. And remember, when the food is gone, the snacks for the day are over.

====== **August 19** ======

If it's not already part of your routine, today marks the day to turn over a new leaf in the kitchen: Start preparing double or triple quantities of whatever you cook. The practice accomplishes several goals. It leaves leftovers, thereby eliminating cooking the next day—that saves money on utilities (to say nothing of the time it saves). It will frequently leave you with food to freeze, as well, and that crop of freezer food is bankable money when you return home from a frantic day and can't face hours of kitchen detail. Rather than ordering pizza or eating out, you'll open the freezer.

♦ Go through your recipe box today and decide which meals are suitable for doubling (i.e., that will leave you leftovers) and which are suitable for tripling (i.e., that will leave you leftovers and freezer food). Use a red pen to mark suitable recipes with a "2" or a "3"—your reminder each time you pull the card of how much extra you're going to make.

◆ Check your freezing supplies—Pyrex and aluminum baking pans, plastic margarine tubs, casserole dishes, Ziploc freezer bags—to ensure you have the supplies to freeze frequently.

Cheap Trick:
Place food for freezing (soups, stews, chilis, casseroles, etc.) inside plastic freezer bags. Use a casserole dish, margarine tub, baking pan, or pot to mold the bag to the desired shape during freezing. Once the food has frozen, pop the bag (and the food it contains) from the mold. This keeps you from filling the freezer with the cookware and containers you'll want available for daily use.

August 20

Should you pay more than $2.50 per pound for cereal? I don't think so, but a lot of people do. In fact many people pay more for cereal than they would for a sirloin steak, or cashews, or salmon. Recently in Seattle, KIRO Television's evening news compared four brands of corn flakes. At the time, Total Post cost $5.80 per pound, Kellogg's Corn Flakes $2.91/pound, Safeway's corn flakes $2.43/pound and Albertson's corn flakes $1.71/pound.

In a blind taste test organized by the station, a small panel of testers tried the four different brands of flakes. Safeway's corn flakes took top taste honors, followed very closely by Albertson's, followed by Post, followed by Kellogg's. After a dietician evaluated all four products and deemed them of equal nutritional value, the station announced Albertson's corn flakes the best buy.

◆ Time for your family to participate in some testing of its own. Add brand and store labels of a variety of cereals to your food-shopping list and pick these up next time you food shop. Pour the cereals out of their boxes and into large Ziploc bags. Mark the underside of each bag with a number and then let your family rate the different cereals over the course of a week. Don't be surprised if a store brand wins the blind test. Don't complain either.

===== **August 21** =====

Listed below are additional breakfast foods costing less than $2.50 per pound. Put these on your food-shopping list and save on what it costs to roll out breakfast every morning. A side effect of all these inexpensive food: They are all healthier than the highly-hyped (and expensive) sugar cereals.

♦ Store-brand graham crackers: $1.70/lb. For breakfast, dip four or five full-length crackers in a glass of milk.
♦ Price/Costco Laguna Low Fat Oat Bran Cookies: $1.85/lb. Three cookies with a glass of milk makes an adequate breakfast. Splurge by adding some fruit.
♦ Toast with peanut butter, jam, honey: about $1/lb for quality bread and toppings.
♦ Fruit of the week: average of $.65/pound. Make breakfast from any fruit that's currently in season and on sale (apples, oranges, bananas, melon, berries). Combine the fruit with cereal or toast for a heartier meal.
♦ Eggs: 40¢/lb.
♦ Bulk granola: $1.70/lb
♦ Hot cereals: $1 to $1.80 for a wide variety of types (many are micro-wave ready in under two minutes).

===== **August 22** =====

Top-level performing arts and sporting events come with ticket prices that, for those of us of modest means, undermine their enjoyment. If $60 tickets run contrary to your definition of what constitutes a good concert, play, symphony, or ball game, devote several hours today unearthing entertainment opportunities you can afford to enjoy.

Local high schools, community colleges, private colleges, and universities offer many quality entertainment opportunities (lectures, concerts, movies, sports events) at bargain-basement prices. Get out the phone books and, starting with the *Public School* listings in the government pages, call all the local schools that are likely to sponsor cultural events, lectures, or sustain sports programs. At community (and private) colleges, the student activities office, student programs office, public events office, or communication center is most likely to coordinate (or monitor) all the institution's events. Call, confess that you are a community member interested in attending more of the school's cultural and sporting events, and ask to be placed on the mailing list to receive schedules/notices of special programs. Naturally, when you connect with the right office, note the number—if your name is dropped from the mailing list in the future, you want quick access to the right office.

Keeping track of a large university's activities is tougher because no single office monitors all events. Call the offices mentioned above and get onto the mailing lists they maintain. Call the university box office and the athletic department for the performing-arts and sporting-events schedules. Call the university paper and ask which day of the week they publish the most comprehensive listing of events. Finally, ask whether a weekly or monthly publication informs university employees about campus news and events. At many universities, this is the best centralized source of information. Call the publication and subscribe.

August 23

Check the jeans around the home front. Are any belonging to you or other family members not worn because they are too faded? Rejuvenate them. Purchase RIT dyes from retailers like Kmart or Walmart or order the dyes (cost $1.80 per dye plus $2 per order for shipping) from RIT Consumer Affairs Department (1437 W Morris St, Indianapolis, IN 46221, 317-231-8044). While you're at it, ask for their literature about fabric care, stain removal, and home-dyeing projects (listing tips for tie dyeing, making Halloween costumes, tea dyeing, and more).

To give your jeans a face lift—or rather a fade lift—toss them in the washing machine with the dye.

Cheap Tricks:
♦ The knees are the first to go—in professional athletes and jeans. Solve the jeans problem with preventive surgery. Apply iron-on patches to the inside of pant legs and you

effectively double their lives. This is especially useful with children's jeans.

♦ To make matching knee-patches for the outside of children's pants, pirate the back pockets of those pants. This is especially useful if you don't have matching remnants for the job.

August 24

Wearing used clothing is something many children may not be proud of, and if you want your progeny to learn to appreciate the benefits of frugal living, it's important that they not become bitter or resentful over the sacrifices imposed on them before they reach the age of understanding. That means making some concessions to their wants.

If new clothing is important to your children's esteem and self-image, let them help you find the clothing they want. Tell them how much money you are willing to devote to their new clothes (give them a budget), let them decide how that money should be spent, using the sale pages from the newspaper and other ideas on how they can get the most from their fixed dollars.

Just because you concede a particular inning doesn't mean you forfeit the game. Practice hemorrhage control elsewhere.

♦ Purchase rough-and-tumble clothing for home use and sports from rummage sales, thrift shops, and secondhand stores. Make sure you remove old name tags before presenting this clothing to your children.

♦ Sew trendy labels into used clothing and older kids will embrace the garments with enthusiasm. Get your hands on labels that impress by: extracting them from your own clothing, pirating them from the clothes of older siblings, requesting them from friends who are donating clothes to charity...

Okay, it's misleading, but what do you say about those stories you once told about Santa Claus? It's an option—you decide whether the end justifies the means.

====== August 25 ======

Maybe they're not as embarrassing as pimples but those unsightly wads of fluff that blemish your clothing when it pills are the major reason many clothes are retired. Toward this end, the properly prepared penny-pincher needs a de-piller to restore woven and knitted garments—sweaters, dresses, sweat shirts, dress shirts, slacks... My extended family has tried many remedies—razors, fuzz-busting shavers, sweater stones, tape—and the only products receiving widespread praise are those like the D-Fuzz-It and the Fuzz-Eat'r. These products use a textured screen that snags pills as the screen is combed over fabric. Order the D-Fuzz-It from the Current Catalog (Current Building, Colorado Springs, CO 80941-0001, 800-525-7170). Cost is about $4 for a pair of combs.

Order the product today. Also, ransack dressers and closets, searching for garments in need of respectability therapy. When the combs arrive, use television time to work through the pile. Because you'll have two combs, recruit whoever is watching with you to help.

====== August 26 ======

When my wife purchases new clothing, she rarely wears it right away. She hangs it from her closet door and studies it over the course of a week. Is it really a good color for her, how will it mix and match with her current wardrobe, does it look swanky at home or cheaply made, will it remain stylish or look ridiculous in a year? These are the questions she consciously and unconsciously ponders over the week.

Eventually the die is cast—it's hot or it's not. Indecision is interpreted as a bad sign: If after a week she still doesn't know whether the garment grabs her, it probably doesn't. Back to the store it goes.

Incorporate this buying habit into your own modus operandi. While it's a technique that can be applied to any purchase, it seems especially well-suited to clothing. Experts say a *third* of all clothing is rarely worn because buyers quickly decide they chose a poor color, size, or style. Leave garments untouched for a while and it's amazing how quickly the love affair you had with them in the store wears off at home.

♦ Add the clothing items you desire to your Master Purchasing List, then wait for them to come on sale over the coming weeks and months. If you still desire an item by the time the price is right, your interest in it is likely to endure. You'll be surprised, however, how often a month's wait changes the picture: Items you recently longed for now seem unworthy of your money. Once again, patience pays off.

═══════ August 27 ═══════

Women who buy name-brand hosiery, lingerie, and intimates from local retailers are spending twice (sometimes thrice) what they should. Start making these purchases by mail. Call the following companies for their mail-order catalogs now:

♦ One Hanes Place, P.O. Box 748, Rural Hall, NC 27098, 800-300-2600 (imperfect and discounted styles of L'eggs, Hanes, Playtex, Bali).
♦ Kayser-Roth Corporation, P.O. Box NN-1, Burlington, NC 27220, 800-575-3497 (imperfect and discounted styles of No Nonsense).
♦ National Wholesale Company, 400 National Blvd., Lexington, NC 27294, 800-480-4673 (big savings on National brand).

For the biggest savings, buy the imperfects. These are commonly half the price of regulars and women report that flaws in most of the imperfects cannot be found. That makes me suspect that the "imperfect" label is a perfect ruse—it gives manufacturers the chance to sell product (most of which is first-quality) to price-sensitive customers without disrupting or angering their network of full-price retailers.

Cheap Tricks:

♦ Women who aren't getting a minimum of eight to 10 days of use from their hose should be looking for a new brand. Durable panty hose usually contain spandex, which is strong, very elastic, and prevents the knees and ankles from bagging.

♦ New nicks in hose or stockings can be kept from running by dabbing nail polish (uncolored) on the spot.

♦ Prevent washing machine damage of hosiery by placing items in a pillow case.

August 28

I challenge you to more tests. Today's laboratory—the laundry room.

Because 90% of the electricity for washing clothes is used to heat water, it's time to chill out. Warm-water washes and cold rinses clean all but the filthiest clothes as well as hot washes and warm rinses. If your water is soft, cold-water washes also clean all but the dirtiest, greasiest clothes. Regardless of the temperature used for washing, always use cold-water rinses—the temperature of the rinse cycle has no affect on cleaning.

Assuming you wash one load of clothes each day, switching from hot to cold water rinses will save $70/year. Switching from hot wash/warm rinse to warm wash/cold rinse will save $135/year—and unless the clothes were truly filthy, they will emerge just as clean.

Run your own tests and prove this to yourself.

August 29

If the water in your home is hard or has a high mineral content, wash your clothes using the amount of laundry detergent the manufacturer recommends. But keep in mind that these instructions were devised to work satisfactorily everywhere in the country.

In most parts of the country, the water is not hard or excessively mineralized, and using half the prescribed amount of laundry powder will not only get your clothes perfectly clean, it also insures those clothes will rinse better (thereby reducing skin rashes).

To quote advice distributed by the water-utility district in Western Washington, "Hardness refers to dissolved minerals (calcium and magnesium) that interfere with the sudsing action of soap. Our water is soft. As a result, you need only about one half the manufacturer's recommended amount of soap in your dishwasher and washing machine to obtain the desired result."

From this day forth, take it upon yourself to cut your yearly detergent consumption (and expenses) in half. Saying to yourself, "This can't possibly work," is an unacceptable rebuttal. I throw down the gauntlet, and the only honorable way to continue your wasteful habits is to take the challenge and prove me wrong.

♦ Get the red stickers out and paste a few on your laundry-detergent box. It's your reminder to take the test. On those stickers you might want to write this equation: $\frac{1}{2}Y=2X$. Translation: Half as much is twice as good.

===== August 30 =====

Yet another day in the laundry room where I hope to destroy another unnecessary habit.

Gather up all the laundry, pull out delicate items and garments likely to bleed, and throw the rest (without sorting by color) into the washing machine. Tests conducted by consumer magazines have reported that when washing with high-quality, modern detergents, sorting by color yields such marginal benefits as to make it unworthy of the effort. And unworthy of the expense. By washing one large load rather than two small ones, you're reducing what you spend on energy detergent, water, and sewage.

Try living an unsorted life. You might like it.

===== August 31 =====

Stained T-shirts and stained jeans—what do you do with them? Tie dye them in reverse.

Using cord or rubber bands, bunch different parts of these stained garments into tight wads. Or fold items back and forth on themselves, accordion-style, and then use cord every four inches to hold the folded garments together. Toss the garments into a bucket containing 2 cups chlorine bleach per 1½ gallons hot water. Stir the solution every 10 to 20 minutes and remove the garments (wear rubber gloves) when they have faded to the desired level. Now launder the garments in the washing machine and, after washing, remove the cords or rubber bands.

Today, gather the materials for the job and some stained items (from both your dresser and from the kids'). Now test this paradox: Can dyeing bring clothes back from the dead?

September

September 1

The information listed below has been distilled from nonpartial product reviews. Product comparisons and reviews can be found in myriad magazines, newsletters, and books. My goal now is not to tell you about each coffee in the crop of 50 that was evaluated or to compare every pasta sauce in the 40 that a magazine recently tested. My mission is to simply direct you toward stellar products that give you the best bang for your buck. My goal, also, is to demonstrate that within every pack of products there are some surprising dogs (often sporting brand names) that bite holes in your budget and give little product satisfaction in return.

It's your job as a consumer to be skeptical of the connection between price and quality that so many people take for granted. It's not unusual for inexpensive products lacking big-dollar marketing muscle to outperform expensive, highly hyped competitors. It's your job as a smart consumer to realize that the expression, "You get what you pay for," is a misleading half-truth.

On the following list you'll find the manufacturer and style of the PRODUCT reviewed, an average PRICE, and a QUALITY rating (using school grades where "A"s are good and "F"s are not).

The last column sums up what you really want to know: Whether you're getting a powerful or pitiful bang for your buck. This amorphous (and admittedly subjective) rating is determined by comparing the quality of an item to its price. STARS are stellar buys, MOONS deliver average value, and BLACK HOLES are best avoided.

PRODUCT: PRICE: QUALITY: BANG FOR BUCK:

Pesto Sauces:

Safeway Select Verdi Vegetable: $.32/srv: A+: Star
Classico di Napoli Tomato & Basil: .41/srv: A: Star
Hunt's Original Traditional (can): .17/srv: B+: Star
Del Monte Traditional (can): .16/srv: B: Star
Newman's Own Sockarooni: .35/srv: A-: Moon
Ragu Hearty Italian Tomato (jar): .26/srv: B: Moon
Di Giorno Marinara (tub): .87/srv: B: BLACKHOLE
Contadina Garden Vegetable: .88/srv: B: BLACKHOLE
Prego Low Sodium: .30/srv: C-: BLACKHOLE
Del Monte Chunky Italian Herb: .16/srv: D: BLACKHOLE

Products tested that delivered less value than the Stars listed above: Rao's Homemade Marinara, Colavita Marinara, Contadina Plum Tomato, Master Choice Plum Tomato with Basil, Contadina Chunky Tomato, Five Brothers Marinara with Burgundy Wine, Francesco Rinaldi Traditional Marinara, Kroger Classic Traditional, Ragu Hearty Italian Tomato, America's Choice Traditional, Ragu Chunky Gardenstyle, Di Giorno Plum Tomato and Mushroom, Kroger Homestyle Traditional, Progresso Spaghetti Sauce, Ragu Old World Style Traditional, Classico di Sicilia Mushrooms and Ripe Olives, Prego Extra Chunky Zesty, Safeway Select Verdi Marinara, Millina's Finest Organic Marinara, Hunt's Light Traditional, Hunt's Classic Italian with Garlic and Herbs, Mama Rizzo's Regular Mushroom and Onion, Del Monte Chunky Italian Herb.

Regular-Roast Caffeinated Coffees:

Eight O'Clock 100% Columbian: $.07/cup: B+: Star
Folgers Cstm Blend (and Cstm Roast): .07/cup: B+: Star
Hills Bros 100% Columbian: .06/cup: B: Star
Safeway's Edwards Premium: .06/cup: B-: Moon
Yuban 100% Columbian: .07/cup: B-: Moon
Folgers Aroma Roast: .06/cup: C: Black Hole
Eight O'Clck Ryle Clmbian Suprmo:.10/cup:D:Black Hole

Products tested that delivered less value than the Stars listed above: Folgers Gourmet Supreme, Gevalia Select Varietal, Columbia, Maxwell House Columbian Supreme, Chase & Sanborn, Folgers Special Roast, MJB Premium, Kroger premium, Gloria Jean's Columbian Supremo, Maxwell House 1892, Maxwell House Lite, Hills Brothers Perfect Balance, Melitta Premium, Albertson's, Hills Brothers High Yield, Eight O'Clock Balanced Blend, Maxwell House Master Blend, ShopRite.

Dark-Roast Coffees:

Peet's Columbia: .11/cup: A+: Star
Millstone Columbian Supremo: .11/cup: A: Star
Starbuck's Columbia (mailorder): .13/cup: A+: Star
Brothers Gourmet Columbian Cafe: .12/cup: A: Star
Folgers French Roast: .07/cup: C: Black Hole
Starbuck's Columbia (store purchased):.13/cup:D:Black Hole
Eight O'Clock French Roast: .06/cup: F: Black Hole

Products tested that delivered less value than the Stars listed above: Maxwell House Rich French Roast, S&W Classico 100% Columbian Espresso, Hills Brothers French Roast, Medaglia D'Oro Caffe Nero.

Study these lists and put to memory the important lessons they teach:

◆ Avoid blindly trusting brand names. Starbuck's Coffee received quality ratings of "A+" and "D" in the same review. Some roasts of Folgers coffees were Stars while others were Black Holes.
◆ Designer/boutique/deli labels mean little. Consider Starbuck's again. Or among the pasta sauces, notice that many deli labels did not offer much value.
◆ Don't disregard store brands. Just like national brands, some of these products are excellent, some are not. Among the pasta sauces, a store brand was the best value going. Among regular coffees, Safeway's store brand was on the cusp of being an excellent buy. Try different store brands—keep using those that satisfy you and move onto other choices (without knocking the entire genre) if you don't like a particular selection.

◆ Price is not indicative of quality. Many expensive items are not worth the marginally better quality they deliver. And many expensive items simply are not as good as cheaper competitors.

═══════ September 2 ═══════

Keep notes. You buy thousands of products each year: peanut butter, orange juice, beer, spaghetti noodles, margarine, ice cream, soap, shampoo, toilet paper, oil. And for each of those products, scores of labels scream for your dollars. If your memory is like mine (more like steel wool than a steel trap) you keep forgetting whether you liked the Janet Lee mayonnaise or not, whether the consumer review of Minute Maid orange juice praised or panned it, whether you've already tried Kroger's peanut butter.

◆ Start your own Best Buys/Worst Buys lists. As you read lists like yesterday's, or reviews in consumer magazines, or articles in the paper, add to your personal list. And as you experiment for yourself to identify products you appreciate and others you detest, make notes.

Obviously there is much you can disregard. If you never buy dark-roast coffees, avoid cluttering your head and your list with best-buy information. You'll also have mainstays you don't think about any more—certain brands of cereal, crackers, toothpaste, or shampoo which have survived the trials of experimentation and please you. Fine, no need to record a done deal.

Nonetheless, we all have gray areas to explore. We're not certain what snacks are the best value, which premium beers are worth a premium price, whether the "nourishers" in shampoo are worth a 10-spot. And for those products that are bought but once or twice a year we are often hard-pressed to remember what reverent or damning facts we once heard about them.

So keep a notebook with the details. For each product listed, make several columns. One column notes whether you liked the product and/or a reliable source recommends it, another column lists whether you disliked the product and/or a reliable source pans it.

Subdivide your list by category. Categories might include Beverages, Baked Goods, Baking Supplies, Canned and Jarred Goods, Candy and Nuts, Car Supplies, Cereals and Breakfast Foods, Chips and Crackers, Cleaners, Condiments, Cosmetics and Toiletries, Dairy Products and Eggs, Dry Goods, Fruits and Vegetables, Frozen Goods, Meat, Miscellaneous, Office Supplies, Paper Products, Pets, Pharmaceuticals, Photographic Supplies, Prepared Meals, Sporting Goods, and Toys.

September 3

It's the season when a harvest's worth of produce pours into the supermarkets and prices you would like to see more often mark fruits and vegetables. According to the Third Commandment of food buying (stock up when the price is right), it's time to buy. Keep your eyes on the specials and when the price of apples, pears, peaches, plums, carrots, peppers, and celery hit the floor, pick them up in quantity.

Of course when it comes to produce, quantity can be ugly if you can't handle it. Today, prepare to process the produce to come: Learn to dry what you can't consume. You don't need much in the way of dedicated hardware to do this. All you really need is your gas or electric oven.

Dry a test batch of fruit using this system:

♦ Slice pears and apples into ¼-inch slices, peaches into ½-inch slices. Slice bananas into quarters along the long axis. Lay the fruit on cake-cooling racks and set the racks in the oven until the fruit reaches the desired dryness (between 12 and 24 hours).

The pilot light of gas ovens provides enough heat for drying, while a light bulb (you'll need to run an extension cord through the oven door) converts an electric oven into a drier. The oven temperature should be between 110°F and 160°F (130°F is ideal), so if you own an oven thermometer, experiment with different bulbs to find the wattage producing the perfect temperature in your oven. Frequently, this is a 75-watt bulb.

Depending on how your oven vents, you may or may not want to keep the oven door cracked. Experiment with a load of fruit keeping the door closed, and try another load using a pencil or stirring spoon to keep the door cracked. Which method yields better results?

◆ If you're likely to dry often, build several drying racks by stretching fiberglass screen-door mesh over wooden frames. Make the racks stackable, allowing 1½ to 2 inches of air space between each.

◆ Drying is not just for fruit. Vegetables like green and red peppers, whose prices can go through the roof when they are out of season, are worth drying also. Carrots and celery dry well, but may not be worth the effort if their prices don't fluctuate wildly over the year.

◆ Store the fruits of your drying in glass jars. Or, if you're squirreling away for the dark days of winter, pack the fruit in thick plastic bags, vacuum out excess air (with your lungs), and freeze the package.

═══════ September 4 ═══════

Some other thoughts about laying away fruits and vegetables now that a buck buys a dozen ears of corn, five pounds of apples, squash the size of a basketball...

◆ If you have the space, start freezing. In one of your cookbooks (or one from the library) find a chart telling how long to blanch beans, corn, squash, beets, broccoli, carrots, greens, and peas. After blanching, cool the vegetables rapidly in cold water, package them (small batches) in heavy plastic bags, and freeze. At 0°F, most vegetables keep between 8 and 12 months.

◆ Dice carrots, celery, onions, lettuce, cabbage, and green peppers purchased at bargain rates and store them (mixed) in appropriately sized bags for soup makings. If you don't want the vegetables freezing together into a solid mass, prefreeze them by spreading them out on a cookie sheet for an hour. Then pour the frozen pieces into a heavy-duty plastic bag and pack them away for long-term freezing.

◆ Pre-freeze large slices of fruit, segments of banana, and whole berries on a cookie sheet for several hours before pouring them together into a mixed bag of fruit. To enhance pancake or waffle batter, grab fruit from the bag, mash the pieces, and pour them into the batter. For fruit shakes combine cold milk, pieces of fruit, and sugar, then blend.

◆ Prepare fillings for pies with bargain fruit. Use cellophane or aluminum foil to line a pie tin and fill the tin with fruit. Wrap the fruit in the liner and freeze. Next time you want a pie, pop your frozen fruit into a pie shell and slide the works into the oven.

September 5

Overseeding your entire lawn every year or two is an inexpensive way to keep it thick and healthy. Grass plants in the lawn are continually dying and overseeding allows new grass, rather than weeds, to fill the vacancies.

Homeowners with new sod yards are particularly good candidates for overseeding. Sods are composed of a mixture of grass species and not all of them may like your soil. Overseeding allows grasses that can grow in your soil to fill in for those grasses that can't. Early to mid-September is the best time of year to do the job, early spring the next-best time.

◆ Call several nurseries today. Tell them you're over-seeding the lawn and want their recommendation of hardy, low-maintenance grasses that thrive in your climate (and soil). Grasses classified as tall fescues (best) and fine fescues (next best) require little maintenance (watering, fertilizing, pest control). Grasses classified as perennial ryegrasses (worst) and Kentucky bluegrass (next worst) are high-maintenance grasses worth avoiding, as are seed mixes with lots of ryegrass.

Another excellent source of information: The Lawn Institute (P.O. Box 108, Pleasant Hill, TN 38578). Send a SASE and request their *Grass Seed Recognition List* and related literature pertaining to low-maintenance grasses.

◆ While researching the types of seeds needed, ask nurseries how much seed is required for overseeding purposes.

◆ Seeds that won't germinate (or that germinate slowly) yrun up water bills, waste time, provide the birds with food, and frustrate you. Here's a trick for fast germination. To each pound of seed, add 1 cup of cool weak tea (use one tea bag to make four cups of tea). Soak the seeds in the tea and refrigerate the works for 24 hours. Spread the seeds on your driveway to let them dry. Once dry, sow normally.

══════ September 6 ══════

A prime rule of clothing purchases: Avoid items requiring dry cleaning. Unfortunately, we all have items—suits, silk shirts, drapes—that keep these businesses solvent. Your chore today is to find the local dry cleaner who will help keep you solvent, as well.

You may be under the impression that a dry cleaner is a dry cleaner is a dry cleaner. Wrong. As is usually the case, the smart shopper will find dry-cleaning outlets that charge half of what competitors charge. It's your job to sleuth out the local deal from the local steal.

Gather up the phone book and your Rolodex, and call all the dry cleaners that are convenient to the routes you or your spouse travel.

◆ During your calls, ask about the per-piece charge of items you frequently clean—blouses, two-piece suits, sweaters. Ask about discounts if, say, you clean more than eight pieces. And ask about per-pound rates.

Most cleaners don't charge by the pound, but a few do; these are likely to be the shops offering true savings. When comparing my local cleaners, I discovered the gaugers charged $5.50 to $6 per blouse and $8.50 to $9.25 per two-piece suit. Meanwhile, an excellent cleaner we occasionally use charges $30 per eight-pound or 10-piece load (it doesn't matter whether the load is a mixture of blouses, sweaters, or suits). The cost is about half what the high-end shops charge.

However, my recent research uncovered an even cheaper cleaner. This new shop charges $2.50 per pound, meaning an eight-pound load costs $20. That's a 33% savings over the shop we currently use.

♦ Price isn't everything, so let new businesses earn your trust. Give them several second-string garments before entrusting them with your varsity lineup.

Safety Tip:
Exposure to "perc", a residue of dry-cleaned goods, is believed to increase the risk of cancer. The degree of risk is controversial but you can all but eliminate any risk by removing dry-cleaned garments from their bags and letting them air several days in a little-used room before moving them to your closet.

══════ September 7 ══════

While trying to nip dry-cleaning expenses, adopt the following practices.

♦ To reduce staining of freshly laundered shirts and blouses, spray the armpits with a light coat of Scotch Guard. To further reduce the stains and odors accumulating here, go extra heavy on the amount of underarm deodorant used. Encourage your spouse to respond in kind.

♦ Garments marked "dry clean only" can frequently be hand-washed in tepid water with a gentle, non-detergent, liquid soap. Test a hidden corner of clothes you're tired of dry cleaning to test whether the colors bleed. Dry these garments with a fan to promote even drying.

══════ September 8 ══════

If your family is satisfied with its stable of cars, use the week ahead to catch up on unfinished business. But if, in the near future, you need a new car (or a different used car), it's time to put machinery in motion.

Why now? Because late fall and early winter are buyers' months—demand for cars is low (Christmas has people distracted and cash poor) while the supply of vehicles is high (the dregs from last year's car crop are still cluttering the lots, and the new models are filling the show rooms).

Before you buy, however, there are decisions to make, reference materials to read, and telephone calls to place. This is important homework. The purchase of a car will probably rate as the largest outlay of the year, and a smart buyer will not only shave several grand off the sticker price of the car, she may also identify a vehicle that costs thousands less to maintain.

Which car should you purchase? That fundamental question can be answered only after considerable soul searching. Unfortunately for most people, settling on a car is a matter of compromising, it's a matter of defining whether a safe car is more or less important than a fast one, whether a vehicle that is cheap to keep roadworthy is more or less important than one that will wow the opposite sex, whether the car will remain in the family for 15 years or five...

People reading this book are likely lean toward economy over extravagance, safety over flash, reliability over recognition, pragmatism over first impression. Even so, zeroing in on the best car to transport your family and possessions leaves you with many choices. Is safety or economy of paramount importance, how large must a vehicle be to handle all your hauling needs, do you buy a car large enough to handle all these needs or most of them?

Reading a variety of reference materials will help you address and answer these questions. Some materials to order or read today:

♦ Send a SASE business envelope to the Highway Loss Data Institute (1005 North Glebe Road, Arlington, VA 22201, 703-247-1600) and request a copy of their brochure, *Injury, Collision, and Theft Losses by Make and Model*. It's a simple brochure packed with powerful statistics about which cars are safest to drive, least likely to be stolen, and most expensive to repair after a collision. Also ask for a copy of the brochure *Shopping for a Safer Car*.

♦ Call AutoAdvisor, a national car-buying service (800-326-1976), and request literature describing their services.

Also, request literature describing the difference between car-buying services and auto brokers. Get out the Yellow Pages (under *Automobile—Buying Service* or *Automobile— Purchasing Consultants*) and call several of the listings. Request a brochure listing services, fees, and guarantees.

When it comes time to buy, consumers who lack knowledge (about the true cost and profit margins of cars), time, negotiating skills, or the fortitude to haggle with dealers will find that good car-buying services save many more dollars than they cost. In the research stage of the game, these same services can be very helpful in steering you away from rolling money pits.

♦ Price will be a crucial factor in determining what car you purchase, but the true cost of a car can be determined only if you know how quickly it will depreciate, the amount of gas it will guzzle, the cost of insuring it, and how often it will need repairs. Consequently, an important part of your research is not only to determine what cars you can afford to buy but which ones you can afford to own.

Go to the library and read through the Annual Auto Issue (April Issue) of *Consumer Reports*, paying particular attention to the predicted reliability of the cars they recommend and the frequency-of-repair records of different cars on the market.

The best single resource for determining what it costs to own particular vehicles is *The Complete Car Cost Guide* (find it in the reference section of the library or order it from IntelliChoice, 800-227-2665). This book evaluates depreciation, gas consumption, insurance costs, and frequency of repairs to derive the average five-year cost of operating each car. When you compare the different cars you're considering, you might make some startling revelations. For example, the 1995 4-door Honda Civic DX lists for $1800 more than the 1995 Hyundai Elantra 4-door sedan (list prices of $11,980 and $10,199 respectively). Over a five-year period, however, the total cost of owning the Honda is $21,377, some $3,655 *less* than the $25,032 it will cost to own the Hyundai for five years.

═══════ September 9 ═══════

Used or new? It's a question you'll want to answer during the confusing process of locating the next tenant for the garage. There are financial advantages to owning older cars—they've depreciated, insuring them is cheap, licensing them is cheap (licensing fees in many states are figured as a percentage of the car's value). Consider the mathematical madness of owning a new car:

You're looking at a vehicle with a suggested retail price of $18,400 but, through shrewd buying and rebates, you're biting only a $15,500 bullet. Of course, if you're financing some 80% of the purchase (say $12,500) on a three-year, 7.5% loan you've just tacked $1,500 in interest payments onto the tab. Then you've got sales tax, licensing, and insurance to think about which is, conservatively figured, another $1,500 claw in your craw. All totalled your car costs $18,500.

Now if your income is being taxed at 28%, you'll need to gross $23,700 to finance this purchase. For the average worker that means nearly 10 months of hard labor to pay for this *one* symbol of freedom. Think carefully about the life you're selling for that freedom.

This being said, there are valid reasons to own new cars—the safety standards of automobiles have improved steadily year by year and, because driving is one of the more lethal chores of modern life, many people view new cars as life savers rather than life wasters. Then, too, the reliability of new cars continues to escalate, and this, too, translates into increased safety out on the road.

Popular frugality dogma states that cars depreciate huge amounts (at least 20% per year) and that a low-mileage, year-old car is a far shrewder buy than a brand new car. That all depends.

It depends on the type of car being purchased—many domestics depreciate rapidly while certain Japanese vehicles (Toyotas, Subarus, Hondas) hardly depreciate at all. And it depends on how good a price you negotiate when purchasing new. Get a new car for invoice price or less (yes, this is possible) and you may well be making up the thousands of dollars that dogma says depreciation robs when you drive the vehicle home. In 1995 you could buy a year-old LX

Escort Wagon with 20,000 miles on it for $8,600, or with a little purchasing fortitude obtain a new LX Escort Wagon for $9,900. The better deal here is gray indeed.

When comparing new and near-new cars, there are no fixed rules. You'll need to study the numbers of your case (use the invoice price of a new car as a yardstick to determine how good the price of a used car is).

Some other pointers to help you determine whether to buy new or used:

◆ If safety is of paramount importance, buying new or near-new may be a necessity—safety improvements like dual air bags make newer cars far safer than cars that are only a few years old. Interestingly, tests conducted by the National Highway Traffic Safety Administration (NHTSA) show that new cars outfitted with air bags greatly reduce injury and death in head-on collisions. Many inexpensive cars that did not test well without air bags rivaled the head-on safety figures of much more expensive cars when outfitted with air bags.

◆ If you're willing to settle for cars that are at least three to four years old, depreciation will have created advantageous discrepancies between what some cars are valued at, and the life they have yet to give. For example, cars like the Buick Century have excellent drive trains and transmissions, and their 3-liter engines are among the most reliable made. Though these cars will go forever, they were not highly demanded and devalued quickly. Net result: a used bargain.

Interview mechanics, or look through *Consumer Reports'* frequency-of-repair records to locate cars that just keep rolling. Check to see how these reliable cars depreciate (use values from *The Kelley Blue Book Used Car Guide*, *N.A.D.A Official Used Car Guide*, or *The Complete Car Cost Guide*).

◆ Small- and medium-sized sedans are often the best values in used cars. Performance cars have probably given their best performances to previous owners. Meanwhile, convertibles and luxury cars remain pricey even when used.

◆ Old cars with relatively low mileage are choice buys. Age pushes the value down, but the mileage is more representative of the vehicle's true age. A properly maintained car with 50,000 miles on it is likely to have the same kick regardless of whether it is three years old or eight. The eight-year-old car, however, will be much cheaper.

September 10

You think a used car is right for you?

♦ Before shopping seriously for a used car, be it with a dealer or private seller, know the general value of the car you want. Study a month's worth of classified ads to learn what your machine sells for on the private market.

In the reference area of the library, look through the *N.A.D.A. Official Used Car Guide*, *The Kelley Blue Book Used Car Guide*, or Edmund's *Used Car Prices* to determine the market value of a particular car. Or get the info you need by calling AAA's *AutoPricing Service* (900-776-4222). Tell them the car model, year, mileage, condition, and accessory package (this is not a free call).

Without such information, it's hard to negotiate down an inflated figure. Equally important, you won't recognize a bargain when you see it.

♦ If you have the luxury of waiting, buy in November, December, or January. During these months buyers are scarce (everyone is cash starved preparing for, or recovering from, Christmas) and sellers may swing at low-ball offers.

September 11

When it comes time to actually shop for a used car, heed the following:

♦ You wouldn't expect it in this age of regulation, but tampering with the odometer is still a frequent (though totally illegal) practice. According to the Washington Department of Licensing, "Each year approximately three million used cars have their odometers rolled back an average of 30,000 miles."

Check that all the numbers across the odometer line up straight. Cockeyed numbers should rouse your suspicion. See if the relative condition of the car matches the odometer reading. How worn are the gas and brake pedals, how do the carpet and paint look, what shape is the upholstery in? A low-mileage car (under 30,000 miles) should not have bald tires. Nor should it have brand new tires. In either case, suspect that the odometer was disconnected, rolled back, or is some way altered.

◆ If you are buying a car from a new-car dealership or a used-car lot, contact the previous owner of the vehicle you're tempted to buy. He or she no longer owns the car and can talk honestly about its shortcomings. The old owner can also give you a guesstimate of the car's mileage when it was traded. This tells you whether the odometer reading is accurate.

Ask the dealer for the previous owner's name, address, and phone number. In most states, the dealer must disclose this information (call the Department of Licensing or Department of Motor Vehicles—dealer division—if you want the specifics for your state).

You can get around a dealer who won't relinquish (or does not know) the last owner's name by paying the Department of Motor Vehicles or Department of Licensing to perform a title search on the car.

◆ Private sellers (see the classified ads of the paper) usually undersell dealers because they don't need to net a profit. Private sellers generally approach the transaction with more honesty and less salesmanship. And you're likely to get more informed answers to the important questions you should be asking. Questions like: Why are you selling the car, what repair work has it required, has it ever been in an accident, how many people have owned the car?

The disadvantage of buying privately? Usually you buy the vehicle "as is," without a warranty. With savvy negotiating, however, you can often get a seller to agree to a short (e.g., one month) warranty. That's long enough to allay fears that the seller has swept a dark secret under the floorboards. Make sure you write down and both sign the conditions of a warranty.

◆ New-car dealerships often have a used-car division where they sell late-model and low-mileage cars. You're likely to get a reliable car and warranty here, but not the best price—these guys have their overhead and profit to make.

◆ No matter who you buy from, promises made about the car's condition, changes to the warranty, and adjustments to the price should be written down. Verbal agreements are as binding as a politician's pledge to balance the budget.

◆ People who buy a used car from a dealer should look for the "Buyer's Guide" sticker the Federal Trade Commission requires dealers to display on the vehicle. Don't see the Buyer's Guide? Then you have motive to distrust the dealer.

The Buyer's Guide notes whether the vehicle comes with a warranty and the limits of that warranty. It advises you to request your right to have the vehicle inspected. It tells you to write any changes made to the warranty or any promises right there on the Buyer's Guide.

Make sure you receive an identical copy of the Buyer's Guide (with all the added changes) when you purchase a used car. This copy overrides any of the provisions listed in the sales contract.

◆ If you are told a vehicle is still under the original manufacturer's warranty or any dealer service contracts, check that these benefits can be transferred from the original owner (read the contracts). Also, have the seller put in writing that the rights are transferrable.

◆ Perhaps the most important step in lemon prevention is to thoroughly inspect a used car before purchase. You're a mechanical idiot? Then rope a knowledgeable friend into examining the car.

If the car is still thumb's up after an initial inspection and you want to buy it, it's time to visit a professional mechanic. This will cost you at least $60, but it is not a step to avoid unless you are a mechanical ace.

Tell the mechanic the situation: You're thinking of buying the car and want a thorough inspection. You want to check the vehicle's compression, emissions, brakes, carburetion, transmission, struts, ball joints, ears, nose, and throat. You also want a report listing the cost of fixing the problems unearthed. If you want to purchase the car after the inspection, the report becomes a lever to drive down the price—you've got hard data here on what it will take to fix the car.

♦ Don't know a reliable professional mechanic? Contact the local chapter of the American Automobile Association (AAA). They can recommend a reliable (though not necessarily the cheapest) garage in your neighborhood.

♦ Never buy a used car without seeing the ownership documents. Does the car's Vehicle Identification Number (VIN) on the driver's side of the dashboard match the VIN on the title and registration?

♦ Check the radio of the vehicle. If it is set on all the hard rock stations, the head banger who had the car last probably drove the car like Hendrix plays the guitar—hard and fast.

♦ For more information on buying used cars read the annual Car Buying Issue of *Consumer Reports* and Consumer Guide's *Used Cars Rating Guide*.

=========== **September 12** ===========

Decided to spring for a new car? Ignorance will be your greatest enemy when it's time to buy the car you want. If you don't understand the process, the games played, the true cost of a car, the margins dealers will accept, what is and is not acceptable behavior on your part, the value of the car you intend to trade in, the dealer add-ons you should not purchase, and the bank rate for financing (if you intend to finance with the dealer), then the likelihood of negotiating a good deal is slim. Although you're unlikely to "beat" a salesman at his game, information is both your offense and defense in getting a fair deal. The hours spent researching all these issues can earn you thousands of dollars in savings.

◆ Sources that will reveal many details you should know about this game include: *How to Buy Your Car for Rock Bottom Prices* by Leslie Sachs. Sachs, who was once a car salesman, gives you an insider's look at the games salesmen play, the money they can exact, and how much you should pay for your car. The yearly New Car Issue (April) of *Consumer Reports* usually runs excellent articles on bargaining effectively for a new car; it also compares how the new cars stack up. The American Automobile Association (AAA) publishes a valuable book to pilot you through the process, entitled *AAA Car Buyer's Handbook* (purchase it at any AAA office). Consumer Guide's yearly *Car Comparisons* and *The Complete Car Cost Guide* are two more excellent resources you'll find at most libraries. Get to the library and read some of these resources.

◆ Even if you have your heart set on one particular vehicle, remember that many cars have twins. General Motors offers many of the same cars as Chevrolets, Buicks, Pontiacs, or Oldsmobiles. Chrysler often clones its cars as Dodges and Plymouths. The Geo Prism is essentially a Toyota Corolla built in America, while the Ford Probe and Mazda MX-6 are twins. The annual car issue of *Consumer Reports* tells which automobiles are twins. If the car you're interested in is twinned, you've upped the odds of landing a deal.

◆ When should you buy a new car? A prime time, according to conventional wisdom, is at the end of a model year when salesmen lament that they are 'giving away' last year's models to make room for the new cars.

Ashley Knapp, owner of the oldest car-buying service in the country, disagrees. According to Knapp, the price of cars steadily escalates throughout the year so the discounted price of these give-aways is rarely no better than what the car would have sold for at the beginning of the model year. Your new car is already a year old and, depreciation-wise, this works against you if you're selling the vehicle several years later. Furthermore, what you're buying at year's end is often the dregs—unpopular colors or option packages.

If you know you're going to buy a new vehicle, Knapp says the best time to purchase is at the beginning of the model year. In fact, before the vehicle even arrives on the lots the manufacturer may be offering come-on prices that will never be seen again. If you intend to sell the car in four or five years, you'll also get a full year of driving out of the vehicle before depreciation takes its bite.

Note: different manufacturers start their model years at different times. Call the dealers to find out when they start stocking their new models.

═══ September 13 ═══

To secure a good price on a car, you need a realistic vision of what price is possible. Consult different experts and you'll get different opinions on what you should pay. According to the book *How to Buy Your Car for Rock Bottom Prices*, the minimum price for a persistent negotiator can be as little as $150 over *full* invoice price (full invoice price is the dealer's cost plus about $500 for freight and shipping charges) or about $650 over *base* invoice price (base invoice price is the dealer's cost and does not include freight charges). Why so little? Surely a dealer can't survive making a mere $150 per car sold. Unbeknownst to most people, dealers typically receive a hidden 3% rebate from the manufacturer after selling the car. On a $10,000 car, that is another $300 made.

According to *Consumer Reports,* the amount you should expect to pay over the full invoice price depends on the make of car. You may have no negotiating power on highly demanded vehicles but, as a rule, you should be able to land most cars for 2% to 4% over full invoice price.

Meanwhile, Ashley Knapp, the owner of Auto Advisor, a car-buying service, suggests using full invoice price as the initial target. Then find out what hidden rebates are in play by reading the current issue of the trade magazine *Automotive News*. The last five pages of the magazine list all the current dealer incentives. Big city libraries are likely to subscribe to the magazine, but if you can't locate it, stop in at any dealership and ask whether you could see a current issue of the magazine. Knapp says that invoice price minus the hidden rebates constitutes the new figure where negotiations should begin. When the haggling is done, you may be a few hundred dollars over this figure— after all, unless there are other incentives at work (this is quite possible), the dealer isn't going to let the vehicle go without earning something.

Find out the invoice price of the car (and options) you want by:

◆ Calling AAA's *Auto Pricing Service* at 900-776-4AAA (they charge you by the length of the call: $1 for the first minute, $1.95 for each additional minute).
◆ Writing *Consumer Reports Auto Price Service* for a cost printout of the car you want ($11 for the first model of car, $10 for the second, and $7 for each additional car).
◆ Visiting the library and looking up dealer costs in either- *Edmund's New Car Prices*, Consumer Guide's *Car Comparisons*, or *The Complete Car Cost Guide.*

September 14

Here's another way to hone in on what you might realistically pay for a new car. Spend a few hours today calling different dealerships and asking for the fleet manager. Tell the fleet manager you want to know the cost of purchasing a company car for your business. Home businesses and cottage industries are as capable of buying a company car as one of the Fortune 500s. Don't own a company? Then perhaps your working spouse could do a little field work from the office—you know, for research purposes.

Figure out an introduction, telling who you are, who you work for, and what your company needs. Be direct and non-apologetic in saying, "I'm calling local dealerships for quotes on a _____ (give them vehicle and options desired)." If certain options are undecided, say so, asking what the option costs.

Some dealers will give you a quote on the spot, some may want you to fax them a request before they fax you a quote, some may take the information down and call you back with a bid. The bids you do receive will typically have most of the fat cut out of them—they're likely to be $100 to $250 over invoice price.

This part of a dealership's business seems to skip most of the games, antics, and showmanship taking place in the consumer-sales division of the company. That's not to say, however, that you can't or shouldn't play one dealer against the other. Be direct, using a line like, "Another dealership offered a better price. My boss wants to know if you'll sharpen your pencil."

You'll either get cooperation or a, "That's the best I can offer." Either way you'll have gathered valuable data today.

===== **September 15** =====

Preferably you'll pay cash for your new or used car.

Even so, you should calculate your monthly payments. That's right. In the future (be that three, five, or 10 years) you'll be replacing this car and you'll need a new cash fund to draw from. Estimate what a future car will cost, then send monthly payments to your own investment program to build that fund.

♦ If you must finance a car, put down as much cash as possible. Putting nothing down (a gimmick often advertised) sounds sweet but the interest you pay for the privilege should give you a bad aftertaste. Also, establish a loan for the shortest term possible: The shorter the term (and the lower the rate) the less you pay in interest.

♦ Before you enter a dealership with the actual intent of buying a car, call a few banks and determine the going rates for car loans. Specify whether you're considering a used or new car—the rates differ. If you decide to finance the car through the dealer, negotiate for market rate; definitely pay no more than 1% over bank rate.

♦ Finally, use the chart on the following page if you are financing a car and can't decide whether to use the bank's financing and pocket the manufacturer's rebate, or whether to sacrifice the rebate in favor of low financing charges available through the manufacturer. This chart is printed with the permission of *The Pocket Change Investor*, a quarterly newsletter promoting savvy spending habits (Good Advice Press, 800-255-0899).

The Great Debate: Rebate or Low Rate?
Go for the rebate if it's more than ...

% Dealer Rate	% Bank Rate	$10,000				$13,500				$17,000			
		Term of Loan in Years											
		2	3	4	5	2	3	4	5	2	3	4	5
3	7	430	647	870	1,100	580	873	1,174	1,484	731	1,099	1,478	1,869
	8	540	812	1,094	1,385	728	1,096	1,477	1,869	917	1,380	1,859	2,354
	9	649	979	1,321	1,674	876	1,322	1,782	2,259	1,103	1,663	2,244	2,845
	10	760	1,147	1,550	1,967	1,025	1,549	2,092	2,655	1,291	1,950	2,634	3,344
	11	871	1,317	1,782	2,264	1,175	1,778	2,405	3,056	1,480	2,238	3,028	3,849
	12	983	1,488	2,016	2,566	1,326	2,009	2,721	3,463	1,670	2,529	3,426	4,361
4	7	323	487	656	831	436	657	886	1,122	550	828	1,116	1,412
	8	433	652	880	1,116	584	880	1,189	1,507	736	1,109	1,497	1,897
	9	542	819	1,107	1,405	732	1,106	1,494	1,897	922	1,392	1,882	2,388
	10	653	987	1,336	1,698	881	1,333	1,804	2,293	1,110	1,679	2,272	2,887
	11	764	1,157	1,568	1,995	1,031	1,562	2,117	2,694	1,299	1,967	2,666	3,392
	12	876	1,328	1,802	2,297	1,182	1,793	2,433	3,101	1,489	2,258	3,064	3,904
5	7	216	326	440	558	292	439	594	753	368	555	748	948
	8	326	491	664	843	440	662	897	1,138	554	836	1,129	1,433
	9	435	658	891	1,132	588	888	1,202	1,528	740	1,119	1,514	1,924
	10	546	826	1,120	1,425	737	1,115	1,512	1,924	928	1,406	1,904	2,423
	11	657	996	1,352	1,722	887	1,344	1,825	2,325	1,117	1,694	2,298	2,928
	12	769	1,167	1,586	2,024	1,038	1,575	2,141	2,732	1,307	1,985	2,696	3,440
6	7	108	164	221	281	146	221	299	379	184	279	376	478
	8	218	329	445	566	294	444	602	764	370	560	757	963
	9	327	496	672	855	442	670	907	1,154	556	843	1,142	1,454
	10	438	664	901	1,148	591	897	1,217	1,550	744	1,130	1,532	1,953
	11	549	834	1,133	1,445	741	1,126	1,530	1,951	933	1,418	1,926	2,458
	12	661	1,005	1,367	1,747	892	1,357	1,846	2,358	1,123	1,709	2,324	2,970

Simple Instructions: No Assembly Required

It's your lucky day. The car dealer's offering you 3% financing for 2 years or a $500 cash rebate, your choice. And the bank just approved a $13,500 loan at 8%. What should you do?

First, find the 3% dealer rate on the chart. Look over to the 8% bank rate, then across to where $13,500 and 2 years meet. It'd take a rebate of $728 or more to beat the dealer's low interest rate, if you were to go for the 2 year bank loan. So you'd go for the dealer financing.

Now let's say the dealer is offering a 4% rate loan, or a $1,000 rebate. Assume that the bank alternative would still be $13,500 at 8%, but this time, you're thinking about a 3 year loan. Which one is the better deal? With $880 as the break-even point, you'd take the bank loan, and go for the dough! To maximize your savings, you'd use that $1,000 rebate as a lump sum pre-payment.

If your loan amount doesn't appear on the chart, all you have to do is some really simple math. For example, the break-even rebate point for a $20,000 loan would be twice as much as for a $10,000 loan at the same interest rate. So to equal 3% dealer financing, you'd need a rebate of $1,080 (2 x $540), assuming an 8% bank loan for 2 years.

But what about interest rates that aren't on the chart? Say you can get 7.5% bank financing on $10,000 for 2 years, or a 3% dealer loan. The rebate would have to be halfway between the $430 at 7% and the $540 at 8% — or $485. At 7.25%, you'd go a quarter of the way up — to $458.

Notes: This table is based on the total cost of loans, and was prepared with *The Banker's Secret Software* ($42.95, 800-255-0899), which will help you save money on your car loan and your mortgage.

═══ September 16 ═══

Study the following advice and commit it to memory. When the day comes to actually purchase your new car, these pointers will keep dealers from taking tropical vacations on your dollars.

◆ The urge to own a car today, pronto, works strongly against you in negotiating a car deal. If the salesman perceives you are emotionally hooked (that you've got to have this car and you've gotta have it today) he's not going to come down to his lowest price. It is only when he knows you're detached enough to walk that he'll keep dropping the price.

Sometimes you just have to get up and leave. Do it slowly, look around longer, give the salesman time to restart the negotiation. He knows if you leave he's unlikely to see you again. And if he has put time and energy in you, he won't let you go if he can make a sale at some price.

What if he doesn't rise to the bait, what if he lets you walk out the door? Worry not. What he offered today will be available to you tomorrow. You just need to call back, and say you needed time to consider his offer and you're ready to talk again.

◆ Many dealers will tack an advertisement allowance or "pack" onto the cost of your car. Negotiate it away. Advertising is a cost of business that should not be passed on.

◆ Dealers use the tremendously successful trick of adding their own options and policies to the factory sticker-price. They may print these dealer add-ons on an official sheet and post it on the car, making it look like you must purchase rust-proofing, fabric protection, processing fees, insurance, extended service contracts, anti-theft protection. Cross them all off and subtract the figures from the cost of the car. Why?

Rustproofing or undercoating is basically a fraud: Cars are rustproofed at the factory and don't need extra protection. What the dealer gets here is primarily pure profit.

Dealer prep and/or glaze and fabric protection amounts to a can of *Scotchguard* sprayed on the upholstery and a wax job. Not much for the $200 it might cost.

Processing fees can be printed on an invoice as if they were a mandatory fee. They rarely are. Eliminate them from the vehicle's cost.

Need accident, life, theft insurance? Fine. Get them elsewhere and you'll land better policies at lower costs.

Extended warranties and service contracts offered by the dealer seem like a good idea but consumer magazines and books consistently advise against them. Extended warranties possess more holes than a sponge and dealers are incredibly adept at finding the holes that shelter them from paying. Documents filed in a lawsuit against Nissan in 1988 revealed dealers paid back only 16.5% on the extended warranty packages that sold for $795. That means the dealers were sponging off huge profits. Rather than buying an extended warranty, buy a car with a good manufacturer's warranty and/or one with a history of few repairs.

◆ When negotiating a deal, successful salespersons will start discussing different option packages, financing possibilities, and trade-in prices. In the process they subtly move you off the bedrock of your knowledge into the quicksand of a high-priced trap. If you suddenly find yourself clueless about whether you're doing splendidly or getting splayed, don't hesitate to dismiss yourself with an, "Excuse me, I need to make a phone call."

Before signing any paperwork, call the Instant-Help, Check-Your-Price-Service of AutoAdvisor by calling 800-326-1976. Over the phone you can explain what you're buying (car, model, accessories), and then receive figures about what you should really be paying as well as advice on how to get that price. It's a $67 can of spinach to keep the dealership from pummeling you.

◆ Factory-installed options are good buys, but think twice about any option the dealer wants to add—stereo, sunroof, etc. Specialty shops do better work for less money (sometimes half the price).

◆ After negotiating on the new car, your resistance to the procedure may have faltered when it comes to dickering over what your trade-in is worth. You may think, "I got a great price on the car; I can give a little on the trade-in." Don't. You deserve what the vehicle is worth. Before buying a new car, check the Blue-Book value of your old one, take it around to used-car lots for their offers, check the classified ads to determine what your year and model of car fetches when sold privately. Use this information to get what your car is worth.

♦ Check the dealer's math if you are financing your car and are quoted a monthly payment—the payment is frequently miscalculated and, mysteriously, those miscalculations rarely work out in your favor.

To help you, come to the dealership armed with either auto-financing tables or amortization tables (available at bookstores and the reference section of libraries) and a pocket calculator. While your salesman visits the financing department to determine your monthly payment, calculate the amount yourself. If you use amortization tables, your figure may not exactly match the dealer's, but it should be darn close.

♦ Before signing a final agreement, check it with a magnifying glass. The boys who write up the final agreement often make mistakes. Sometimes the agreed-upon price gets listed incorrectly, or extras you crossed off get added back on, or a higher financing charge than the one you settled upon gets used. Give that contract Gestapo treatment.

♦ Even if you do sign, the agreement is not binding *until* you drive the car off the lot. Until that time, the dealer must refund your deposit and return a trade-in should you back out.

Therefore, you don't want to take home a new car until it is prepared as promised and until all the financing details are settled. If it is late and the salesman tells you to take the car home and return tomorrow to finish the details, don't relent. You've got a nervous salesman and a big negotiating lever when the car remains with the dealer. Take the vehicle home and you break the lever.

September 17

If you lack the stomach or time for the car-purchasing game, use the services of a reputable automotive consulting and purchasing firm. A good service can help you identify the best vehicle for your needs, *and* because they truly know what cars should sell for and have several dealerships bidding for your business, they should guarantee the lowest price going (their guarantee should stipulate a refund of their fee if you can beat their price).

Unless you're a shrewd and knowledgeable operator, the fee paid to a national car-buying service like AutoAdviser (800-326-1976 or 206-323-1976) is likely to save you substantially more than the $335 cost.

Yet another purchasing strategy comes from Ashley Knapp, the owner of AutoAdvisor. He calls it the Ten-Minute Negotiation. The trick here is to change the rules of car buying. This requires accurate information about the cost of the desired car and some role-playing skills, but it eliminates most of chicanery associated with the car-buying process. Here's how it works.

◆ Do your homework: Decide on a car and test drive it; prearrange your financing; and know the invoice price, freight charges, and hidden rebates associated with your dream machine.

◆ When it's time to buy, arrive at the dealership in a respectable vehicle, dressed to impress. Have a photocopied sheet in hand showing the car desired and listing the model, color, and options desired. Be polite but be in a hurry—you are an important person with little time to waste. Write your name and phone number on the sheet and tell the attending salesman, "I want to buy this car at this price (list the best price your research says is possible). This price, of course does not include taxes or licensing, but I need this price or something extremely close to it."

Then say, "I'd like to get the car as soon as possible— my financing is ready—but I can wait while you order or trade for the car."

Tell the salesman to talk to Mr. Honda, or Mr. Ford, or whoever must be consulted to get you that price.

◆ Now dismiss yourself. Salesmen will lure you to stay. Don't. Be polite, gentle, friendly, and trusting, but leave. "I'm sorry, life is crazy, work... family... You can understand that. Talk to Mr. Honda. Get me that price. Call me later—I'd love to buy a car from you."

◆ Run the same routine at several dealerships. Get in fast, get out fast, then go home and harvest the calls. Some salesmen won't respond, so call another salesman at the same dealership, "Steve wasn't interested, but I'm still primed: my financing is ready and you've got a sale if you get me that price."

◆ Salesmen who do call will try to chisel information from you. Cut to the quick, "Sorry, Steve, I'm in the middle of a deadline. Did you get the price I asked for? Can we do it for $X?"

You're likely to hear, "Well, I don't know."

"Steve, that was the whole point, to find out. Why did you call if you don't know? Please, go back to Mr. Honda and find out. That's the car I want, that's the price my budget can afford...You have a family, Steve?... Do you make a ton of money?... Then you can appreciate trying to provide for a family within a budget. My budget says I can buy that car at that price. Please... Go to bat for me. Talk to Mr. Honda. Let me know if you can get that price."

Your angle is price, price, price. Don't give up the floor. And don't buy lines like "We've got the best service center in the region." You're not purchasing service. You're buying the car from the dealer providing the best price. Later, you'll get it serviced by whoever you decide gives the best service. The two issues are unrelated.

September 18

An African saying notes, "It's better to repair than purchase anew."

It doesn't take Marilyn vos Savant to explain that a dime's worth of glue to repair a possession beats a $10 expenditure on its replacement. Which means every household needs a rudimentary repair kit. Today, check that your repair kit is stocked with an all-star team of glues and tapes capable of handling most of your repair needs. The following fixers will pay back dividends a hundredfold greater than what you invest in them—that's an even better investment than having purchased Microsoft stock when the company went public. Put those items you don't yet own on the Master Purchasing List (see January 1) and get them when travels take you near a major hardware store.

Over 15,000 glues infest the marketplace, but a handful of general-purpose, household glues will handle 90% of your repair needs.

♦ **Epoxy cement**, a two-tube glue that you mix, is a star player of that team. It creates a very strong, waterproof bond that sticks to most hard surfaces (metal, plastics, wood, porcelain). It also fills gaps on surfaces that won't be flexed. Slow-setting epoxies (24 hours to cure) are the strongest, but the five-minute varieties still receive adequate grades for strength. The quick sets are better when bonding parts and pieces that cannot be clamped. Elmer's, Duro, and Devcon are all widely available, good-quality epoxies.

♦ **Contact cement**, a glue brushed onto each of the two surfaces being glued together, has extremely diverse uses in bonding flexible materials (like patches to tires or rafts) and rigid materials (like tiles to counter tops). It is waterproof and lets you bond materials in a matter of minutes.

♦ **Wood glues**, both white glue (like Elmer's Glue-All) *and* yellow carpenter's glue are inexpensive, strong adhesives for interior use on a wide variety of semi-porous materials—wood, paper, particle board, cardboard, styrofoam. Carpenter's glue has a shorter clamping time, is more water-resistant, and sands easier than white glue.

♦ **Cyanoacrylates**, like *Super Glue* or *Krazy Glue*, are not as useful as late-night TV ads crack them up to be, but they are handy for items that can't be clamped—porcelain, pottery, fingers, eyelids....

Along with these glues, the complete repair kit needs a diverse supply of tapes.

♦ **Duct tape** changed the face of the repair world because this one item has 1,001 applications for splinting breaks, patching holes, reinforcing worn areas, repairing tears, sealing leaks, covering nicks, and clamping odd-shaped items. All duct tapes have threads laminated inside them to increase strength. The mesh pattern of really good tape resembles the mesh pattern of a window screen..

♦ **Masking tape**, another essential around the home, can be used for far more than masking walls and windows that should not be painted. Use it to clamp odd-shaped items during gluing, splice wires (if electrical tape is not available), patch car hoses, tape paper products together.

♦ **Packaging tape**, while less useful for actual repairs, is extremely handy for shipping, sealing storage boxes, and reinforcing storage boxes. Every household needs at least one roll of clear packaging tape.

♦ **Electrical tape** does not handle a wide array of odd jobs, but when you repair or splice electrical wires, this is the tape of preference. And because you're dealing with electricity, get the best product for the job—you don't really want to play with fire.

===== September 19 =====

Today, track down several more invaluable items for your home repair kit.

♦ The most valuable members of my home repair kit are liquid-urethane compounds. These compounds come out of a tube as a viscous, clear syrup about the consistency of cold honey and dry into a tough, flexible rubber. Liquid urethanes can be used to patch holes in tarps, rafts, tents, inner tubes, tennis and running shoes, hiking and rubber boots, waders, and balls. They can be used to reglue surfaces (like a shoe sole separating from the upper); build up eroded surfaces (like the heel of a running shoe); and patch holes (like those in clothing, packs, shoe uppers, and gloves).

A few of these compounds like *Shoo Goo* and *Goop* can be found at hardware stores and both are excellent for repairing the spines of dilapidated books; creating pads of paper (see November 27); or reinforcing rough, porous materials.

The hands-down best products in the genre, however, are those made by the McNett Corporation (1405 Frazer, Bellingham, WA 98226) like *Aquaseal* or *Seamgrip*. These compounds cost more and are slow to cure, but there is no comparison in how well they bond to slick, non-porous materials like soles of running shoes, the rubber of balls, the surface of hip waders. Find these products at hunting, fishing, diving, backpacking, or marine-supply shops. Or order them from the manufacturer (360-671-2227) or REI (800-426-4840).

When creating a patch with any liquid-urethane compound, lay down masking tape to form neat boundaries. When patching a gaping hole, rub tape to the underside so that the glue can pool and cure without draining away.

◆ The all-purpose glue my neighbor, the fix-up guy on our block, promotes with fanatical fervor is *Marine Tex*, an epoxy putty. It bonds materials like glue, yet acts like putty to repair leaks in fuel tanks, water tanks, piping, food containers, cracks in the crankcase of engines.... It bonds to metal, plastic, fiberglass, wood, glass and is impervious to water, oil, grease, fuel, brine, and detergents. The glue has both incredible tensile and compressive strength and won't shatter under heavy blows. Get it from marine-supply stores or contact the manufacturer (Travaco Laboratories, 345 Eastern Ave., Chelsea, MA 02150, 617-884-7740).

September 20

Keep your possessions in good repair, and both the need and desire to replace them (always an expensive proposition) will vanish. Today it's time to work on furniture.

◆ Scratched furniture. Scrapes in wood can be hidden with beeswax or with crayons, shoe polish, or felt-tip markers matching the wood color. Scratches in dark woods can also be hidden by rubbing on a paste made from instant coffee crystals and water. Scratches in valuable furniture can be hidden by working with high-quality touch-up pens available through large furniture dealers.

◆ Loose furniture joints. One loose joint leads to another, so fix wobbles whenever you encounter them. Don't nail these joints; glue them with yellow carpenter's glue or white wood glue. Remove old glue—glue adheres by absorbing into the wood and attaching itself to the wood fibers. Always put joints being glued under pressure with clamps, elastic tie down straps (bungee cords), hose clamps, rubber bands, or other devices capable of compressing the area.

♦ White rings on furniture. These water marks have discolored the finish but not the underlying wood. Use mineral oil (or baby oil) and a soft rag to remove furniture wax. Then, using a new rag, rub the ring with isopropyl alcohol. Rub fast and gently if the finish becomes tacky. A stubborn ring that won't lift may need light sanding with 600-grit sandpaper and baby oil. Wax the area when finished.

Note: Before working on a visible surface, test this procedure on a hidden part of the furniture.

♦ Dented wood. Lift minor dents in wood by covering them with a wet rag and briefly laying an iron (set on high) over the rag. Furniture patch sticks (available at hardware stores) will fill larger nicks. Rub wax over the patch and buff.

September 21

Light bulbs are rated in watts, a measure of the power they consume, but wattage does not tell how much light is produced—lumens tell that story. Lumens per watt, meanwhile, measure efficiency (like miles per gallon) and different types of light bulbs can be as different in efficiency as the Geo Metro and a Winnebago.

Incandescent light bulbs (the common bulb found in homes) have changed little in the 110 years since Edison's day—90% of the electricity that feeds them is still wasted in heat. They produce about 17 to 23 lumens per watt. Fluorescent bulbs, on the other hand, are three to four times more efficient, yielding 67 to 83 lumens per watt.

Adding fluorescent lights to high-use rooms like the kitchen is easy if you're building a house, but how do you capitalize on their efficiency in older homes? With compact fluorescents.

Compact fluorescents screw into the same fixtures as normal incandescent bulbs, but one of these bulbs will produce the same lumen output as a 75-watt incandescent. Assuming average power rates of 8¢ per kilowatt hour, one compact fluorescent burned for four hours a day will save you $6.66/year, $13.32/year if the light is burned eight hours a day.

Unfortunately, these bulbs are expensive. An 18-watt bulb, for example, can cost $15 to $18, so they won't pay off in locations where the light is "on" only a few minutes per day. In locations where the bulb burns daily for long hours, however, compact fluorescents will pay for themselves in a year or two. And because these bulbs have incredible longevity (their average life is 10 times longer than an incandescent bulb) you won't be paying that steep, upfront cost for a long time to come.

Circular fluorescents, like the GE *Circlite*, convert lamps with large shades (table lamps or hanging lights) to fluorescent bulbs. These circular fluorescents produce the lumen output of a 75- or 100-watt incandescent bulb with one-third the power. Replace the old bulb with a screw-in fluorescent adapter (ballast), snap the circular bulb onto the adapter, and cover the apparatus with the lamp shade.

Like compact fluorescents, circular fluorescents last about 10 times longer than normal incandescent bulbs (10,000 hours versus 1,000 hours). Purchased at large hardware and electric-supply stores, they cost $9 to $15.

♦ Many utility companies participate in rebate programs to tempt their customers into replacing incandescent bulbs with compact fluorescents. For a utility company, this is a wise conservation program; for you, it's a chance to get the bulbs cheaply. Currently, my utility company offers a $7 per bulb rebate on compact fluorescents. Call your utility to see what deals are awaiting you.

September 22

Make the rounds of the house today surveying the kitchen lights, hallway fixtures, bedroom lamps, outdoor and indoor security lights.... Which ones are "on" long enough each night (at least a few hours) to justify replacing with a compact or circular fluorescent?

◆ Unfortunately, finding a suitable fluorescent for each spot is not necessarily easy. Compact fluorescents don't fit every lamp or fixture, they may not be bright enough for some applications, or the lamp shade may not fit over them. It will take some looking to locate bulbs you can live with.

So, to the Yellow Pages you go (*Light Bulbs and Tubes*). Call the larger stores and ask about their selection of different fluorescents. Do they have compact fluorescents, circular fluorescents, fluorescent floods, fluorescents suitable for outdoor security use...? How many of these lights are displayed? Visit the store(s) offering big selections and good displays.

◆ For information on compact and circular fluorescents (and local dealers) you can call General Electric (800-626-2000) and Lights of America (800-321-8100).

◆ The recessed ceiling fixtures you may have in some of your rooms or hallways can be filled with bulbs like the Lumatech fluorescent flood lamps (800-932-0637 or 510-654-4300). Ranging in price from $20 to $40, this is not a cheap option *unless* that particular light stays on much of the day. A more economical solution will employ a 15- or 18-watt compact fluorescent (globe or capsule style) and a reflector that bounces the light lost to the fixture into the room.

◆ Be aware that fluorescents don't hit their full lumen output until they've been on for several minutes. Also, leave them on unless you will be leaving a room for longer than 20 minutes—otherwise the wear and tear on the ballast is not offset by the energy saved.

Buying Tips:
◆ Not all compact fluorescents turn on without flickering first. Avoid this nuisance in preference of bulbs that light up straight away.

◆ Get lights with reusable ballasts and replaceable bulbs. The bulbs die long before the ballasts and you want to be able to replace the cheapest part (which is the bulb).

◆ Buy bulbs encased in glass. Those with clear, plastic exteriors can yellow over time, ruining the quality of the white light.

September 23

Incandescent bulbs turned on and off with a dimmer will last far longer than those operated with a normal switch. The dimmer reduces the power surge that destroys the filament of many bulbs. It also lets you operate the bulb at lower voltages—dropping the voltage just 3% below maximum extends bulb life by 40%. A variety of inexpensive, easily installed dimmer switches can replace the light switches in hallways, bedrooms, and living rooms. For lamps, dimmers that clamp quickly to the power cord or attach to the socket are options.

◆ Wander the house and determine which lamps, bedrooms, hallways, and living rooms would benefit from a dimmer. Call the local hardware stores to see who has the best selection of dimmers before putting mileage on the car.

◆ For most home applications, dimmers with mechanical controls are the best choice. Alladin 710 slide dimmer ($14) and Alladin 120 rotary dimmer ($7.50) are both good products. For lamps, the Leviton 6356 lamp dimmer ($24) and the Alladin 510 socket dimmer ($7.95) are among the better-rated products.

◆ These dimmers require no real genius to install. If you can read instructions (I know, that eliminates most men) you can handle the job.

Note: Unplug lamps before installing a dimmer. Shut off power at the circuit box before working on wall switches. A small mistake here could be your last mistake.

September 24

A joke says that the two happiest days of a homeowner's life are the day he buys a home and the day he sells it. That's because homes—especially old ones—can be black holes that demand ever-larger slices of your income. The tips over the next week work to remedy that. They'll give you inexpensive ideas for dealing with home repairs and maintenance.

Today, tackle your door problems.

♦ Swinging doors. Bedroom and bathroom doors that swing open or closed by themselves don't need a cross to be exorcised, they need a hammer. Remove the hinge pin from one hinge (place a nail in the bottom of the hinge and force the pin up with taps of the hammer), lay the pin on a concrete floor, and bend it *slightly* by striking it with a hammer. Reinsert the pin and the swinging will be gone or reduced. If the door still swings slowly, repeat the procedure with the other hinge pin.

♦ Rattling doors. The racket of a rattling door gets irritating over time. Fix the problem by bending out the tongue of the strike plate (use a screwdriver or pliers) until it exerts pressure against the edge of the door. Open and close the door several times to fine tune how much you should uncurl the tongue.

♦ Non-latching doors. It gets embarrassing when you're on the throne and, surprise, the door pops open. Inspect the hinges first and tighten any loose screws. If the problem persists, the door latch is not sliding properly into the hole on the strike plate. Study the latch as you close the door to see which edge of the strike plate's hole is binding the latch. Now use a file to enlarge the hole so that the latch slides in.

September 25

The work order for the day is counter tops.

Repair burns and chips in your counters with *Seamfil* (Kampel Enterprises, Wellsville, PA, 717-432-9688). The kit comes with filler, a wide assortment of colors, mixing charts to match colors, and additives for a glossy finish (it cures naturally to a matte finish).

A cheaper alternative is to fill small nicks and cracks with a wood-patching compound like *Zar Wood Patch* (United Gilsonite Laboratories, Scranton, PA, 1-800-272-3235). Color the compound to the desired shade with watercolors or acrylic paints from an art-supply store.

Large, deep burns and chips may be difficult to patch adequately. Consider cutting out the damaged area and laying in a stainless-steel insert that will serve as a trivet for hot pots. Just Manufacturing Company (Franklin Park, IL, 847-678-5150) makes several sizes of Hot Pad Inserts that nestle into holes cut into the counter top.

September 26

Worried about termites? You should be. In the U.S. alone they cause over $1 billion in home damage each year. To ensure these are not your dollars, do the following:

♦ Relocate all wood piles that are beneath or alongside your house. Cover attic vents with small mesh screens. Ventilate all crawl spaces, and check that the plastic vapor barrier under your house adequately covers the ground.

♦ Treat the wooden sills on basement windows or replace them with concrete sills. Contact your local hardware store for their recommendation on how to treat wooden sills.

September 27

Clean your chimneys and/or stovepipes at least once a winter (twice if you burn regularly). Scraping out creosote deposits eliminates the possibility that a hot or sparking fire could cause a chimney fire. As long as you can work on the roof without danger of falling, it's an easy job.

♦ Purchase a wire-bristled chimney brush at the hardware store and attach it to a 10-foot length of aluminum conduit (3/4" diameter). Tie and/or tape the brush securely to the pole so you don't accidentally leave the brush behind in the chimney (an ugly problem to fix but an easy one to prevent).

♦ Inside, make sure you have the doors to the fireplace or stove closed (fireplaces that don't have glass doors should be blocked off with cardboard). Outside, remove screens covering the chimney, insert the brush, and scrub it with vigorous up-and-down strokes.

September 28

Cleaning the gutters is one of those menial chores needing attention several times a year. If you're unable to negotiate the roof or yoyo up and down a ladder, you'll hire someone for the job.

Minimize those cleanings by laying long strips of plastic mesh like *Gutter Guard* over the top of your gutters. The product is inexpensive (about $2.50 for a 25-foot by 6-inch roll), available at large hardware stores, and dramatically reduces the number of gutter cleanings you will need.

September 29

Sliding heavy furniture around on hardwood floors commonly causes scratches. Chairs are particularly bad offenders: Heavy stuffed chairs can scar floors as kids push them around during play, and dining room chairs frequently gouge the floor as adults scoot to and from the table.

◆ Protect what you've invested in hardwood floors today by purchasing several square feet of felt, cutting small pads for the bottom of furniture legs, and gluing these pads on. Contact cement makes the job quick and easy. Brush a layer of glue onto one side of the felt pads and to the bottom of furniture legs. After five minutes apply a second coat of glue to the felt pad. Wait until the glue looks glossy and is ever-so-slightly tacky to touch (about 15 minutes). Align the glued surface of the pad over the glued surface of the leg and press them together. The glue bonds instantly when the two surfaces connect.

September 30

It's fast, it's easy, and, if you own a forced-air heating system, changing the air filter is something you should do each month. A dirty air filter increases the load on your heater's blower which increases your electric bill and decreases the life of your heater.

As you pull out the old air filter, note which way its air-flow arrow points (you may want to attach a piece of tape to the furnace noting the direction of the air flow). Slip in a new air filter from the hardware store, with its air-flow arrow pointing in the correct direction, and you're done. If your heater uses a permanent filter, you should clean it each month. Check the unit's manual for instructions.

Besides changing the filter...

◆ Place air filters on your Master Purchasing List (note the dimensions needed). When the filters come on sale (expect prices between 70¢ and $1), stock up for a year.

◆ On your daily calendar, note a time during each wintertime month to change the filter.

Cheap Trick:

If you don't want to trash your old filters, clean them. Lay a sheet of wire-mesh screening (with about a ½" mesh) or chicken wire over the filters and use a canister-styled vacuum to clean them.

October

October 1

One of the most significant energy-saving tasks for the do-it-yourselfer is to check the insulation wrapping the ductwork carrying heat (or cooling) from the furnace (air conditioner) to each room of the house. Uninsulated ducts running through crawl spaces, basements, and attics can loose 40% of their heat (cooling) before reaching the intended room. Pare your utility bills by making sure all ductwork has been wrapped with rolls of foil-backed fiberglass insulation (minimum loft of 2½ inches).

♦ Don old clothes, grab a flashlight and ruler, and head to the grottos (crawl spaces, basement, attic). Find the ducts and, using the ruler, check several segments to make sure they are adequately wrapped. If there is less than 2½ inches of insulation, wrap the ducts with more. By using rolls of one-inch foil-backed fiberglass insulation and a 50% overlap (foil side out) you can add two inches of insulation with no obvious seams for heat to escape. Use duct tape to attach and seal the insulation when starting or ending a roll. It's easy (but itchy) work and it's an investment that will pay for itself during one heating season.

♦ Use the phone to price the insulation at local home-improvement/hardware stores. Ask about the lengths, widths, thicknesses, and prices of fiberglass insulation to wrap heat ducts. Also, if you have friends in the construction/contracting business, ask if they can purchase materials for less.

October 2

The U.S. Department of Energy recommends that walls and floors of houses be insulated to values of R-19 (the R-value measures the resistance to heat flow: the higher the number, the greater the resistance). Ceilings should be insulated to R-30 in Southern US, R-38 in middle latitudes of the country, and R-49 in northern latitudes.

◆ Do-it-yourselfers wishing to improve the energy efficiency of an older house can accomplish this by adding insulation in the attic and beneath the floors. Check that the insulation in these spaces meets the U.S. Department of Energy's recommended R-values listed above. Measure the average depth of the insulation in the attic and below the floor, write down the measurements and the type of insulation used, and call a building-supply store for an estimate of the R-values. Alternately, check the charts published in either *How to Weatherize Your Home or Apartment* or *All About Insulation.* Both booklets are published by the Massachusetts Audubon Society (Educational Resources, 208 South Great Road, Lincoln, MA 01773). Cost is $4.25 each (shipping included). These booklets are filled with other practical money-saving tips the average homeowner can perform, making them worth the investment.

October 3

Tackle these miscellaneous chores and save energy and money this winter:

◆ Hot-water pipes passing through basements or crawl spaces should be wrapped with insulation. Covering them with foam-wrap insulation has about a one-year payback. An even cheaper alternative is to slice fiberglass batting (lengthwise) into strips 7½ inches wide. Wrap these strips around the pipes and secure them with contractor's sheathing tape. Note: Don't use foam tubing on the pipes of a steam boiler—the foam can melt.

◆ Reduce heat loss in the garage by tacking foam pipe insulation (3/4-inch diameter) to the bottom of the garage door. Set the pipe insulation about ½ inch from the outside edge of the door.

◆ Aluminum foil reflectors behind radiators bounce the heat out into the room. Reflectors cost you under a dollar per radiator to make and will lower wintertime heating bills by $4 per radiator. To make your own reflector, tape aluminum foil to cardboard. Or buy strips of thin foam insulation with a bright foil coating. Place these reflectors behind the radiator, foil coating facing the room.

◆ Don't forget to pull down the shades every night—it's absolutely free and, on average, saves $5 per window per heating season.

October 4

Chores to keep the ice man outside this winter.

◆ Keep the chimney damper closed. Heat rises, so an open damper allows for more heat loss than a hole in the wall twice its size. Close the damper when the fireplace is not in use. Install a glass door across the fireplace to further block heat from flying away. Better still, cut a custom plug made of rigid foam insulation or plywood (backed with fiberglass insulation) to lodge into the chimney just below the damper. Leave a cord dangling from the plug, reminding (and helping) you to remove the plug when it's fire time.

◆ Lay insulation over the attic-side of your attic door (or hatch) and weatherstrip the edges.

◆ Insulate or caulk the areas where water pipes and wires enter the house.

♦ Insulate your electrical outlets. Purchase inexpensive gaskets at the hardware store (under 25¢ each), turn off the power, remove the face plates of the electrical outlets, slip a gasket in place, and replace the face plate. Each gasket placed will save you about $1/year.

=====   ## October 5   =====

It requires 540 BTUs to heat one gallon of ground water to the tank temperature of your water heater. Using average utility rates, those BTUs cost 1.25¢. Avoid these terrible habits that squander that hot water:

♦ Running the hot water while shaving. The practice can waste 15 gallons of hot water (19¢). Instead, plug the sink and pour in a gallon of hot water. Running the hot water while washing hands and face is less offensive but can still waste 5 to 7 gallons (6¢). Travel the house placing red dots on the faucets. When family members ask about these, tell them what you want.

♦ Running the hot water continuously while washing/rinsing dishes. It's another awful habit that can easily consume up to 16 gallons of hot water (20¢). If those dishes are headed for the dishwasher, just scrape off the food scraps with no prerinsing at all.

♦ Failing to fix hot-water drips. You're going to fix it someday, so do it now. A drip every second wastes 75 gallons per week (94¢). That's a lot to tolerate when a 20¢ gasket solves the problem.

♦ Overfilling bathtubs. A quick shower is the least expensive way to bathe. If you want the lingering luxury of a lengthy soak, however, remember that five inches of water (about 20 gallons) will immerse you nicely. You don't need to fill the tub to its 45-gallon capacity. Put red dots on the bath faucets with a reminder like "½" to remind you that the tub need not be more than ½ full.

♦ Washing clothing in warm or hot water. A large load of wash consumes 40 to 50 gallons of water. If that water is warm or hot, the energy costs can run upward of 50¢ per load (assuming average electric rates). With modern detergents you'll get all but the filthiest clothes clean with the cold/cold or warm/cold cycles. In the process, you'll save money—90% of the cost of washing goes into heating water.

======= ## October 6 =======

Put the money meter on a shower and a 10-minute drench costs 50¢ (assuming average electric rates). By itself, that may not seem extravagant but multiply the figure by the number of family members taking daily showers and a family of four may be looking at a $600 shower bill by year's end. Habits to reduce the cost of showering:

◆ Run the shower at low pressure. You'll get just as clean and slash your water consumption. My shower can blast out five gallons of water per minute but I run it at a pressure delivering less than two gallons per minute.

◆ Go military. Get in, get wet, shut off the shower, soap up, and rinse. It's short, sweet, and cheap. Showers with a single control that mix hot and cold water (common in newer houses) make it easy to maintain the right temperature as you turn the water on and off. Showers with separate knobs controlling the hot and cold water require too much fiddling to get the temperature right. Get a new showerhead with a lever to turn on and off the water (cost $12 to $15 at hardware stores).

Low-flow shower heads will give you the luxury of a pressurized shower while still being stingy about water use. They're also great for damage control in bathrooms where guests and kids are apt to hemorrhage money.

◆ Low-flow shower heads use no more than 2.5 gallons of water a minute and top-rated models that have different spray patterns and massage patterns cost $25 to $40. Units in this arena to consider include the Teledyne Water Pik, Model SM-62-P or Model SM-82-W ($30 and $37, respectively, 800-525-2774); Pollenex Power Shower, Model PS320 ($25, 800-767-6027); and the Interbath Intouch II Massage

($25, 800-800-2132). The Interbath is the stingiest of the lot, doling out a maximum of 2.1 gallons per minute.

♦ Highly rated low-flow units lacking Yuppi-massage features or myriad spray patterns but delivering a good, strong shower include the Whedon Saver Shower, Model DS1C ($12, 800-541-2184); Interbath Classic II Deluxe, Model E26300 ($10, 800-800-2132); and the Teledyne Water Pik Super Saver, Model SS-1 ($10, 800-525-2774).

♦ It's worth visiting the library to read what the most recent review of low-flow shower heads in magazines like *Consumer Reports* recommend. Such sources help you determine the features you'll find most useful. They'll also help you realize that quality is not connected to cost: Some of the worst-rated units are pricey and some of the best-rated units are cheap.

♦ Installation of a low-flow showerhead is simple: Screw off the old head (wrench or pliers necessary), screw on the new one, tighten (but don't overtighten) with a wrench. Now shower off all that sweat you've generated. Consider applying a silicone gasket maker to the threads of the shower pipe before screwing on the new showerhead. This waterproofs the threads without the need to overtighten the parts. Let the gasket maker, which comes out of a tube as a thick liquid, dry before turning on the shower.

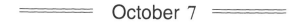

October 7

As a gardener you may have diligently sprinkled bone meal over the tops of your bulbs every fall. If so, stop. Bone meal is not all that it's been cracked up to be and studies indicate that the bulbs need nitrogen rather than the phosphorus of bone meal.

The money-saving implication of all this? Stop using bone meal, start using the compost you've created by burying your food scraps and yard waste (see June 9).

♦ Fill up buckets with the fertile soil you've created and spread it over the bulb beds at a ratio of about a bushel's worth of compost per 50 square feet.

♦ Make a springtime entry in next year's calendar to do this again when the new growth is just emerging.

══════ **October 8** ══════

Time to drop first mention of the dreaded—Christmas. Call U.S. Box Corporation in New York (800-221-0999 or 718-387-1510) for a free catalog. This company wholesales wrapping paper, tissue, bows, and ribbons. If you find items of interest here, co-op with friends and neighbors to get your order up to the $150 minimum.

══════ **October 9** ══════

The Great Chicago Fire of 1871 claimed 250 lives and razed 17,430 buildings. Since 1922 the week containing the anniversary day of that fire, October 9, has been proclaimed National Fire Prevention Week. Considering both the physical and financial havoc fire can wreak, devoting the following week to fire prevention and fire preparedness will be time and money well spent.

Kitchen fires are the principal cause of fires in the home. Statistics state that nearly 80% of all home fires start in the kitchen. The leading reason these fires start in the first place? Unattended cooking. People leave food cooking on the burners while attending other chores, or in the oven while out of the house.

Other causes of cooking fires: paper products, potholders, towels, cookbooks, curtains, and food packaging were not kept a safe distance from the stove top.

Kitchen tips to implement or adopt today:

♦ Whenever cooking food is left unattended (and especially if you're broiling or frying), carry a wooden spoon or potholder with you as a reminder of the danger you've left behind.
♦ Keep a proper-sized lid next to the stove whenever you're cooking on the stove top. It will smother a pan fire.
♦ Avoid crumb and grease fires—clean the toaster and stove often.

◆ Pot handles sticking over the edge of your stove can be hit in passing or grabbed by young children. To avoid burns and stove-top fires, always turn pot handles toward the back of the stove.

◆ Oven fires should be smothered by closing the oven door and turning off the heat. Same goes for the microwave. Grab the fire extinguisher and prepare to call 9-1-1 if the fire does not extinguish itself immediately.

◆ Keep a large box (two pounds or more) of baking soda (sodium bicarbonate) within arm's reach of the stove. Should a pan or grease fire erupt, liberal use of the baking soda will smother it. Do not try to put out grease fires with water.

October 10

The other major causes of home fires involve heating equipment (portable heaters), smoking, and child play.

To reduce heating hazards:

◆ Buy only heaters with a label from an independent testing lab and automatic shut-offs (in case the heater is knocked over).

◆ Keep heaters a yard away from walls, furniture, paper, and curtains.

◆ Unplug the heater when it's not in use.

◆ Don't leave portable heaters unattended, and don't leave them on while you sleep.

To reduce smoking hazards:

◆ Don't smoke in bed or while lying on a couch. And don't smoke indoors while drowsy.

◆ Keep many large, sturdy ashtrays around the home and empty them often.

◆ Pour water into ashtrays before dumping the contents into the trash.

To reduce child-play hazards:

◆ Store matches and lighters out of children's reach.

- Don't store matches or lighters where children who are left alone could find them.
- Teach children to tell an adult whenever they find lighters or matches.
- Purchase lighters with child-safety features. The largest number of fatal child-play accidents are started by children using lighters, but 85% of children under the age of five are incapable of operating lighters with child-safety features.

October 11

Fires inside your home can blaze out of control in less than a minute. The speed at which fire consumes a home explains why 4,000 Americans die in home fires every year and why the majority of those deaths occur at night in homes lacking smoke detectors. Statistics prove that owning a working smoke detector cuts your chance of dying in a home fire in half. That's an awfully good return on a device costing $10 to $20.

If you don't own smoke detectors:

- Decide how many are needed. You should have at least one detector for every level of the home and one in every bedroom. Put the number of units needed on your Master Purchasing List, then monitor the sales.
- Battery-powered detectors can be attached to the ceiling in a matter of minutes with a drill and screwdriver.
- After installing smoke detectors, you may get a break on your insurance premiums. Call your insurance agent.

If your home has smoke detectors:

- Make sure it has enough. You should have one detector for every level of the home and one in each bedroom.
- Test your units. Walk the home now and make sure the units and batteries are working. This should be done a minimum of five or six times a year. Pull out next year's calendar and write a reminder every two months, "Test smoke detectors." The batteries should also be changed once a year.

◆ Vacuum your detectors. Dust desensitizes the units—use a canister-styled vacuum to clean them every year.

══════ October 12 ══════

Because home fires can blaze out of control so quickly, extinguishers to instantly control flames constitute inexpensive home and health insurance.

If your home lacks extinguishers:

◆ Put them on the Master Purchasing List now. You might want to give them or request them as a gift for Christmas, birthdays, Mother's Day, Father's Day... Some points to consider.
◆ The majority of home fires start in the kitchen. Here, you'll want a bicarbonate extinguisher within easy reach but away from sources of heat.
◆ The garage and shop are two other locations where fires frequently start. Keep multi-purpose extinguishers handy in each of these locations.

If you own fire extinguishers:

◆ Walk the home. Remembering that fires can blaze beyond the point of no control in under 60 seconds, evaluate whether you have enough units and whether they are easily reached.
◆ Check each extinguisher. Read the gauge to be sure each is adequately charged and ready for use.

Homemade "extinguishers" to prepare today:

◆ Purchase several large boxes (two pounds or larger) of baking soda (sodium bicarbonate). Keep a box handy by the kitchen stove and position others in the garage or shop wherever sparks from grinders or the flames of propane torches create potential hazards.
◆ Fill water pails with a mixture of fine sand and baking soda (one pound baking soda per three pounds sand makes an ideal mixture). Keep these pails in convenient locations in both the basement and garage. In the event

of oil, grease, or petroleum fires, smother the flames with the mixture.

═══════ October 13 ═══════

Despite your efforts to avoid and to control home fires, are you prepared should the worst happen? Have you planned for worst-case scenarios? Have you taught your kids what to do?

Anyone who hasn't mapped out escape routes from the home, prepared second-story escapes (should all the ground-floor exits be blocked), and run their children through fire drills needs to do so today.

♦ Take young children to the fire station today. Visiting the station, seeing the equipment, and talking to fire fighters will be interesting and educational. At the station, gather literature on fire prevention and preparedness.

♦ Teach teenagers how to assess and fight a manageable fire. Coach them on the use of fire extinguishers, baking soda, pot lids, water, and blankets for fighting fires. Establish procedures for notifying the family, clearing the house (without gathering possessions), and calling for help (9-1-1). Most importantly, stress to teenagers how quickly the battle is lost, how susceptible they are to smoke inhalation, and why fleeing is better than fighting.

♦ Work with all family members, young and old alike, on exiting the house. Discuss the ground-floor exits and, if they are blocked, the second-floor escape routes. Address what is to be done once the house is exited (where will you gather, who is to call for help...).

♦ Practice what you preach. Don't make it academic: Run through the motions, crawl on the ground to avoid smoke inhalation, gather up the family and evacuate through different exits, make each child flee the house alone. Make it interesting: Time the kids with a stopwatch as they exit the house through different exits—turning drills into a competition will make it fun.

◆ Open your calendar and list "fire drill" on three different dates over the next year. During each fire drill, review situations that could dictate how the house is evacuated. Again, make it fun by timing everyone's efforts.

═══ October 14 ═══

One problem yesterday's drills may have illuminated is this: How do you evacuate the upper floors of a house (or apartment) when flames block access to the ground floor? Could each bedroom be safely evacuated if the inhabitants awoke and found flames trapping them in that room?

◆ Fire escape ladders (rope or chain ladders with plastic or aluminum rungs) offer one solution. These ladders hook onto the window sill and about 15 feet of hanging rungs see you to the ground. Most of these ladders roll up and store under a bed or in a dresser. Get literature from the fire department describing what to look for in such a ladder, then look for the ladders at large hardware stores or stores listed under *Safety Equipment* in the Yellow Pages.

◆ The cost of escape ladders ($60 for low-end, 15-foot models) is a deterrent. Because families may need several ladders to properly protect their upstairs and because the odds of needing the ladders is slight, most families take the gamble and ignore the purchase.

The odds may be slight but, should the ladders be needed, the consequences are dire. If you dismiss the ladders, at least furnish each upstairs bedroom with an evacuation rope. An evacuation rope of your own design is not as idiot-proof as a commercial escape ladder but does offer an inexpensive, workable solution. Here's how I handled the situation for our two upstairs bedrooms:

— Above the window of each bedroom (on the exterior of the house and into the header above the window) I screwed a 3/8" thick, eye bolt (the threaded shank of this eyebolt should be 3 to 3½ inches long).

— In an emergency, we would tie (using three or four half hitches) or clip (using a climber's carabiner) the evacuation rope to the eye bolt and lower ourselves to the ground, Batman style (i.e., feet flat on the side of the house, hands on the rope).

— I used about 20 feet of ½-inch thick rope for our two-story bedrooms. Important: Make knots in the rope every 10" to give your hands something to grab while descending the rope. Without the knots, hands will slip and burn on the rope.

— It's a system requiring some coordination and arm strength, but most children and adults can descend such a rope with a little practice. Important: Don't practice from the second-story windows. Hang the rope and master the Batman technique at heights where a mistake won't result in a hospital visit.

◆ If your kids are incapable of climbing down a rope ladder or an evacuation rope (too young, disabled, etc.), keep a lowering rope (about 25 feet long and 3/8" in diameter) in each upstairs room. In an emergency, this rope can be tied snugly around your child's chest (a bowline knot is recommended but a big wad of granny knots will work in a crisis). Lift the child out the window and lower her with the rope.

October 15

What possessions, records, documents, files, and pictures would you miss most if your home burned? Make a list.

Today it's time to protect all items on your list that can be backed up. Backup copies will then be stored in a safety deposit box or at a second location (e.g., a friend's or relative's basement). That makes finding a friend or relative willing to let you store a box of valuables the first order of business. Reciprocate by encouraging your friend/relative to store valuables of their own at your house.

Now gather the items to be stored. Some possibilities:

◆ Computer diskettes (or backup tape) with a complete copy of your computer's software and data files. Back up your computer often and keep the most recent backup off the premises.

◆ Slides, prints, or negatives of the family. When my wife's childhood house burned down, what she missed most were the family pictures of her childhood years. As a result, we keep the second string pictures we take off the premises so that we'd still have a good selection of images if our house burned. We also keep the negatives of all the prints we take in the safety deposit box so that we can make reprints of all lost images. Finally, we've made some duplicate videotapes of the kids growing up.

◆ Photocopies of licenses, financial cards, membership cards, passports, birth certificates, and the like. This includes photocopies of credit cards, drivers' licenses, social security cards, voter registration cards, will, living will, and durable power of attorney.

◆ A videotape of the inside of your house. Show each room in detail with closeups of shelves, closets, and drawers. The tape serves as an insurance record of your valuables. Borrow a video camera, if necessary.

For security reasons you will want financial records, account statements, insurance policies, birth certificates, passports, important account numbers, and your marriage license stored in a safety deposit box.

═══════ October 16 ═══════

Besides changing the oil, routinely inspecting your vehicle's radiator fluid and the condition of the radiator hoses is another critical maintenance chore: without coolant circulating through the engine, you can quickly transform valuable machinery into worthless scrap metal. Get out the owner's manuals to your vehicles and learn how to check the coolant level of each.

If the radiator fluid is low, add a 50/50 mixture of antifreeze and water. And if the fluid looks muddy rather than lime green, change the fluid (an easy task, usually described in the owner's manual). See a mechanic if you're frequently adding fluid or if the fluid is often muddy.

The rubber hoses leading from the radiator to the engine (and the other engine hoses, for that matter) should not be cracked, brittle, bulging, or mushy when squeezed.

Other radiator facts:

◆ In the coldest parts of the country, or when an extreme cold snap strikes, alter the mixture in your radiator to 70% antifreeze, 30% water. But don't make the mistake of pouring pure antifreeze into the radiator—undiluted ethylene glycol freezes at 8°F.

◆ Drain and replace your radiator fluid every other year. After about two years the liquid's anti-corrosion elements are spent.

===== **October 17** =====

Because flus can cause complications with people over 65 years of age as well as those with respiratory problems, high-risk people should get an annual flu shot. It's cheap insurance against the major problems a flu can precipitate. These shots are unlikely to give you a low-grade case of the flu. Recently, a double-blind study showed that people receiving flu shots suffered no more side effects than those receiving a placebo shot.

◆ Decide whether any one in your extended family (children with respiratory problems, family members coming off a serious injury, elderly relatives) is a good candidate for a flu shot.

◆ Got a family member who would benefit from a shot? Call your medical clinic and ask whether they charge you for only the cost of the shot ($10-$12) or if there is a visitation fee as well. If you will be charged for the visit, call your county's public health clinic (Blue Pages in the phone book) and schedule an appointment during the next few weeks.

═══ October 18 ═══

Take advantage of this beautiful season with a few walks. While you walk, collect attractive leaves, branches, and ferns.

Back at home, use light taps of a hammer to tenderize the ends of the stems of your 'finds.' Now, in a jar or vase, mix one part glycerine (found at pharmacies) with three parts hot water and make a centerpiece for the table by placing the stems of these plants in the solution.

After several days the color and texture of the leaves will change. When they are completely soft, stop using the leaves as a centerpiece and use them for floral arrangements, in cards, on wreaths...

If stored in a cool dark place, these preserved leaves will last for years.

═══ October 19 ═══

One reason mowers commonly visit mechanics during the spring is because they were improperly stored during the winter. Assuming you've already mowed for the last time this winter, give the machine the following TLC for the hibernation ahead:

◆ With the engine warm, change the oil. Run the new oil through the engine for a minute.
◆ Drain the gas (depending on the mower, you may need to hold it upside down), then run the machine until the gas is completely used (gas left in the mower over the winter can coat the carburetor with varnish).
◆ Take out the spark plug, pour 15 or 20 drops of lubricating oil down the cylinder, and crank the engine a few times to disperse the oil. Clean and regap the plug before reinserting it.
◆ Scrape matted grass off the bottom of the housing. Use a rag and the old motor oil you just removed to wipe down the blade and the bottom of the housing (prevents rusting).
◆ Store the machine in a dry (and not overly cold) place.

====== **October** 20 ======

Death. It's the part of life which is utterly unalterable but for which we are never fully prepared. Unfortunately, many of us—particularly those under 40—are not even partly prepared for the Big Sleep, even though tomorrow we could simply be in the wrong place at the wrong time and become one of the 40,000 Americans who die on the highway each year. That means the people we care most about—our family—will be the ones who pay for our unwillingness to face the facts of life head on. Over the next several days that will change: You'll be getting yourself (and your spouse) ready for that day when the Landlord decides to call in the mortgage.

◆ The average cost of a funeral (over $4,300) and burial (over $2,200) make death one of the larger expenditures a family faces. An easy way to drive the price down is to make your own arrangements. Use the luxury of time to comparison shop for goods and services you want instead of giving the onus to a grieving relative who will feel guilty cutting financial corners.

You may not care if you're buried in a cardboard box or an orange crate but, to a spouse or relative, penny-pinching may smack of disrespect. So make your own plans for the end. If you are married, make your plans with your spouse.

◆ A traditional funeral entails holding the body for the service, a casket, embalming (not always necessary), and a sizeable price tag. Increasing numbers of people are now opting for immediate burial or for direct cremation of the body. The survivors often organize a memorial service later (without the body present).

Different funeral homes offering the same basic package (moving the body to the funeral parlor and later to the cemetery, holding the body for a day or more, a low-cost container, payment to the funeral director) will charge prices as low as $500 and as high as $1,500. An outer burial container (required by many cemeteries), a plot, and other cemetery charges will be additional.

Direct cremations at different funeral homes offering the same services (moving the body to the parlor and later to the crematory, holding the body for a day or more, payment of the funeral director, delivery of the cremains) can also cost between $500 and $1,550. Containers for transporting the body may be extra.

♦ In 1988, the American Association for Retired Persons (AARP) reported, "A task force in Phoenix found that the same traditional funeral (a hardwood casket, transportation of the body, memorial observances, and the funeral director's charges) cost as little as $1,100 and as much as $4,500 at different homes in that city."

Some homes rely on prestige to scalp you. Others exact outrageous profits because people don't comparison shop for death services. You should. Shop for funeral goods and services like you would a washing machine—look around. By law, funeral homes must give a general price list (GPL) to visitors who request one (cemeteries, however, are not required to publish their prices for a burial plot or a monument). While funeral homes are not required to *mail* GPLs to consumers who request the list over the phone, about half of all funeral homes will. Get on the horn now, call six to 10 homes listed in the *Yellow Pages*, and request their GPL.

When those lists arrive, compare the *total* costs at different homes. Funerals are a combination of goods (caskets and outer burial containers) and services (transportation, use of the facilities, care of the body, services of the funeral director). To these costs you will still need to add cemetery costs (burial plot, monument, care of grave site) which can be hard to obtain since cemeteries are not required to publish their prices.

Decide (in general terms) on the goods and services you would want. Do you want to be buried or cremated? Do you want low-, medium-, or high-end goods and services? Write down your wishes (maybe even the name of the funeral home that seemed most forthright in its practices and prices), discuss these with your spouse, and file the information where it will be found (with death-related documents in the home).

October 21

Contemplating your demise may be emotionally distressing, but it is financially worthwhile. True, the money saved may not help *you* where you're headed, but it will help your survivors. And you'll want your loved ones, not a funeral home, to inherit the bulk of your fortune. Therefore, consider joining one of the 150 nonprofit memorial societies around the U.S. and Canada which help members obtain a dignified funeral (or cremation) at an affordable price. Most societies have done all the local price shopping so that members know where to obtain funeral, burial, and/or cremation services at the lowest cost.

Other societies negotiate lower prices with a local funeral home and offer members several "package deals." In Seattle, $10 makes you a lifetime member of the People's Memorial Association (2366 Eastlake E., 409 Areis Bldg., Seattle, WA 98102-3366, 206-325-0489). Upon death, your survivors can choose one of several plans: cremation for $497 (includes pickup of the body and delivery of the remains), limited mortuary service Plan 1 (minimum casket, delivery to local cemetery without graveside committal) for $629, limited mortuary service Plan 2 (includes graveside committal) for $708 and full mortuary service for $769. These prices are about half the going rate for the same goods and services elsewhere in the Seattle market.

Memorial societies have reciprocal agreements with other societies. If you move, you become a member of the closest society. If you die while traveling, the nearest society will help with funeral arrangements.

Get the name and the address of the memorial society closest to you by sending a SASE business envelope to Funeral and Memorial Societies of America, P.O. Box 10, Hinesburg, VT 05461-0010.

October 22

It's only fair to warn consumers that the death industry is infested with unscrupulous deadbeats. A report published by the Federal Trade Commission, the regulatory body overseeing mortuaries, estimated that only 30% of the industry complied with all aspects of the funeral rules established in 1984 to protect the public. Some examples:

♦ Derivations of the "show-how-much-you-care" or the "do-you-really-want to-skimp-on-their-final-farewell" sales pitch are commonly used to upgrade survivors to costly goods and services. While it's inane to express love by what you spend on a funeral, the ploy works.

♦ Most people purchase mid-range products. In the case of caskets, a top-end box may run $6,000 while the low-end option may cost $600—which leaves a large mid-range. Interestingly, funeral directors know that by introducing the average buyer to the high-end casket first, Mr. Average will settle for a casket costing half as much ($3,000). By introducing the average buyer to the low-end product first, Mr. Average will settle for a casket costing twice as much ($1,200). Through salesmanship, the funeral director has wrung an extra $1,800 from the average buyer.

♦ Spokespersons for the Funeral and Memorial Societies of America say that funeral homes routinely mislead consumers to believe that: Embalming is mandatory (depending on the state, it may not be), that caskets must be purchased even if cremation is planned (caskets can be rented for funerals, then bodies can be cremated in inexpensive alternative containers), high-end caskets prevent bodies from decomposing (untrue), cremation plans must be handled by a funeral director (most states allow survivors to save substantial sums by cutting out the middle men and contacting crematoriums directly).

♦ Most cemeteries require a liner or a vault to cover the casket (both keep the earth from sagging around the grave site as the casket deteriorates). Funeral directors often steer you toward the more expensive vaults, stating they retard the deterioration of the body. Retard, yes: prevent, no. And because the body *is* going to decompose, opt for the more affordable liners.

♦ As testimony about what is truly the best bang for the buck in the death industry and what a crock the show-them-how-much-you-care argument is, consider this: *The Funeral Monitor*, a trade magazine for the industry, reports that most funeral directors planning for their own death opt for the cheapest of all services—immediate cremation.

◆ Want to keep the sharks from having a feeding frenzy on your body? Get your library to order *Understanding the Tricks of the Funeral Trade—Self Defense for Consumers* (Upper Access Book Publishers, P.O. Box 457, Hinesburg, VT 05461, 800-356-9315). If the library lacks the budget for this 53-minute video ($29.95), order it yourself (it will save you more than it cost), then donate it to the library.

October 23

Did you know that in over 40 states, families, friends, or religious groups can handle all death arrangements without "hiring" a funeral director? You can transport the deceased yourself to the cemetery or crematory (after you've attended to the necessary paperwork). The process saves a lot of money. More importantly, families who care for their dead report that the personal involvement in the process has a healing power that is absent in the clinical atmosphere of a funeral home.

In earlier days, families and friends routinely cared for their own dead, meaning there is nothing new or unusual about the process. The present system of using a funeral director is really the new kid on the block.

The book *Caring for Your Own Dead* by Lisa Carlson ($16.95 from Upper Access Book Publishers, P.O. Box 457, Hinesburg, VT 05461, 800-356-9315) elaborates on these benefits. It also details the legal requirements for each state, describes how to obtain permits and fill out death certificates, and explains cremation and burial procedures.

Because death expenses are so high, it is worth having a copy of this book in your library. Think of it as insurance—in case the worst happens.

October 24

Donate your body to science and, abra cadaver, funeral and burial expenses disappear. Most state universities with medical research and training schools operate a willed-body program. Programs differ but most of them work like this: Upon death, the university picks up the body (no charge for local pick up); later, when the research is completed, the university cremates and buries the body in one of its plots or, if the survivors wish, returns the remains to the family.

For more information about these programs, call the nearest university with a medical school and ask about their body-donation program. The book *Caring For Your Own Dead* (mentioned earlier) lists the medical schools around the country (addresses and phone numbers included) with such programs.

Not all members of a willed-body program will be accepted when they die. Infectious diseases, trauma, and obesity are among the reasons bodies may be rejected. Work out contingency plans.

Also, if you are part of your region's organ donation program (as opposed to a full-body donation program) you do not avoid funeral expenses. After the organs and tissues have been recovered, the family must make arrangements for the body.

October 25

Aristotle said, "Men are divided between those who are as thrifty as if they would live forever, and those who are as extravagant as if they were going to die tomorrow."

Well, even if you budget for the possibility of life everlasting, prepare your estate for the possibility of meeting Gabriel tomorrow. Why? So your affairs are handled in an orderly fashion; property is distributed to family and friends according to your wishes; and inconvenience, expenses, and taxes are all minimized.

Without a will or living trust, state law controls what happens to your estate and the government and lawyers alike may have a feeding frenzy at the expense of the people you love.

♦ Many books encourage you to write your own will. For a couple with uncomplicated assets and the wish to make a spouse the beneficiary of the entire estate, a do-it-yourself document may suffice. Call the library today and check out recent books on the topic. If there are no new books on the topic, visit a major bookstore. Even if you decide not to write your own will, the material will prepare you for working with a lawyer on this task.

===== **October 26** =====

The claims made by books that anyone can write his or her will are but half truths. After preparing our wills, my wife reports anyone can do it, just like anyone can rebuild an engine. Unfortunately, most people lack the time to learn the intricacies of federal estate taxes, state taxes, and of substitutes and complements to wills (joint tenancy, community-property agreements, revocable living trusts). Consequently, most families are better served by hiring an attorney practiced in estate planning.

Of course if you let a lawyer work on your estate for more than a few hours, there may be little estate left to pass on. It may take longer than a night, but before meeting with a lawyer, Foster Pepper & Shefelman, a Northwestern law firm specializing in estate-planning, recommends you answer the following questions:

◆ What is the net value of your estate?
◆ Will you leave your estate to someone (spouse) with no strings attached?
◆ Who will administer your estate? List backups.
◆ What personal property will you leave to specific people?
◆ What will you leave to charity?
◆ Do you want to avoid probate?
◆ Are your financial records comprehensive and located where they'll be found by your personal representative?
◆ Do you want a personal statement in your will?
◆ Are you donating your organs for research or transplantation?
◆ In the event of terminal illness, should life-support procedures be terminated?
◆ Who should manage your affairs in the event of incapacitation?
◆ Who should inherit your estate if your entire immediate family dies in a common disaster?
◆ Should property left to children be kept in a common fund or in separate funds for each child?

- At what age should children receive their inheritance outright?
- Who is the trustee (and backup trustee) of your children's trust?
- Who is the guardian (and backup guardian) of your minor children?

===== **October** 27 =====

A bad roll of the dice—say an accident on the highway—could instantly transport any one of us from the driver's seat to the vegetable bin. Suddenly, we may need family or friends to tend our affairs.

Uglier still, if disaster struck and you hadn't filled out the appropriate papers, even your spouse might lack the legal power to handle your affairs, sell jointly held property to pay expenses, make decisions in your business matters, or tap into your pensions to pay mounting bills. And relatives working in your behalf might need to ask the courts to appoint a guardian and conservator—a process that could take months, cost dearly, and create endless frustrations.

Prepare for these horrible possibilities while you are healthy. While a lawyer drafts your will, ask her to draft an inexpensive document called a *durable power of attorney*. This empowers an appointee to make decisions (legal, medical, and financial) in your behalf. Everyone over age 18 should have this document prepared. Who knows when a car hurtling down the highway or a tumble down the stairs will forever change your future?

- Fill-in-the-blank forms assigning durable power of attorney to an appointee are better than nothing, but, should you become disabled, these boiler-plate forms could easily become a false economy. An attorney knowledgeable about estate matters will list powers and clarify tax issues that wouldn't be addressed in a standardized form.

══════ October 28 ══════

You've answered unpleasant questions and contemplated dire situations over the past few days. Now find a lawyer. Estate planning for the rich can get complicated. If you're reading this book, however, your empire is probably not vast enough to warrant a city slicker whose high-rise office dictates a $250/hour fee. For middle-income Americans, most general practitioners licensed in your state can handle the job for $125 to $200.

Although my wife and I live just outside of Seattle, we hired a respected lawyer from the hamlet of Stanwood some 35 miles north of Seattle. Being a small-town lawyer with small-town overhead, our lawyer spent a lot of time discussing our needs before drafting both our wills for a combined total of $175.

◆ Ways to track down a lawyer for the task: get a referral from a friend; check the *Attorneys' Referral & Information* in the Yellow Pages and call listings under General Practice or Wills, Estate Planning, and Probate; contact friends from college days who have gone into law (this shouldn't be hard considering how many graduates bite the big-buck lure of the profession).

══════ October 29 ══════

The activities over the past week have been grim, but there are excellent financial reasons to complete this unpleasant planning. There are also non-financial reasons; one pertains to the immutable laws of Mr. Murphy. Fate, according to Murphy, will deliver the future you are least prepared for. Get ready for D-Day and Fate is likely to let you wrinkle until the ripe age of 99. So, as you tackle this last grizzly issue, consider all of this to be "life insurance" rather than "death planning."

◆ To pull the plug or not to pull the plug? That is the question of the day and the question behind a *living will* (or directive to physicians).

If two physicians agree you have an incurable injury or a terminal illness, and that life-sustaining procedures are artificially prolonging the moment of death, what would you have them do? Sign a living will and you opt to pull the plug (i.e., withhold or withdraw life-sustaining procedures).

The topic is an emotionally charged one brimming with moral and religious issues. Nonetheless, most people aren't interested in being kept alive artificially against their will. They want to die with dignity and without bankrupting their survivors (life support can easily cost over $2,000 per day).

If you are such a believer, make out a living will and give a copy to both the executor of your estate and your doctor. Books from the library feature living wills you can copy. Alternately, get forms from either the Funeral and Memorial Societies of America (P.O. Box 10, Hinesburg, VT 05461-0010) or Choice in Dying (Box 397, Newark, NJ 07101-9792, 800-989-9455).

═══ October 30 ═══

How much does your heating bill rise with each degree you push up the thermostat? Would you believe 3%? That means you can put a 15% dent in your heating bill this winter by keeping the daytime temperature at 65°F (instead of 70°F) and the nighttime temperature at 55° or 60°F (instead of 60° or 65°F). That's worth shivering (or wearing an extra sweater) for.

♦ Polypropylene and polyester long underwear hug the body and create dead air (and therefore insulation) right next to the skin where it does the most warming. Good long johns keep you warmer than a bulky, but baggy, sweater. Avoid wool long underwear: it's itchy. Cotton and silk get the thumbs down if you also intend to use your long johns for skiing, hiking, hunting, or fishing—both fabrics are dangerously cold once wet. Look for the following design features: a turtle neck or a snug crew neck to reduce the amount of heat escaping out the top, adequate length in the sleeves and pant legs to cover wrists and ankles, long-bodied tops that tuck well below the waist, bottoms that don't creep down the hips as you walk. Mail-order outlets for such underwear include: REI (800-426-4840), L.L. Bean (800-221-4221), and Campmor (800-525-4784).

♦ A hot-water bottle will also contribute toward keeping the thermostat down. Place the bottle on your belly between a T-shirt and sweat shirt while vegetating (reading, watching TV). Rewarming the bottle is more convenient (and economical) with a microwave oven. Remove the cap, prop the bottle against the side of the microwave, and nuke it. Once hot, slip the bottle under your sweat shirt for hours of atomic luxury. The same bottle can preheat your bed at night.

♦ Blankets in the TV and reading rooms will keep you comfortable in a cold house.

♦ Thick comforters or electric blankets will give you a warm sleep in a cold house.

♦ If you refuse to set the nighttime temperature at 55°F because rising to a cold house is too painful, replace your thermostat with a clock thermostat costing between $50 and $100. The change will pay for itself in a year. Set the clock to activate the furnace an hour before you awaken.

════ October 31 ════

The damage sweets inflict upon teeth is not a function of how much sugar you consume, but of how long the teeth are exposed to sugar. So... encourage your children to gorge on Halloween treats over the next few days. Dole out candy slowly over the course of weeks and you'll keep resupplying bacteria with the foods needed to dig in deep.

By the same rationale, big candy bars devoured in bites do less damage than small sucking candies that keep the teeth coated with a sugary film.

November

The first few days after the major sugar holidays (Halloween, Christmas, Valentine's Day, and Easter) you'll find the seasonal candy at supermarkets, drugstores, and discount retailers steeply discounted. If you want candy around for snacks, it's time to restock the reservoir. Buy in bulk, store the candy in the freezer, and ration its outflow.

♦ Call the different supermarkets, drugstores, and discount retailers (Kmart, Target) and find out who has discounted candy reserves. For future reference, note in your Rolodex who the good prospects are. Now pay a visit.

♦ Open your daily calendar. On each day following a major sugar holiday, leave a reminder that it's time to restock the candy shelf.

Dentists and hygienists give us a lot of flack about plaque. Plaque, a sticky film of bacteria and salivary components that adheres to teeth, is the major cause of cavities and gum disease. Its evils account for the loss of teeth in 35% of all senior citizens. Plaque also hardens into tartar, a crusty coating over the teeth that contributes to gum disease and loss of teeth. Control disease-producing plaque and you'll prevent (even eliminate) most dental problems. The good news: Prevention is cheap and will spare you horrendous dental bills later in life. The bad news: Brushing, flossing, and professional cleanings (twice yearly) are still the most effective weapons.

♦ Of course brushing and flossing are effective only if the job is done right. Find out if everyone in the family is doing these jobs right by purchasing disclosing tablets (available at drugstores) and making everyone use them tonight after the nightly cleaning ritual. The dye in the tablets stains any plaque remaining on the teeth after cleaning. Check the gumline, spaces between teeth, molars, and backs of teeth closely.

With a mirror, show your kids and spouse the areas that are being missed and coach them on how to use a brush and floss to erase these sites.

Cheap Trick:
A much cheaper substitute for disclosing tablets is red food coloring. Spread petroleum jelly on your lips (keeps your lips from turning Dracula red), then add seven or eight drops of red food color to ½ teaspoon of water. Swish the solution around in your mouth for 60 seconds before checking for plaque deposits (they'll be red).

November 3

Over the next week, promote better brushing and flossing habits throughout the family. Even if you have dental insurance, each cavity prevented can amount to $30 or $40 saved. And if you don't have dental insurance, you've got big-time incentive to paste those pearlies because those little holes cost, on average, $125 to $150 to plug.

♦ Brushing properly not only saves your teeth, it keeps gums from developing woes that could cost megabucks later in life (gum surgery, for example, can run upward of $12,000). Here is a recap of what you've heard umpteen times but are probably not doing.

Place the brush at a 45-degree angle at the intersection of the tooth and gum. Gently vibrate the brush in small circles, cleaning one or two teeth at a time. The goal is not to polish the flat surfaces of your ivories but to thoroughly clean the boundary between the gum and each tooth. Finish your brushing with a gentle scrubbing of the chewing surfaces.

The gumlines alongside molars and the backs of teeth need just as much attention as the smile surfaces. To clean all these surfaces, devote at least three or four minutes to the job.

Brush twice a day if possible, but if you do it just once, brush at night: Oust the army of bacteria before giving them the evening to dig in.

Use small, soft-bristled toothbrushes. Giant brushes won't speed up the chore and they are not as effective at scouring the little grottos sheltering plaque. Meanwhile, hard bristles damage your gums.

◆ Flossing cleans between the teeth and below the gumline in places where a brush can't reach. For the long-term health of your mouth, flossing is just as important as brushing. Make a habit of doing it daily and, be it through bribes or arm-bending, make your kids floss regularly. (Note: an easy way for parents to floss the teeth of young children is to lay them down on their backs, and do the job while sitting beside them.)

As with brushing, do it right. Use a gentle sawing motion while moving the floss in the gap between the teeth. At the gumline, bend the floss into a "C" and cup one tooth while continuing the back and forth motion. Curve the floss around the other tooth and floss it in kind. Go slow and scrape the teeth at and below the gumlines without abusing the gums.

November 4

I think my parents erred by sheltering me from dental bills as a kid. They should have required that I help pay for the cavities I incurred: It was my responsibility to clean my teeth and I should have suffered part of the financial burden when I blew it. Had the payment for my transgressions affected my piggy bank, I would have paid more attention to dental hygiene.

To make your kids more conscientious about their brushing, establish cavity-fees for your children. When they have cavities, they pay you a certain amount. Make that amount large enough to hurt. Also incorporate bonuses for perfect checkups—that gives children a double incentive to adhere to the daily drudgery of brushing and flossing.

◆ Draw up the terms today. Stick red reminder dots on all the toothbrushes in the family. When kids and spouse ask what the dots are all about, fill them in on the family's new dental plan.

═══ November 5 ═══

A good hand brushing can be just as effective as an electric brushing but, truth be told, the average person does a much better job with a quality electric brush. Not all electric brushes are created equally but two which have proved themselves extremely effective in clinical tests are the *Interplak* (in which the stem remains stationary while the bristles of the brush rotate) and the *Sonicare* (in which the brush vibrates at a high frequency). In clinical tests both these brushes have been shown to remove as much as 98% of the plaque (most people using a brush eliminate only 50%). They also stimulate and tighten the gums.

These brushes aren't cheap ($60 to $80 for the Interplak and $100 to $120 for the Sonicare) but hygienists swear there is a huge difference in the quality of cleaning they see between clients using the electric brushes and clients brushing by hand. Given the price of filling a cavity (average cost: $130) think of a quality brush as inexpensive prevention. Put one of these brushes on your Master Purchasing List, price them over the phone at various department stores, look at the different models and decide which one fits your family's needs best, and be ready to jump when the right unit comes on sale.

Note: While the Interplak (800-334-4031) is cheaper than the Sonicare (800-682-7664), it is more likely to develop mechanical problems.

═══ November 6 ═══

Take the money-saving dental quiz today. Adopt those tips that will save you money.

Quiz:

1) What's the best rated toothpaste for preventing cavities?
2) Is brushing without toothpaste like washing hair without shampoo?
3) Which produces better results: holding your toothbrush like a pencil or gripping it like a scrub brush?
4) A dab of baking soda is an inexpensive toothpaste, but do dentists endorse it?
5) Wax, unwaxed, flavored, tape, generic...which floss is best?
6) Should you finish meals and snacks by rinsing your mouth with water?
7) Should you use mouthwashes, like Listerene, that are known to reduce plaque and gingivitis (inflammation of the gums)?
8) Are children's toothpastes a marketing scam to squeeze more money out of you?

Answers:

1) Despite what ads may lead you to believe, there is no *one* best paste. Currently many dentists are steering patients away from pastes advertised to control tartar (too abrasive) toward those billed as sensitive-tooth formulas. Whether you use a formula for tartar control or sensitive teeth, you can buy by price among any fluoride toothpaste approved by the American Dental Association (ADA), an independent body that rigorously tests the products it approves. Products that don't sport the ADA's seal (most generics don't) should be avoided because you don't know whether they use an inactive fluoride, employ overly abrasive cleaners, or whether they simply haven't been tested by the ADA.
2) Nope. Toothpaste is a small part of the formula. Brushing well with no toothpaste at all but plenty of water still gives your teeth a good cleaning. And using just a

pea-sized dab of toothpaste will give your teeth as good a cleaning as an inch-long strand of paste.

3) Foreign research shows that the pencil grip gets teeth as clean but causes less gum damage. This grip promotes a vibrating motion more than a scrubbing one.

4) True. Wet your brush, dab it in the powder, and save money. Baking soda is ten times cheaper than toothpaste—which makes up for its taste being ten times worse. To improve the flavor, mix baking soda and fluoride mouthwash into a thick paste and store it in an empty film canister.

5) Although people with widely-spaced teeth may prefer tapes and those with tightly packed ivories may opt for waxed string, for most people it doesn't matter which floss they use. Most store brands are sound investments that cost about half as much as brand names. If you happen upon one store brand that frays easily, try another.

6) It's a good idea. It's fast, easy, washes out substantial quantities of bacteria, and it's free.

7) Not if you're conscientious about brushing and flossing. If you're delinquent, however, post-meal swishing is better than nothing.

8) In this case, no. Children's enamel is soft and some adult pastes are too abrasive.

November 7

As much as I hate the lip-smacking and bubble-popping that goes along with most gum chewing, I should report this to you. Chewing gum, according to the American Dental Association, can help reduce tooth decay. Chewing after eating gets saliva flowing and saliva neutralizes those acids contributing to tooth decay. Saliva also contains calcium and phosphate which help maintain the tooth enamel. The ADA recommends sugarless gum.

No, this is not a substitute for flossing and brushing. However, a quick chew after lunch apparently keeps the bacteria at bay. Consider including a stick of sugarless gum in the sack lunches packed for kids and spouse.

═══ November 8 ═══

"Prevention is better than cure."

The British say that. So do the dentists—which is why they recommend that a hygienist give your teeth a professional cleaning twice a year (people with diagnosed gum problems will need three or four cleanings per year).

Even with proper brushing and flossing, you won't remove all the plaque coating your teeth at or below the gumline. That spells future trouble unless you scrape it off regularly. Professional cleanings are cheap medicine compared to treating future gum disease and tooth loss. An added bonus: Most dental policies pick up the tab.

Pull out the daily calendar, call the hygienist, and get the entire family scheduled for their semi-annual cleaning.

Cheap Trick:

If you don't have dental insurance covering these important preventative cleanings, any local college or university dental hygiene program offers professional cleanings for less than half the going street price. The hygienist program at my local community college, for example, charges $35 for a routine cleaning (which includes X-rays and an examination with the attending dentist). Fees for comparable services in the private sector run over $100. Meanwhile, cleanings attacking periodontal scaling cost $50 through the community college and over $400 through private practice.

═══ November 9 ═══

Fluoride, a mineral that combines with and strengthens tooth enamel, has decreased cavities in children by nearly 40%. The best way to get fluoride is through drinking water, but if your water lacks fluoride, talk to your doctor or dentist about fluoride drops or tablets. It is especially important for children to get fluoride when the permanent teeth are forming (before age six).

Sealants are the other big, modern advance in preventing cavities. These plastics, which are used to cap the top of children's molars, can reduce cavities by as much as 80%.

Sealants protect the permanent molars from bacteria and decay by filling in macroscopic and microscopic pits and crevices that trap food and bacteria. For children, whose tooth enamel is considerably softer than adults', sealants are a tremendous preventive weapon.

Get the first four permanent molars sealed after they emerge (around age six) and the second four permanent molars sealed as they come in (around age 12). Cost runs $20 to $25 per tooth ($10/tooth if you use hygienists in training at a local college). It's a bargain considering the initial cost of treating cavities. Furthermore, all cavities will need refilling later in life, making their actual cost considerably higher.

That leaves you with two items on your platter today. Check that your kids are getting adequate fluoride protection (call your dentist and municipal water district). And schedule appointments to have unprotected molars sealed.

Cheap Trick:

Children's teeth get X-rayed yearly with little thought to whether the X-rays are needed and whether you can afford the $35 expense. Children with a history of little tooth decay don't need yearly X-rays. Stop the habit by having a message printed across their charts: "No X-rays unless confirmed by parent."

This message can also stop the unnecessary X-raying of baby teeth. With baby teeth, problems that require attention before the tooth falls out are generally visible without film. A more acceptable time to take a child's first X-rays is around age six after the first permanent molars emerge.

November 10

"My desires will always exceed my income."

The quote comes from Shelley Ensz of Edina, Minnesota who once sent me a letter with money-saving tips. Shelley repeats the line to herself when she shops and finds herself desiring impulse items that are not on her list.

Desires are a vacuous hole, and if you relent to them, they'll break you. Making more money, as witnessed by millions of Americans who earn a generous salary but are chased by an avalanche of debt, is not the solution. Saying "no" to desires is. Every time you shop, you traverse a field of dreams that can blow holes in your budget—foods and clothes you don't need, toys the kids don't need, decorations the house doesn't need.

This book is peppered with tips to help you prevent making purchases that were not premeditated, but accepting the truth of this quote and repeating it when impulses beckon, is a huge step in staying solvent.

♦ Use this quote to protect your money by keeping a copy of it in your wallet. Cut a sheet of paper down to a size that is slightly larger than a dollar bill. On one side of that sheet, print the quote (or some facsimile) in large, bold letters. On the other side of the sheet, list the financial goals that are truly important to you: buying a home, taking a vacation, buying a car, retiring early. If you want to get elaborate, tape pictures representing those goals onto the sheet.

Kept with the money in your wallet, this sheet reminds you of what's at stake whenever you're considering an imprudent expenditure.

November 11

By the time people with normal vision turn 45, most need glasses to read. This side effect of aging eyes is completely normal and is corrected by glasses that magnify print. You can pay more than $100 for reading glasses from a specialist or you can pay $15 to $25 for good-quality, over-the-counter models (available at department stores and mass merchandisers around the country). These glasses are effective, perfectly safe, and meet regulations monitored by the American National Standards Institute and the FDA.

If you or your spouse are squinting more or are reading books out at arm's length (especially now that the long nights of winter make for more hours of dim light), visit a department store and test their reading glasses.

Over-the-counter reading glasses use numbers between 1.00 and 4.00 to denote their magnification. Find the strength that's right for you by reading a book with fine print. Start at low magnification (1.00) and try on different glasses until you hone in on the strength that works best for you.

Note: You can buy reading glasses without a prescription, but it's wise to have your eyes checked by a specialist whenever your vision changes.

===== ## November 12 =====

It's the day when merchants huddle around the cash register singing *What a Friend We Have in Jesus* and companies boast about their fourth-quarter earnings. And it's the time of year when the average adult will, according to surveys conducted by MasterCard, spend nearly $500 each (that's $1,000 per couple) on presents. That figure doesn't even include ancillary expenses—ornaments, wrapping paper, parties, cards....

While many of you will consider it heresy to talk Christmas before Turkey Day, with corporate America perched for its jugular attack, it takes planning to unplug the colossal Christmas cash machine. Wait too long and cost-cutting doors will start slamming. Today, plan how to spend less and derive more from Christmas.

♦ This evening, call members of the extended family to discuss gift-giving strategies. My two brothers, sister, and I now draw names so that each of our families has one (and only one) family to buy for.

♦ Another topic to discuss with extended families and friends—instead of exchanging gifts, consider exchanging time. Possible services: a promissory note to write more letters to distant family members (or to call them more often); baby-sitting coupons; a coupon for housework or yardwork; pledges to cut wood, tune a car, give massages; lessons in computers, skiing, chess.... These inexpensive gifts are not only more appreciated than yet another toaster, they draw you closer to friends and family. That's a gift imbued with the spirit of Christmas.

♦ Two years ago my siblings and I held a Christmas competition: We agreed that gifts would be inexpensive (under $5), could be purchased new or secondhand, and that after Christmas we would honor whomever we thought had found the best present for the least money. The game helped everyone's budget; it also made both the giving and the getting more fun. (We excluded children from this game.)

◆ Another topic of discussion with your extended family: Must all gifts be purchased? We all own nice, used items that could make siblings, nieces, and nephews happy. The trouble? We're scared of insulting loved ones or of being called a cheapskate. Discuss that option; if others like it, everyone benefits. If they don't—well, at least you know.

November 13

Call the library and reserve this book: *Unplug the Christmas Machine* by Jo Robinson and Jean Coppock Staeheli. It's loaded with ideas on how to replace the dollars and stress of the holidays with meaning and spirit. Prepare yourself for the greed-fest of Christmas by reading this book before Thanksgiving.

November 14

A curious fact: People who pay for their purchases with plastic spend, on average, 30% more than people who finger the cash passing through their fingers. Apparently plastic makes the pain of spending easy to bear. So...

◆ Hang your credit card on the tree as an ornament. To give the card an appropriate face lift, stick on a small bow and tape on a hanging loop.

◆ Give your budget seasonal shelter by storing the credit cards in your safety deposit box.

Once you've pried those cards from your wallet, set your Christmas budget. Write down whom you will buy for, what other Christmas expenses you will incur (parties, decorations, wrapping supplies), and the total number of dollars you intend to spend. Go to the bank, withdraw this amount of cash, and put it in an envelope.

Take all Christmas-related expenditures from this envelope, and here's the important part: When the cash is gone, your giving is over. Period. Corporate America may accuse you of having a stunted heart, but the intent of Christmas was never to generate debt. It was to celebrate a birth.

November 15

On your list of people you intend to give to this Christmas, you'll find several families. Rather than giving to the individuals in the family, give a family gift. Possibilities:

◆ A magazine subscription the entire family can enjoy—something broadening like *National Geographic*, something factual like *Consumer Reports*, or something to fuel the family's special interest like *Backpacker* or *Ski*.
◆ A big jar filled with candies or bean soup makings.
◆ Homemade candies, jam, salad dressing, cider, baked goods, beer...
◆ A homemade freezer meal (casserole, lasagna) that your friends can enjoy in the future.
◆ A game the entire family can play (Taboo, Pictionary, backgammon, cribbage, puzzles).
◆ Books that will interest the entire family (a book describing various card games, a book of one-minute mysteries, a book of brain teasers, this book).
◆ Computer software, music album, coupon book.

November 16

Parents and grandparents are tough buys. What do you give people who have everything they need?

◆ **Pictures.** Try a yearly calendar made from family pictures. Many photocopy stores can turn color copies of your pictures into yearly calendars. Gather your best shots from the year and organize them into a calendar.

◆ **Time.** Parents and grandparents will value time more than your presents. Coupons volunteering time to do housework, yard work, heavy work, car maintenance... are good picks.

◆ **Dining or Entertainment.** Give a gift certificate (and a two-for-one coupon) for a restaurant, play, or movie.

November 17

Entertainment Publications (2125 Butterfield Road, Troy, MI 48084, 800-445-4137) compiles coupon books for over 115 major cities around North America. The two-for-one coupons can be used at restaurants, hotels, tourist attractions, and entertainment clubs. Buy a book for your city (average cost, $34) and use coupons as gifts. Give kids a gift certificate to go bowling and a coupon so they can take a friend free. Give friends a gift certificate to a restaurant and a two-for-one coupon to make the dinner out affordable. You can fashion dozens of affordable gifts from one coupon book and have coupons left over to treat yourself to some half-price entertainment.

If the idea proves interesting, order a coupon book now. Call the local number for Entertainment (listed in your phone directory) or order a book from the national office.

November 18

If you haven't done so already, start saving the colored comics from the Sunday newspaper—come Christmas, use the stash as giftwrapping. Also, start saving attractive shopping bags—cut up, they make beautiful giftwrapping. Other sources of inexpensive wrapping paper:

◆ Save all those craft projects that come home from school with the kids. File the stellar projects with the family memorabilia; use the rest as wrapping paper.

◆ Make many different-sized cloth bags (with drawstring closures) from scraps of colorful fabric or from steeply discounted remnants purchased at a fabric store. Use these bags to 'wrap' presents. Granted, the bags are more expensive than paper, but they are reusable. After two or three years, the money saved on gift wrap (and the time saved wrapping) pays off.

◆ Buy a large roll of butcher paper (white or colored) at a paper supply house. The cheapest paper you can find is perfectly suitable (so are cut-up grocery bags). Let your kids draw Christmas motifs on strips of paper as recreation. Crayons, pastels, magic markers, and poster paints are all fair mediums. Decorating the paper with unusual stickers, rubber stamps, and cut-out images from old magazines (glued on) also works. Finally, blotting paper with different shaped designs cut from sponges and dipped in poster paint makes beautiful paper.

◆ Use inexpensive shelf paper (see previous tip) to wrap gifts, then personalize them. Write recipes on the presents of people who enjoy cooking; paste faces cut out of *People Magazine* onto the presents of movie lovers; paste magazine pictures of old cars onto the presents of car lovers. With imagination and old magazines, you can personalize all your gifts using inexpensive paper as the foundation.

◆ After Thanksgiving the paper bags from many grocery stores are printed with a Christmas motif. Use those bags for wrapping paper.

◆ Call home-decorating stores and ask them to save their wallpaper scraps and samples for you. It's all great wrapping paper.

◆ Rubber stamps of the alphabet are useful for all wrapping occasions. At Christmas, use the rubber stamps to spell Merry Christmas, Emmanuel, Noel, or Santa across butcher paper. The stamps are equally useful for birthdays, Valentine's Day, Easter, Mother's Day, anniversaries....

═══════════ November 19 ═══════════

The question undoubtedly arises with each Christmas party you attend: Should you bring the hosts a present? If you do, should they reciprocate and send you a gift later?

When you throw your own Christmas bash, be rid of all ambiguities. Mention the gift situation on the invitation. A few ways of handling this:

♦ "No gifts please." It's short, sweet, and gets everyone off the hook.

♦ "No gifts unless you'd like to bring a clean, used toy that we will deliver to the XYZ charity." It's a thoughtful gesture that spreads the spirit of Christmas to the less fortunate.

♦ "Please bring one white-elephant gift per family. Make it an outrageous/tacky/comical item from around home that you no longer want."
At the party, play the white-elephant gift game. Guests gather in a circle with the gifts piled in the center. Going one at a time around the circle, a family is asked to either choose and open a gift from the pile, or to take a gift another family has already opened (any family who has their gift taken then selects and opens a new gift from the pile).
When the game is complete (after much laughter) everyone has a new white elephant to take home.

November 20

How efficient are you with your cooking practices? Test yourself; then incorporate what you learn. While these practices deal with small savings, day after day little savings add up. Like the Danish say, "He who does not save pennies will never have pounds."

1) How much heat are you losing when you open the oven door to peek in?
2) True or False: A watched pot never boils.
3) Which stove-top burner is most efficient?
4) Name several energy-efficient ways to bake potatoes.
5) True or False: Dried pastas are reconstituted in about eight minutes by boiling noodles in an uncovered pot.
6) How do you make a stove-top burner as efficient as a microwave?

7) True or False: Preheating an oven is a waste of time and money.

8) When is the best time to use the self-cleaning function of an oven?

Answers:

1) A quick peek lets out 20% of the heat. Learn to trust your timer. When done, however, open the oven door and use the heat you've already paid for to warm the house.

2) False. It just seems like it never boils because you've removed the lid. Without a lid, it takes 20% more time (and energy) to bring liquid to a boil.

3) The one that most closely matches the size of the pot. Using a big burner with a small pot pours heat out into thin air.

4) Most energy efficient of all is to "bake" them in the microwave. Impaling potatoes (lengthwise) with clean nails, and cooking them in conventional ovens with the nails in place reduces cooking time by 15 minutes. Or, reduce baking time about 40% by cutting the potatoes in half and baking them, cut side down, on a greased cookie sheet.

5) True, but there is a smarter alternative. Bring salted water to a boil, add pasta, cover the pot, and turn off the heat. Noodles will cook in 12 to 15 minutes.

6) With a pressure cooker. Pressure cookers reduce stove-top cooking times by two thirds. Purchasing a pressure cooker and learning how to use it will save you loads of money (and time) over the years.

7) True (except in the case of baked goods). Main courses can be preheated along with the oven.

8) Directly after baking—the oven is already preheated.

═══════ November 21 ═══════

Some of the more common automobile problems that mechanics deal with throughout the winter are caused by water in the gas. If your car suddenly starts to sputter and lurch, adding gas drier (like *Prestone Gas-Drier* or *Heet*) to the gas may save you from expensive repair bills.

Gas drier is an alcohol, which binds with the water in gas and then burns its way out of your vehicle. For wintertime preventive maintenance, many mechanics recommend adding a bottle of drier to the gas every few fill-ups.

Other ways to minimize moisture in your gas: Keep your vehicle in a garage and your fuel tank as full as possible throughout the winter. Unfortunately, it's not uncommon to pump bad gas from the filling station into the tank, so keep a bottle of gas drier in the vehicle for first aid.

Scores of companies market a gas drier and prices fluctuate widely. Buy by price among any of the name brands, stocking up (of course) when the price is right. Add the stuff to your shopping list—even if you opt not to add it regularly to the gas, you'll want an emergency supply.

November 22

Buying your film (and, if possible, your processing) through the Eastern mail-order houses will have you capturing family's Kodachrome moments at half price.

Example: When purchased through the mail, 36 exposures of the Kodachrome and Fujichrome slide films I use cost $5.34 and $3.89 respectively. The cheaper, local department stores sell both those films for about $8. I also purchase the manufacturer's processing mailers from these mail-order houses—cost is currently $4.39 for the Kodachrome mailers, $3.72 for Fujichrome mailers. To have a local department store, pharmacy, or lab process my slides costs me $8 a roll. Furthermore, those stores are sending my film to the same labs where my pre-paid mailers go.

Mail-order houses that have given me no trouble over the years include: Adorama (42 W. 18th St., New York, NY 10011, 800-223-2500); B&H Photo (119 W. 17th St., New York, NY 10011, 800-221-5662); Bi-Rite (15 E. 39th St., New York, NY 10016-7080, 800-223-1970); Focus Camera (4419 13th Ave., Brooklyn, NY 11219, 800-221-0828).

♦ Copy these mail-order addresses onto a Rolodex card and file it in your phone file under Photo Supplies. Call a few of these firms for a per/roll price quote of your favorite film, and if applicable, what a pre-paid processing mailer for that film runs. Pencil these costs onto the card for future reference.

◆ Whenever you order film, call several of these firms for price quotes—the best deal changes monthly. Also be sure to ask about shipping and handling costs. After placing an order, have your salesperson read back the following information: your name and address, the exact specifics of the item(s) ordered, and your credit card number. Ask for the total cost and the order number identifying this transaction (if there are problems that number will help).

◆ These companies also sell cameras, lenses, camcorders, and slide projectors at costs that are extremely competitive. Get their price quotes when you're purchasing hardware.

November 23

When it comes to processing print film on a local level, you will be hard pressed to beat the price/quality combination of warehouse stores like Costco. Can't use the Costco option? Then try Walmart. You'll pay a bit more and receive even slightly better quality prints.

If you're not opposed to sending your film through the mail, you can still beat both of these options. York Photo (400 Rayon Drive, Parkersburg, WV 26101, 304-424-9675) may be the king of value, offering some of the least expensive processing anywhere and top-quality work.

Skrudland (5311 Fleming Court, Austin, TX 78744, 512-444-0958) and A Positive Kolor (11037 Penrose Street, Sun Valley, CA 91352, 818-768-5700) also do topnotch work for low prices.

◆ Contact these labs and request their literature, price sheets, and mailers.

November 24

We all have books that, once digested, integrate into the waste stream of our home. While many people give their unwanted books away, those with money-smarts trade their

:OⱢ

d pages for coveted ones. Accomplish this through
ₑ following avenues.

veral friends and ask if they want to horse
ch other's dogs. Ask them to cull their
backs, outgrown children's books, unneeded
ₐnd unused cookbooks. Then, drop by and

book stores and thrift shops in the area
and   trading policies. Some shops are happy
to tra   ₁sed books for two of yours. List these
stores ₁   ₜ for future reference.

═══ ₒvember 25 ═══

Keep up the reading, but keep down the expense—that's
sound advice for anyone who spends substantial sums on
new books each year. Here's how.

◆ Call your local library now and ask how to request
books over the phone. Typically, you need only mention that
you're interested in having a book held and it will be
done—you can wander by in a few days and claim it. In the
event that the book is checked out, ask to be placed on a
waiting list and to be notified when it's available. And if
the book is not in your library system, ask whether it can
be located through an inter-library loan (ILL).

◆ Another trick for making the library easier to use is
to bring home a pile of the library's Book Request Forms.
When you want a particular title, fill out a form and mail
it back to the library. Write on the card that you are
willing to wait for an inter-library loan if the book is not in
the system. Then wait. You'll be notified when your request
arrives.

◆ Even should you prefer using the phone to reserve
library books, keep some of the library's Book Request
Forms at home. The next time you visit a bookstore, bring
a few forms with you. When you find an interesting book,
note the title and author on the form. Once home, mail the

completed forms to the library. Then wait to be notified when your books become available.

♦ Call the local used-book stores (check the Yellow Pages under *Books—Used & Rare*). Inquire about the titles they carry, their specialties, pricing policies, and whether you can trade in your own used books. List the promising stores in your Rolodex.

♦ Make the same kind of calls to the Goodwill, St. Vincent De Paul, and other thrift stores. Add those that claim to have good book sections to your Rolodex. When rounds take you past these stores, stop in and stock up on 25¢ and 50¢ paperbacks.

♦ Occasionally check the classified ads (Thursday and Friday papers) under Garage Sales or Rummage Sales, then visit a few neighborhood happenings. Typically, you'll find tables of books with paperbacks selling for a quarter, hardbacks for a half-dollar, encyclopedia sets for a ten spot.

===== **November 26** =====

It's one of the banes of modern living, but now you'll have at least one reason to look forward to junk mail. This Amazon of paper is going to provide you with a lifetime supply of envelopes. All you need for the harvest is a pair of scissors, a roll of cellophane tape, and a felt-tipped pen (black with a ¼"-wide tip is best).

Any junk mail arriving in a 9"x11" or 10"x13" envelope constitutes a catch. Open envelopes you're interested in reading. Go right to work on those pieces you don't care to read by cutting the envelope roughly in half. Cut (transversely) across the long axis of the envelope, positioning the cut so one of the two pieces is devoid (or has a minimum) of printing. Should any printing remain on your "envelope," make it the back surface and darken out the printing with the felt-tipped pen.

To use your envelope, seal its top slit with cellophane tape. Alternately, roll the open slit of the envelope over once and tape the fold you've formed to the back of the envelope.

Note: For simple correspondence, keep your envelopes relatively narrow (roughly the dimensions of a business envelope). Envelopes that are wider than 6 1/8" cost more to mail (43¢ versus 32¢ for the first ounce).

═══════ November 27 ═══════

Yet another blessing of junk mail—it provides the raw materials for a forever supply of scratch paper and paper pads.

◆ Designate a place (perhaps in the office) to stack paper with an unused side. As those reams of paper received in the mail arrive, add all 8½"x11" sheets with an unused side to the pile. Also add to the pile all trash-bound sheets generated at home with a blank side. Dip into the new pile whenever a family member needs scratch paper, drawing paper, doodling paper, paper for lists.... Why use fresh sheets costing about a penny apiece when the paper you normally toss can handle the job?

◆ The paper collected above can also be bound into pads by means of a simple trick. Grab a ½-inch stack of like-sized sheets (e.g., 8½"x11") and tap the stack on a hard surface until the bottom edges of the sheets are flush. Clamp the wad together using giant paper clips or clothes pins (keep the edges of the pad flush). Stand the pad between two large books that are leaning against each other in an A-frame configuration. Spread a paper-thin layer of a liquid-urethane compound like *Goop* or *Shoe Goo* (see September 19) across the top of the pad. Let the compound harden and, *voilà*, you've created a pad of paper. Although it takes the liquid urethane several hours to cure, you can actually lay up a dozen pads of paper in about 20 minutes—that's less time than a trip to the store.

═══════ November 28 ═══════

If your family is about to bud (or has just budded), dozens of the baby products you'll be contemplating are luxuries at best, a waste of money at worst. Here are some you can easily live without.

♦ **Bassinets**. If given one, use it, but clothes baskets or a large drawer covered with a quilt does the job. Or just place your child in a crib from day one.

♦ **Formula**. Pediatricians usually prefer that babies be breast fed. This minimizes food allergies, infections, and possibly even the likelihood of obesity in childhood. It's also free.

♦ **Jarred baby foods**. They are convenient for occasional use but expensive for everyday use. It's easy and economical to mash or puree foods you've prepared for the rest of the family (use a fork, blender, or food processor). It's also easy to puree larger quantities of food and freeze the excess in ice-cube trays. Once frozen, pop the cubes into a freezer bag. Later, you can place a cube in a dish, defrost it, and serve.

♦ **Baby food grinders**. While they are useful for pureeing your fare into food an infant can stomach, most foods are easily mashed with a fork.

♦ **Baby juices**. These juices cost two to three times more than those marketed to adults. And if you follow the pediatrician's advice of diluting adult juices half and half with water, adult juices are cheaper still. Some infant juices are fortified with additional vitamins, but if you're feeding your child properly, the added vitamins are unnecessary.

♦ **Baby applesauce**. Baby formulas are considerably more expensive than normal applesauce. Buy the adult version.

♦ **Traveling crib**. An inflatable plastic wading pool (available at most department stores) makes an inexpensive replacement for a portable travel crib. Inflate it, cover it with a sheet, tuck the edges of the sheet under the bottom of the pool, and put your infant (or young toddler) in it.

♦ **Baby bathtubs**. The kitchen sink works fine for infants if you line it with a towel. Infants are about as mobile as plants and don't collect dirt quickly, so don't bother with the mutual torture of frequent baths. Toddlers can be washed in a tub; placing them in a plastic clothes basket (inside the tub), keeps them from sliding around.

♦ **Baby soaps**. They are costly and unneeded. Use a plain-Jane soap that is low in scents, additives, and antibacterial agents.

♦ **Baby shampoo**. While they may sting eyes less, the "No Tears" claim of manufaturers is more hype than fact. Adult shampoos won't melt your baby's eyes or hair, so don't hesitate using them. Because babies don't have much hair, go easy on the amount of shampoo used.

♦ **Talcum powder**. These powders neither prevent nor cure bottom rashes. In fact, an infant's skin is sometimes irritated by powder. Finally, talcum powder is potentially dangerous—airborne particles are harmful to an infant's lungs and have caused cases of pneumonia and death.

♦ **Infant swings**. Generations of parents managed to pacify children during the first months of life without this Yuppie rage. Nonetheless, some parents swear by them and if their opinions override my good advice, buy a windup swing—they are cheaper to buy and operate (no batteries needed).

♦ **Walkers**. They have the highest accident rate of any group of baby products (nearly 25,000 injuries per year). While using them, children routinely crash down stairs, tumble into pools, and tip over onto concrete floors. Save your money (and your child).

♦ **Changing tables**. Any elevated surface—the top of a dresser or dryer—will do. Worried about kids falling off these unofficial platforms? Build a rail around your changing area. But the best solution is not to leave your child attended—gather everything needed for a diaper change before setting your child down.

♦ **Diaper wraps**. You'll hear radically different opinions about the fancy (and expensive) diaper wraps used with cloth diapers: everything from 'Made in Heaven' to 'Spawned in Hell.' I side with the latter group. In my experience the reason these wraps 'breathe' (a much-touted feature), is because they leak. After trying several brands, my wife and I reverted to cheap, plastic overpants. Coated-nylon overpants are also excellent and, though more expensive, last longer. Neither of these inexpensive overpants breathe but I've yet to hear a doctor or nurse object to their use.

November 29

Making your own diaper or wet wipes is not only extremely simple, it's extremely inexpensive. Your use for these wipes will grow with your children—by the time they're out of diapers, there will be other body parts (hands and faces) to clean.

To make diaper wipes, use a serrated knife to saw a normal roll of paper towels into two half-sized rolls. Pull the cardboard core from the center and place one of the mini rolls into a large coffee can (or if you purchase bulk margarine, a similarly sized plastic margarine tub). Feed the center sheet of the roll through an 'X' cut in the can's plastic lid.

Mix 1 to 1½ teaspoons liquid dishwashing detergent with about 1½ cups water and pour the solution over the towels. Leave the towels alone for about 30 minutes, allowing the water to be absorbed evenly throughout the roll. Add water as needed to get the towels to the moisture level you like—the exact quantity needed will vary according to the brand of towel used.

To make the exterior of the coffee can more attractive and to keep the interior from rusting, paint the can first.

═══ November 30 ═══

To diaper or to pamper—that is the question.

When cost is the yardstick, "diapers" is the clear-cut answer. Children have their diapers changed about 5,300 times during the first two-and-a-half years of life. Disposable diapers, at an average cost of 25¢ each (sale prices are a little less, non-sale prices considerably more) are the most convenient but most expensive diapering option, costing you about $1,325.

Compare that to the cost of home laundering diapers which exacts the following expenses: $240 for diapers and overpants, utility fees for two loads of diapers per week, and detergent fees (40¢ per load). Add this up clothe diapers with home laundering costs about $495 (9.3¢ per diaper change) for your first child, $254 (4.7¢ per diaper change) for a second child.

In light of the savings, take a serious look at laundering your own diapers.

♦ Call several department stores and research the cost of cloth diapers and nylon overpants. You'll want at least a four-day supply of diapers which translates to 45 to 70 diapers (quantity depends on the age of the baby, thickness of the diapers purchased, and how often you need to double diaper your child). You'll also need a diaper pail, diaper pins, and nylon overpants (about eight for infants, six for toddlers).

♦ Look up *Diaper Services* in the Yellow Pages and inquire whether you can purchase their retired diapers. These diapers may be slightly tattered but will still offer plenty of life. Best of all, they are inexpensive (10 diapers for about $6.50) and of better quality than most department-store diapers.

♦ The job of laundering those evil parcels spawned by your angels behind is not nearly as evil as legend has it. Throw dirty diapers (be they wetted or be they soiled) in the toilet bowl and, using the latex gloves sitting atop the diaper pail, give them a quick rinse. Now toss them into the pail where they can soak (water only) until wash day.

On wash day: Pour the entire contents of the diaper pail into the washing machine and, using a spin cycle, remove all the water.

Add normal amounts of detergent and ½ cup of bleach to the diapers and, using a normal cycle, wash the diapers. Most sterility-minded Americans use hot-water washes and warm-water rinses, but warm washes and cold rinses will work just fine. One friend washes *and* rinses diapers in cold water. "Never had a problem getting the diapers perfectly clean," she reports. Try it once.

Machine-dry the diapers (air-dried diapers are stiff and scratchy).

If your child is getting rashes from the diapers, include an additional step. Before drying, run one more rinse/spin cycle with a capful of vinegar added to the rinse water. The vinegar neutralizes any detergent or bleach left in the diapers. If the diapers come out smelling of vinegar, you used too much.

December

What creates the most guilt every year about this time? Christmas cards must be near the top of the list. Getting them out on time is your problem, lowering the cost of these guilt-producers, however, is in my domain.

♦ **Forget cards.** Send a personal letter (or even one of the ubiquitous photocopied letters) instead.

♦ **Make cards**. Collect autumn leaves, ivy leaves, fern boughs, cedar sprigs, and/or holly leaves. Paint the backs of your leaves or sprigs with poster or acrylic paint and lay the plant (paint side down) on a nice sheet of paper. Cover the leaf (or sprig) with a paper towel, then use a wallpaper seam roller or a spoon to press the paint from leaf to paper. Note: Next year gather leaves earlier in the fall and freeze them until you need them.

♦ **Make postcards.** Use the process just described and press painted leaves against card stock rather than paper. A postcard under 4¼"x6" in size is 37% cheaper than a letter to mail (also see December 27).

♦ **More about poscards.** Make Christmas postcards from a family snapshot. Photographic prints (used as postcards) cost less than store-bought cards, and your friends would rather see a picture of your family than of Santa stuffing a stocking.

♦ **Kid cards.** Using construction paper as the foundation of your cards, whip your child labor into pasting wide strips of colored ribbon onto the paper. Green ribbon cut in a series of ever-smaller trapezoids will form a Christmas tree. Three short lengths of ribbon can be cut and pasted to form a holly leaf. Multi colored strips of ribbon, cut and pasted appropriately, form a Christmas bulb (ornament).

Alternately, give the kids free reign to design whatever they please using construction paper, fabric remnants, beads, sequins, lace, and yarn.

December 2

All those ornaments for the tree—it's yet another expense affiliated with Christmas. And here, as is normally the case, the brilliance of the brain can triumph over the wad of the wallet. Get ready to drape your tree with some of these inexpensive ornaments.

♦ **Ginger-bread ornaments.** Use a straw to poke holes in the head of each character before baking. After baking, decorate the cookies with colored frosting, and hang the figures by threading ribbon through the straw holes.

♦ **Pine-cone ornaments.** Hang unadorned cones, or paint them with gold or silver spray paint.

♦ **Egg ornaments.** Put a pin prick on both ends of the egg and blow the raw egg out into a mixing bowl. Paint the eggs gold, silver, red or green. Hang the shells by ribbon loops glued to the top.

♦ **Paper ornaments.** Cut up last year's Christmas cards into seasonal shapes: Santas, stars, sleighs, gifts. Punch holes in the top and thread the card with a hanging ribbon.

♦ **Shell ornaments.** It's hard to improve upon the shapes of nature. Drill a hanging hole through the shell or glue a loop of ribbon to the hanging point.

December 3

Call several friends and neighbors today and make arrangements for a cookie exchange. Here's how it works: You make quantities of just one kind of cookie, then trade equal numbers of your cookies for the cookies others have made. The process saves everyone money—rather than buying the ingredients for many cookies, you can buy bulk quantities of the ingredients needed for just one type. Equally important, the exchange saves you time—it's far faster to mass produce 250 shortbread cookies than it is to make five different recipes. Finally there's a quality of cooperation and sharing here that enhances the season.

═══ December 4 ═══

What's the cheapest way to weather a cold? Ignore cold medicines that claim to do everything. Instead, identify which active ingredients fight the symptoms you are suffering at the time. Buy single-ingredient medications (preferably generics) to ease those symptoms.

People with colds normally suffer from congestion, sore throats, fever/headache/muscle ache, *or* coughs. They don't, however, suffer from all these symptoms simultaneously. If you're congested and take a drug with both a decongestant and a cough suppressant, you'll pay much more for that medication than for a simple decongestant. Likewise, some companies add aspirin or acetaminophen to their decongestants and charge you a fortune for the pain relief that a penny's worth of aspirin delivers.

When you have a cold, fight muscle aches, fevers, and headaches with pain relievers containing aspirin, acetaminophen, or ibuprofen. Stymie sore throats with medicated lozenges and sprays containing phenol compounds, benzocaine, hexylresorcinol, or menthol. Stop coughs with suppressants containing dextromethorphan, codeine, diphenhydramine; medicated lozenges containing menthol; or with expectorants containing guaifenesin. And relieve congestion with topical decongestants containing phenylephrine, oxymetazoline or xylometazoline, or with oral decongestants containing pseudoephedrine.

♦ Check your medicine cabinet to see if you are stocked with a medication to deal with each category of discomfort: aches and fever, sore throats, coughing, and congestion. If not, place the medications needed on the Master Purchasing List (see January 1) and purchase them when pharmacies place them on sale.

Cheap Trick:
Hard candies and saltwater gargles (warm water) will give you about the same sore-throat relief as lozenges and sprays packed with phenol compounds, benzocaine, or menthol. A saltwater gargle can also provide throat relief (use no more than ¼ teaspoon of salt per cup of water).

December 5

Yesterday's advice for fighting a cold applies to flus as well. According to the *University of California at Berkeley Wellness Letter*, one of the most-respected health newsletters, flu medicines are made from basically the same ingredients as cold medications. Also, flu medications are often expensive combination medicines containing a fever-lowering pain reliever, an antihistamine, and a cough suppressant.

Avoid the high cost of these combination medicines by sticking to single-ingredient medications that relieve the symptoms you're suffering at the time (see yesterday's entry for the active ingredients you need).

Cheap Trick:
Both flus and colds are "self limiting." In other words, they run their cycle and go away on their own. Nothing a doctor prescribes (this includes antibiotics) actually shortens the time you are sick. Save yourself a doctor's visit and let the illness run its course. The bite of a flu will last three or four days while the worst of a cold can last five or six days (lesser symptoms may last for weeks).

December 6

If you're not a generic drug user it's time to become one. The vast majority of generic drugs give you the same benefits as brand-name medications at half the price, sometimes less. For example, the prescription medication Inderal can sell for $44 per hundred tablets while its generic equivalent, propranolol, can be purchased for under $7 per hundred.

Do generics work? Yes. Nearly half of them are made by the very companies that developed the brand-name product. The other half are sold by firms specializing in generics. These firms must prove to the U.S. Food and Drug Administration (FDA) that their products are bioequivalent (work in and on the body in the same way) to their brand-name brethren.

A scandal in the late 1980s, in which several FDA employees accepted bribes from generic-drug companies, rocked the public's confidence in generics. But the FDA has purged itself, and the evidence shows the vast majority of generics will deliver the same therapeutic value as brand-name drugs. A few generics are controversial in their efficacy. This, combined with the fact that the brand-name companies work hard at spreading misinformation about generics, has many people reluctant to try them. If you have any doubts, most pharmacists will give you an informed (and honest) opinion about whether the generic drug you need will deliver the same results as a name brand. Ask.

Of the 500 generic drugs available, the ones with the spottiest results are those that: 1) regulate epilepsy 2) govern heart rhythm 3) replace thyroid hormone.

Cheap Trick:
Tell your doctor when he or she is writing your prescription that you would like to take a generic medication if one is available. Your comment serves two purposes. First, if your doctor has no objections, it will eliminate doubts you might have. Second, some doctors habitually check a box on their prescription form stating that the prescription be dispensed as written. If the doctor checks this box and lists a brand-name drug, a pharmacist cannot substitute a generic for you. By asking about generics, you'll tip the doctor not to check that box.

═══ December 7 ═══

A rose by any other name is still a rose. Keep that thought in mind when evaluating over-the-counter medications. You'll get the same headache relief from 325 milligrams of aspirin regardless of whether it's labelled Bayer or Brand X. Meanwhile, 200 mg of ibuprofen will give you the same relief whether the bottle reads Advil or Acme, and 325 mg of acetaminophen will perform the same work whether the pills are Tylenol or TyTabs.

Buy your generics from a reputable pharmacy or chain and you can rest assured the medication will duplicate the efficacy of the name brand. That applies to the gamut of medications: pain relievers, decongestants, cough suppressants, antihistamines. If you're unsure whether a $7 bottle of Robitussin will give you the same cough relief as a $4 bottle of Robicop, ask the pharmacist which one, on a cost-benefit basis, is the smart buy.

Generally, over-the-counter generics cost about half as much as the name brands. Following are a few examples from the pharmacy I frequent: Afrin nose spray is $7.43 versus $3.39 for the same quantity of generic, Bayer Aspirin is $8.49 for 200 tablets versus $3.99 for 300 tablets of generic. Advil is $10.99 for 250 tablets versus $7.57 for 500 tablets of generic ibuprofen.

♦ Make a list of over-the-counter medications you use, listing everything from aspirin to zinc. Call several pharmacists and ask whether the name brand has the generics beat in any of these categories.

♦ Of course a medicine a child won't take is not cheap no matter how inexpensive it is. Ask your pharmacist about the children's medications you need and see if any of the options (generics, pills, chewables, liquids) have putrid reputations. Occasionally the frugal buy is the costlier option.

Cheap Trick:

The "extra strength" rage is a marketing maneuver to lure bigger bills out of your wallet. Example: 100 tablets of Anacin delivering 400 mg of aspirin per tablet cost $5.89 while 40 maximum-strength Anacin delivering 500 mg of aspirin per tablet cost $5.39. Milligram for milligram, maximum-strength Anacin is nearly twice as expensive, making that pill hard to swallow.

If you have an "extra-strength" headache, three tablets of aspirin or acetaminophen (usually 325 mg each) give you nearly the same dosage as two extra-strength tablets (usually 500 mg each).

═══ December 8 ═══

Shop around for medications taken regularly. Prices vary considerably among pharmacies and no single outlet has the best price on every drug. Recently, when my wife needed an expensive allergy medication, I found a $32 difference between the cheapest and costliest quote. Then I checked prices with several reputable mail-order pharmacies and found two that undersold the cheapest local store. By ordering through the mail, we also avoided state sales tax (an additional 8.2% savings), and the mileage costs of driving to the pharmacy.

Order over-the-counter and prescription medications through the mail from sources like Medi-Mail (800-331-1458), Wonder Laboratories (800-992-1672), Action Mail-Order Drug Company (800-452-1976) and AARP Pharmacy Services (800-456-2277). You needn't be a member of AARP to use their pharmacy. For prescription medications, enclose the doctor's prescription with your order.

◆ Make a list of regularly used drugs, ointments, vitamin supplements, and medications. Call several local pharmacies and mail-order firms to determine where you will buy these supplies in the future. Be sure to ask mail-order firms about their shipping fees. Currently, the AARP Pharmacy Service charges only $1 for shipping, regardless of the order size.

═══ December 9 ═══

Because of the visitation costs, it doesn't make sense to see the doctor every time your child develops a sniffle or cough. When is a child sick enough for a doctor's visit?

According to many doctors, a child who is well enough to play several hours during the course of the day is probably not sick enough to warrant a visit. A child who is completely listless and has no interest in any sort of play warrants a telephone call to the doctor.

Also call when: 1) children younger than three months of age have rectal temperatures over 100.2°F, 2) children between three and six months have rectal temperatures over 101°F, 3) children over six months have rectal temperatures over 102°F.

===== **December 10** =====

Women would do well to ignore the advice I dish out on cosmetics. I am, after all, a man (a cheap one at that) so most of what I say about the cosmetics industry is unflattering.

Woman's Day, however, a magazine I browse in supermarket lines for its money-saving advice, interviewed its own makeup artist for her thoughts about reducing cosmetic expenses. Her advice? Buy inexpensive lip liners, lip gloss, lip balms, translucent powders, and mascaras.

What cosmetics were worth a splurge? According to the magazine, a foundation to match your skin type and tone, lip brush, eye-makeup remover, and a flattering color of rich-formula lipstick.

===== **December 11** =====

No one in your family need ever invest in expensive face moisturizers and creams again. Here's a technique that pricey spas use to keep skin soft and smooth. Encourage all family members who worry about such matters to try this tonight.

Rub small amounts of petroleum jelly onto your clean, wet face. As you rub in the jelly, keep wetting your face with a little warm water. Dab your face with a towel when you're done. The finished effect will not feel greasy.

The technique also works great for hands.

Cheap Trick:
At such a low cost and without a mouthful of unpronounceable chemicals, you may not believe they can work. According to dermatologists, however, two of the best skin moisturizers are baby oil (mineral oil) and petroleum jelly. Dermatologists also give *Crisco* shortening excellent marks as a moisturizer. Just watch out if you notice your spouse salivating when you moisturize.

December 12

What is shampoo? Mainly detergent with a few minor ingredients like scents. What is dishwashing detergent? Much the same stuff. Considering that they are both basically detergent, you can legitimately ask whether you should pay five times more for *Nexxus Therappe* than for *Ivory Dishwashing Liquid.* No you shouldn't. In fact, if you wash your hair with detergents formulated for washing dishes, many will leave your hair perfectly clean and shiny.

Don't want to contract dishpan scalp? Then simply stick to a cheap shampoo. When *Consumer Reports* evaluated 60 of the best-selling shampoos—shampoos ranging in price from $1.50 per 15 ounces to $10 per 16 ounces—the professional beauticians who did the blind testing gave 54 of the shampoos nearly identical marks. Price played no bearing on the performance; in fact, one of the $10 shampoos was at the bottom of the pack. No shampoo gave hair more luster than another. Incidentally, the magazine included Ivory Dishwashing Liquid in the shampoo test and its performance was rated as very good.

What about the notion that protein shampoos and secret conditioners "nourish" your hair? Rubbish. Hair is dead by the time you see it; you can nourish it only by eating properly.

The moral: If you pay much more than $2 per 15-ounce bottle of shampoo (sale price of about $1 per bottle), switch loyalties. Take a look at shampoos made by Ivory, Revlon, Alberto VO5, or Wella Balsam. Find one with a scent you like and switch.

December 13

Keep facial tissue in the house for visiting guests, but when you blow your own nose (or wipe the makeup from your eyes) use bathroom tissue (toilet paper) instead of facial tissue. Two squares of double-ply TP folded over on itself several times gives enough paper for a good nose blow or eye wipe, yet costs three times less than facial tissue (the sale cost of two sheets of two-ply TP runs .16¢ versus the .57¢/sheet sale cost of facial tissue). As for softness, the two papers are nearly identical. Facial tissue is much stronger than TP when wet, but for tissue headed to the trash after a blow, that strength is a non-issue.

◆ Rolls of toilet paper adorning the tops of dressers or bathroom counters won't earn Martha Stewart's endorsement for fashion, so dress them up. Place several boxes of Kleenex Ultra on your On-Deck shopping list (see July 12). When you find these cube-shaped boxes of facial tissues on sale (about 90¢ per box) purchase several in colors and designs you like.

After the facial tissues are used, open the box along one of its glued sides, insert a roll of toilet paper with its cardboard core removed, feed tissue from the *center* of the roll through the box's top slit, and paste (or tape) the box shut. You've just given a homely roll of bathroom tissue a handsome shell.

====== December 14 ======

Go to your paper towel dispenser, take off the roll, and stash it away. Alternately, tie a shoelace around the roll so you cannot, conveniently, tear off a sheet. Time to start living without these throw-away luxuries. Options:

◆ Lay dish towels and small hand towels in convenient locations in the kitchen (e.g., across the cupboard door below the sink, on the handle of the oven).

◆ Use old washcloths or diapers to wipe down counters and mop up spills. Wash as necessary.

◆ Place a roll of toilet paper or a box of facial tissues in the kitchen. On the rare occasions when you need paper to mop up spills, these products do the job with less waste and more economy.

====== December 15 ======

If you rely on paper napkins, hide them deep in a cupboard where they are not easily reached, and pull out cloth napkins. Proper management of these cloth napkins will allow you to use them for at least a week before they're ready for washing.

♦ Make it the law of the land that after meals all family members refold their napkins and leave them at their seats.

♦ We use a variation of that theme: After each meal, our napkins go into our personal napkin holders. At the next meal, there is no question whose napkin is whose—my wife grabs the lion holder and I, symbolically, reach for the monkey.

♦ Use paper napkins only for picnics and messy meals (spare ribs, spaghetti) but make them go twice as far by tearing them in half before setting the table. Open them and tear (or cut) them along the crease.

December 16

Pick an evening this week when your family will sort through the old toys, games, books, sports equipment, and clothing you intend to donate to charity. Before that evening do some research with your children: Find a worthy group, shelter, or non-profit organization that will receive your donation.

From a spiritual point of view, making a yearly donation to charity emphasizes the meaning of Christmas—that it's a season of hope and a time to share with those who are less fortunate. On the practical side, the donation makes room for the new by purging the old. When the purging stops we start outgrowing our homes. That's an expense few can afford.

December 17

Still short a few Christmas presents? Following are last-minute suggestions for young children that will keep everyone in good cheer.

♦ Bead sets—they're challenging and cheap.

♦ Outing coupons to the zoo, aquarium, movies, children's museum, planetarium, puppet show, sporting event...

♦ Coupon to take a child fishing (redeemable later, of course).

♦ Baseball/football cards.

♦ Stamp-collecting albums (check with the Post Office and inquire about their beginner's stamp collecting kit).

♦ Sandbox toys: buckets, shovels, measuring cups, molds.

♦ Lessons (music, swimming, gymnastics, skiing, ballet...).

♦ Subscription to a children's magazine: *Your Big Backyard* (ages 3-5), *Sesame Street* (ages 3-6), *Highlights for Children* (ages 6-10), *Ranger Rick* (ages 6-12), *American Girl* (ages 7-12), *Sports Illustrated for Kids* (ages 7-14). Call your reference librarian for ordering addresses, phone numbers, or other recommendations.

♦ Marbles (in a bag) with the rules to a game like Ringler. Rules for Ringler: Place 13 marbles in the center of a circle (10-feet in diameter). Arrange the marbles in a cross formation with three marbles along each arm of the cross and the thirteenth marble in the center of the cross. The first player to hit seven marbles (shooting from the edge of the circle) wins.

♦ Classic toys that have withstood the test of time: jacks, pick-up sticks, kites, hand puppets, rubber stamps, origami books, poster paints, crayons, colored chalk (for outside drawing), charcoal, colored glues (by Elmer's), packs of construction paper and scissors, tiny decks of cards, jump rope and jump-rope rhymes (check the library), books of magic, tops, yoyos (with description of yoyo tricks), dolls, doll clothing, doll-house furniture, trucks, children's jewelry, bubble solution, dress-up clothing.

♦ Record yourself reading children's stories.

♦ Bird feeder for the window of the house, or a bug farm.

December 18

In the same vein as yesterday's entry, following are inexpensive, last-minute gift ideas for teen-agers.

◆ Lessons sharing one of your skills: skiing, crafts, music, auto repair, cooking, typing, computers, sewing, basketball, chess.

◆ Tutoring in a difficult/interesting subject.

◆ Hair ornaments, antique combs, and clips from a thrift store.

◆ Art supplies (pens, pastels, oil paints, charcoals).

◆ Tickets to a local event: major- or minor-league sports, local talk shows, community theater.

◆ Gift certificate to a movie, bowling alley, local carnival, regional water slide, skating rink.

◆ Coupon to take them skiing, inner tubing, fishing, canoeing, water skiing... (redeemable in summer).

◆ Subscription to *Zillions*: Consumer Reports for Children.

December 19

Finally, some last-minute gift suggestions for adults.

◆ Teas, spices, candy, foreign foods—you'll find specialty and gourmet foods to satisfy all tastes.

◆ Large-type books (good for the elderly).

◆ Homemade freezer meal (chili, lasagna, casserole, soup). Place meal in a foil pan so it is oven-ready. Include cooking instructions. You'll be thought of twice—once when the gift is delivered, again when it is eaten.

◆ Homemade relish, jam, pesto, or salad dressing packaged in a nice jar.

◆ Homemade breads, cinnamon rolls, or cookies.

◆ Map showing how to get to a family's house from all directions. Put in mass transit options, freeway exits, and street directions. Include the phone number. Give 10 copies and the master copy as a gift.

◆ Volunteer an afternoon of your time to a cause/charity the person believes in.

◆ Language tapes—for a commuter with a language interest.

◆ Books on tape. Assuming your library has books on tape, supply the recipient with one of the library's audio books every other month. Great for commuters.

◆ Fix it afternoon. An afternoon of handy work.

- House or yard work—a coupon to polish, mend, weed, iron, wash, mow, rake...
- Lessons in one of your skills: skiing, sailing, cooking, tennis...
- Your professional services if you're a lawyer, mechanic, typist, computer jock.
- Quality coffee beans.
- Borrowing coupon for temporary use of your Nintendo, ping pong table, pool table, computer games, canoe, or 90-foot yacht.
- Baby-sitting certificate.
- Books. There's a book for every interest. Know a family wanting to live on one income? Give them this book.

December 20

Take this quiz today; save on batteries from now on.

1) Should you buy inexpensive general-purpose batteries, medium-priced heavy-duty batteries, or expensive alkaline cylinders?
2) What brand of alkaline batteries is best?
3) Should you stockpile batteries when they are on sale?
4) Are rechargeable nickel-cadmium (nicad) batteries worth the high initial cost?
5) Should you use nicads in emergency devices?
6) Are all nicads created equal?
7) How do you minimize battery use in the devices you already own?
8) Are alkaline batteries rechargeable?
9) How do you ensure the batteries you buy are fresh?

Answers:

1) The cheapest batteries to buy are the most expensive to operate. Tests in which the same device was powered by different types of batteries showed: alkaline batteries cost 13¢ an hour to operate, heavy-duty batteries cost 26¢ an hour to operate, and general-purpose batteries cost 35¢ an hour to operate.

2) Despite what advertisers would have you believe, there is little difference among the major brands. Go with the cheapest or, preferably, with what is on sale.

3) Yes and no. Heavy-duty batteries have about a nine-month shelf life, alkalines will store nicely for about two years.

4) In an often-used device that devours batteries, rechargeables pay for themselves in several months. Unfortunately, nicads don't store a lot of energy (about one third the amount of an alkaline), so you'll be moving batteries between device and charger quite often.

5) Nicads leak their charge quickly (about 1% of their charge per day) which makes them unsuitable for devices seeing occasional use—like the emergency flashlight in a car.

6) In the AA sizes, most nicads store about 500 milliamps of juice. In the C and D sizes, significant differences exist because many manufacturers pack the extra volume with air. Look for high-capacity C and D cells at stores like Radio Shack. They weigh about twice as much as the Twinkie (air-filled) models, store about twice as much energy, and are worth the extra cost.

7) Many battery-driven devices run off household current if you connect them to a suitable AC adapter (transformer). Even a device that did not come with an adapter will often accept one: Check for an adapter outlet marked with a direct current (DC) voltage rating, like "DC 6V" or "DC 9V." At Radio Shack, fixed-voltage adapters cost about $8 while universal adapters, which can be set at many different voltage levels, cost about $13. It won't take many battery changes to recoup the cost of these adapters.

8) Most alkaline batteries are not rechargeable, but Rayovac does make a rechargeable alkaline battery that has some decided advantages over nicads (see tomorrow's entry).

9) Some batteries come with built-in battery testers, but guess who pays for that expensive packaging. Instead, buy batteries from outlets like K-Mart that, due to low prices, never have batteries that sit long enough to grow stale.

December 21

Make the rounds of the house checking out battery-powered toys, lights, Walkmans, noise makers, and calculators. Evaluate each item, noting the size and number of batteries required. Note also which of these devices is heavily used and, therefore, a definite candidate for rechargeable batteries. Use your math skills (i.e., your toes and fingers) to calculate how many rechargeable batteries your household needs; put those batteries on your shopping list. Include a charger as well (if your house needs an assortment of battery sizes, get a universal charger that can handle AA, C, and D cells alike).

A question to answer before you stock the household with rechargeable power: Will you be investing in nickel-cadmium (nicad) batteries or rechargeable alkalines?

Nicads have been on the market many years and because they can be charged and discharged hundreds of times they are, indeed, economical. They do, however, present drawbacks including: lower voltages (not all appliances work on nicads because these rechargeables discharge 1.25 volts instead of the 1.5 volts discharged by an alkaline), reduced storage capacity (each charge holds only a third of the energy of an alkaline), leakage of charge (nicads discharge 1% of their energy per day), and a faulty memory (if you don't discharge nicads fully, they quickly forget how to fully discharge).

The Renewal batteries (a rechargeable alkaline, widely available through mass merchandisers) address many of these drawbacks. Because they output 1.5 volts, they will operate any battery-powered device. Because they don't have the memory problem of nicads (in fact, you'll significantly extend their life by recharging them often), you needn't worry about discharging them fully. And because they don't leak their charge, a flashlight that's been sitting in the car for a year will illuminate when it must.

Unfortunately, the Renewal batteries aren't perfect. In the first third of life they pack about 75% of the energy of a normal alkaline; late in life they will hold only 30% of the charge of a normal alkaline. And unlike nicads which will recharge hundreds of times, expect only 25 to 30 recharges from Renewal batteries.

Four AA Renewal Batteries cost about $5 to $6 (4AA nicads cost $10 to $11), an AA charger (don't use your nicad recharger) runs about $14 ($8 for nicads), and a universal charger runs $25 ($17 for nicads).

December 22

Checked your tire pressure lately? Over 50% of American cars suffer from saggy tires. Under-inflation can increase a tire's rolling resistance (and hence its gas consumption) by 5%. That same rolling resistance ultimately shortens the life of tires (by as much as half) and increases engine strain.

That is a hat trick of reasons to check tire pressure each winter month. Why so often? For every 10°F fall in temperature, your tire pressure drops one-pound per square inch.

Check tires when they are cold and keep them inflated to the figures recommended in your owner's manual (between 30 and 34 psi for most cars). Note the tires that are low and how many pounds of pressure they require. By the time you reach a filling station, road friction will have warmed the tires. Take a new reading of the underinflated tires and add to this reading the pounds of pressure that were needed when the tire was cold.

While you're checking the pressure, observe the wear pattern of your tires. The pattern can warn you of a variety of problems. A tire wearing quickly in the center—but not on the edges—is overinflated, while a tire wearing on both edges—but not in the center—is underinflated. A tire with irregular and uneven wear patches is improperly balanced. If one tire is wearing on one edge, either the tire is faulty or, more likely, you have a steering or front-end alignment problem (take your car to a mechanic and have the front end checked). If both tires on the front or back are wearing on an outside or an inside edge, the toe setting needs adjustment (another job for the shop).

For more information:
Request a free copy of the *Consumer Tire Guide* from the Tire Industry Safety Council, P.O. Box 1801, Washington, D.C. 20013.

══════ December 23 ══════

Run the car's air conditioner for at least five minutes each week. This sounds uninviting during the chilly months, but adopt the habit all the same—it maintains the coolant pressure in your air conditioner and, down the road, reduces the number of expensive repairs your air conditioner will require.

══════ December 24 ══════

We all have little simple pleasures we enjoy. Maybe it's a long, hot soak in the bathtub; or a back rub from our spouse; or time alone with a book; or maybe it's a particular delicacy shared with a particular person... One of my simple pleasures is to pour myself an Irish Cream, before visiting the sofa for a talk with my wife. The liqueur is a cue not to discuss day-to-day issues but to dream and philosophize. By the time we leave the sofa, we both feel uplifted and refreshed—which is exactly what a simple pleasure should accomplish.

◆ Make a list of your own simple pleasures today. Now give yourself permission to enjoy a few of these pleasures each week by actually scheduling them on your daily calendar. Some—like devoting 10 minutes to early-morning stretches or meditation—might give your outlook of the coming day a real boost. Others—like a few minutes to talk or read at day's end—might be all you need to put a positive spin on the day's craziness.

◆ Incidentally, if Irish Cream happens to be one of your simple pleasures, here's how to make it on the cheap. Combine in a blender 1½ cups whiskey, 1 cup sweetened condensed milk, 1 cup Irish-cream-flavored Coffee Mate, 1 teaspoon powdered instant coffee, 2 tablespoons liquid chocolate syrup, 1 teaspoon almond extract, and 1 teaspoon vanilla extract. Blend and store in the refrigerator (keeps for at least two months). Print the recipe right on the storage bottle used.

December 25

"Want what you have and you'll always have what you want."

♦ Read that quote several times. Get a pencil and piece of paper while you're thinking about its meaning, then write down your thoughts. This need not read like poetry or an Emerson essay.

For me, the quote triggers the following observations: that I already own what's truly important (health, family, food enough, shelter enough, and a Subaru Legacy); that contentedness is a condition that most people can attain; that contentment is not a place we get to but a state of mind; that by closing my eyes to advertisers and my ears to the toy talk of peers, I can avoid wanting things I've lived happily without all my life; that desire is the root of discontent; that those who don't see that they already have enough are unlikely to see it later when they have more; that without a philosophy like this one, the capacity to spend will grow as fast as the capacity to earn.

♦ Transfer this quote onto an index card and tape it to the headboard of your bed. Take a moment each day (when you encounter the card) to reflect over its meaning. In a few weeks when you've grown blind to the quote, take it down.

December 26

You may be so sick of shopping that even the thought of the post-Christmas sales is torture. Nonetheless, a great time to shop for *next* Christmas is the week following *this* Christmas. Pull out the weekly calendar and schedule some mornings to buy next year's decorations and stocking stuffers. Maybe you'll even find some major gifts. Stash the loot in the attic. Now enjoy the reprieve until next year.

══════ December 27 ══════

While cleaning up after Christmas, gather all the cards you received. Here are a few ways to use them.

◆ Tear off (and dispose of) the backs of these cards and you have a crop of postcards for next Christmas. You won't have to buy cards *and* you'll save on postage (postcards fly for 37% less than letters). Note who sent you the card in the first place (pencil their initials on the corner of the postcard), so that you can have the fun of sending the card back to the original sender (or to avoid this fate if it embarrasses you). Card dimensions must be over 3.5" X 5" and under 4¼" X 6".

◆ Turn Christmas cards into holiday place mats by sandwiching several between pieces of clear, plastic contact paper. Make holiday coasters by cutting cards into desired shapes, laminating the card between sheets of contact paper, and trimming the edges.

◆ Create jigsaw puzzles for children by gluing large cards onto cardboard and then cutting the works into assorted shapes.

◆ Also, save the holiday stamps from the envelopes that delivered all those cards. Paste stamps onto a star-shaped piece of construction paper, or felt. Next year that collage of stamps can be used as a tree ornament.

══════ December 28 ══════

Frugality is a topic you'll never completely master. Every aspect of life, every subject, every transaction has its money-saving angles. Make it part of your continuing education to keep expanding your knowledge. Newsletters can help.

Although books gather together more information and index that information for easier reference, newsletters have a benefit of their own—their arrival each month (or quarter) helps remotivate you and reaffirm that your choice to work the home was a wise one. That benefit alone—to say nothing of the money saved—is worth the subscription price of a newsletter.

Quite a number of frugality/downscaling newsletters are on the market. Write for a sample issue of each; decide for yourself which one speaks to you.

♦ *Simple Living*, 2319 N 45th Street Box 149, Seattle, WA 98103. My favorite newsletter. The articles in this quarterly are sometimes philosophic, sometimes pragmatic, and always useful. The articles are thoughtful and often written by top names in the simplicity movement. Subscription price is $16/year, samples $4 (check, money order).

♦ *The Pocket Change Investor*, Good Advice Press, Box 78, Elizaville, NY 12523. Another superb quarterly that deals with more nuts-and-bolts, hard numbers, and banking information than Simple Living. It will save you far more than the $13/year it costs. Send $1 for a sample issue.

♦ *At-Home Dad*, 61 Brightwood Ave, North Andover, MA 01845, 508-685-7931. A quarterly newsletter costing $12/year that addresses the issues, problems, worries, and successes of fathers who stay home with their children.

♦ *The Penny Pincher*, 2 Hilltop Rd, Mendham, NJ 07945, 201-543-1114. A newsletter packed with tips, addresses, to-do lists, and resources for saving money. This monthly newsletter costs $15/year. For a sample issue, send $1 and a self-addressed business envelope with two stamps on it.

♦ *The Cheap Report*, P.O. Box 394, Antioch, CA 94509. Ten issues, $12/year. For a sample, send $1.20 and a SASE.

♦ *The Cheapskate Monthly*, P.O. Box 2135, Paramount, CA 90723, 310-630-8845. A monthly costing $16/year. For a free sample, send SAE with 55¢ postage.

December 29

For your continuing education, books deliver more frugality information per dollar than newsletters. The better frugality/simple-living titles will save you a hundred times what you invest—especially if you reread them occasionally and reference them as you're faced with new expenses.

Search libraries and bookstores for books filed under the headings of home economics, frugality, and voluntary simplicity. Following are some of my favorites:

◆ *Your Money or Your Life* by Joe Dominguez and Vicki Robin ($11). A landmark book for reexamining your relationship with money. It's a philosophic look at how you spend your time and your money that can really round out and buttress your objections to a life that revolves around earning a big paycheck and amassing a closet full of consumer goods. This book will get you focused on what matters—namely, using the little time you've been allotted to fill your life with meaning rather than clutter.

◆ *Cheap Tricks: 100s of Ways You Can Save 1000s of Dollars* by Andy Dappen (Brier Books, $15, see order form at the end of this book). The previous book lays down the "why" of it all. This one shares the "how" of it all—how to stretch your money so you needn't spend your life chained to the time clock. It lists over 2000 ideas for saving money on everything from appliances to zinfandels (and everything in between). Because I wrote the book my recommendation is meaningless, but the publisher frequently receives letters saying it's the best book of practical tips on the market.

◆ *The Simple Living Guide* by Janet Luhrs (Broadway Books, 800-223-5780, $18). Luhrs, the editor of the *Simple Living* newsletter, writes about simplifying issues pertaining to money, housing, health, clutter, time use and more. She gives topics a welcomed philosophic grounding while showering you with pragmatic advice.

◆ *365 TV-Free Activities You Can Do With Your Child* ($8) and *365 Outdoor Activities You Can Do With Your Child* ($7), both by Steve and Ruth Bennett (Bob Adams, Inc., 800-872-5627 or 617-767-8100). These outstanding, activity-oriented books can unplug your kids from the television. Buy at least one, and don't let it collect dust.

◆ Other books you should read: *Voluntary Simplicity* by Duane Elgin; *How to Get What You Want in Life with the*

Money You Already Have by Carol Keeffe; *The Tightwad Gazette* books by Amy Dacyczyn; *Mary Ellen's Ideas that Really Work* by Mary Ellen Pinkham; *6001 Food Facts and Chef's Secrets* by Myles H. Bader; *1001 Ways to be Romantic* by Gregory Godek; *The Complete Car Cost Guide* by IntelliChoice; *The Wholesale by Mail Book* by HarperCollins Publishers; *The Doctors Book of Home Remedies* by Sid Kirchheimer and Rodale Press.

═══ December 30 ═══

Many of the activities in this book should be done each year. Grab next year's calendar, and go through each activity in this book, noting in your new calendar when a particular activity should be done again. When finished, you'll have many of the coming year's assignments in place—you'll know when to clean your heating filters, drain sludge from your hot water heater, shop for Christmas, stock up on sale items, maintain your lawn mower, overseed your yard....

═══ December 31 ═══

You've been reading my ideas all year long. Now I'm soliciting your help. What other practical advice and hands-on activities would people like you who 'work the home' want to know? Share your wisdom and tips so that future books like **More Daily Secrets of Living Well on One Income** are packed with valuable ideas.

◆ Write down your best money-saving ideas, activities, or practices and mail them to me c/o Brier Books (address on order form in the back).

◆ Even if you don't send me ideas, get on the mailing list for subsequent books (see mailing-list form in back). You'll get pre-publication notifications to order new books from the publisher for 20% off the cover price.

Index

The Author

Andy Dappen is the author of *Cheap Tricks*, a book many critics call the best frugality title available.

He is also a journalist whose articles have appeared in *Reader's Digest*, *Ladies' Home Journal*, *Sports Illustrated*, *Men's Health*, *Hemispheres*, *Bottom Line Personal*, *Bottom Line Tomorrow*, *Moneysworth*, *American Woman*, *Travel-Holiday*, and other national magazines.

Although his earnings as a free-lance writer would be enviable only in a third-world country, by practicing the money-stretching advice this book preaches, Dappen's family lives comfortably on his single income.

More importantly, they live a fulfilling life. Dappen and his wife have time to parent their two children, pursue hobbies outside of work, travel widely (though cheaply), and volunteer time to their community.

Want to Be...
on our mailing list?

You're reluctant to place your name on another mailing list. "More junk mail," you think, "who needs it?"

Our junk mail, however, delivers good news. Our pre-publication notices of new books like, *More Daily Secrets for Living Well on One Income* (the sequel to this one) will offer those who return this form a substantial discount. And if you've benefited from this book, you'll find our future titles just as valuable.

Okay, you convinced me. Please mail me notice of your introductory offer (20% off list price) when *More Daily Secrets...* is ready for distribution.

Name:_____

Address_____

City:_____State:_____Zip:_____

Phone:_____

Clip (or copy) this page. Return it to **Brier Books**, P.O. Box 180, Mountlake Terrace, WA 98043.

Order Form

Help family and friends live a saner, richer life by giving them a copy of either:

- ◆   *Shattering the Two-Income Myth*
  or
- ◆   *Cheap Tricks: 100s of Ways You Can Save 1000s of Dollars*

Our promise. If, upon reading our books, you don't believe they will save you thousands of dollars, send them back for a full refund. You must be satisfied.

The risk is ours. You have nothing to lose.

Orders. Send this form with a check or money order to: Brier Books, P.O. Box 180, Mountlake Terrace, WA 98043.

Name:_____

Mailing
Address:_____

City:_____State:_____Zip:_____

Send me:

_____ copies of *Cheap Tricks* ($14.95 each).

_____ copies of *Shattering the Two-Income Myth* ($14.95 each).

Subtotal:_____

[Washington State residents only: Add 8.6% sales tax] Tax:_____

Shipping and handling:_____

[**Book Rate**: Add $2 for first book and $1 for each additional book (books will arrive in about 3 weeks).
Air Mail: Add $3.50 for first book and $2 for each additional one (books will arrive in 1 to 2 weeks).]

TOTAL ENCLOSED:_____

Questions? Call us at 800-742-4847 during business hours (Pacific Standard Time).